The Shining Path

A BOOK IN
THE SERIES
*Latin America
in Translation/
en Traducción/
em Tradução*

*Sponsored by
the Duke–
University of
North Carolina
Joint Program in
Latin American
Studies*

Gustavo
Gorriti

Translated,
with an
introduction,
by Robin Kirk

THE
SHINING
PATH

A HISTORY OF
THE MILLENARIAN
WAR IN PERU

*With a new preface
by the author*

The University of
North Carolina Press
Chapel Hill and London

© 1999 The University of North Carolina Press

Originally published in Spanish with the title
Sendero: Historia de la guerra milenaria en el Perú
(Lima: Editorial Apoyo, 1990).

Manufactured in the United States of America

Translation of the books in the series Latin America in
Translation / en Traducción / em Tradução, a collaboration
between the Duke–University of North Carolina Joint Program
in Latin American Studies and the university presses of Duke
and the University of North Carolina, is supported by a
grant from the Andrew W. Mellon Foundation.

The paper in this book meets the guidelines for permanence
and durability of the Committee on Production Guidelines for
Book Longevity of the Council on Library Resources.

Library of Congress Cataloging-in-Publication Data
Gorriti Ellenbogen, Gustavo.
  [Sendero. English]
  The Shining Path : a history of the millenarian war in Peru /
Gustavo Gorriti ; translated, with an introduction, by Robin Kirk.
    p. cm. — (Latin America in translation/en traducción/em tradução)
    Includes bibliographical references and index.
    ISBN 0-8078-2373-2 (cloth : alk. paper)
    ISBN 0-8078-4676-7 (pbk. : alk. paper)
    1. Sendero Luminoso (Guerrilla group)   2. Peru—Politics
and government—1968–1980.   3. Peru—Politics and government—
1980–   4. Guerrillas—Peru.   I. Title.   II. Series.
F3448.2.G67   1999   98-4360
322'.5'0985—dc21   CIP

03 02 01 00 99   5 4 3 2 1

Ayacucho seems more
closely tied to death than
life. . . . It has always been
a place of battle and death.
Revolutions begin in Arequipa
—an old Peruvian saying goes—
but when they reach Ayacucho
they are serious matters.
    CARLETON BEALS
    Fire in the Andes, 1934

But in contemplating history
as the slaughter-bench at which
the happiness of peoples, the
wisdom of states, and the virtue
of individuals have been sacrificed,
a question necessarily arises: To
what principle, to what final
purpose, have these monstrous
sacrifices been offered?
    G. W. F. HEGEL
    Reason in History

Contents

Introduction

More than one friend who has visited Peru recently has commented on the changes since Gustavo Gorriti first saw *The Shining Path* in print in 1990. Where once alarm and anxiety reigned, foreign graduate students now eagerly conduct interviews. U.S. chicken chains no longer report bomb attacks. Computers and cell phones and pagers and photocopiers beep and buzz and rattle on limitless current. The financiers who once shunned the former Inca Empire now see gold, literally, in its gorges and riverbeds and figuratively in its unwhitened, unbrightened, unaccessorized, and undeodorized populace.

Underneath this skin of giddy globality, though, has everything really changed? To be sure, Abimael Guzmán, the Shining Path leader and a vivid and unsettling presence in these pages, broods on a prison island off Lima. What remains of his army is in a jungle redoubt, capable no longer of remaking society, only killing its weakest sporadically. Many of the villages they and the army razed have reemerged from the rubble. The Shining Path never seized power; a Nisei agronomist named Alberto Fujimori did, and in 1992 filled the vacuum guerrillas labored so hard to create.

Yet the poverty, corruption, and institutional rivalries described in *The Shining Path* continue, as well as those remarkable and rare examples of quiet proficiency and wisdom that Gorriti took such pains to identify for this book. Although Peru, at its worst, tests the limits of what humankind can endure, it also proves, again and again, that once those limits are passed, the story continues, made up in equal parts of character, chance, and odds few in the First World are ever obliged to face.

Some of the more memorable individuals Gorriti describes are the police and State Security officials called on to detect and dismantle the incipient insurgency. Among them is Eduardo Ipinze, whom Gorriti describes as a "Latin Elliot Ness," who, at the outset, "appeared to be the incarnation of the ideal of the modern, honest, and efficient policeman that the country needed." Appearance was deceptive, as was so often the case in the period covered by *The Shining Path*, essentially 1979 to Christmas 1982. Ipinze had been corrupted by the largest narcotics ring ever organized in Peru. As damaging to his country, however, was Ipinze's dedication, as head of the Investigative Police, to annihilating his institutional rivals, not guerrillas.

In contrast, José María de la Jara, the first interior minister under Peru's re-established democracy and called "Bonbon" for his rotund figure, took seriously his role as "defender of society" and tried, despite fierce opposition from within his own political party, to defuse the ticking bomb of rebellion. More than any interior minister who followed, De la Jara managed to slow the Shining Path. Significantly, his methods were not repression and brutality, but a tenacious support for democracy and the law, feared by guerrillas as well as De la Jara's enemies within the security forces. But the Bonbon failed. When he resigned, Gorriti writes, any attempt for a "democratic reform of the mechanisms of state security" ended.

But the man who dominates this book, inescapably, is Guzmán. Perhaps Gorriti's most notable achievement is to have so accurately and richly described the fugitive Shining Path leader without ever having met or even glimpsed him. Through a close analysis of Guzmán's writings, interviews with those who knew this philosophy professor as a member of the San Cristóbal de Huamanga National University faculty, and Shining Path documents and government intelligence analyses, Gorriti draws a full and convincing portrait, no less frightening for being taken essentially from meticulous research, never personal contact.

Gorriti introduces us to Guzmán in the first pages of the book, writing of the professor's brief arrest during a general strike in 1979. But he waits until the chapter called "Mohammed, Mao, Macbeth" to evoke the Guzmán that dominates the rest of *The Shining Path*. To do it, he depends on the guerrilla leader's first and perhaps only true love: the political writings that were the bedrock of Shining Path military strategy. Gorriti's use of these documents is brilliant. To those of us who, like me, are bored quickly with the jargon and historical murk of Communist theory building, these tracts can seem as dry and dusty as an Ayacucho plain. But Gorriti not only places them firmly and convincingly in their Communist and military context, but draws out the human passions at work within the Shining Path and Peru at the moment they were being written and debated.

These passions were not, as Gorriti underscores, merely the result of growing pains and the predictable rivalries of any political machine built on the far margin of real power, although these forces were certainly present. Beneath the veneer of pseudoscientific certainty lies a deep faith and a palpable hatred. Guzmán's task, at the very outset of rebellion, was to stiffen the resolve of his followers to embark upon destruction. Some among them, writes Gorriti, had already been figuratively "beheaded . . . (but the) realization that the actions they were about to take would irrevocably seal their future acted as a powerful stimulus to uncertainty." Much had already happened. "Old friendships and long-standing camaraderies had been undone; homes and any hope for a normal life had been abandoned. Nevertheless, all of this journey had only reached the beginning that they now faced. For the Shining Path, this was the meeting on Rooster Island."

On Rooster Island, the conquistador Pizarro had drawn a line in the sand with a sword to separate those who would go on to wrest the Inca Empire from its founders from those who feared quick defeat and death in the mountains frowning on them from the east. Guzmán drew his line with words. The prudent met their political death at his literary hands, much as thousands of Chinese had seen their careers and families extinguished by the dazibaos and public humiliations of the Cultural Revolution, Guzmán's model. He was relentless in his campaign against those he labeled "revisionists" and champions of the "rightist line in development"—in other words, anyone who questioned him. Those who survived were confirmed as wheels in what he would later call "his killing machine."

With his own ruthlessness against former colleagues and friends, Guzmán demonstrated the true measure of the sacrifice he would ask of his cadres as the price of victory. In the previous century, Abraham Lincoln had called it the "killer arithmetic" necessary to preserve the Union, and only found the men willing to apply it after discarding officers who proved too squeamish. Guzmán's innovation, if it could be called such a thing, was to place not only his fighters and their uniformed opponents in the equation, but the people themselves, the ones he and the Shining Path were pledged to conduct into the promised land of Maoist utopia. After weeks of brutal criticism and self-criticism sessions, during which the killer-scholar used quotes from Shakespeare, Marx, Mao, the Peruvian hero Andrés Cáceres, and Washington Irving's "The Life of Mohammed" to finish off and bury internal opposition, he declared the Shining Path was ready to draw Peru into the "powerful vortex" of revolution.

In Gorriti's subsequent chapters, the state's attempts to detour Guzmán's plans were occasionally successful, usually uncertain, and in the end thoroughly inadequate. Consistently, Peru's leaders underestimated Guzmán and failed to perceive that they played their roles in the theories he had devised too faithfully. Above all, after the Bonbon's departure, they failed to use the best tools at their disposal—democracy, the rule of law, and careful intelligence work—to trap and disarm the Shining Path at its most vulnerable.

The country's leadership did not pay the price of incompetence. Farmers did, and community leaders, police officers, mayors, Protestant ministers, and students. They felt the full force of Guzmán's extremism and the equally consuming rage of the army, sent to quell the rebellion at the close of Gorriti's book. Guzmán showed the lengths he was willing to push his cadres to at Lucanamarca in 1984, where "the masses," he later commented, conveniently "overflowed" and murdered more than sixty people. Peru's elected leaders and their military henchmen did it at spots whose names are still tinged with horror: El Frontón, Accomarca, Pucayacu, Cayara. By 1990, massacres, extrajudicial executions, battles and forced disappearances had converted much of southern and central Peru into a wasteland, with

30,000 dead. More than 600,000 families fled their homes for the "misery belts" surrounding cities like Huamanga, Ica, and Lima. The list of ghost towns was long, each with its shocking story.

At the time, I was covering Peru for a U.S. newspaper. I remember particularly the story of Umaru, obliterated by an army offensive and mentioned only by the handful of ragged refugees who had escaped to Lima. Perhaps some among them had supported the Shining Path. Others hadn't. Their former mayor spoke no longer of the relatives and neighbors he had lost, but only the church organ that had been seized in the fighting, the bellows and pipes and pedals that had once been Umaru's pride and distinction but now only served to measure the true scale and particularity of their loss. Lima was blacked out regularly by Shining Path attacks on the electrical towers feeding it from the Mantaro River. Pundits raised the possibility of a Shining Path takeover. Ever on the lookout for the sensational, foreign correspondents quoted its messages hopefully, seeing in the graffiti-stained walls of Lima's Central Highway proof positive that a big story was on the way along with the end of democratic Peru.

There was both more and less to this fear than people supposed at the time. But I can say without doubt, since I lived in Peru at the time, that the arrival of Gorriti's *The Shining Path* underscored the degree to which many of us had been operating out of an almost complete ignorance of the force set loose in Peru. To say that I devoured this book as soon as I got my hands on it is an understatement. Upon release, it became *the* book to read, the only book. It put to rest persistent fallacies still passed around as insight—that the Shining Path strove to reestablish Inca rule, that it was led by peasants, that it was funded from abroad, that its willingness to kill "the masses" it claimed to represent was disinformation designed to discredit (this last from the group's handful of international supporters). Beyond any reasonable doubt, it demonstrated that what Peru faced was not a demented, drugged-out cabal of Sino-savages (as some among the local press routinely described them), but a determined cadre of Peruvians willing to pledge their lives to apply Guzmán's so-called scientific certainties.

Gorriti made them human. He also gave them a story, the character, context, and motive that placed them firmly in Peru's tumultuous history and soil. Up to the publication of *The Shining Path*, little of what had been written outside the pages of the magazine *Caretas*, where Gorriti did much of the leg work for the book as a reporter, had captured the narrative in the destruction. Bombs, deaths, attacks jumbled in people's minds, a blind force, a *chaqwa* to use the Quechua term, seemingly headed only for chaos. Indeed, destruction was among Guzmán's fondest aims; but there was also grim method at work, a conscious planning to the rubble, and this is what Gorriti has captured and scored here, the text of the music that President Gonzalo, as Guzmán was known, played for his fellow Peruvians.

For Gorriti, this book was not without its price. In *El Diario*, the Shining Path newspaper, Gorriti was a favorite target, excoriated with all of Guzmán's infamous flair for hyperbole. Perhaps more dangerous to this journalist's well-being in the long run, however, was the evidence, so convincing in these pages, of Gorriti's ability to analyze and, when necessary, expertly ridicule those in power. Since the publication of *The Shining Path*, he has honed these skills. After publishing a series of investigative pieces on President Alberto Fujimori and his shadowy security adviser, Vladimiro Montesinos, a former drug cartel lawyer, Gorriti became Enemy Number One to Peru's new regime. He was arrested after the 1992 "self-coup" during which Fujimori dissolved Congress and Peru's judiciary. Gorriti was forced to leave the country with his family for safety.

In 1996, he became deputy editor of Panama's *La Prensa*. There, Gorriti developed and led an investigative unit that published a series about the collapse of a local bank, used by a Colombian cocaine cartel to launder money. The most controversial article showed that the Cali cartel had funneled $51,000 to the election campaign of President Ernesto Pérez Balladares. The president initially denied taking money from drug traffickers but later had to make a humiliating public retraction.

In response, the Panamanian government filed an expulsion order aimed at ridding the country's leaders of what they considered a pesky foreigner. There was even well-founded information that the Panamanian government knew of a Peruvian plot to assassinate Gorriti and chose to expel him rather than risk being linked to his murder.

Characteristically, Gorriti refused to be cowed. For weeks, he was forced to live in his office, to make the task of the police sent to deport him more difficult. "Could I have avoided the type of reporting I did and concentrated on tamer subjects?" he wrote at the time in a *New York Times* opinion piece. "Sure. Could it still have been good journalism, while acceptable to the political authorities? Not impossible. Would it have presented a fundamentally incomplete view of reality? Certainly. Would I have felt it to be a betrayal of the fundamental tenets of a free press? Absolutely."

Gorriti saw his case not as unique but as part of a wider problem in countries like Venezuela, Colombia, Peru, and Argentina. "These are countries," he wrote, "with imperfect, or even cosmetic, democracies. There is no real balance of power; indeed, the judiciaries have been unable to stop government corruption that grew exponentially when companies were privatized. In these countries, the independent press—particularly investigative journalists—has a critical role to play. But cosmetic democracy is only comfortable with cosmetic press freedom. That is the reason why many journalists throughout Latin America have to struggle so hard to defend their work, and often their lives, from harassment and threats." The Panamanian government eventually backed down, and Gorriti remains as of this writing at *La Prensa*.

Journalists continue to struggle to defend their work in Peru, threatened by the likes of Fujimori and his creole Rasputin. What Peru gained from its lost decade, besides a close knowledge of grief, is a jumble. The Shining Path was finally defeated not by the army and its blind blows, but the police and the people themselves, who rebelled against the rebels and made the countryside, Mao's launch pad of revolt, hostile to them. What it lost is all too clear in these pages: a chance, perhaps fragile and doomed from the outset, at a more equitable society. For all of its admittedly laudable ideals—justice for the disenfranchised, bread for the hungry, respect for the downtrodden—the Shining Path sowed only misery for Peruvians. In that task, it received timely and energetic aid from the army, which tilled with matching fervor.

Finally, a word on this translation. Translation can be an irritating endeavor, both for the translator and the subject of his or her attentions, the writer. There can never be an absolute transparency between two languages, only an aspiration to narrow the distance to it. Inevitably, the journey from one to another form of expression loses something of the original. With lesser writers, this transition can be complicated by sloppy thought and ungainly expression. With *The Shining Path*, however, I can say that any faults here are my own, and the felicities wholly Gorriti's. I could not have asked for a clearer, more absorbing text to work from. At times, it caused me great sadness; it also caused me to laugh out loud. Throughout, it betrayed not only the considerable skills of a writer at the height of his powers, but the compassion of a man striving to understand and to explain the terrible and the beautiful workings of the country that raised him.

Robin Kirk

Preface to the English Edition

This book was first published in Peru in July 1990, at a time when the Shining Path insurgency was fast coming to affect the survival of the country as a whole. If the 1980s had witnessed the seemingly unstoppable growth of the insurgency, at the turn of the 1990s the Shining Path purported to have achieved a level of strategic parity with the Peruvian state. The new decade, the rebels proclaimed, would witness their conquest of power. That, in turn, would mark the beginning of the strategic counteroffensive of world revolution. The crumbling of the Berlin Wall, the Soviet Union's collapse, the Tienanmen massacre only showed, from their point of view, the decrepitude of worldwide revisionism. Pure Marxism-Leninism-Maoism was, the Shining Path contended, alive and well in the Andes and would eventually prevail all over the world. Regardless of grandiose claims, for most Peruvians the Shining Path insurgency continued to be a deadly paradox: so alien to Latin American political discourse and, at the same time, so effective, as events were proving.

At the time, the insurgency's very obscurity seemed to add to its power. Few people understood what the Shining Path was all about, what its doctrine and strategy were, who Abimael Guzmán really was, and how all of this related with Peru. For some, the questions were more pragmatic, though no less anguishing. If the Shining Path was a devastating infection of Peru's social tissue, was there anything that could be done to stop it? These questions acquired an air of urgency, as the internal war was increasingly shifting its center of gravity from the provinces to Lima. Its quite specific terrors, the fear of sudden, horrifying violence, were going to be felt more and more by Lima's inhabitants within the next two years.

That was the Peruvian quandary when this book appeared. It was widely and (if I might be excused for saying so) even avidly read for reasons pertaining to the book's contents as well as to the circumstance. Although *Sendero* described events that had taken place eight to ten years earlier, it related very much to the distressing questions that were very much on Peruvians' minds at the time. It explained, by dint of revealing and ordering both known and unknown facts, how the Shining Path insurgency had been able to take hold in what appeared to be a refractory reality. It told about the actions, countermeasures, perceptions, and misperceptions on both sides and about the results they engendered. It also addressed more general questions, such as the role of strategy, doctrine, organization, and will in the creation and growth of revolutionary movements and how these related to social conditions.

This book was originally intended to be part of a three-volume project that would cover the whole insurrectionary process, from the founding of Peru's Communist Party to the latter stages of the internal war in Peru. That intention was not realized because, in a sense, the project also became a victim of the war. When Alberto Fujimori, democratically elected as Peru's president in 1990, waged his April 5, 1992, self-coup, I was captured by an army intelligence squad and technically disappeared for nearly fifty hours. This is not the place to explain in detail the background of that criminal action, but it was directly related to my previous work as an investigative journalist. It was ordered by Vladimiro Montesinos, who at the time had already become the power behind the throne in Peru and who saw (in the window for impunity created by an ongoing coup d'état) an opportunity for revenge for exposés I had written in the past. I emerged alive and relatively well from that experience. Moreover, I managed to save my files and hide them in the nick of time. Then I had them safely carried out of Peru, but several months elapsed before I had them with me in a safe environment, in the United States.

Then, Abimael Guzmán, the Shining Path's leader, was captured in a masterful stroke planned and executed by a small police unit and its very capable leader, Benedicto Jiménez, and the course of the internal war changed dramatically from one day to the next. As I wrote in reaction to the event: "Could just one masterful lightning stroke implode the long anthill-like insurrectionary build-up of the Shining Path? Could carefully built strategic initiative and favorable strategic momentum—both of which the Shining Path unfortunately had—be lost in a moment if a dashing action rendered the queen-bee a prisoner and the red beehive steerless? If the second defeats the years; and if audaciousness defeats deliberateness; there was an added drama in there because of the fact that the Shining Path was widely regarded as a movement which had been rowing against the stream of history, and actually making progress against the current. Militant anachronism subduing reality, defiant Stalinism reincarnated and making elaborate progress in a wounded country. Could this disappear in a wink? As Sendero's prophet—the one who claimed to interpret the allegedly inexorable laws of history—was stared at in his human stature, abruptly diminished by defeat, you couldn't help but think on whether a group of policemen had not only made an arrest but simultaneously stated a philosophical case: That accident is central to History, and that single events can defy and eventually alter powerful trends of progression or regression in human affairs."

Together with Guzmán, the central archives of the Shining Path were captured. Therefore, the ability of scholars to investigate and understand the organization was fundamentally changed. Documentation whose existence I could previously only infer was now out of the Shining Path's hands. Any history of the war written without access to these files would be necessarily incomplete and would have an assured obsolescence. Of course, those files were, and are for now, in the possession of Peru's National Intelligence Service, and we will have to wait until democracy is fully restored in Peru before independent scholars will have access to them.

So, this book ended up as a single volume. This is, perhaps, as it should be. It is a self-contained book that examines in depth a crucial moment of Peru's history and, in doing so, explicates events and phenomena that have relevance for other realities and other research perspectives. As an in-depth study of the early stages of a revolutionary movement attacking an incipient democratic regime, it will hold, I hope, some interest to those studying other processes that share some of these elements.

But, for me, the primary reason that drove me to write the book in the first place still holds and justifies both the writing exertions and the consequences endured afterward: that the tragedies recounted would not be forgotten and that the record of lives and hopes shattered would endure as long as the memory of the internal war itself, so that time would not distort what really took place.

Gustavo Gorriti
Panama City, Panama
July 1, 1998

Preface

This book is an account of the biggest insurrection in the history of Peru. It is not an interpretation or an analysis of a series of more or less well known and accepted events, but rather the recovery and ordering of little-known deeds. For this reason, the greatest service this work aspires to is to unify deeds and actions with the context and meaning in which they occurred, and thus contribute to general knowledge. By this, I do not mean to say that analysis is entirely absent from this war tale. As the patient and diligent reader will note, I try again and again to connect, associate, and match details, to compare and establish analogies between the actions I describe and the theories behind them with other events and theories from other times and places, as long as this helps make the story understandable. However, I have tried to do this only sparingly and without altering the purpose of the story.

I decided to write this book after attending a Lima seminar where I perceived as a journalist how the multitude of tragedies we were writing about were becoming repetitive and dulling our readers' interest and sympathies, particularly presented as they were in the inevitably disconnected and episodic style of a weekly publication. As a consequence, not only were the suffering and horror then engulfing people, villages, and whole regions forgotten, but new events drew less and less attention. It became difficult to take seriously the warning signals meant for the rest of the country.

Yet, though it seemed only fair to rescue this tragedy from oblivion, the more compelling reason to begin work on this book—evident to me at the same moment—was that in this war, deceptively small, deceptively primitive, I discerned that the very future of the country was at stake, with a finality and irreversibility unmatched since Spanish had been first spoken within our borders. The group that had launched the war did so with imperial designs on society as well as history, and—in contrast to those ubiquitous groups of more or less innocuous lunatics—waged it with a methodical consistency and discipline that had carried to victory, at other times and places, groups with equally unlikely initial and apparent disadvantages. I have not attempted to prove this idea in these pages, but instead leave the events to speak for themselves. Nevertheless, this book's subtitle, "A History of the Millenarian War in Peru," is drawn from this perception.

The final reason for writing this book was my recognition—as I see it even today—that this war is one of the least understood chapters of Peru's history, even by those who waged it and their victims. This is due in part to the very nature of the conflict, but also owes much to the fact that the leading actors, their organizations and institutions, and the way in which these entities function are unknown; what is crucial is not how they present themselves but how they really are. I thought and continue to think that it is necessary to try and remove from this tragedy the accumulated darkness of ignorance.

Security and Access to Sources

To write this book, I have used extensively and with passion the experiences, methods, and sources I have gained through many years of working in investigative journalism. Throughout the book, there are many footnotes and references to documents, institutions, and occasionally people whose identities must be kept in reserve or secret. I have used these references only when I have deemed that to leave a citation out would impoverish the text.

The documents that served as this book's foundation have been donated to the Princeton University library. A large number of them will be available to academic researchers and journalists as of 1991. Another collection—documents that could contain information potentially harmful to individuals—has been deposited separately within the same library, and will be made available in the year 2004.

A fundamental concern of this book has been to guarantee the safety of those who entrusted me with information in confidence. In the same way, I have endeavored not to write anything that would endanger anyone regardless of his or her position in this war. This is why those who requested that their identities not be revealed were identified with pseudonyms, marked by italic type in the text (for example, *Sergio Escalante* is a pseudonym). I have also used pseudonyms for people whose past or present allegiances are unknown to one or all sides in the war, and finally, for those who were simply unnoticed witnesses to various events. To ensure safety, in some cases I have given the same person two or more pseudonyms or combined two individuals under a single name. I must add that some of those I have protected in this manner have carried out acts repugnant even to those with the most pragmatic moral beliefs. My guiding reason for protecting even them has been that the aim of this book is to serve as a medium or as a catalyst, to comprehend, to rethink, and to know, and not to kill, spread fear, or persecute anyone. Those individuals whose acts, political allegiances, or duties were public are of course identified with their real names.

Acknowledgments

Though it is always a solitary endeavor, the work of writing is rarely possible without an array of help that supports and complements the work of the writer. Here, I would like to recognize and thank those individuals and institutions who contributed to the completion of this book.

The long period of research and writing was made possible thanks to the generous help of a research grant from the Harry Frank Guggenheim Foundation. To this foundation, and particularly to Program Director Karen Colvard, whose admirable work is the search for academic research projects worthy of support, I send my lasting thanks.

In Boston, writer Douglas Bauer read with care several early drafts that were later partially incorporated into this book. His comments were a great help to me. In an even earlier stage, Felipe Mac Gregor, S.J., urged me toward a deeper study of the theme, after examining the already considerable (1982–83) archive of documentary material. I want to express my gratitude for this early stimulus, decisive in the undertaking of this endeavor.

Most of the writing of the book took place during a prolonged stay at Harvard University, in Cambridge, Massachusetts, while I was a fellow first at the Center for International Affairs and later as an associate at the Committee on Latin American and Iberian Studies. The teaching and administrative staff at both programs offered me invaluable encouragement and understanding during the most difficult periods in my work. Without forgetting the appreciation that others deserve, I would like to give special thanks to Leslie H. Brown, director of the Fellows' Programs of the Center for International Matters; and John Womack Jr., director of the Committee for Latin American and Iberian Studies. Samuel P. Huntington, at the time director of the Center for International Matters, urged on and inspired the continuation of this work.

Different parts of this manuscript were read and commented upon by the following people: David Scott Palmer, Boston University; Peter Johnson, Princeton University; Cynthia McClintock, George Washington University; Jorge Domínguez, John Womack Jr., Jim Brennan, Ronald Berg, and Robert Leiken, Harvard University; and Susan Kaufman Purcell, the Council on Foreign Relations in New York. Writers Carlos Fuentes, Roberto Toscano, and José Rodríguez Elizondo, the latter a longtime colleague at the newsweekly *Caretas* and now with the United Nations in Spain, stoically endured the infliction of the manuscript and gave observations as insightful as they were valuable. On more advanced drafts, and on specific points, the commentaries of Héctor López Martínez and Rafael Merino Bartet were extremely useful.

This book, and the journalistic vision that underlies it, owes much to the teaching and example set by Howard Simons, the legendary managing editor of the *Washington Post* during the Nixon presidency and Watergate investigation, which he contributed to in a decisive manner. He later became the curator of the Nieman Foundation for Journalism at Harvard, where he devoted much of his effort—with the combination of bravura, generosity, piercing ingenuity, and alert intelligence that characterized him throughout his life—to defending reporters persecuted for doing what in established democracies is no longer simply a right but a necessity: free expression, criticism, investigation. Thanks to his ability to mobilize dozens of editors, publishers, and politicians, Howard managed to defend the freedom, and in more than one occasion the lives, of journalists in, among other places, South Africa, Panama, China, and Guatemala. In 1989, after being diagnosed with an incurable illness, Howard chose not to submit himself to any treatment, with the familiar logic that to prolong his life would increase the suffering of his loved ones and diminish his own dignity. To the memory of this master reporter, of the dear friend, my gratitude, my fond memory.

Although I have the impression that the director of *Caretas*, Enrique Zileri, was not entirely in agreement with my departure from weekly journalism in his magazine to dedicate myself to this book, I owe him special recognition. It was during those intense weeks, enduring the sleepless deadline nights of *Caretas*, that I learned what I know about journalism; and it was for *Caretas* that I began to cover the theme of this book. From these years of work, I cherish a great admiration for Zileri's quality as a journalist, expressed in the bohemian energy at the close of the issue, intuition and the sudden inspiration for the perfect photo, the irreverent and exact emphasis, the creative bellowing and the eccentricities that made *Caretas* many things but never boring. And from another perspective, for those of us who have worked in the relatively new territory of investigative journalism in Peru, the demands of an editor like Zileri with respect to the veracity of the detail, the imagination to consider new angles, new ways of getting close to the news, were without question invaluable.

I have conducted dozens of interviews of as many people for this book, in some cases openly and in other cases in secret. In them, I acquired frequently not only facts but also an enriched vision that directed and gave perspective to my work. I would like to express my appreciation to all of those who gave of their time and ' trust, who shared memories, notes, and in some cases documents, hoping that a truthful account of the events of this war would be written.

I must convey my special gratitude to those people whose long-ago or continuing political activism in Ayacucho's leftist parties allowed them to test, closely and with intensity, the early stages of these events; and who shared their recollections with generosity and patience. My special thanks go to Carlos Tapia, Juan Granda, Germán Medina, Manuel Granados, and others, who because they still live in Ayacucho must remain in anonymity.

I must close with the necessary qualification that, despite this still incomplete list of intellectual debts, the responsibility for occasional errors or limitations in this book is mine alone.

Abbreviations

Apra	American Popular Revolutionary Alliance
APS	Popular Socialist Action
ARI	Leftist Revolutionary Association
CCP–Red Flag	Peruvian Peasant Federation
CGTP	General Confederation of Workers
CIA	U.S. Central Intelligence Agency
CTR	Confederation of Revolutionary Workers
CTP	Peruvian Federation of Workers
Dimin	Interior Ministry Intelligence Center
ELN	National Liberation Army
EPL	Popular Liberation Army
ERP	People's Revolutionary Army
FER	Federation of Revolutionary Students
FEUNTA	Student Federation of the Altiplano
FOCEP	Peruvian Workers, Peasants, and Students Front
FUE	United Student Federation
GC	Civil Guard
JOOPP-ZE	Joint Operative Command of the Emergency Zone
MIR	Leftist Revolutionary Movement
MOTC	Movement of Laborers, Workers, and Peasants
PCP	Communist Party of Peru
PIP	Peruvian Investigative Police
PPC	Popular Christian Party
PRT	Workers Revolutionary Party
PSR	Socialist Revolutionary Party
SIN	National Intelligence Service
Sinamos	National System for Social Mobilization
Sinchis	Civil Guard special forces
SL	Sendero Luminoso (Shining Path)
Sutep	Peruvian Teachers Union
UDP	Peruvian Democratic Unity
UI	Left Unity
UNIR	National Union of the Revolutionary Left
UNSCH	San Cristóbal de Huamanga National University

The Shining Path

The Arrest

It was January 1979. State Security, reinforced with other units, was deployed throughout Lima to search houses and offices and arrest leftist politicians and members of the Peruvian General Confederation of Workers (CGTP). Nevertheless, the union leadership continued to call for a seventy-two-hour general strike on January 9. Tense, on edge, the military government had put into play all the tools at its command to stifle the strike. A new plan to respond to urban disturbances, inspired by the lessons of previous strikes, had been put in motion for the first time. The plan emphasized the need to maintain open access to the city's northern, southern, and central highways by massively deploying police and military units while at the same time forcing public transportation to continue uninterrupted despite strike roadblocks. Troops had been assigned to protect public buses. Military drivers prepared to take over in case there were not enough civilian drivers to be found.

The military's attitude was meant to be decisive, demonstrating the depth of its resolve with deeds. In it, there was also a message to the Constitutional Assembly, a warning about the precarious nature of the democratic opening and underscoring who was still in charge. The interior minister and vice-minister, generals Fernando Velit and Jorge Lassús, had received the new operation plans from the Joint Chiefs of Staff. With the unmistakable arrogance that characterized the military regime, maximum repressive might, they took charge of issuing orders to their police subordinates.

Several magazines had been closed. Other "information media" were warned by the military commanders of the central and coastal security zones to "refrain from disseminating news" that could provoke "the perturbation of order." But the most threatening warning was the military's decision to submit to court martial anyone who "participated in or incited others to commit acts that alter public order." News bulletins released incessantly by press controlled by the military government warned the population that troops had been authorized to make use of their weapons to put down any disturbance.

Put in the context of events earlier that month, these threats were not empty. A case of espionage acknowledged by the government of Chile, culminating with the Chilean ambassador to Peru being declared a persona non grata, had captured the public's attention. Julio Vargas Garayar, a junior officer in the Peruvian air force, had been condemned to death and would be shot by firing squad within the month. Relations with Chile were at their lowest ebb since the almost war of 1975. Once again, preparations for war had intensified. There was talk of postponing general elections. Some politicians, like Luis Bedoya Reyes, accepted this possibility in principle. The American Popular Revolutionary Alliance (Apra), in contrast, did not; but in order to ensure that elections would take place, the party ordered the union it controlled, the Peruvian Federation of Workers (CTP), to openly oppose the strike and try to make it fail.

This combination of events doomed the strike. On January 10, after its failure was evident, the CGTP chose to call off the strike. It was the third strike in under thirty months, and the only one to end in defeat. Yet just as the two previous strikes had prodded the military government forward with the transfer to democratic rule, paradoxically this last one had the same result. In contrast to the rancor of past years, the moderating effect exerted by the Constitutional Assembly was extremely clear for most officers. Clearer still was that the decisive help given by unions controlled by the Apra would force the strike to abort. Yet this help was conditioned on sticking to the timetable for general elections.

Among State Security top brass, a small group of detectives wanted to take advantage of their virtually unlimited sphere of action during the strike to carry out unrelated investigations whose importance could be crucial. For example, in matters concerning the Shining Path. Information reaching State Security through intelligence channels in Ayacucho indicated that the Shining Path was making serious preparations for armed insurrection. And while the military scoffed at these persistent rumors, some veteran detectives who had followed the Shining Path sporadically over the years and who continued to receive information from inside the Maoist organization judged that to fail to take into account these preparations was a serious error.

On his own authority, the division chief, Commander Modesto Canchaya, ordered a tactical group whose mission was to arrest Ricardo Letts, a Revolutionary Vanguard leader, to add to its original objective the task of locating and capturing Abimael Guzmán, the Shining Path leader. It was known that Guzmán was in Lima, but not where he was staying. At dawn on January 7, detectives divided into various teams to look for him simultaneously in his most likely haunts: the home of his father-in-law, Carlos La Torre (the fifth block of Pershing Street); at the Lima campus of the Enrique Guzmán y Valle (La Cantuta) University; and a sister's home.[1]

Just as night fell and a woman left the La Torre residence, the police pushed her aside and burst in. Abimael Guzmán was there, working at a desk. There was no resistance, but neither was there any sign of surprise or tension. A State Security agent recognized him immediately. Nevertheless, the inevitable by-the-book question was asked. Your documents? The truth was he didn't have them, Guzmán replied, "claiming to have lost them."[2] Wearing a white *guayabera*, courteous and cooperative, Guzmán agreed to accompany his captors. At half past nine, the police and their captive set out for State Security headquarters.

The investigative police major who directed the search came from a different unit and only barely understood the importance of the capture. Although a junior officer suggested that they seize the papers Guzmán had been working on and make a thorough house search, the major decided that it was unnecessary to further inconvenience such a well-mannered family.

Officer *Pablo Aguirre* learned of Guzmán's arrest by telephone and prepared himself to meet the professor upon his arrival at State Security.[3] *Aguirre,* who had spent his entire career in State Security, had an appearance incongruous with his tenure there. Disheveled, with extravagantly long nails on his index fingers, like those of a bookie, *Aguirre* was considered by several of his superiors to be an outstanding analyst of the radical left and above all a living library on the theme. With his graying, kinky hair, smoking one cigarette after another, displaying in his manner of dress every indication of someone fallen on hard times, *Aguirre's* features became animated at the beginning of any discussion of the Shining Path or the radical left. With the intonation and gestures of those eloquent veterans of the La Victoria neighborhood recalling with passionate precision Alianza Lima's most memorable games, Officer *Aguirre* would describe without hesitation every conference, plenary session, and broadside by the Shining Path, Red Flag, Red Motherland, and Puka Llacta (Red Fatherland). *Aguirre* had interrogated and later chatted for long hours with Guzmán when he had been arrested in 1969 and 1970.

Calm, serene in his white *guayabera*, Guzmán climbed to the second floor of the building annexed to the Lima Prefecture, where the State Security offices were located. The faded tile floors of the offices and hallways gave off a sensation of deterioration and early ruin abruptly imposed on the walls and furniture.

Aguirre found Guzmán in the office of Julio Pantoja Cuevas, a division chief. It was there that the first interrogation would take place. Upon entering, Officer *Aguirre* greeted him with the respectful deference everyone had shown toward this prisoner. Guzmán remembered him immediately and greeted him warmly.

"Friend *Aguirre*, how can you do this to me?" said Guzmán in feigned reproach.

"Why, Professor Guzmán?"

"You know very well that I'm not involved in these things. What do we gain with strikes?"[4]

Aguirre had to admit that Guzmán was right. However, he hoped that over the next several days they would be able to discuss things that the professor was indeed involved in. But as *Aguirre* observed him, summing up the situation with his expert eye, he began to doubt that it would be possible to make any progress. It was enough to see Guzmán's "enormous calm," *Aguirre* remembers.

Outside the office, there was no calm. While Guzmán was still on his way to State Security, efforts to win his release had already begun.

That day, Laura Caller, a tenacious and crusading lawyer for trade unionists and peasant organizations, received almost simultaneous visits from Guzmán's parents-in-law and members of his organization, the Communist Party of Peru (PCP–Shining Path), already known as the Shining Path. The comrade had been arrested, she was told. "Abimael?" Yes, the comrade. Laura Caller and Abimael Guzmán had known each other for a long time. Caller had successfully defended Guzmán and many others arrested and tried after the 1969 protests in Ayacucho and Huanta. She had also defended other Shining Path defendants throughout the 1970s, in cases arising from the bitter battles between the Shining Path and other leftist groups for control of the San Cristóbal de Huamanga National University and other Ayacucho organizations. In the great majority of these cases, Caller, an expert lawyer and highly respected in legal circles, had won. Although she and Guzmán differed strongly in their political views, their friendship and professional ties had prevailed.

Caller perceived that Guzmán's family and the Shining Path members had different concerns, yet both were equally upset. It made sense. In the context of a strike that he had honored, Guzmán's mere arrest was worrisome in itself. With the military government in crisis, ploys and drastic measures were a possibility. They had to act immediately, and in coordination.

The first thing she told them was that they needed to hire a different lawyer, "someone beyond suspicion and with influence."[5] A "progressive bourgeois," in other words. She recommended *Horacio Alvarado*, all of the above as well as an excellent lawyer.

Both the family and the Shining Path agreed, and Caller got in touch with *Alvarado*. He agreed immediately to assume Guzmán's defense and concurred with Caller that it was necessary to invoke the aid of influential people as soon as possible.

Alvarado had been a judge and university professor. His writ of habeas corpus, prepared between Monday, January 8, and Tuesday, January 9, was approved without delay by a deferential judge. The legal machinery began to turn at full speed.

Other events were also in motion. One of *Alvarado's* close family members was a rear admiral in the Peruvian navy. He was persuaded to press for Guzmán's release. He was told that Guzmán was merely the leader of a tiny faction of provincial Marxists, had never harmed anyone, and, furthermore, was against the strike. Really, he was simply a university professor with innocuous political whims. Graciously, the rear admiral agreed to pursue the matter and went personally to State Security to express his "interest in the situation" of Dr. Abimael Guzmán, an apparent victim of confusion and perhaps excess police zeal, and to ask that this situation be resolved "as soon as possible"—precisely the formula, euphemistically veiled, used by the military to tell their police servants to speed the release of this or that person.

The rear admiral was not the only high official to visit State Security on Guzmán's behalf. Three generals—two from the army and one from the Investigative Police—came with the same purpose. They had been mobilized independently, by the family or the organization, not by the lawyer. Yet they served the shared purpose well. "They pulled all the strings," *Aguirre* remembers. "Abimael has friends everywhere! If you disagree, tell me why he's never been caught?"[6]

Since January 10, a Wednesday, the State Security detectives had little doubt that Guzmán would not remain in custody for long. To stave off the habeas corpus, and above all the combined pressure for his release, they did not have a single piece of available, concrete incriminatory evidence. And so, as a lieutenant began to type up the paperwork for Guzmán's release, *Aguirre* resigned himself to converting his planned interrogation session into a mere conversation.

It was a "friendly conversation," interrupted only by a brief taking of pictures and the reading of the deposition, less than one page typed. Without any hope of success, *Aguirre* tried to lead Guzmán into making incriminatory statements. "Come on, professor, we all know that you have extreme views and that you won't budge." A courteous nod. "We know you are preparing for armed struggle." "Correct, we are on that road," Guzmán responded. "Now, it's up to the masses to decide when to begin."

Nevertheless, when he answered questions for the police deposition, he admitted only to "belonging to a Marxist-Leninist ideological line, but he emphatically denies belonging to or leading the faction called PCP–For the Shining Path of Mariátegui, and therefore the deponent claims to be unaware of the armed-struggle platform of that faction."[7]

Nothing more could be done. "Perhaps if indications that he had been planning armed struggle had been found, it would have been possible to continue the investigation," *Aguirre* says. Since the questioning of detainees arrested in relation to the strike continued, *Aguirre* left the office where Guzmán was kept. When he returned, he was told that Guzmán had just been released. It was January 11, 1979.

He had left in the company of his in-laws and his lawyer, who escorted him to the Prefecture gate. There, more people waited, greeting him with effusive handshakes and surrounding him as they moved fluidly between the pedestrians and the cars, until they were lost to view and disappeared in the traffic, the city. Until today.

1

Return to Democracy

Weariness and disenchantment with the military government gave way to hope for a fresh start over the first weeks of the new decade. An eagerness for democracy took hold, with all the self-confidence of an early adulthood won after a perilous schooling. The past decade had seen the social fabric fray, rip in places, all had changed; yet the nation emerged more robust, more complex, more capable. An increase in exports and the economic recovery accomplished under Economy Minister Javier Silva Ruete and Central Reserve Bank president Manuel Moreyra prompted some qualified observers to speculate that, under a democratic government, the economy was sure to perform beyond expectations. For example, economist Roberto Abusada wrote, "There is no reason why Peru could not grow 10 percent or more per year."[1] A few months later, Abusada was to become one of the most important members of the new government's economic team. As such, he became a protagonist and witness to the sad contrast between his hopeful analysis and the reality of the following years.[2]

Among civilian elites, the attitude and thinking that predominated was that the imminent transition to democracy meant growth, not a rupture. An article written by ex–foreign minister Carlos García Bedoya,[3] at the time one of the most prestigious civilians who had served the military government, asserted that the 1970s had brought the demolition of old hierarchies, the elimination of historical flaws, and the incorporation of vast majorities long kept on the peripheries of national life. Starting where the military government left off, the future civilian government had a foundation upon which to build a modern, free society.

It's not possible to deny a certain merit to the argument, but its negative implications should also be noted: it condoned even as it stimulated the pendulum swing between civilian and military rule, suppressed rational analysis in the interest of diplomacy, and persisted in the distorted understanding of history endemic to Peru, which has paid the price generation after generation.

One of the photos used to illustrate the article expresses now a very different message from what it expressed then. In it appear some civilian experts who served the second stage of the military government. In the center is Alvaro Meneses, then president of the National Bank and later a notorious fugitive in the Banco Ambrosiano embezzlement scandal. It's perhaps a somewhat exaggerated symbol of an entire new class that enriched itself by plundering the state over the course of a decade.

These were weeks, months of optimism about the country's historic destiny. Among the presidential candidates, Fernando Belaunde best sensed the collective spirit. After twelve years of the generals' frequently artificial-sounding severity, his unassuming style appeared authentic and warm. "Work and let others work" was his slogan, summing up the reigning mood even when interpreted maliciously. At the time and until 1982, it was common to hear emphatic declarations that Belaunde was "a sir" (in contrast to those other yokels) and a "luxury president," perhaps the highest compliment Lima society could bestow.

A gradual yet intense foreboding about the natural world provided counterpoint to upbeat political and social expectations. An article published a decade earlier by American seismologist Brian Brady had predicted a cataclysmic earthquake for 1980. Since January of that year, fear of an imminent disaster deaf to entreaties for mercy took hold; by February, there was widespread belief that a telluric apocalypse was imminent. In March, with the earth intact and Brady's prophetic reputation in shambles, at least in Peru attention focused once again on human events.

The presidential campaign had begun with the new year. Within Popular Action, Belaunde's political party, there was obviously no question about who would become the official candidate. But Fernando Belaunde was also interested in presenting himself as a candidate of the Popular Christian Party (PPC). In the end, his conversations with Luis Bedoya Reyes, the PPC boss who was offered the post of vice-president, bore no fruit. The first opinion polls had given a slight advantage to Belaunde, 20 percent compared with Bedoya's 18 percent. With this virtual tie, and without taking into account the factions within each party opposed to a union, it was difficult to agree on who would occupy key jobs or make campaign decisions.

Both parties nipped at the heels of the Apra, polling at 24 percent and at the time considered the probable victor. The military government clearly favored the Apra. It was even assumed that the recent death of Apra founder Víctor Raúl Haya de la Torre would rebound paradoxically to the Apra's electoral advantage, laying to rest old hatreds and freeing the energies of a new generation of leaders.

In January, the Apra's ticket was announced. It was led by Armando Villanueva, a veteran militant and leader who had a reputation as a tough guy. But the battle for dominance among Haya de la Torre's heirs had shaken the party. Villanueva's victory over Andrés Townsend, who had only partially resigned himself to becoming the Apra's candidate for vice-president, did not end the clash between opposing factions, also battling over control of the party and its direction. At the time, Villanueva supported a return to the Apra's "light-filled springs," using party vernacular, and spoke in the rhetoric of the left as he appeared to promise a social democratic administration. Townsend was decidedly anti-Communist and closer to a Christian democrat perspective.

Up to the very moment the official candidate list was announced (with no shortage of arrogance called "the roll," Venezuelan style), the dispute within the Apra raged. Hostilities festered between the party's political factions, like a deeply divided family. At the beginning of February, the slap that Helena Távara, Townsend's pugnacious mother-in-law, had aimed at Alan García in the Apra headquarters known as the People's House kept political gossips titillated for weeks, although it did nothing to shake Villanueva's dominance.

The most conspicuous battles were settled once the candidates were formally registered. Yet they were replaced by systematic sabotage carried out by the pro-Townsend faction and by a war of rumors and graffiti waged through personal attacks. Wall graffiti deriding Villanueva's Chilean wife was added to whisperings about a supposed military veto of his candidacy on those grounds.

Nevertheless, Villanueva's candidacy flourished. As the year began, it was believed that his lead in the polls would grow during the campaign. Many of the newly wealthy, that emerging plutocracy created and nourished by government debenture loans and illegal commissions awarded during military rule, left behind without a murmur the anti-Apra stance they had assumed during the Velasco years and began making contributions to the Apra's campaign.

No single individual was more important than Carlos Langberg, a Peruvian recently returned from Mexico with a rumored fabulous fortune, close contacts with the military government, and a disturbing affinity for violence. Langberg paid a large part of the Apra's campaign expenses and supervised the production of television advertisements, many made by a team he brought from Mexico.

In 1982, when a magazine investigation revealed Langberg's key role in the largest single case of cocaine trafficking known to date,[4] he had become a figure of decisive power within the Apra, both threatening and overwhelming. His subsequent fall meant the fall of what was possibly the most important Peruvian drug-trafficking syndicate that had existed up to that moment. Within the Apra, it sparked the internal renewal movement that would thrust Alan García to party leadership and the presidency of the Republic soon afterward. But that is another story.

The Marxist left was more disorganized, more unstable, than it had been for Constitutional Assembly elections. The various coalitions and groupings drew together, drew apart, and drew together again within a few months, leaving behind a wake of acronyms and complex affiliations and ruptures. In January, Left Unity (UI) presented a ticket featuring Genaro Ledesma, Jorge del Prado, and Antonio Meza Cuadra, of the Socialist Revolutionary Party (PSR). The alliance between the Peruvian Workers, Peasants, and Students Front (FOCEP) and the pro-Soviet Communist Party lasted less than a month. The Trotskyites united behind the candidacy of Hugo Blanco of the Workers Revolutionary Party (PRT), which during one stage of the campaign had on its ticket Alfonso Barrantes, who represented the Leftist Revolutionary Association (ARI). Several pro-Maoist groups joined within the National Union of the Revolutionary Left (UNIR). The various factions of Revolutionary Vanguard and other groups on the heterodox left came together in the Peruvian Democratic Unity (UDP). Finally, Genaro Ledesma continued to be FOCEP's candidate after its break from the UI.

This electoral ferment, a reflection of substantial though disorderly development, had dazzled the Marxist left and within a few months had produced some of the most important changes in its history. Trotskyites and Maoists, Third Worlders and pro-Soviets together entered the democratic system and, in so doing, were slowly yet inescapably united. The dogmatic disputes they shared, immutable as long as they remained in clandestinity, lost importance before the imperative of articulating a parliamentary strategy. At times imperceptibly, at times acknowledged by all, rivalries and doctrinal differences gave way, and the positioning of groups and political parties increasingly reflected electoral maneuvering rather than ideological schisms.

This process was only partially voluntary and was marked by frequent hesitation. But it was decisive. And if one had to select a moment to symbolize this transition, I would choose the Maoist coalition UNIR's final 1980 presidential campaign rally, when veteran teachers' union leader Horacio Zeballos brandished a stick rifle from the stage as he spoke to his party.

Within the context of the campaign, few declarations about abandoning violence and embracing legality could have been more eloquent. At the same time, however, Zeballos's skeletal frame, perhaps already on the brink of death and waving about a toy rifle, gave ammunition to the sworn anti-Communists who remained convinced that the Marxists' electoral intentions were simply part of their strategy to take simultaneous advantage of all legal and illegal means to victory.

Yet the situation was precisely the opposite. Whether willingly or not, those on the left had successfully joined the system. And they began to have a stake in maintaining the system's stability and a practical responsibility for solving daily problems. As part of the government, the left would have an important role to play in changing the nation's course; in turn, it would undergo substantial change. The following years simply reinforced this evolution. The brandishing of a stick rifle on the eve of elections symbolized the send-off of one era and the beginning of another.

If the Shining Path had not existed, the left's incorporation into the system would have been more visible and complete, and today the Marxist left would be a pillar of democratic stability, part of a lively and vibrant political process, and an entirely peaceful one.

But it did exist. The Shining Path saved its most strident attacks for leftist organizations that took part in elections, denouncing them for abandoning the revolutionary path. Which was, of course, entirely correct. For such groups, especially those with Maoist pasts, these puritan accusations—which they once would have shared—were at the very least unpleasant and slightly distorted their incorporation into the system.

While such harassment was extremely irritating to those Marxists turning toward legality, for the Shining Path it was absolutely necessary to attack these much larger groups, and thus steal away and chip at their support. That's why the left's presidential campaign had to advance along with a parallel battle of shouts, insults, stonings, and beatings with Shining Path militants (and their sympathizers, like Puka Llacta) who remained in semiclandestinity.

Several incidents, especially in Ayacucho, illustrated the passionate intensity of the confrontation between these diverging leftists. In October 1979, the UDP and other leftist groups organized a night rally in Ayacucho's central square. In the morning of that same day, UDP leaders and members had challenged the Shining Path to a debate in a patio of Huamanga University's Engineering Department. Carlos Malpica challenged Julio Casanova. Although Casanova was present, a student who was a Shining Path member rose to debate in his place. But Malpica made it clear that he would only debate another professor. Casanova did not acknowledge the challenge.

When it became clear that the verbal jousting was not to be, Javier Diez Canseco took center stage and in his familiar vehement style attacked the Shining Path. A Shining Path rock struck Diez Canseco's face, causing a minor though eye-catching forehead wound. Immediately, a brawl began. It ended with the Shining Path's eviction from the patio. The UDP members marched their banners triumphantly through Ayacucho's streets, working themselves up for an evening rally.

But the rally went badly from the beginning. Since that afternoon, the UDP leaders had fought over the roles the speakers were to play and their order of presentation. Finally, it was decided that Carlos Tapia would speak briefly as the representative from Ayacucho and that Alfonso Barrantes would close the rally. Juan Granda introduced the speakers. As the rally was about to begin, it started to pour and people sheltered themselves in doorways. When it appeared as if the rally would fall apart, peasant leader Julio Orozco Huamaní (who, a few years later, would be arrested and "disappeared" as the war intensified) fell back on an Andean ritual to stop the rain. "Coca leaves were burned and it stopped raining."[5]

But just as the heavens appeared to comply, a group of about twenty to thirty Shining Path militants attacked the rally-goers with homemade explosives. At first, the UDP members were too shocked to respond (this was the first time that explosives had been used in open attacks), but they quickly regrouped and their shock troops, armed with sticks and plywood shields, rousted the Shining Path militants from the square and chased them through the connecting streets.

The UDP's election campaign intensified over the following months, at each step coming up against the Shining Path's unrelenting hostility. In the city of Ayacucho and the surrounding towns and countryside, graffiti celebrating the armed struggle went up next to insults meant for the UDP ("Apra, UDP, and CIA, the same bullshit"). The campaign continued in a tense climate where the threat of a clash with the Shining Path, with blows or stone throwing, was always imminent. "With Tapia, we got around in a Volkswagen. If they had broken one of the windows, our campaign would have ended."[6]

In Ayacucho city, Tapia and Granda also put up graffiti, competing with the Shining Path brush masters by covering over their slogans. They were accompanied by a small phalanx of United Student Federation (FUE) veterans, sufficient for the occasional street brawl. Always with the Shining Path.[7]

But when they ventured out into the countryside in their tenacious Beetle, going everywhere, especially in the final weeks of the campaign, they went alone. "If we went to Cangallo, Chuschi, or Vischongo, we would return the same day, to attend other rallies."[8] And although in many districts they faced an uphill battle against the Shining Path, in others they managed to establish a certain presence. In Chuschi, the UDP organized a musical group, while in Vischongo it established good relations with local folk healers. There, a UDP teacher had organized various students from local communities to do grass-roots work. In both towns, the UDP could count on rallies of between 100 and 200 people and had made friendships with communal authorities.

Nevertheless, in both towns, and even more so in other areas, the Shining Path's influence was perceptible. Most educated residents worked for the Shining Path, and other organizations acknowledged its influence. In constant local conflicts,

UDP militants held out for as long as possible. When they were overwhelmed, they would call on Tapia and Granda to breathe new ardor into their alternative message.

On one trip to Chuschi, a group of five young men of about eighteen or nineteen years of age stood around the Volkswagen with hostile gazes. The local UDP members told Tapia and Granda that these were Shining Path members. Tapia and Granda returned their "ugly looks." After glaring at each other for awhile, the Shining Path members retreated but without leaving town.

Everywhere, on walls, on blackboards, and in rumors, word of the imminence of armed insurrection spread. Almost every day at about four or five in the morning, Shining Path groups would run through Ayacucho's streets shouting synchronized slogans in support of "armed struggle." There was talk of an armed camp in Socos, for example, and other places. The patio chalkboard in Higuera contained summonses to members of the Popular Juvenile Movement to come discuss matters related to the insurrection, complete with date and place. To the UDP, all this appeared less than serious. "We thought they would never go beyond painting graffiti . . . clearly we were wrong."[9] Another UDP leader remembers having chided the Shining Path after yet another victorious scuffle. "How are you going to begin the armed struggle if we just beat the shit out of you? We have held rallies in Chuschi, in Tambo, in Huanta, and they could do nothing with us."[10]

Yet even as these incidents occurred, the entire Shining Path organization was making intense preparations for war. And the UDP cells in Ayacucho's towns and provinces were later swept away in the insurrection—sometimes by the Shining Path, but more frequently by the security forces.

Nationally, the election campaign gained momentum. The tenuous rumors of insurrection brought before the public's attention were ignored or considered improbable at best.

As the left, divided in several fronts, frittered away its chance to consolidate more votes,[11] the battle for victory concentrated increasingly on the campaigns of Villanueva and Belaunde.

Little by little, Belaunde began to gain ground in the polls and Villanueva to fall back. Drawing on the illusion of returning to the years prior to the 1968 military coup, Belaunde's attitude drew in more voters and more strongly than his competitor. In contrast to the years of military rule, when politicians adopted the stern voice, gestures, and tone of the barracks, Belaunde spoke with the modulation and gravitas of a wise and still-vigorous grandfather. In contrast, Villanueva projected a brusque and hard image that appeared little different from a military man and perhaps even more dangerous. Campaign advertising underscored the electorate's first impression: Belaunde spoke of shovels, of simple but healthy work, of pastoral vistas lovingly remembered in all their detail by the architect who had gazed upon them. The Apra's ads featured youths with varying hues of blonde hair, a disquieting fanatical brilliance in their eyes, beginning to sing a march in part military and in part mystical, while in a park, young couples, mature couples, passersby, and street vendors slowly gathered. All appeared surprised in that countrylike atmosphere, which they left behind to parade toward an implicitly ferocious future. The ad was modeled on the movie *Cabaret* and had a different purpose, but in the end the results were the same.

It was not the moment for barracks posturing. Despite the economic recovery, the military government had released its hold on power seriously discredited. The fear once inspired by the image they fostered of limitless power and efficiency had dissolved, at least in the wake of the general strikes. *Monkeys and Monkeyshine*, a humor magazine, found in Morales Bermúdez an ideal subject for some of the bloodiest and most effective needling—or direct hits—in the history of Lima political humor.

In addition, revelations about corruption dogged the Morales Bermúdez government until the very end. In May, just before the elections, Interior Minister General Fernando Velit had to resign, buffeted by published reports (in *X* Magazine) tying him to a sordid case of contraband. A Civil Guard (GC) general, the GC director's brother, was the principal suspect. Two years later, Velit would again be accused (by *Caretas*) of involvement in a much more important case: protection given to a drug-trafficking organization run by Carlos Langberg.

The city stank, literally. The prolonged city sanitation workers strike had caused a huge accumulation of trash. In a city marked by strong smells (many visitors believed ammonia to be central Lima's characteristic odor), the garbage stench was suffocating. Yet it wasn't merely a noxious conflict, but a bloody one. In a clash between striking workers and police, four were killed.

In May, Belaunde's popularity noticeably surpassed Villanueva's. The final efforts of the Apra and its sympathizers (a Lima march, the support of Alfredo Barnechea, host of a popular television show) were counterproductive and resulted in more votes for Belaunde. During Popular Action's final campaign rally, the taste of victory was palpable. High on a stage and cheered by the fervent crowd were the same people who twelve years earlier had been deposed by the military and later scorned and ridiculed by these same people, government bureaucrats and their own impassioned multitudes. At the time, the resurrection of Belaundism seemed inconceivable. Nevertheless, there they certainly were, names from yesteryear, acclaimed by a sea of faces that stretched from the stage.

Accompanying Belaunde and soaking in the applause and enthusiastic roars was Manuel Ulloa, owner of the newspaper *Expreso*, financier, and businessman. Intelligent as he was undisciplined, he was soon to be the next government's prime minister and economy minister. Alongside were Javier Arias Stella, the doctor who would become foreign relations minister; Javier Alva Orlandini, the Cajamarcan politician who had been the military's most spirited opponent and would again become the consummate apparatchik, a master manipulator of Popular Action's parliamentary majority and out-of-town calamities for the benefit of his cosmopolitan party colleagues; and José María de la Jara, the short, chubby, and combative Popular Action secretary-general when Belaunde's first government was toppled. Although De la Jara was the son of a famed parliamentary orator, he stuttered. A combative journalist, he wrote in a bombastic style. And he was an individual of great integrity, whose exile had thrust him into painful financial straits and even penury. De la Jara had decided not to become a candidate for parliament, prevented perhaps by his lack of oratorical skill. Incongruously, he was to become the new government's interior minister, the defender of society.

On May 18, election day, Belaunde won easily, amassing 45 percent of the vote. Villanueva came in a distant second, with 27 percent, while Bedoya Reyes came in third with only 9 percent. Candidates presented by the left won a combined 14 percent. Individually, the Marxist group that won the most votes was Hugo Blanco's PRT (3.9 percent). After it came UNIR (3.2 percent), Left Unity (2.84 percent), and the UDP (2.39 percent). FOCEP received only 1.47 percent, and neither the Popular Socialist Action (APS) nor the Socialist Party received more than 1 percent of the vote.[12]

Widespread enthusiasm paired with Belaunde's clear mandate definitively swept away fears that the military would go back on its promise to relinquish power. This very real apprehension had provoked ominous rumors of a "third phase" of military rule as the year began.

The fearful could now be included in the ranks of the Armed Forces. Several of the highest-ranking officers, including Rafael Hoyos Rubio, the army's commanding general, had participated in the coup that unseated Belaunde in 1968 and were later active participants during both periods of military rule. But in the many meetings held to bury the hatchet, Belaunde had expressed emphatically that the past's transgressions were forgotten and that Hoyos Rubio would remain as commanding general. Anxiety, however, was slow to subside, despite the fact that Belaunde kept scrupulously to his word.

Between the night of May 18, when crowds of ephemeral Popular Action supporters celebrated the candidate's victory, and the afternoon of July 28, when Belaunde once again entered the Government Palace with the presidential sash draped across his chest, there was a period of high hopes. It was a myopic time, as are almost all enthusiasms of this nature. But much about it was moving: people hoped for more than what their politicians could possibly deliver in even the best of times. We shared an inexplicable belief that the distance separating our present straits from a better future was not so great; with the simple application of the correct techniques and precise mechanisms, it could be crossed.

On the evening of Popular Action's victory, in the midst of a crowd singing campaign jingles in front of the building where Belaunde lived, one young woman appeared to have entered a rhythmic ecstasy. The party's name, which she chanted as she jumped from one foot to another, was like a kind of mantra that would open the way to a brighter future.

Not one among these enthusiastic youths knew that war had begun the day before, and that their future, and the future of the rest of the nation, would be much more shaped by a mysterious incident that took place on election eve in a remote village than by the impressive victory, won the length and breadth of the country, that they celebrated.

The burning of the ballot boxes in Chuschi, on May 17, 1980. The first shot, treacherously muffled, began the fire of the millenarian war.

2

Chuschi

Burn of ballots
thus start of vol

At dawn on May 17, the day before general elections, five hooded men entered the Chuschi voter registration office, subdued and tied up the registrar, then burned the registry and ballot boxes. The attack began at two in the morning and was over in less than thirty minutes.

The registrar managed to untie himself. With bells pealing, he raised the alarm. A brief meeting was called and residents searched the area. They knew who they were looking for since the registrar had recognized his attackers, the same kids who had threatened him since May 15. That very morning, they had warned him that they would break into his office that night. The registrar didn't believe them until he was bound and gagged.

Between 7 and 8 A.M., four youths were captured in an abandoned shack near town.[1] Two were locals, from the neighboring village of Quispillacta.[2] The youths denied having participated in the attack, but the search revealed that one was carrying an official electoral seal. The attack had been led by a teacher from another town who eluded capture.[3]

Town authorities notified Cangallo, the provincial capital, and an army truck arrived later to pick up the detainees.[4] The four youths were taken to Cangallo, and there the incident seemed to end. Even the Ayacucho press failed to mention the attack until four days later and gave it no importance.[5]

And so the war began. For the Shining Path, the action was the first spark of destiny's fire. This was the genesis of the blaze on the symbolic plains of the bourgeoisie and all betrayed revolutions. Over the following years, as the embers flamed throughout the country, the search for an explanation returned repeatedly to this primordial spark. Why Chuschi? What symbolic detail separated this distant village from all others to mark the war's beginning? Did Chuschi unite the basic characteristics of semifeudal oppression in the countryside, the delay of progress in Andean towns, or was it the first cradle of Shining Path activity in the countryside?

Few towns in the Peruvian Andes had been more studied than Chuschi in the years before the war. Unfortunately, as happens frequently in academic research, almost all of the in-depth studies had been published in English in the United States and remained relatively unknown in Peru.[6]

Chuschi was a relatively prosperous and stable community.[7] It had never been subjected to the dependence, exploitation, or patronage of hacienda rule. To the contrary, its inhabitants had once invaded a small hacienda bordering community lands. It was essentially an independent community. Although linked by highway to Ayacucho only since 1966, Chuschi had been "an important market, administrative, and ceremonial center for at least 400 years."[8] People from neighboring communities traveled by foot from one to two days simply to buy and sell goods in Chuschi's Friday market.[9] A good number of Ayacucho's residents had ancestors who were mitimae, including the Chuschans. Shaped by the demographic commotion that followed the Inca conquest, the area is populated by the descendants of the indigenous populations of Canas, Cusco; Cañaris, Ecuador; Aymaraes and Angaraes in Apurímac and Huancavelica; coastal Moches; and the original Taquiguas from the area. Chuschi and Cancha-cancha share an origin in Aymaraes while neighboring Quispillacta has its origins in the Canas mitimaes.

According to documents, border disputes between Chuschi and Quispillacta date from 1593.[10] In 1959, the communities battled over pastures on the high moors, and three Quispillacta villagers were killed. Starting in 1980, the counterinsurgency war first stretched to the breaking point the rivalry between the two communities and then brought an apparent reconciliation based on their shared tragedy, the first in 400 years.

Starting in the 1940s, an active community of migrants to Lima maintained close contact with their hometowns, looking out for their interests in the capital. Many influential families lived in the same Lima neighborhood, first in San Cosme and then in a "young town" known as "October 7," seized by squatters in 1963.

Some migrants with experience in unions and knowledge of how political decisions were made in Lima remained involved in hometown affairs and became much more active after Velasco Alvarado seized power. Two of them returned to the community and led an aggressive campaign to expropriate the lands and cattle held by the Catholic Church in Chuschi (the church owned 100 acres of the best land and 800 head of cattle, cared for by the community). A bitter fight ensued, during which the local priest managed to get the community leaders jailed on more than one occasion. Nevertheless, the leaders prevailed. The priest was transferred in 1972 (clearly thrown out) and the church's holdings passed to a community cooperative. Nevertheless, the cooperative was short-lived. The traditional community structure later took control of the church's land and cattle.[11]

The legal battle and intensely contentious feelings raised by the dispute prompted the virtual ecclesiastical abandonment of Chuschi and aided the spread of a Pentecostal sect. From humble beginnings at the end of the 1960s, by 1980 it had grown to include more that 200 people within a population numbering barely more than 1,000.[12] In Quispillacta, the conversion to Protestantism had been even more intense and far-reaching. Meanwhile, the Shining Path gained much more influence in Quispillacta than Chuschi, a development that, it must be noted, puts into doubt the stereotype of the fierce anticommunism of Third World Protestant sects.

The Shining Path began organizing in Chuschi in the first years of the 1970s via teachers sent there. Their number had increased substantially since the opening of a high school at the end of the 1960s. Before, the town had only seven elementary school teachers, but by the 1970s there were nineteen.[13] Three were born in the community and the rest were from elsewhere. Most of the teachers belonged to the Peruvian Teachers Union (Sutep). As was customary, some had been sent there by the government as punishment for their union activities. Only a few Sutep teachers belonged to the Shining Path. However, as was true in other instances and groups, these few were better organized than anyone else.

In 1975, American anthropologist Billie Jean Isbell, who had returned to Chuschi to continue her research and organize a bilingual studies center financed by the Catholic University, was virtually thrown out along with her Peruvian and North American team. The movement against them in Chuschi was led almost exclusively by the teachers. Because she and her group attempted to resist, a series of incidents and bureaucratic confrontations ensued, creating tensions that made their stay impossible.

Curiously, Isbell had avoided previous contact with the teachers, hoping to forge a deeper relationship with the community without appearing attached to other educators: *qualas*, mixed-race, strangers, people whom she claimed the community looked on with suspicion and even disdain. "They told me [the teachers] were only their employees, and they could fire them at will . . . there was very little interaction between the two groups."[14] Identifying herself with the closed world of the community, in its own way unyielding and suspicious of mixed-bloods, Isbell trusted that she would be protected by their same defense mechanisms. "I too felt that I was somehow protected by peasant ideology from the outside world."[15] Isbell shared a Rousseauian fantasy common among anthropologists, ingenuous but always poignant.

Accused by the teachers, one of whom was the town mayor and a businessman of some means, of being "CIA agents" and exploiters, the anthropologists discovered that despite the mestizos' relatively small numbers, they had real power. The passive neutrality exhibited by the rest of the community gave them no protection.

Although their expulsion was, without a doubt, orchestrated by the Shining Path, not only party-affiliated teachers were involved. The teacher-mayor, who emerged as the most strident among the anthropologists' enemies, denounced them to the Velasco government as spies, something that the Shining Path would never have done given its unconditional opposition to the government. During the war years, that same mayor was forced to flee because of Shining Path threats.

Between 1975 and 1980, the Shining Path's influence in Chuschi grew much less visibly than in other towns and villages in Cangallo and Vilcashuamán. The community's relative prosperity, ceaseless commercial traffic, traditional independence, and, above all, the political astuteness and experience of the Lima migrants who had returned made the guerrillas' advance more difficult. The UDP was one competitor, and one UDP activist had won an important position in the Cangallo Agrarian League and the Departmental Federation, both organizations sponsored by the Velasco government.

Why, then, did the Shining Path choose to distinguish Chuschi as the stage to launch its campaign? I believe it was simply that there was an opportunity: a decision had been made to attack electoral symbols, and the ballot boxes and registry were kept in Chuschi. And the fact that Chuschi was not a Shining Path stronghold was more advantage than problem. The action, and the likelihood of a repressive reaction, would stir things up, polarize the debate, and obligate people to renounce passivity. Which is precisely what happened over the following years.

Mohammed, Mao, Macbeth

Between March and May 1980, on the eve of battle and with the opposing forces tensed for war, the Shining Path held a series of meetings led by Abimael Guzmán. The first was the Central Committee's second plenary (or the second plenary session), which began on March 17, 1980, lasted until month's end, and was the most important. After the insurrection began, there were other party meetings, to conduct a "general overview of the first actions" and to develop further the principal agreements (and problems) discussed in the second plenary session.

These meetings encompassed every Shining Path debate held, decision made, and reaction noted during the first year of its existence as an insurrection. While it is true that the party followed the route laid out in Convention I ("To Define and to Decide") in September 1979, the second plenary session's singular intensity stems from its proximity to imminent action, the irreversible step over the threshold.

In order to describe these meetings, I have guided myself as much by documents published by the Shining Path as other manuscripts, notes, and some interviews. The manuscripts that record these party meetings follow the Shining Path's schematic model. Although neither the actual content of the comments made nor the identity of those present (even by their pseudonyms) is revealed, the debate's thematic structure and development are described in detail. Such a system permitted an exact distribution of the agreements made to lower levels in the organization without compromising internal security or the integrity of the political ideas. The precision and organization of the information ensured that militants who had attended meetings could disseminate the reports without forgetting any of the points, accord each their proper emphasis, and transmit the information from the top of the hierarchy to the bottom without distortion.[1]

The preparatory meeting for the Central Committee's second plenary began on March 17 with a report by the Political Bureau, prefaced by the mandatory sacred quotations. In this case, however, the theme and circumstance bestowed a special importance to each gesture, each word. Despite this context, the first quotation did not allude to inevitable victory but to the eventual necessity of sacrifice, a theme that would be hammered home over the following years. The quotation was from Marx, on the defeat of the Paris Commune.

> The making of history would clearly be very comfortable if the struggle
> was begun with nothing more than the absolute assurance of victory.
>
> The bourgeois scum at Versailles had given the Parisians an alternative:
> either accept the challenge or surrender without fighting. The demoralization
> of the working class in the latter case would have been a much greater shame
> than the loss of as many leaders as you may imagine.[2]

The second quotation was from Lenin, and also alluded to the necessity for the party and the working class to prepare themselves to meet setbacks and failures. "To suffer a defeat, begin again, remake everything . . . we must tell the truth no matter how bitter and hard." The third quotation was classic Mao, on the historical necessity of the "two-line struggle" in order to achieve the "just" political line.

The choice of quotations seems to reflect a high level of uneasiness within the organization. Although the most important purges of the opposition within the old guard had already taken place, it was clear that doubt still crackled among influential groups within the Shining Path leadership. The knowledge that their immediate actions would irrevocably sign and seal their future was a powerful stimulus for uncertainty. The warnings that pervade tragedy's beginnings struggled to reveal themselves through dreamed omens and auguries and the fatigue of the predawn watch. The party's path had already been long and fraught, the "two-line struggle" wearying and full of sorrow. Long-standing friendships and old camaraderies had been dismantled; homes had been abandoned along with any semblance of a normal life. Yet this long journey had brought them only to a beginning, which now confronted them.

This was the Shining Path's Rooster Island meeting. For his part, Guzmán went to it fully aware that emotion and enthusiasm were more important than reason.

His way of neutralizing caution and lingering doubt was to convince his followers that they stood at the threshold of a grand historic quest.

As was customary, the agenda reserved an extended period of time to a review of what had been discussed and approved during previous events. Subsequently, the Central Committee's second plenary session was dedicated to a discussion of the following points:[3]

1. Actual situation of the party and its union to mass struggle
2. To develop by actions the militarization of the party
3. A general readjustment of the party to focus on military matters
4. Action plan for the BAS (Beginning of the Armed Struggle)
5. Rectification Campaign
6. Agreements

The meeting's general goal was the agenda's second point: "To develop by actions the militarization of the party." The general readjustment of the party would then serve to define the form of the "action plan."

The plenary session began on March 18, with a long methodological reflection taken from Mao. In addressing the problem of linking theoretical reflection to praxis, Mao not only emphasized the traditional Marxist affirmation that "theoretical knowledge, acquired through practice, should be returned to practice," but also that "what is most important is that this must manifest itself in the jump from rational understanding to revolutionary practice." To do it presupposed the long and difficult path that Guzmán had preached about through the years and that he had been urging them to put into action.

> Unless we understand its true circumstances, its nature, and its relationship with other things . . . we won't be able to accomplish a thing, bring it to a happy conclusion. . . . In dealing with something, we must examine its essence and consider its appearance only as a guide that brings us to an entrance. . . . Materialist philosophy assumes that the law dictating the unity of contrasting opposites is a fundamental universal law. This law had universal validity, as much in nature and society as in man's thought, . . . this law propels the movement of things and change. . . . Analytic method is dialectic. We understand analysis to mean the analysis of contradictions. . . . Many of our comrades, unaccustomed to thinking in an analytic way, don't want to analyze repeatedly and deeply and study complex things, but rather prefer to formulate simplistic conclusions that are absolutely affirmative or absolutely negative. . . . Things in the world are complex and are shaped by many factors. We must examine problems from different vantage points, not from just one.

Though it took place on the verge of war, this decisive meeting did not begin with a conventional military discussion of missions to be carried out and the means to bring them off successfully, but with more general considerations on dynamic interrelationships and the way theory and practice could reinforce one another. This was Maoism's methodological key. By underscoring this quotation at such an important moment for his organization, Guzmán sought to instill it as a guiding principle in the Shining Path's method of waging war, just as it had been in China and later in Vietnam.

Later, after the slogans had been unfurled, the essence of the discussion began.

Was the party prepared to begin armed struggle? A faction within the Central Committee was less than convinced, and pointed out the party's obvious weakness and military inexperience. "This is a matter," Guzmán noted, "of dispute with the developing rightist line."

The "correct" position (Guzmán's, it is understood) asserted that the revolutionary conditions existed, but it was necessary to catalyze them with armed actions carried out before deploying guerrillas to the field. The means to accomplish this had been achieved already: the reconstituted party and "advances since plenary IX."

As far as the "elaboration of the plan" of action went, the key question was whether "the masses will support armed actions . . . and how will the masses be incorporated, mobilized, politicized, organized, and provided with weapons." In this regard, Guzmán's analysis and directive were emphatic. "Ties between the party and masses exist and are developing, particularly in the countryside. . . . [The incorporation of the masses] is resolved through a long process, as the armed struggle develops and the new state forms."

The process had already begun, directed at the "militarization of the party through actions, [readjusting] in order to concentrate on military aspects. . . . it is an immediate task and in essence has already begun. . . . The party has advanced and is able to take on the BAS (Beginning of the Armed Struggle)."

In this context, the "two-line struggle" was necessary to readjust the party's internal mechanisms. The next step was to develop the "Rectification Campaign" following the "Seven Unifiers."

During the debate that followed, several concrete matters emerged. An incident in Andahuaylas, related to party leadership, was mentioned and the location of the Shining Path leadership was discussed. Later, Guzmán called on the opposition to specify whether "they were for armed struggle or not, or if they are but don't consider it pertinent today." The notes make a reference to comments made by some Political Bureau members, with a terse comment: "Retreat and persistence."

On March 19, before Guzmán resumed the previous day's discussion, several Central Committee members made the required statements expressing their "rejection of the rightist positions disclosed." The rest of the day was dedicated to a long Guzmán lecture on the "two-line struggle," drawing parallels between the present debate and "the fight against opportunism" in China, singling out the Political Bureau's dissident members, and at the same time explaining that, since the party developed with the "two-line struggle," the Central Committee simply reflected this reality.

On March 20, Guzmán challenged the opposition within the Political Bureau, and debate centered on them, on party leadership. Throughout the day, with the agenda clearly controlled by Guzmán, the "defeat of the leadership" and "its system" was discussed. In the first of a series of dramatic gestures Guzmán was to employ, pages from Shakespeare's *Julius Caesar* were read, to illustrate the ways in which conspiracy takes shape. Afterward, they discussed the "so-called positive movement's" position—apparently, the position of those opposed to Guzmán. They asserted, now openly, that neither the organization within the masses nor the party was ready to face up to an insurrection.

On March 21, Guzmán began a spirited argument, emphasizing "our decision to go forward and reach a conclusion, come what may." He continued by referring to "a document sent by a deserter." The "deserter" was *Juan Enríquez*, one of Guzmán's longtime lieutenants who had broken with him shortly before the meeting. *Enríquez* had led the opposition to the "inception plan," declaring Guzmán a "Hoxhist," and gathered about him a group within the Central Committee's Political Bureau. Perhaps, this group could have pulled together a majority and thus changed the country's history, but it lacked cohesion and was flattened by the reverential fear Guzmán inspired. The final blow came when "the deserter" left the organization and fled the country, not before writing a letter, according to rumor drafted with the collaboration of a patriarch of the "sacred family." After the debate, Guzmán spoke once again, to describe what he called "the destruction of the rightist opportunist platform and tactics" and warn of the need "in battle, to locate and differentiate well between individuals."[4]

On March 22, the decisive confrontation of this internal battle took place. The day had begun with quotations on the theme of the virtues of optimism. Guzmán had his followers read classic Mao quotations like "Changsha," "Three Brief Poems," and "The Mountains of Chingkang." But along with these excerpts, he also had them read selections from the memoirs of Field Marshal Andrés A. Cáceres, to demonstrate "the need to inspire the greatest optimism in our leaders."

Next, Guzmán drew parallels with the debate between the "positive movement" and those who had confronted Mao at the beginning of his rural campaign. What was at stake in Peru was at least as important, since "we fight for communism, not just for a national democratic revolution."

As unreachable as their objective seemed and as puny their means at the battle's start, an ideology based on justice and intense conviction were the tools they would use to distill victory from the alchemy of history's hurricane. This was the formula used repeatedly over the centuries. As a dramatic example, Guzmán had them read selections from a small and forgotten book by Washington Irving called *The Life of Mahomet*, to demonstrate "how men united behind a cause behave and further it with weapons in their hands, to establish a new order."[5]

Rip Van Winkle's creator would surely have been fascinated to see that the little book written 150 years earlier was being used in an isolated corner of the globe to ignite the warrior spirit of an obscure rebel group on the brink of committing itself to destiny.

Even Irving himself thought *The Life of Mahomet* was a minor work. He made no pretense of adding to academic knowledge on Mohammed or Islam. For him, it was a simple story about the beginnings of one of the most important feats in history. Nevertheless, this self-imposed limitation allowed some of Irving's unfairly forgotten qualities to emerge effortlessly: his excellent command of the language, his talent for detailed description, and his fine sense of humor. This small book stylishly mixes legend and history with irony and admiration. The description of the grandeur of Muslim culture at its peak is brushed on with a delicate mockery of the religion's beliefs and glimpses of Mohammed's character, especially his amorous passion, in which Guzmán would have found an uncomfortable parallel and some of his old comrades would have found amusing at the very least. More probable, however, is that Guzmán would have made a selective reading of the text, given that he had in mind only romantic hyperbole and not irony.[6] This was particularly true in describing the Muslims' amazing zenith as the historic equivalent of "the tempests which sweep the earth and sea, wrecking tall ships and rending lofty towers."[7] It captured the imagination and enthusiasm of the gathered Shining Path members, making them feel like the still ignored but nevertheless formidable source of the storm.

After this, cornering the "positive movement" was no problem. They were not only blocking "the frame of mind, cohesion, and optimism that we could develop," but, by "resisting from within" and "applying outside pressure," they had colluded with "the deserter." It was a potent accusation. The Central Committee's immediate response was "to have no further contact with the deserter." Another member of the Shining Path's old guard had been converted into an untouchable.

The second part of the Central Committee meeting was held between March 23 and 26. At first, it seemed as if the internal problems were a thing of the past and that the discussion would focus on how to "develop through actions the militarization of the party." March 23 was dedicated entirely to theoretical and doctrinal analysis. The texts read and commented upon were taken from Lenin's *Selected Military Works* and a speech made by Stalin on July 3, 1941, delivered shortly after the Nazi invasion of the Soviet Union. This text was chosen to make the Shining Path militants understand the nature of the war that they were about to create: total, a never-before-seen level of violence and destruction. Guzmán emphasized that only by agreeing to accept for themselves and especially for strangers to them higher casualties and a much more intense level of suffering than the enemy could the party erase the tactical and material disadvantage it had with the enemy and forge a "combat machine" able to grow and build itself on the nourishment provided by the old order's collapse and destruction. Stalin's position—willing to raze his own lands, destroy his country's infrastructure, and absorb the most shocking human losses in order to defeat the Nazi invader—was the example it had to keep in mind.

On March 24, the meeting centered on analyzing the recent past of armed insurrection in Peru. After a "general overview of the guerrillas in the 1960s; Peru: insurrection, revolution, guerrillas," those in attendance began to study this theme in detail. Well-known peasant activist Hugo Blanco's organization in La Convención, Cuzco, was studied under the agenda item "our revolution's path and 'land or death.'" Peasant mobilizations in 1963–64 were examined by referring to *Los Andes: Land or Death*, a book by Hugo Neyra. Finally, the most important part of the discussion examined the differences between the essentially Maoist model of insurrection developed by the Shining Path and the strategies employed by the movements mentioned already. In the context of this meeting, the purpose of a comparative analysis was to highlight the defects of these other movements for the Shining Path members, relate them to fundamental ideological defects, and explain their defeats as a necessary consequence of these defects and not the enemy's merits.

March 25 was dedicated to "the current peasant struggle." The first session was an analysis of "the agrarian law's failure and its results." On this point, Guzmán maintained that tensions and inequalities created by the application of the Agrarian Reform had generated conditions ripe for violent upheaval in the countryside.

The central theme of the plenary session convocation, "developing through actions the militarization of the party," should have been introduced on March 26. However, Guzmán chose this moment to break apart the internal conflict. In an apparently long and aggressive speech, Guzmán demanded they "resolve . . . problems caused by the Political Bureau." Those Political Bureau members who persisted in their opposition should "define their position on the deserter" before the party. If not, the party faced the "danger of a split." With this ominous warning at such a serious moment, the meeting was suspended until the following day.

On March 27, the confrontation reached the breaking point. In case *Julius Caesar* had not proved sufficient in illustrating to those in his audience how conspiracies were born and took shape, Guzmán had them read passages from *Macbeth*, where "it describes how treason grows and begins to form in the mind. To see how the seeds of injurious actions are sown." No one should be surprised to see a formerly admired and respected leader converted "objectively" into a traitor. This was not only possible but historically probable. And it was obvious that the party should be as hard on traitors as it was on the enemy.

It seems that here any effort at coordinated resistance was demolished. During the day, there were no more debates about the "two-line struggle." But literary classics continued to argue in favor of Guzmán's thesis. To focus on the following point, ties between the party and the masses, Guzmán had those present read several long segments from Aeschylus's *Prometheus Bound*, to demonstrate not only "this example of the capacity of unyielding rebellion" but also the necessary role of the masses. "It is not possible to separate the masses from the rebels."

The second plenary session ended the following day. Added to the intense and majestic message of Shakespeare, Irving, and Aeschylus, the combination of partial objectivity, attention to detail, and thematic organization had once again delivered several days' worth of victory to Guzmán. These authors had never been more necessary to him. And his final report nailed down and tied in anything that might still have remained confused: there was a "tie" between "a line and the two-line struggle," between "developing through actions the militarization of the party" and the rightist group. The worst aspect, as he said, was that those of the "right" increasingly acted like a "figurehead and within their dark headquarters. A clan."

His insinuation clearly points at one of the trunks of the "sacred family" tree, an impression accentuated when Guzmán emphasized the need to "destroy and de-molish the deserter's line and blow up this camp clan."[8] The Central Committee backed Guzmán completely.

There were seven final agreements: the reports were confirmed, along with the "contributions" gleaned from debate; it was agreed to "develop through actions the militarization of the party" (which is to say, go to war) and, as a consequence, to call for "the general readjustment of the party in order to concentrate on military aspects"; "to approve the action plan for the BAS (Beginning of the Armed Strug-gle) in accordance with what was discussed"; and "to develop the Rectification Campaign" (the promise of a self-criticizing hairshirt for those who were defeated). With the incorporation of one person, the number of Shining Path members belonging to the Political Bureau was increased to six. It was agreed to convoke in the near future a Military School and, finally, to hold another Central Committee meeting "immediately after the school, in order to finish off pending problems."

There were four exhortations made to party militants and party-generated orga-nizations: "The masses clamor to organize rebellion"; "Actions speak"; "Let us begin to tear down the walls" (organizing groups to take up immediate action); and "Raise the banner of optimism and let enthusiasm overflow." These exhortations were conveyed and reinforced, repeated in slogans with liturgical care, and were sung, this above all, in musical marches composed soon afterward.

Red flags were drawn in notebooks and covered the walls. Above them, the universal exhortation proclaimed: "Let us begin to tear down the walls and unfurl the first light of dawn." A dawn dipped in blood, of course.

The Military School

The party's Military School began on April 2. The Shining Path's future military leaders were there, and this was where they were to acquire their basic training. Yet this "school" had very little in common with a conventional military school.

The school remained in session until April 19, a total of seventeen intense and decisive days for the Shining Path. A conventional military academy, or a training camp for irregular troops, would certainly have attempted to take advantage of the most time possible to instruct the students in purely technical military skills: the preparation of explosives, demolition techniques, the setting of ambushes, the tactical use of different weapons, weapons operation, marksmanship, the use of silencers, secret communications techniques, how to post sentries, ways to follow individuals and avoid being followed.

It will be made clear later in this book that the Shining Path did not fail to pay attention to these matters. Yet it dealt with them as necessarily subordinate to ideology. Under the Central Committee's direct supervision, the purpose of the Military School was not to saturate everyone in lethal technology—given that what was necessary would be learned in the hard school of actual experience or, at the very least, in lower level classes—but rather to relate and overlap ideology with its military manifestation at every level. For the Shining Path, this was critical and warranted its undivided attention even on the eve of war.

That ideology was paramount was drilled into cadres with the ritual quotations invoked from the first day forward. The first was the celebrated lines of Mao that had figured so prominently in disputes with the supporters of the Cuban line in the 1960s and early 1970s: "When the party line is correct, we have it all: if we have no guns, we shall get them and if we do not have power, we shall conquer it. If the line is incorrect, we will lose everything that we have gained." The other quotations also came from Mao, offering attacks on "opportunism" and a recognition of its inevitability. These were just the quotations needed for the school's objectives.

After a report on the development and conclusions of the Central Committee's plenary session, they moved onto two long "self-criticism" sessions for Central Committee members "with problems," which was to say the side conquered by Guzmán. Once their penitence had concluded on April 3, those attending the school had their say, to express their opinions on the party's situation, especially the "two-line struggle and its manifestation in the Central Committee." Each leader then launched into the bittersweet exercise of self-criticism, "insofar as it relates to the problems we are dealing with."

The next day was devoted entirely to "developing battles against the right . . . a hard fight against eggshells and we will sweep them away." Most of this fight was devoted to renewed self-criticism by the vanquished members of the Central Committee who, under the vigilant stares of the others, continued to discover the inexhaustible springs of personal sin.

The process continued, inflexible, for several more days, until April 9. Almost every day, the "rightist opportunists" on the Central Committee had to repeat and delve deeper into their self-criticisms before the young Military School pupils, admit new errors, and then once again turn to self-criticism for having failed to have discovered them earlier. Prisoners of the system, as so many other Communist leaders were in the not so distant past and in almost every party in the world, they were only drawn deeper into the web of blame—which, it should be said, didn't necessarily have to be real, but was nevertheless demanding. Veteran leaders would bow their heads to some fierce youth, possibly a not very smart student in school or university, who would point accusingly, charge them with straying in a potentially suspicious way from communism's true course, in the gray area between the involuntary and the intentional. The veteran would rise afterward to speak, thanking the accuser for having drawn out and recognized these faults, adding humbly that, nevertheless, this comrade had not yet seen all the errors, given that in effect . . .

Created as an efficient method of post facto analysis, designed to annul any artificial defenses erected by the ego, criticism and self-criticism has become one of the most efficient methods history has known for the control of groups and individuals, especially strong and motivated ones, since the first years of the Stalinist hegemony. Otherwise legendarily brave combatants ended by publicly humiliating themselves with extravagant admissions of guilt, asking vehemently to be put to death, only undecided about whether it would be too much to ask that a Bolshevik bullet be contaminated by their contemptible brains. From the Moscow trials in the 1930s to Cultural Revolution China in the 1960s, these tormented displays of personal self-destruction were only possible thanks to the constant and systematic use of the rituals of surveillance, accusation, defense, recognition of guilt, humiliation, and penitence that took place through criticism and self-criticism.

In contrast to the Christian way of viewing sin, the secular theology of Marxism according to Stalin, and Mao held that one could be "objectively" guilty even though "subjectively" one believed oneself to be acting correctly. A party cadre's honesty is measured by the degree to which, once an "objective" responsibility is pointed out, the cadre cooperates with the party in picking apart conduct, in discovering the elusive roots of failure or treachery. Under collective pressure, the jump to extravagance and hysteria, to believing that one could emerge to the surface by delving deeper, was often inevitable. And honest and upright cadres would without doubt be more vulnerable to the destruction of self-criticism than colder and more cynical ones.

There was yet another reason to submerge oneself in the excesses of self-criticism. The supposed honesty and objectivity of the exercise was a way not only to recognize one's errors but also to affirm oneself before others as a true Communist. Of course, every militant went through more or less routine versions of criticism and self-criticism. In this context, "objective" wanderings, even serious ones, were theoretically subject to redemption.

Finally, the humiliated penitent was, in some form, conscious of fulfilling a useful and necessary historic role. Hadn't Mao said, "If there were no contradictions in the party and battles to resolve those contradictions, the party's life would reach an end"? A moment's error was the devil's advocate of history. In this way, if it was one's fate to occupy this unenviable but indispensable role, one had to behave as a good Communist and perform the duty with diligence and thoroughness.

In Peru, every Marxist movement had taken part in this obligatory ritual with more or less intensity. Yet none had applied the Shining Path's systematic and comprehensive consistency at once molded to its political objectives. Few within the organization had failed to cross through this dark passage, except, of course, Guzmán. And this was yet another tacit rule inherited from Stalinism and perfected by Mao. The only one exempted from the corrosive effects of criticism and self-criticism, the only one whose ceremonial self-criticisms were rejected with emotion, were those of the president, the chief, the guide. He, according to Orwell, "was more equal than the rest." As far as the others were concerned, criticism and self-criticism sessions would accompany them without pause for the rest of their lives within the party, would weaken them, and, given the very nature of the exercise, would obligate them to cooperate in their own annihilation.

The hunt for heresies and penitence: this was the Military School's first week. The meeting's nadir came on April 6, with a reading of Mao's quotations on the perfidious maneuvers of rightist opposition and from Stalin's "Against Trotskyism," followed by speeches from school students. On April 7, now completely possessed by the spirit of the "two-line struggle," students wrote and read calls for "the defense of the state of being a Communist," followed by another hemorrhaging of self-criticism. Subsequently, and after an additional reading of pertinent quotations from Mao "on sectarianism and subjectivism," Guzmán could summarize what they had achieved by predicting a "crushing defeat for rightism; rotund success for the left. The Rectification Campaign is on the move." The next day, April 8, was devoted to activities to incorporate consciousness. Nevertheless, an interesting fact was revealed. One point of discussion was to determine "the situation of the four comrades who mounted a 'defense.'" If we assume that it is probable that these individuals were the nucleus of opposition in the Political Bureau and the Central Committee, it becomes clear that Guzmán met a challenge from a substantial faction within party leadership. If this was so, and the available facts suggest it to be true, then on this momentous day Guzmán had faced down one of the greatest challenges to his control of the party; and the method he chose to combat it was just what Mao would have counseled: draw support from midlevel cadres and the party's grass-roots members.

Starting on April 9, the school began to examine fundamentally military matters. After lectures and debate on Maoist military philosophy (prolonged war, the path to surrounding cities from the countryside, bases of support), pupils began to discuss the imminent start of armed struggle within the frame of Marxism. Mao's early experiences ("Autumn Harvest," "Rural Investigation in Hunan") and Lenin's thesis on revolutionary conditions and the Communist Party's role in them were studied to explain "how to begin armed struggle from nothing."

On April 11, in a characteristic tactical role, Guzmán once again focused the energies of those gathered on another example of internal fighting, what he termed "the second beheading." If the overwhelmed, punished, and defeated opposition expected a minimum of fair play, it meant it did not know Guzmán. He read the following celebrated paragraph from Mariátegui: "I am a revolutionary. But I believe that between men of pure thought and firm beliefs it is easy to understand and value one another. But with the political sectors I will never understand it is another matter: these mediocre reformists, domesticated socialism, those Pharisee democrats."[9]

After pausing to make sure his words had soaked in, Guzmán announced that the moment's task was to clean out the "colossal mountain of garbage" that, according to Engels's metaphor, was left behind by the ideological struggles within the workers' movement. The task of ideological policing lasted all day and concluded, inflexibly, with another round of self-criticism from those members of the wretched historical detritus. Guzmán's triumphant final summary: "We have demonstrated one more way to fight against beheaded rightism."

Over the last five days, between April 14 and 19, time was dedicated to exclusively military matters. The first theme broached was the way to "construct a revolutionary army," whose axis had to be "the party's absolute leadership of the army" through permanent "political work in the army."

They then debated the insurrection's "Inception Plan." The plan counted on a small number of armed actions to catalyze a larger number of "measures of force." The principles were "to raise the harvest" (of someone else's crop, it is understood); to direct land takeovers; "to combat the reactionary government by targeting local authorities" (at the district level); and, months later, to begin guerrilla actions. More pressing matters included a discussion of what actions to take to reinforce an "electoral boycott," which would take shape a month later as the war's first action. However, the boycott had a minor impact.

Initial battles should be executed and channeled through "seedling forms" of revolutionary actions. Armed actions or force should be directed by detachments, embryos of the future "First Company," and administrative actions by "supply committees."

In the Shining Path's schematic terms, the plan took into account:

First, the political tasks to carry out, and this is to begin armed struggle, boycott elections, stimulate armed struggle on the ground with weapons, and establish foundations for the new, especially the new power; second, forms of struggle: guerrilla warfare, sabotage, propaganda and armed rabble-rousing, selective annihilation; third, military and organic forms: military detachments with and without modern weapons; fourth, timetable, starting day and plan duration, simultaneous actions on specific dates; fifth, slogans: "Armed struggle!"; "A government of workers and peasants!"; and "Down with the new reactionary government!"[10]

Another important part of the discussion was to anticipate the state's response. The Shining Path knew that the military government's weakness and, above all, the transition to democracy would make a strong response exceedingly improbable. It was on this basis that it agreed upon the action plan, which went from "the beginning up to the breaking of the first boundary."

April 16 and 17 were dedicated to an immersion in the postulates of Maoist military philosophy and their application to the Peruvian case, in particular the dialectical relationship between strategic and tactical categories. While the Peruvian state, like the proverbial "paper tiger," could be strategically scorned because of its structural weakness, at the same time it had to be taken seriously for tactical reasons in those cases where its means and power could be those of a real tiger.

In real terms, strategic disdain paired with tactical caution created the necessary paradox of having to maintain a tactical initiative within the global context of a "strategic defense" that would last several years. The purpose of tactical aggression was to create "with our effort many cases of superiority and local initiative, depriving the enemy again and again of this superiority and initiative and pushing it into inferiority and passivity."[11]

There was another vital factor: the qualities of the war leader or, in Marxist terms, the "subjective leadership." According to Mao, "in addition to the objective material conditions, the victor necessarily owes triumph to a correct subjective leadership while the vanquished owes defeat to an erroneous subjective leadership. . . . Armed with correct leadership and correct ideology, we can achieve more victories and transform our inferiority into superiority and our passivity into initiative."[12] As far as the "correct subjective leadership" went, none of the school participants, not even those who had been beheaded, seem to have harbored the least doubt about the abilities of a leader who had waged such conscientious "beheadings" over the previous days.

The final days of the Military School dealt with the way to organize guerrillas and basic principles of insurrectional war, including the Maoist categories of prolonged war on internal ideology and tactical offensives against outsiders.[13] During discussion of this last point, a review was made of the ways to fight a guerrilla war (surprise attacks and ambushes) and ended with a review of the "ten military principles," "general and concrete rules," and the "great expansion of strategy and tactics."

On April 18, the historical markers of imminent armed struggle were examined. Pupils once again reviewed, in order: "the battle in La Convención, 1962–63"; "the peasant movement of 1963–64"; "guerrillas in 1965"; "contemporary grass-roots struggle"; and, finally, "internal party organization and the Beginning of the Armed Struggle."

A day later, on April 19, the Military School was concluded. Early on, there was a debate on the school's "significance." Afterward, militants talked about the changes wrought in them by those seventeen intense days. Without exception, all were filled with emotion, seized by the intensity of their roles as universal protagonists, their destiny.

At the closing ceremony, Abimael Guzmán gave the speech that would later gain fame as his most polished oratorical piece, known as "We Are the Initiators." There are several versions. Here, I include some of the most deeply felt passages from a reliable source:

> Comrades: Our work with hands unarmed has concluded. . . . A period has ended. Here we seal what had been done; let us open the future, actions are the key, power the objective. This we will accomplish ourselves, history demands it, class exhorts it, the people have prepared for it and want it; we must do our duty and we shall. We are the initiators.
>
> Revolution will find its nest in our homeland; we will make sure of it. . . . we begin the strategic offensive for world revolution, the next fifty years will see imperialism's dominion swept away along with all exploiters. . . . the people's war will grow every day until the old order is pulled down, the world is entering a new era: the strategic offensive of world revolution. This is of transcendental importance.
>
> President Mao stated: "the storm approaches, the wind roars in the tower." . . . The peak takes shape, revolution's invincible flames will grow until they turn to lead, to steel, and, from the din of battle and its unquenchable fire will come the light, from darkness will come radiance and there will be a new world. The reactionaries dream of hyena blood: agitated fantasies rattle their gloomy nights. Their hearts beat in sinister hecatombs. They arm themselves to the teeth, but they cannot prevail, their destiny is weighed and measured.

. . . The people rear up, arm themselves, and rise in revolution to put the noose around the neck of imperialism and the reactionaries, seizing them by the throat and garroting them. They are strangled, necessarily. The flesh of the reactionaries will rot away, converted into ragged threads, and this black filth will sink into the mud; that which remains will be burned and the ashes scattered by the earth's winds so that only the sinister memory will remain of that which will never return, because it neither can nor should return.

. . . The trumpets begin to sound, the roar of the masses grows, and will continue to grow, it will deafen us, it will take us into a powerful vortex. . . . there will be a great rupture and we will be the makers of a definitive dawn. We will convert the black fire into red and the red into light. This we shall do, this is the rebirth. Comrades, we are reborn!

We have learned to manipulate history, law, contradictions. . . . The progress of the world, the country, and the party are pages in the same book. That is why our future is assured. . . .

We are the initiators. Let us begin by saying we are the initiators. We will end by saying we are the initiators. . . . Comrades, the hour has come, there is nothing further to discuss, debate has ended. It is time to act, it is the moment of rupture, and we will not carry it out with the slow meditation that comes too late, or in halls or silent rooms. We will make it in the heat of battle. . . .

Marxist–Leninist–Mao Tse-tung thought, the international proletariat, and the peoples of the world, the working class, and the people of the nation, the party with its committees, cells, and leaders: all of the great actions of the centuries have culminated here at this moment in history. The promise unfolds, the future unfurls: BAS 80.

Guzmán had not been, after all, off course when he gave them Irving's *Mahomet* to read. The speech's prophetic structure and millenarian tone is clear; with the change of a few words, it could have been delivered a hundred years ago to declare a holy war and invoke divine protection, the eye of destiny, the blessings that come after required tests and sacrifice. This was the rebellion of the mystic commissars; they set out that day. In any case, the members of that ecstatic gathering felt fervently that they were the messengers of the millennium, and signed on:

The Communists of the party's first Military School, seal of peacetime and gateway to the people's war, we stand at the head of battle as the initiators, under the leadership of the party we accept the tempering of the invincible iron legions of Peru's Red Army. Glory to Marxist–Leninist–Mao Tse-tung thought! Long live the Communist party of Peru! Led by Comrade Gonzalo, we begin armed struggle!

It is not difficult to conjure at this moment the militants who attended the first Military School: youths, the majority very young, captured by the intense emotion of people convinced that they fight for a transcendent noble cause that will at some precise moment deliver humankind to paradise. They were few and had little, but there was no more motivated, convinced, or determined group in the country and perhaps the hemisphere. Over the following years, members of this group, many themselves perishing in the task, would carry out or provoke the greatest violence, the most calamitous wounds in the country's history. Pain with no possibility for redemption, unrelieved suffering. In doing so, many continued to believe in this utopian vision, what on April 19, 1980, appeared to them with absolute certainty. Others, with flesh and bones destroyed, their own or those of others, stopped believing. Yet that was no longer of any consequence.

4

Expectations and the
Transfer of Power

Work on the transfer of power and the return to civilian rule continued between Popular Action and the military government. After a twelve-year hiatus, the Parliament prepared to reassume its former function. Veteran bureaucrats, partially retrained through the work of the Constitutional Assembly, assumed once again deliberate and solemn administrative control of the building on the Plaza of the Inquisition. Most had taken part in electoral politics since the 1950s or even earlier. With some exceptions, the list of new senators and representatives didn't differ greatly from that read by the secretaries and readers of the roll call in the tempestuous days preceding General Velasco's 1968 coup. The proverbial Peruvian political pendulum, at times overused as a metaphor, was this time apt. As a group, few returned enriched by the previous twelve years. Most of those in the party preparing to rule could perhaps best be described by the words once used to refer to those Bourbon émigrés who "had neither forgotten nor learned anything." In truth, for many Popular Action members returning to government, the year preceding 1980 had not been 1979 but 1968.

Among those who had remained in government throughout military rule were some Popular Action members now elected to Parliament, individuals who had accepted low or intermediate posts. The others, in the majority, had simply been witnesses and passive subjects of the Velasco and Morales administrations. They had sat back and watched the first moments of enthusiasm and sweeping reform, speaking out in opposition only to defend the former government. They later witnessed, again without taking part in any way, the military government's despondency and disintegration.

In short, their return to power was won with the same knowledge, political methods, and policies used before Velasco's coup. This was what they knew how to do. In any case, anything that smacked of the alternative methods of government used by the military was seen as bad form at the very least.

They were a heterogeneous mix, and reflected the striking diversity of an important part of the Peruvian elite. A minority came from traditional leading families, especially from Lima and Arequipa, or were the children or grandchildren of prestigious immigrants. Many were bound by family ties, particularly with Belaunde, or owed their connection to the president to the friendship he shared with a parent or grandparent, friendships that in more than one case had begun while working in the service of Nicolás de Piérola, the political boss of Belaunde's youth. Others were leading professionals and colleagues of the man known as the Architect from his earliest student days. They were the core of Popular Action, a mix of aristocrats and technocrats (frequently combined in the same person) implicitly separated by class from other party members and with a different kind of relationship to Belaunde.

In contrast, most Popular Action parliamentarians and members belonged to the provincial and urban middle class. While they lacked the cosmopolitan or genealogical brilliance of their "coreligionists," following the Popular Action manner of speech, perhaps because of this they had more experience within the party's committees. And they were determined to stand up and be noticed. From the beginning, their natural leader was Javier Alva Orlandini, the epitome of a Popular Action apparatchik and provincial political boss.

From the very first moment of electoral victory, Alva maneuvered to place his allies, populists tied to him by classic patronage relationships, in influential positions. He had the backing of a substantial group of Popular Action parliamentarians and also the majority within the party's committees; and he was not shy about wielding power (an indispensable trait for any political operator). Once the parliamentarians began their work, he humiliated Popular Action's candidate for Senate president, neurologist Oscar Trelles, holding up the votes necessary for his election. Only after negotiations that in essence compelled a recognition of Alva's decisive role in directing the parliamentary majority did he give the order to his allies to vote in Trelles's favor. The message was very clear. A good number of undecided provincial parliamentarians rushed to ally themselves with Alva.

Alva was particularly interested in control of the Interior Ministry. Interior minister during Belaunde's first administration, he was very familiar with the opportunities this post offered for control and influence. The only problem was that between him and José María de la Jara, the man nominated to head the ministry, there was little affection.

De la Jara had offered the post of vice-minister to historian Héctor López Martínez, a longtime friend, and Belaunde had immediately accepted. Nevertheless, once Alva Orlandini learned of the nomination, he invited De la Jara to lunch at the Crillón Hotel. There, surrounded by several of his Senate allies, he told the soon-to-be minister that López Martínez was unacceptable. He had collaborated with the military government, and remained the director of the newspaper *El Comercio*, still controlled by the military.

De la Jara was the antithesis incarnate of Alva Orlandini. But he had passion and fighting spirit to spare. Without giving any explanations to Alva Orlandini, he told him that López Martínez "would stay." Minutes later, the lunch ended with the men stalking out, in the words of one invitee. De la Jara called Belaunde and made López Martínez's appointment a condition of his appointment. Well acquainted with López Martínez's character as well as the fact that he remained at *El Comercio* with the support of the Miró Quesada family and was preparing the way for the family to recover the newspaper (and, in fact, López Martínez returned to *El Comercio* after leaving the Interior Ministry), Belaunde spoke with Alva Orlandini and pushed through De la Jara's choice.

Bad blood between the two Popular Action leaders thickened when De la Jara began to name new police force chiefs. Alva wanted to retain General Humberto Passano, head of the Civil Guard, his friend. De la Jara turned him down and stuck to his decision.

Weeks after assuming control of the Interior Ministry, De la Jara and López Martínez had begun to tackle the critical task of naming new police force chiefs. Their method was anything but scientific. Recommendations rained in. Almost every Popular Action potentate had candidates and people to protect politically. Eligible officers maneuvered to the limits of their powers, trying to curry favor and put obstacles in the way of their rivals. Both confused and surprised, De la Jara and López threw their hands up and decided "in part guided by recommendations and in part by instinct"[1] to name General Juan Balaguer to head the Civil Guard, Eduardo Ipinze to the Investigative Police, and Julio Estrada to the Republican Guard. For all practical purposes, the peace of the Republic rested on the shoulders of these men.

Balaguer had served during the last months of the Morales Bermúdez government as the head of the agency charged with reviving the region devastated by the 1970 earthquake and massive landslide. As such, he had ministerial rank. If anyone had guessed that in this former rank there rested the seeds of a problem, they would have been completely correct. Balaguer carried with him an aura of energy and hardness fostered by the stereotypical forbidding demeanor and harsh voice he had adopted and shared with so many Latin American military and police officers. After twelve years of military government, the value of this manner had depreciated. Yet in the absence of an alternative, it still seemed authentic. His time as a minister had exacerbated one of his largest flaws, vanity. The mental machinations of this strictly vertical bureaucracy had finished him off. For Balaguer and his generals, institutional progress was measured by the protocolary honors awarded to his team and the administrative offices placed under his control, which became his principal concern. The tools put at the disposal of the police, the quality of training, the well-being of its members, were secondary.

Ipinze raised fewer doubts. He was a relatively young general, with the bearing and reputation of a Latin Elliot Ness, and had risen rapidly through the ranks as chief of a "brigade" specialized in criminal investigations. His penchant for personally directing raids and arrests had brought him excellent press. To the public, Ipinze was the incarnation of the ideal modern policeman, just the sort of honest, efficient officer the country needed.

However, there was another side to the story only known by a few within the police department and some branches of the intelligence services. After heading up the "brigade," Ipinze had moved to the "division"[2] that oversaw the crackdown on drug trafficking in 1978, just as several national syndicates began to take shape and trade intensified. As was learned several years later, Ipinze firmed up his ties to a then unknown public accountant, Reynaldo Rodríguez López, presumably via José Jorge Zárate,[3] another police officer, during this period. Rodríguez López was already well on his way to setting up what would be, as of 1982 and perhaps even beforehand, the most powerful and best organized drug-trafficking network in Peru. Although it is possible that corruption had begun to work its way into Ipinze earlier, this is when his leap to criminal behavior took place.[4]

Corruption immediately contaminated the drug-trafficking "division." That this would happen was perhaps inevitable given the economic power of the drug trade, but the initiative taken by the police chief not only greatly accelerated this process but also gave it an official uniform. The nucleus of honest cops that usually manages to survive such spontaneous periods of corruption was either pushed aside or transferred. The quality of police work suffered immediate decay.

By 1978, the Drug Enforcement Administration (DEA), part of the United States Justice Department, had already sent a team of agents to Lima to coordinate investigations and exchange intelligence on drug-trafficking networks with Peruvian police. The team leader was veteran police officer William Wetherington. When it became evident that the corruption within the narcotics command made any cooperation impossible, Wetherington tried to develop investigations into drug trafficking with the Peruvian Investigative Police (PIP), then under the command of PIP General Edgar Luque Freyre.

Luque cooperated enthusiastically and won the approval of his superiors to begin joint investigations with the DEA. During one such investigation, a rookie agent, José Vásquez Vargas, who was tailing Alfonso Rivera Llorente, one of the most powerful drug traffickers of the time, was ambushed by his target and his gang, tortured, and killed. One of the killers was David Barrios Esponda, an active-duty PIP officer.[5]

In the rush to capture Rivera Llorente, who fled the country immediately after the murder, Luque acted with the utmost zeal and risked more than a police officer normally would. Clearly, the tacit and initially silent war had been openly declared between the leadership of the drug-trafficking and intelligence departments and above all between Luque and Ipinze. Luque captured various police suspects and, flaunting his institution's unwritten rules, ordered them "strung up," which is to say interrogated using a standardized form of torture common in Peruvian police stations. It consists of suspending the victim in the air by arms bound behind the back, from a rope tied to the elbows and wrists. The pain in the shoulders, which often pop out of joint, is extreme, and the pressure on the diaphragm creates a sensation of suffocation heightened by blows, shoves, and insults.

Later, Luque obtained the cooperation of an important Colombian drug trafficker, Franco Giraldo, captured just outside Lima. Giraldo was willing to talk about where Rivera Llorente was hiding in exchange for his freedom and immediate return to Colombia. Luque agreed and Giraldo left for Colombia, where he was murdered.

That made a personal confrontation between Ipinze and Luque inevitable. Ipinze and his people, more numerous and astute than those around Luque, attributed the operation's failure to more than police incompetence. According to them, Luque had committed a crime by releasing a prisoner without a judge's authorization. Technically, they were right. As far as Luque and his team were concerned, the information on Franco Giraldo's secret mission had been leaked to Colombian drug traffickers by corrupt PIP officers, probably people from within the narcotics division. Confronted by the explosion of internal conflict, then PIP chief Manuel Lezama, who didn't want to impose a decision on his own, called a "council of generals" to discuss the problem.

In the meeting, the discussion quickly became heated. Ipinze, an aggressive man who found it served his purpose to let his passions get the better of him, answered Luque's accusations with a shove, an act that resonated for several years in institutional folklore. Smaller than Ipinze and above all less belligerent, Luque was struck dumb and only managed to lodge a protest with Lezama. A weak-willed man who let himself be ordered around by his military chiefs, Luque tried halfheartedly to punish Ipinze but never managed to do so. With this single gesture, Ipinze emerged triumphant from the conflict. The intelligence department abandoned its drug-trafficking investigations, and inquiries into the Rivera Llorente-Giraldo case were shipwrecked.[6] For those in the know, however, it was clear that the ensuing years would revolve around the rivalry between Luque and Ipinze.

Ignoring the history behind this episode, acting with the best of intentions and a most revealing naiveté, De la Jara and López Martínez named Ipinze to head the PIP under the new democratic government.[7]

Julio Estrada, chief of the Republican Guard, was an essentially innocuous person. Like almost all the top officials of his generation, he had been drawn from the army's middle ranks. Despite the fact that the Republican Guard was meant to be a neighborhood police force, it was the smallest force within the police. In the perennial battle of intrainstitutional skirmish and confrontation, the Republican Guard had always closed ranks with the army in order to neutralize the Civil Guard. While the Civil Guard had always assumed the role of a Cinderella (at least according to its members) in its relationship with the armed forces and above all the army, other police branches related to it as the evil stepmother. Each institution's chiefs of staff shared the belief that "institutional objectives" demanded that they assume the most public duties possible while at the same time blocking rival institutions from doing the same, amassing resources and denying access to their rivals. In the wake of the lobbying efforts carried out at the Constitutional Assembly, each of the forces saw itself in ascendance and was prepared to maximize its prerogatives while cutting off any competition. Among other things, this provoked frequent street clashes between police officers over the following months, some violent.

Meanwhile, once the police chiefs were named to this future ministry, the transfer of power concentrated on passing along information on administrative matters and priorities in police work. It should have also included the transfer, with detailed explanations, of the intelligence archives on subversive groups. But this never occurred. The way that this stockpile of information was pilfered from the stores of the new civilian government constitutes a chapter both sad and incriminating: a military government awarded this new democracy a Trojan horse carrying an insurrection it neither understood nor clearly detected.

5

The Vanished Files

On the night of July 27, 1980, Héctor López Martínez left the executive offices of *El Comercio* and moved to the Interior Ministry. The short trip between downtown Lima and the Córpac offices—an old airport refurbished to house police headquarters and Peru's prefectures—separated his former job under the military government from the new one under the emerging Belaunde administration. On a personal level, it was a rapid transition, but not at all surprising given the terms of the transfer of government: brief, almost exaggeratedly courteous, without questions or uncomfortable demands, and with an ease that at moments made it seem more like a transfer of command rather than the delivery of a government from a military dictatorship to a newborn democracy.

At the first hour of July 28 and a democratic government, López Martínez was already seated at the epicenter of the country's police apparatus, taking the pulse of the visible and invisible veins of the system of social control: the three branches of the police force, their intelligence offices, the prefectures, subprefectures, and offices of appointed governors; each should have been alert to the subtlest variations in the national mood, the first sign of social disturbance, emerging conspiracies. Without alarm, López Martínez began to gather bent antennae, loose threads.

Two months before the formal transfer of power, since June 1, López Martínez had begun to "receive" the Interior Ministry from the military government's last interior minister, army general César Iglesias. In several of the meetings held over the following months, Iglesias had expressed to López Martínez his uneasiness over what he termed "the advance of subversion."[1]

Nevertheless, López Martínez realized that among the things that the new government should inherit were Interior Ministry intelligence files, which were not there. Weeks earlier, after wrapping up a meeting with Iglesias, he had been shown the Interior Ministry offices by the interior vice-minister, army brigade general Luis Sánchez Obregón. Upon arriving at the Interior Ministry Intelligence Center (Dimin)—a three-floor building attached to the main office, equipped with a narrow staircase on an outside wall—López Martínez had asked after the ministry's intelligence files. "They have been evacuated," answered the vice-minister. An empty space in one of the Dimin's largest rooms marked the spot just where, López Martínez learned, the files had been kept.[2]

That same night, López Martínez broached the matter with Belaunde in the apartment the president-elect occupied in the "Olivar Tower" apartment complex in San Isidro, converted into the headquarters of the "high-level" political negotiations that preceded the official transfer of power. Genuinely concerned by the possibility that the military would take a step backward in the democratic transition (a fear the military capitalized on skillfully at the time and for the next few months), Belaunde told him that it was better "not to make waves." The matter of the intelligence files was not mentioned again until 1983, when the issue of whether they existed was no longer relevant.

Fear was not the only reason why the new government chose not to make the issue of the vanished files a matter of national importance. There was also an element of form: it appeared crass for a democratic government to put undue emphasis on retrieving files containing confidential information, much of it obtained secretly. Some of Belaunde's close associates even made the predictable nervous jokes that the files had disappeared because of the number of reports dedicated to recording their activities. At a time when both populists and soldiers were cultivating amnesia, invoking elaborate courtesies to communicate, the mention of documents that could contain a good part of the recent past's crude history was perceived as akin to an attack on common decency.

The huge room remained empty. With time, new desks and chairs began to fill it, their occupants draped across, reading newspapers, summarizing them as "information reviews," and solemnly stamping them "classified" or "top secret" in the upper margin.

Despite the enthusiasm and democratic ebullience of these days, López Martínez and José María de la Jara had reason to lament the absence of this information only a few hours after officially taking over the Interior Ministry. On the evening of July

28, during a cocktail party at the Venezuelan Embassy, where both were present, the first act of sabotage against the electrical power network left Lima dark. It was the beginning of what would, a short time later, become a genuine tradition during the war: the violent play between light and the night.

During the blackout, De la Jara and López Martínez immediately assumed their new roles as the supreme guardians of the collective peace. After returning to the Interior Ministry offices, they wrote the first orders dispatching citywide police patrols.

The next day, the minister and vice-minister summoned their police chiefs, particularly those from the PIP, to coordinate a sabotage investigation and find out what the police knew. To their surprise, few detectives were willing to comment. Not a single one was introduced as a specialist in the area of State Security.

Both amused and upset, De la Jara and López Martínez realized that the police, and above all the PIP, feared reprisals from the populist government, especially from De la Jara, the ultimate exile. Although he reassured them that he held no grudges against his persecutors and had accepted his appointment without regard for what was past, to some officers present his statements suggested a sinister cunning. "No one wanted to appear tied to State Security," López Martínez remembered, "and only several months later did General Luque show his cards."[3] But Luque was enmeshed in an institutional battle on the verge of being lost to the sitting PIP chief, General Eduardo Ipinze, and the group he represented. At stake was much more than ego. In this predicament, Luque could not hope for victory, despite having offered his services when no one else was willing to do so.

And so, along with their inexperience—accentuated by De la Jara's lack of relish for the job, repulsed as he was by the gruff demeanor expected of interior ministers—both minister and vice-minister spent their first crucial weeks of training and command groping their way around the newborn guerrilla insurgency. They felt the first tremors with growing intensity, unable to identify their origin or any cause with the detail or depth one would have expected in their positions. The files had disappeared and the few police officers who knew something kept silent out of fear. In that way, several weeks passed.

When did the military know about the Shining Path? Did it realize or ignore the fact that an insurrection was imminent? When the issue of the vanished files became public in 1983, one of the numerous conspiracy theories woven or unraveled each week in Lima held that the military knew perfectly well what was coming and permitted a Shining Path insurrection to explode in order to pressure and indirectly humiliate the civilian government. This would ensure that at a given moment, when the civilian government was discredited, its own failures would be forgotten and it would be called once again to action.

However, this was not the case. A disaster typical of these types of events had occurred within the intelligence services: essential information existed and was shared, but was not deemed important.

In terms of internal security, the Shining Path had a relatively low priority compared with the Morales Bermúdez administration's other concerns. Half-hidden in the virulent thicket of other Marxist organizations, less visible in—or completely separated from—work stoppages and strikes, the Shining Path's plan for insurrection, so openly plotted out, seemed at the very least difficult to accomplish.

Nevertheless, a more or less steady stream of reports on the organization had been filed, even before the break with Saturnino Paredes and the definitive split with Red Flag. Its activity was recorded by local police or civilian informers working with the National Intelligence Service (SIN). Yet everything points to the fact that the information received was considered unimportant.

Beginning in 1977, details warning about Shining Path preparations for armed struggle started to arrive at the various intelligence services. On March 16, 1977, a navy intelligence service reported on "politicized students from . . . the Communist Party of José Carlos Mariátegui [sic] (Shining Path) directed by Luis Kawata Kawata [sic]. . . . Frequently they carry out continuous visits [sic] to the jungle (Santa Rosa, Pichari, San Francisco) that borders the valleys of La Convención and Quillabamba, where they practice marksmanship with light weapons explaining that they are wild animal hunters."[4] With the speculative style typical of creole informants, the report added that "the possibility exists that some students have ties to drug trafficking, and intend to finance arms purchases and carry out agitation and propaganda activities in the central mountains since the area dwellers provide the necessary conditions."[5] The report was sent to the SIN classified as B/B/2.[6]

On June 27, 1977, another intelligence report included information about a meeting of Shining Path militants in a Lima "young town," Playa Rímac, held on June 20. There, a delegate from the Lima Regional Committee indicated that "the only solution for the people is popular war, for which we should prepare ourselves ideologically and militarily. . . . the end of the current government will . . . deliver power to one of the reactionary political parties or perhaps a right-wing coalition."[7] The report was classified as B/B/3.

On July 19, 1977, an army intelligence report forwarded information about the sabotage of two Cangallo bridges between July 6 and 8, "having an understanding that these actions of force are taken against the Agrarian Reform, against the increase in the cost of living, against the rise in the price of gasoline, fares, and other internal problems." After adding that "at this time, the people of Ayacucho are being stirred up by the Coalition for the Defense of Ayacucho," the report said "it is understood that university students are taking part in trips to the areas of San Fernando and Pomacocha, possibly with the goal of carrying out explosives training and to proselytize."[8] This ambiguous bureaucratic style, the disjuncture between information and any conclusion, was typical of similar documents.

On December 28, SIN report 3219, titled "Possible guerrilla indoctrination in Cusco," suggested that grass-roots schools were being set up in the city. The information was specific. The Shining Path cadre responsible for classes asserted that in Lima there were "around 500 grass-roots schools operating in secret, given that problems cannot be solved with strikes, marches, or graffiti on walls, the situation obligates us to raise the consciousness of the people in preparation for popular war." According to the report, there were already eight grass-roots schools functioning in Cusco.[9]

On December 6, 1978, Report 17-DPE from the Civil Guard's Central Intelligence office reviewed the panorama of Marxist activity in Ayacucho and mentioned the Shining Path's recently held eighth plenary, emphasizing that the most important agreement "was to culminate and lay the groundwork for armed struggle to begin." The report described the way the Shining Path had divided Ayacucho city into zones as well as how different guerrilla-generated organizations functioned. Describing the Shining Path as a "dangerous and subversive" organization, it added that it was impossible to rule out a "possible guerrilla action." Further on, however, the report erroneously indicated that Red Flag had "come to an agreement to initiate armed struggle in the rural sector, for which it should be establishing support bases in the Apurímac River jungle."[10] The report linked this organization to agitation in rural areas, as well as attacks on Civil Guard stations in Vischongo on November 20, 1978, and the Cangallo province police station that same month.

On April 30, 1979, an army intelligence report gave a detailed account of a clandestine meeting in the Ayacucho home of Shining Path peasant activist Manuel Llamojha Mitma, which included Shining Path cadres, community members, and teachers from Pomacocha, Vilcashuamán, and Vischongo. The information, which had to come from an informant present at the meeting, referred in detail to Shining Path plans to continue forcing the Civil Guard to abandon its posts in Ayacucho's provinces. It indicated that a "commission of three people" would soon travel to Ocros, Chumbes, and Concepción "with the goal of planning the Civil Guard's eviction, recognizing that the number of Civil Guard personnel at these posts is low." During the meeting, the semiopen operation of the grass-roots schools in Vilcashuamán and Vischongo, where the Civil Guard had already been evicted, was discussed, and a peasant leader affirmed that they were "ready and prepared so that together with the teachers they could declare a 'civil war.' "[11]

On May 24, 1979, Civil Guard Central Intelligence prepared a new summary of the substantial increase in agitation and attacks on Civil Guard posts in the department. The report concluded by affirming that "acts of sabotage, clashes with the forces of order, and probable attacks on GC posts" could be expected, although the report insisted that these actions would be the fruit of coordination between the Shining Path and Red Flag.[12]

The combined weight of these reports, evaluated with a bureaucratic caution even greater than that exercised in their preparation, finally prompted the military government to convoke a high-level meeting to discuss social upheaval in Ayacucho. As *Caretas*, no. 566, reported, "On Wednesday, August 15, the President of the Republic presided over an Internal Front meeting dedicated especially to an analysis of a problem involving strange characters appearing in some districts in Ayacucho and Huancavelica." The article added that "usually exaggerated intelligence reports made reference to a guerrilla outbreak in a zone plagued by long-standing poverty and wicked freezes." Nevertheless, the article added that "after more careful investigation, a better overview of the situation was made. . . . It has to do, rather, with the nonviolent removal of political and police authorities of some districts located in an undetermined region between Ayacucho and Huancavelica, with the massive support of the population."[13]

Given that the article was obviously based on a source with access to privileged information from the Government Palace, it appears clear that the military government—weary and in retreat and, on top of that, overwhelmed by urban union agitation—did not want to hear the reports coming in from the countryside. For their part, the intelligence services were habitually sensitive to the mood changes of those in power and were inclined to please them to the extent possible. They tried not to insist on supplying unwelcome information about what was happening in Ayacucho. In addition, it is clear that the intelligence services had only a fragmentary understanding. Faced with the military government's irritated lack of interest in new problems, they did not persist in broadening their inquiry despite the evident seriousness of some of the symptoms.

Despite everything, some information continued to reach the intelligence services. On September 6, 1979, a SIN message indicated that "a group of university students, members of the Shining Path political sect, is giving talks on guerrilla warfare in a building located in northern Lima." The message added that a selected group practiced "with firearms in the Ancón beach resort dunes where it conducts exercises in handling weapons (without munitions)."[14] The message was evaluated and given a prudent B/B/2.

Based on this information, it was difficult to avoid the realization that the air was heavy with portent, rumors of storm—that the proverbial "old mole" of Marxist metaphor was actively rooting around just under the surface. But the military government preferred not to listen. And it wasn't for reasons of tragedy but because of the more prosaic combination of fatigue and a loss of reflex due to the lethargy of twelve uninterrupted years of power, the last four of which had been dedicated to retreat and stagnation. Disenchanted with its own rhetoric, harassed by protest, and whittled down by the growing influence of corruption in its ranks, the military government's energies were absorbed in carrying out the most peaceful transition to civilian rule possible while at the same time guaranteeing its separate courts and privileges and reacting only to what was most visibly urgent.

But rumors and night marches, public statements by Shining Path leaders and militants, did have an impact in Ayacucho. Although a significant portion of the population—almost the entire Marxist left among them—did not take seriously these proclamations of an imminent "people's war," others did not undervalue the announcements of a revolt. In September 1979, the military commander of the zone, apparently acting on his own initiative, ordered and carried out a "special intelligence operation" to assess the extent of "subversive activities" in Vilcashuamán, Pomacocha, and Vischongo.

The "agent report" was written in October.[15] Most of the text is dedicated to descriptions of the physical and social geography, and evokes the style and structure of a high school term paper. But in other details, the report is interesting and revealing, as much for what the agent saw as for what he stopped looking at.

In Vilcashuamán, the agent noted that "the Civil Guard post does not exist. . . . at present, it has been replaced by the 'Peasant Patrol' . . . made up of forty people or members." Along with maintaining order, punishing cattle rustling, and making sure that community decisions were carried out by the authorities, among the duties of the patrol was the "protection of community leaders in order to prevent 'repression' from police authorities, communicating immediately through . . . a system of contacts." The agent discovered that the patrols had been extremely efficient in carrying out their duties. He also noted that most of the community's collective work was done according to tradition, indicating that "all the community members participate in this service. The teachers who own plots of land also fulfill the same obligations as members of the community."

The agent observed that "Sute [sic] teachers are the main educators on political matters because of their relationship with the parents (community members) and students as well as the community labor they also participate in without exception." Apart from the eviction of the police from their posts, he also noted more clues to Shining Path influence, and indicated that "as a result of the substitution made by Sute-Vilcashuamán, the director of NEC-10-35 was thrown out and declared persona non grata by the Communal Assembly."[16] These observations well described the Shining Path's local influence and control. But the agent also presented other clues to the threat of insurrection. Despite the fact that he asserted that the patrols "maintained a certain level of vigilance over strange or suspicious people who took no part in communal life for . . . fear that leaders who had outstanding warrants would be arrested," he found no evidence "of paramilitary training camps or weapons storehouses."

His observations on Pomacocha were similar to those made on Vilcashuamán, although he specified that while the Shining Path predominated in Vilcashuamán, in Pomacocha "Red Flag, led by Saturnino Paredes Macedo, was more popular." After pointing out that the Vischongo Civil Guard post had been closed since November 1978, he commented that the district government was in the hands of the "Coalition for the Defense of the People's Interests," made up of members of the local community, Sute-Vischongo, the local women's committee, and the "Unified Front of High School Students." He also wrote that political influence was divided between the Shining Path and Red Flag. Finally, he received information that the area communities (Vilcashuamán, Pomacocha, and Vischongo) had recently unified, but he gave it no importance. His search for training camps and uniformed guerrillas had been fruitless.[17]

On October 2, 1979, basing himself in large part on the agent's report, one of the area military commanders prepared an intelligence report about the "establishment of a liberated zone" in Pomacocha. The report drew on reliable and alarming information, like the violent expulsion of the police from Vischongo and Pomacocha—and the later abandonment of the Civil Guard posts in Vilcashuamán, Carhuanca, and Huambalpa. He also observed correctly that these actions had been "supported directly by Sutep and San Cristóbal de Huamanga National University (UNSCH) students." A matter of immediate concern stemmed from having watched about thirty armed soldiers mount sweeps in the gorge created by the Apurímac River to capture "approximately forty deserters belonging to the Andahuaylas barracks who had fled with weapons and munitions."[18] He added that "the Ayacucho political and police authorities are incapable of controlling the spread of subversive actions." But he made no mention of the Shining Path as the organization behind these actions, and instead focused on Red Flag, at the time concentrating its attention on its leader's performance: Saturnino Paredes Macedo, then attending the Constitutional Assembly. It was a curious blindness, but not entirely inexplicable.

The final results of this investigation were communicated in a report prepared by the army general command. The paperwork generated up to that moment begged some sort of bureaucratic response. The intelligence reports appear in the final section of the army summary, converted into part of Operation "Morochuco." This final report was written in Lima on October 12, 1979. Its initial analysis was surprising. The movements in Vilcashuamán, Vischongo, Cangallo, and Pomacocha were "autonomous, spontaneous [sic] rebellions . . . pursued with the objective of living within a communitarian liberalism in accord with the laws of the Inca Empire."[19] How the author of the report came to this picturesque interpretation remains unexplained.

Nevertheless, part of the report was objective: the expulsion of the police from

Vischongo by a throng of peasants, students, and teachers was mentioned. There was also information on the expulsion of the Civil Guard from Vilcashuamán, carried out by a joint mobilization made up of the communities of Vischongo, Pomacocha, Chito, Chanin, "and others," the same ones that had thrown out the director of the Educational Nucleus of the area for "having dismissed teachers pledged to honor the Sutep strike."[20] The report added that every stranger was questioned, and that "if that person is suspected of belonging to the government, his movements are watched and all types of information are withheld."

In referring to the political organizations with local influence, the report specifies that the Shining Path "has occupied all the leadership positions in Sutep in Cangallo province and Ayacucho department, because of the fact that the Shining Path controls the UNSCH Federation and the Education Department. The teachers sent to these locations are, for the most part, from the area and do political work in the cities and countryside."[21] The report added that "the Sutep in Vilcas, Vischongo, and Cangallo is directed by Shining Path militants, who do not permit any compromise with other leftist forces." But it also made the point that Red Flag, "conducted and directed by Saturnino Paredes Macedo, is carrying out political work specifically within the peasant sector, and has managed to dominate the leadership in Pomacocha, Vischongo, Chito, Chanin."

Referring to activities "that reveal the subversive situation," the report concludes that "neither instructors nor indoctrination and paramilitary preparation zones or places have been detected" and that "no political organization orients and recruits individuals for subversive actions." Commenting on the possible presence of foreigners in the area, the report makes mention only of an Albanian delegation that attended the Peruvian Peasant Federation (CCP–Red Flag) conference in Pomacocha. The report added that "there are no controlled areas or support bases" and that community life continued "in harmony with that established by the Laws of the Nation" and that "there are no weapons or weapons caches in community hands." It explained that the ten uniformed individuals armed with light automatic rifles (FAL) and Uzi weapons who entered the "San Agustín" farm on July 15, 1979, who were "identified as guerrillas indoctrinating peasants in communism and inciting them into seizing lands," were members of an army patrol "who were carrying out a mission to recover FAL Number 76911, which had been stolen from a soldier . . . on June 5, 1979."[22] In light of what the future held for the "San Agustín" farm and its inhabitants, this part of the report appears to contain the first confused auguries of coming tragedy.

These were the conclusions of the most focused and specific intelligence work carried out at the time, when all of the Shining Path's energies were tensed, in preparation for war. From today's perspective, the agent's point of view appears at moments not only seriously deficient but intentionally in error. Yet it is improbable that this was the case. In all intelligence work, and especially in strictly hierarchical organizations like the army, one of the considerations that frequently precedes report preparation is an attempt to ensure that the information will not exasperate superior officers. And the military government wanted to know nothing about massive conspiracies that would reveal a field mined beyond anyone's worst nightmare. To this logic was added another, more important one: all dictatorships—and the Morales Bermúdez regime was no exception—brandish the defense of the country's internal security as a leading argument to legitimate their rule. With the professional soldiers about to deliver to the nation the Trojan horse of an insurrection ready to explode after a long incubation during their government, any pretense at historical legitimacy was undermined.

There was also a perceptual problem. The military could only conceive of guerrillas in terms of a classic Castro-style movement. The symptoms it looked for were the presence of strangers wearing olive drab uniforms, training camps, arms deposits. It could not imagine a different style of guerrilla war; and when these guerrillas were literally under the noses of the military, it had no way to see them. It was not a case of physical blindness—all the basic information was there, it had been recorded—but intellectual blindness.

From the dawn of the art of war, one of the greatest ambitions of any strategist in preparing a campaign has been to get the enemy to convince itself that it is well informed on the strategists' plans. To blind the eyes and comprehension of spies—and through them the enemy—through elaborate forms of camouflage, illusion, and trickery has always been among the highest expression of the military arts. Scant months before the actual outbreak of war, with its organizational apparatus virtually ready, the Shining Path had achieved—perhaps without realizing it—its first victory.

Information continued to arrive over the following months. On December 18, 1979, a report sent by the SIN indicated that "versions exist . . . that in the districts of Vilcashuamán, Vischongo, Carhuanca . . . Pomacocha, and Chito, there are subversive organizations and guerrilla training camps." But, loyal to implanted stereotypes, the informant added: "The districts of Vilcashuamán, Vischongo . . . are tourist centers (archaeological ruins) and so they are visited by a large number of foreigners, and it has happened that among them are international Communist elements who take advantage of tourism to visit the areas referred to."[23] Even if the Shining Path itself had spread this disinformation, it couldn't have done a better job. But the informers and their bosses had put their gaze on the horizon, awaiting a literal repetition of Che Guevara's undertaking in Bolivia. And they didn't look around them.

Reports, fragmentary but insistent, did not come in only from Ayacucho. On January 17, 1980, a SIN report from Puno reviewed a clash between UNIR activists, among them Horacio Zeballos, and Puka Llacta students at the Altiplano Technical

University. When the UNIR activists tried to enter the university, "they were rebuffed by the Student Federation of the Altiplano (FEUNTA) students armed with sticks and stones." The UNIR members had no recourse but to hold their rally outside the university, where the speakers "criticized the FEUNTA university students for having chanted the 'Popular war from the countryside to the city' slogan, labeling them infantile dreamers of a popular war from the countryside to the city."[24]

The basic information reappeared regularly and with insistence, although still lost among apparently trivial details. For example, on February 18, 1980, after discussing a rally held by Víctor Quintanilla's strengthened faction, part of the Coalition for the Defense of the People of Ayacucho, in the city's central square "in which a thousand people took part," a SIN report added that "recently the Communist Party of Peru (PCP-SL) organized a 'celebration of student unity' with the participation of UNSCH students in the student cafeteria; the entry fee went to cover the cost of political work, like the trips of commissions to various communities in the region, with the goal of organizing the so-called grass-roots schools and beginning preparations to give incentives in order to carry out armed struggle in the near future."[25]

At other times, the same information was mixed with apparent attempts at personal vengeance or obvious errors. On February 21, 1980, for example, a report from a group tied to the army on "actions that the Shining Path movement is developing" emphatically affirmed that "subversive actions are carried out under the direction of *Walter Tristán* . . . who works . . . in the Transportation and Communications Ministry." The report continued by indicating that the Shining Path members "are training for the campaign and land seizures in Ongoy, Acobamba, and Miraflores (Andahuaylas). They also receive support from miners from the central mountains. In the city of Lima, their main support rezts [*sic*] on San Marcos University (UNMSM) and the Callao Technical University." With the same emphasis used for the first point, the report adds that "they propose to prevent the elections and become the armed wing of Red Homeland."[26] However, next to this elemental mistake, the report indicates that "the PCP 'Pucallacta' is preparing peasant guerrillas to support the Shining Path movement."[27]

The same informer—if we can judge by the report's tone—wrote a similar document for air force intelligence on February 22. With more details and the help of maps, the report combines reliable facts with serious errors. After pointing out that "the Communist Party Peru [*sic*] Shining Path is preparing a guerrilla war conceived within the Maoist idea of 'war from the countryside to the city and war from the urban periphery (young towns) to the urban center (residential areas),'" the report repeats information about the supposed alliance with Red Homeland, adding that the goal was to create a "political military coalition similar to the Nicaraguan Sandinista Front for National Liberation."[28]

After correctly mentioning the principal recruiting areas (some of the universities where the Shining Path had influence) as well as areas where there was training and armed actions (for the first time, the Upper Huallaga was mentioned together with Ayacucho, Huancavelica, and Andahuaylas), the informer once again mentioned government employee *Walter Tristán*, no longer supposedly the subversives' supreme leader but the one responsible for purchasing and storing weapons. "This functionary . . . obtains maps of roads, highways, installations, and essential services with the complicity of his secretary. . . . One of the actions carried out in Huancavelica was the seizure of dynamite crates." Noteworthy about this report, plagued with errors and contaminated by obvious personal dislikes, is that the map included to show the Shining Path's zones of operation precisely recorded areas that would be the primary and secondary theaters of war three years later.[29]

On April 4, 1980, a SIN report sounded a muffled alarm. According to information given by one informant, a Shining Path member had announced that his group "will boycott the May 1980 elections; at the same time he said that on May 18, 1980, armed struggle would begin in the country, against the new civilian government; that for this reason the forces of war . . . are distributed equally throughout strategic zones, awaiting orders to begin guerrilla war."[30]

Five days later, on April 9, a Republican Guard intelligence report, written by a new source and sent to the SIN with the epigraph "Possible beginning of the popular war from the countryside to the city: Ayacucho," gave further details and added several crucial new ones. After reporting that the Shining Path "was advocating the start of the so-called 'Popular war from the countryside to the city' as the only way to take power," the report added a dramatic detail: "A possible date for the beginning of the popular war would be the second half of the current month, simultaneously throughout the Republic, giving priority to Ayacucho (Paras, Chuschi, San Miguel). Lately, they have been making final arrangements."[31]

Two intelligence reports from different sources, yet on the same subject and separated by a mere five days, gave the date and location of an imminent guerrilla explosion, with forty days' warning. One could not ask much more of information. Nevertheless, no decisions were made and not a single action was taken.[32]

Among other things, all of the reports mentioned here had been removed when soldiers decided to "evacuate" the Dimin intelligence files. By then, the insurrection had begun, and news of attacks and actions piled on top of yesterday's forgotten predictions. If this intelligence had been put at the service of the new civilian authorities, eager and anxious for it, the negligence of the military government's security apparatus would have been evident, and it would certainly have been mentioned, if not denounced, by De la Jara in public. And this institutional embarrassment, this "loss of face," was what the military apparently tried to avoid by carting off the files and leaving the new government in darkness.

6

The Dogs of War

War had begun, but one side didn't realize it. Its attention was focused on the transfer of government, its energy on a smooth transition and the turns and twists of the disputes that continued within the political parties. After the Apra's depressing electoral defeat, hostilities between the followers of Armando Villanueva and Andrés Townsend erupted with increasing openness and rancor. Despite his defeat, Villanueva managed to prevail and maintain control, helped in large part by the Apra tradition of discipline from above. Andrés Townsend and a group of followers—who initially appeared to be many, but ended up being few—left the party and tried to start a parallel Apra movement, which in the following months suffered a constant drain of supporters until it dissolved soon after Alan García's electoral victory in 1985. Villanueva's triumph was only partial, however, and he ceded control of the Apra National Committee to Fernando León de Vivero, a member of the Apra's old guard. Without a doubt, however, in these months of depression, doubt, and debt, Carlos Langberg's influence over the party became decisive. That would continue until the middle of 1982.

On June 16, the Shining Path literally opened fire in Lima. A group "of about 200 youths . . . screaming MOTC [Movement of Laborers, Workers, and Peasants] slogans"[1] surrounded and set afire the San Martín de Porres municipal building, pelting it with a brief but effective hail of Molotov cocktails. As the building burned, the arsonists marched away chanting guerrilla slogans. A few minutes later, after Mayor Oscar Nagamine arrived to inspect the damage, the Shining Path members had dispersed along the overcrowded streets of this fast-growing and chaotic district.

San Martín de Porres was one of the urban areas in Lima where the Shining Path achieved a certain strength and presence in the years preceding the war. This relationship continued over the following years. Willy Fernández Melo, a mayor elected by popular vote, would eventually be detained by Dircote and accused of cooperating with the Shining Path. A brother of his was arrested on the basis of more concrete evidence and was among those killed in El Frontón prison on June 19, 1986.

Although the attackers had chanted Shining Path slogans, the flyers thrown about the streets were signed by the MOTC. This resulted in jumbled reports, which referred to the MOTC as an independent party. Even some people associated with the legal Marxist left did not immediately link the MOTC to the Shining Path. For its part, the Shining Path leadership had chosen to begin the insurrection in the cities under the banner of the MOTC in order to try and give it the stamp of a grass-roots uprising, a massive movement.

On May 1, 1980, during the international workers day celebration, the MOTC had released a flyer that turned out to be the Shining Path's last public document before the insurrection began. The choice of date and "front group" inscribed the imminent uprising within the core tradition of Marxism and not as peripheral heresy.

The document, "The Celebration of May First by the Revolutionary Proletariat," was not just the public, formal announcement of the coming start of hostilities, but also a faithful portrait of an organization in an accelerated trajectory of change and readjustment. The image of José Carlos Mariátegui still presided over the document's cover, but it was an ever more silent icon. The process that would end by subordinating Mariátegui to Gonzalo was already well advanced.

The document's introduction emphasized that "Marxist–Leninist–Mao Tsetung[2] thought is the ideology of the international proletariat and the general political line of the revolution[3] is its application to our concrete reality," which was to say "in all its glory the task of the coming revolution is . . . TO BEGIN ARMED STRUGGLE. To begin the hard and prolonged Agrarian War that follows the path of surrounding the cities from the countryside, creating revolutionary bases of support." As is evident, it would be difficult to state the matter more clearly. Nevertheless, to wipe away any doubt, the introduction underscores the contemporary, immediate nature of its cure. In an attack on other Marxist parties (still divided between "revisionists" and "revolutionaries") for "ideological falsifications" and attempting to "make us believe in electoral illusions," the MOTC document called for an active boycott of the coming elections, with "mass mobilizations . . . to develop the growing grass-roots protest to begin armed struggle for the next uprising of the masses. . . . Through the party, it is the proletariat's job to take up arms and direct the revolution's principal force, the poor peasantry." In bookish Marxist-Leninist jargon, deeds had been announced to the letter. The "boycott" materialized with the action in Chuschi and others less reported on election day; the charred and blackened walls and furniture that the stupefied Mayor Nagamine contemplated on June 16 were the first act of the "popular uprising" of the Lima "proletariat."

The document did contain writings by Lenin and Guzmán, presented in a supremely academic way. At the end of every paragraph of Lenin's article (written on the celebration of May First in Saint Petersburg in 1913) was inserted another containing commentary and new ideas clearly penned by Guzmán. The result was not only revealing about the Shining Path's immediate military intentions but also threw light on important views and worries within the organization.

Among the leading problems that the "revolution" in Peru confronted, the document asserted, was "the break between those who went to combat in the decades of the 1960s and 1970s, with the middle occupied with opportunism, and with the permitted liquidation of leaders." The main reason for concern, the Shining Path's obsession for taking care of and protecting the leadership (in contrast to the militants, who are replaceable), was then expressed explicitly: "The reaction has two ways to crush guerrillas: (1) to win the masses, (2) to liquidate the leadership, because as long as it remains, it will return, an experience drawn from the Algerian revolution [sic]."[4]

To take care of the leadership was, therefore, vital. But the leadership would only serve the interests of revolution if it remained capable of analyzing the exact moment to launch armed struggle, and if it had been able to create an organization powerful and experienced enough to conduct it to victory. On this point, Lenin's analysis of the revolutionary situation in Russia in 1913 and Bolsheviks' ability to direct the situation as it became a crisis were adjusted to an analysis of Peru in 1980 and the Shining Path's ability to make Peru burn.

In the 1913 pamphlet, Lenin noted that the situation in Russia was revolutionary not just because of the "sharpened oppression, hunger, misery, the absence of rights, and outrages against the people," but essentially because these characteristics were found "in flagrant contradiction of the state of productive forces in Russia, with the degree of awareness and the level of the demands made by the masses, awoken in the year 1905." "Oppression," Lenin continued, "no matter how big, does not always stem from the revolutionary situation in a country. *For the revolution to explode, it is not enough for those from below to not want to live as before. In addition, there is a need for those from above to not be able to administer and govern as before.* This is exactly what we observe today in Russia."[5]

Lenin's observation—without doubt penetrating and expressed with economy and simplicity—was transposed to Peruvian reality in Guzmán's commentary, where he declared it, of course, a perfect fit.

> What is crucial is that the suffering of those from below from exploitation be tied to the inability of those from above to govern. . . . These two conditions exist in our country; therefore, there is a revolutionary situation. Moreover, we live in a developing revolutionary situation, which demands that we follow our own path: TO BEGIN ARMED STRUGGLE. Elections have never given the working class or the people power and it can only be conquered through prolonged and hard armed struggle. . . . The state's foundation has fractured. The substantive problems ailing the country have to do with this. . . . The crisis derives from there.[6]

Without transition and unexpectedly, Guzmán continued with observations that unconsciously reveal the Shining Path's long-term strategy: "The Peruvian state's planning goes up to 2005. The population increase, the two halves of the decade of the 1980s (80–85 and 85–90): *a critical decade that must define solutions to problems. . . .* We must keep in mind the decade of the 1980s, the fracture of the state's foundation, its incapacity to resolve the country's problems."[7]

That is to say that for Guzmán, the grand theater of war and the most important objectives within were clearly defined on the eve of insurrection. This meant: (1) during the 1980s, the Peruvian state's inability to govern would become not only visible, but critical; (2) the Shining Path insurrection would develop in this sequence of events; (3) the "solution to the problem" would be defined during this decade, which is to say that the growth curve of the Shining Path insurrection would exceed that of its vulnerability once strategic equilibrium was achieved;[8] (4) the first great stage, "strategic defense," would take place throughout the "critical decade," divided as it was into two moments (which, as will become evident later in this book, were for their part carefully planned out) that corresponded, *grosso modo,* to presidential elections mandated by the constitution.

Upon writing these lines in July 1989, with almost the entire decade in perspective and a somber prospect in view for the rest, it is impossible for me to avoid comparisons between the ingenuously optimistic prophecies of, for example, Roberto Abusada[9] (shared by most of the political elite or those in the process of converting themselves into leaders) and Guzmán's, made at about the same time. They were diametrically opposed. Guzmán guessed correctly, although not completely. Being correct did not mean everything was predetermined. But the story of the war will gradually reveal why Guzmán prevailed.

Even when the social situation was revolutionary—in Marxist-Leninist language, the "objective conditions" were present—more was needed to lead revolution forward. "Neither the oppression of those from below nor the crisis of those from above," Lenin had noted, "are enough to produce revolution . . . if a given country lacks a revolutionary class capable of transforming the passive state of oppression (into an active one) of revolution." For Lenin, the "revolutionary class" was the industrial proletariat, and its brain and motor were the clandestine party. In the document, Guzmán's commentary expands on the clandestine party's role.

> The objective conditions exist. . . . Subjective conditions enter into play, the instruments of revolution, particularly the PARTY. . . . Opportunists do not see the necessity of the principal instrument of revolution: the party. . . . The Communist Party was small, some claimed it had "two or three hundred," this is what a Communist Party is; . . . we don't want a broad party, this is an election-mongering party. In our country, the party is composed of more peasants than workers. . . . They don't speak of a legalized party . . . or of other forms of this type, that induce idleness. Communist Party members speak . . . of beginning armed struggle. . . . Our problem is to fight for revolution and in the next uprising, principally of peasants, to Begin Armed Struggle.[10]

So the imminent start of insurrection had not been detected only by a few intelligence service operatives and informants. It had been proclaimed publicly, and not simply with a slogan, but in the form of an annotated treatise, the kind of document those individuals with an eye on history tend to believe is necessary at the moment of deciding their fates.

Autumn Harvest

A call for insurrection had also been written on the wall—literally scrawled on almost every available surface in the central squares and nearby walls of Ayacucho's cities and towns, especially those in Cangallo and Víctor Fajardo provinces, which would be the geographical center of action during the first months of insurrection. While the final preparations for the transfer of power were made in Lima in July, author Piedad Pareja traveled by land between the capital of Ayacucho and the Canarias mining center, owned by her family and where she had recently assumed managerial control. Pareja, who had studied and written about the Peruvian trade-union movement, had a capacity for observation doubly sharpened by her academic training and her then embattled management position. While the conflict that gripped Canarias was soon to become a crisis and make her stay at the mine impossible, for a time she was able to gather valuable information.

Slogans scrawled on the walls were overwhelmingly in favor of the Shining Path, interspersed with a few lone UDP, Apra, and even pro–Hugo Blanco graffiti. In Huahua Puquio, Mollobamba, Cangallo, Huancapi, Cayara, Huaylla, Tiquihua, and Canaria, graffiti calling for an "Election boycott," "To begin armed struggle," and "Develop growing popular protest to serve armed struggle" dominated the walls.[11] Their sermon was the one that most obviously resonated in those provincial hamlets.

And it resonated in more than graffiti and enthusiastic shouts. After the Chuschi action, activity intensified in Ayacucho. Individual acts remained part mischievousness, part openly violent, but tending more each time toward the latter. On June 1, the Civil Guard health clinic had been stoned and on June 14 the Tourist Hotel was the target. But on June 21, the Popular Action offices were attacked with dynamite, wounding one. On July 6, a school was attacked with dynamite. On July 8, the highway linking the refinery with the Canarias mine was bombed simultaneously in several places.

At the same time, Shining Path activists made an effort to carry out actions in the four provinces central to their movement—Huamanga, Cangallo, Huanta, and Huancapi—that involved mobs, crowds, even rabble, in an effort to achieve through "overflows" a transition from the protest methods used during peacetime to the violent, irreversible actions that led to war. "To aim at popular overflow," in their words, "is to develop the mass struggle that goes much further than what is permitted by the reactionary state order and exceeds the reigning system's legal order."[12]

In the cities, the "overflow" had to be won through violent rallies and marches or in "spontaneous" looting, combined with increased doses of terrorist activity, sabotage, and propaganda as explicit as it was symbolic. In the countryside, the initial wave of action should be "the gathering of harvests," which is to say raids on ranches or agricultural communities by groups of peasants led by a Shining Path nucleus; the looting of machines, tools, tack, and anything else that could be carried away, later given to "distribution committees" directed by party cadres; the humiliation of or physical violence against owners or their representatives; and, most important, the harvest of seized fields and the distribution of crops among militants. Combining the atavistic call of pillage with the seal of "revolutionary justice," these actions placed those who took part irreversibly outside the law.

Together with the elections and transfer of power, the mountain harvest season had been one of the most important reasons for choosing a time to begin the insurrection. For symbolic as well as dogmatic reasons (and perhaps for similar pragmatic reasons), Guzmán paralleled Mao's first insurrectional steps almost literally. In August and September 1927, as the Communist insurrection in Shanghai and later the Canton commune were suffocated bloodily, Mao Tse-tung led a massive uprising of peasants in his home province of Hunan, which later became known as "The Rising Up of the Autumn Harvest" ("rising up" in the Spanish translation meaning as much insurrection as the confiscation of crops). The "rising up" was defeated, and Mao had to flee, with some cadres and troops, to the provincial border, the Ching-kan-shan Mountains, where he united his forces with troops under the command of the Communist general Chu-teh and established his first "base of support." Fifty-three years later, after Mao's experiments had been converted into canon, a similar "raising" in the Southern Hemisphere autumn of Peru's mountains began to unfold.

On July 10, the San Germán de Ayrabamba ranch in Cangallo was attacked by about fifteen armed Shining Path members. The ranch, with 300 acres planted, belonged to César Parodi Vasallo, an agronomist who was not present. The Shining Path militants captured Carlos Parodi, the foreman, his wife, and their four children, and looted the ranch (their haul included two hunting rifles, a radio transmitter, and money).[13]

Three days later, the Vilcashuamán Civil Guard chief received a call for help. Benigno Medina, owner of the "San Agustín de Ayzarca" ranch near the community of Parcco, had been told that his ranch would be attacked and burned to the ground. "San Agustín" was where intelligence reports had noted the presence of armed individuals in 1979, individuals later identified by an officer in charge of Operative Plan Morochuco as soldiers hunting a deserter. The ranch was, in any case, on the edge of a rural area where the Shining Path had carried out its most sustained and uninterrupted work. Over the following years, it was again and again to appear, always tragically, at the war's epicenter.

The Vilcashuamán police chief sent three officers to Ayzarca to "take the relevant statements." Passing Parcco, they detained two people apparently believed to have participated in the attack on the Ayrabamba ranch. When, hours later, the police returned to Vilcashuamán, they were ambushed at a spot known as Lachapujas. No one was wounded, but the detainees managed to escape.[14] For their part, the police didn't feel it was necessary to give Benigno Medina permanent protection, an understandable decision as long as violence remained more rumor and threat than spilled blood. Nevertheless, for the Shining Path, Medina's fate was already weighed and measured.

On July 28, Peru's national independence day, the military government ended and the democratic one began. According to law, the former president had to deliver the presidential sash to the Senate president, who would place it on the new president. But this was not done. Morales Bermúdez had not been elected, but was a dictator, and protocol underscored the contrast in legitimacy. The Senate president took the sash symbolically from the electorate and went with it to Belaunde as Morales Bermúdez and his generals silently left the Government Palace and the ministries. In peace, but without glory.

Once again, it was a moment of shared enthusiasm. The contrast between

Belaunde's mature, smiling image and the somber and dour one of the officers emphasized the difference between democracy and dictatorship. Never again, it was said, repeated, and felt, would the democratic government be turned upside down.

That night, Belaunde swore in his cabinet on a Government Palace balcony, facing a Central Plaza filled by people. Applause was divided equally as each minister took the oath. De la Jara, a living symbol of the government's intention not to support itself by repression but by law and the force of its convictions, was among those who received the most applause. Grass-roots members of Popular Action were particularly fond of him, for the moral courage he had displayed after Velasco's coup, for knowing that he had suffered exile to a greater degree than other militants, and because they realized that his wife's recent death threw a shadow over his hour of victory. There was also much that was poignant about De la Jara's small, rotund figure. He had the body of a cherub decked out in a tie and brass-covered chest, and he was assuming a role traditionally reserved for hard-line, dour, or crafty civilians and soldiers, or all of the above. He was the brave little tailor beginning his task. And of course, the fact that this democratic government had De la Jara as its interior minister made many people in Peru, as they had at other brief moments in history, feel as if they had embarked on the path to democratic utopia.

Unlike the rest of the country, enthusiasm hadn't jelled in Ayacucho that day. During a military parade in the Central Plaza, as over 5,000 people watched, someone threw what looked like five bombs with fuses lit at soldiers from "Los Cabitos," the local base, as they marched past the university. Some in the crowd stampeded, and panic could have spread if Civil Guardsman Miguel Alcántara had not quickly pulled out the fuses. The bombs turned out to be thin lengths of cane wrapped "in dynamite paper."[15]

That same day, the radio antenna on the hill known as Yanaorcco was dynamited. Also bombed were the Cangallo Provincial Council and the Huancapi Provincial Council.

On the other side of the country, in Cerro de Pasco, and on the same day, a Shining Path contingent attacked the Atacocha mining company and took 350 sticks of dynamite along with fuses and cord. It was the first assault on a mine since the beginning of the insurrection. The following day, at a Transportation Ministry warehouse in Pomabamba, Ayacucho, another Shining Path band overwhelmed workers and took 2,200 sticks of dynamite, gun powder, and fuses.

The police had responded in almost every case. In Huancapi, they managed to capture the suspected perpetrators of the dynamite attacks. A bit before, in Ayacucho, Germán Medina, the doctor who would be elected to the Chamber of Deputies for the United Left in 1985, had received a telegram from the president of the Peruvian Medical Federation indicating that a Huancapi doctor had been detained. Medina was instructed to check into the matter and press for his release. At first, Medina did not believe the news. There was no doctor in Huancapi. Nevertheless, he contacted the departmental prefect, Marciano Cavero. That afternoon, Cavero notified him that the detainee was Dr. Eduardo Mata Mendoza, former director of the Cangallo Hospital.

The news surprised Medina and his Ayacucho colleagues. Mata had resigned from his post not long before. "He had come to Ayacucho the previous Christmas and he had told us that he would resign his post at the Cangallo Hospital, that he would go to Lima to complete his residency. I remember this very well, because this meant Cangallo would be left without a doctor."[16] After Mata and his wife left Cangallo, Medina had attended a farewell party for the couple in Ayacucho.[17]

His wife was Yeny María Rodríguez Neyra, who also worked in Cangallo as a social worker and studied psychology at San Marcos University..Both were among those cadres the Shining Path sent first to fight. Instead of going to Lima, the couple delved into the Cangallo and Huancapi countryside. To avoid being recognized, Mata dressed in typical Andean garb: a poncho, tire-soled sandals, a hat. Having the features and fair skin of someone from the coast was not a problem in Cangallo, where the defeated conquerors who had supported Almagro had settled and left a physical mark still evident today. Identifying himself as "Víctor Paniagua," Mata had been captured with his wife and another student.[18] A fourth prisoner confessed to following the doctor's orders.

This couple's short-lived odyssey handily illustrates how the Shining Path protected its cadres as the insurrection began. According to various testimonies, Mata came from the ranks of the Leftist Revolutionary Movement (MIR), but then joined the Shining Path. His rank in the Cangallo subzone was undoubtedly that of an important cadre. That the president of the Peruvian Medical Federation would learn in Lima of Mata's imprisonment just a few hours later shows the velocity the Shining Path was able to use as a defense strategy. In the same way that it had used state institutions to grow, it also used, when possible, professional organizations to defend its own members, hiding their political affiliation or appealing to common feelings of solidarity within the left in reaction to any arrest. In this case, the association's defense reflexes were efficiently induced, and the Medical Federation asked its Ayacucho affiliates to mobilize themselves to gain Mata's release. The doctors took up a collection. With Medina leading them, they traveled to Huancapi to press for their colleague's freedom and organize a defense.[19]

Relationships within the family were a completely different story. The Matas had a child who was a few months old and with the mother when she was arrested. An acquaintance was called and "entrusted" with the child, to "bring it up."[20] Many similar cases occurred over the next years. When couples entered clandestinity together, their children remained under the care of relatives when possible or with friends. According to available evidence, the Shining Path made no effort to take care of or see to the necessities of the children of its cadres. Apparently, abandoning one's progeny for the proletariat, or the hypothetical abstraction that goes under that name, could prove one's commitment to the cause.[21] Even if it is pointless conjecture, one cannot help wondering if things would have been different if Guzmán and Augusta La Torre had managed to have children.

In Huancapi, Mata made no effort to explain to Medina and the other doctors why he had been there and not in Lima. Only when the prosecutor explained to them that he had been arrested "with a poncho on, with dynamite nearby, painting graffiti" did Mata deny having any explosives, "and told us that he had gone to visit some relatives."[22]

Despite the pervasive atmosphere of amnesty that existed then and the little to no importance accorded Shining Path attacks, the doctors had to make an effort to mount a defense. After several visits, and after having managed to get Mata transferred to Cangallo, they finally got him released. Mata wasted no time in disappearing, and his Ayacucho colleagues never saw him alive again. "Afterward, we saw him in the morgue."[23] But that was in 1982, when Mata fell in the attack on the Ayacucho prison. His wife would be arrested several more times in the future.

Hoxha and Guzmán

The war had begun, although few took it seriously. During most of 1980, the mere mention of the Shining Path provoked jokes in Lima, even on the legal left, at the time testing its alliance and open to the promise of growing influence within the system. As the year ended, the accumulation of actions obligated the government to recognize the problem; yet it remained phrased as an essentially rabid effort at agitation by a hysterical group outside history and situated on the political and psychological margins, a group easily defeated once earnest action was taken against it. News of more disturbing endeavors, like the takeover and looting of the Ayrabamba ranch, was little disseminated in Lima or wasn't linked to others that happened at the same time in Ayacucho and the rest of the country.

The Shining Path advanced, meanwhile, its first steps beyond the Rubicon taken with caution and extreme care, coordinating almost every action and immediately examining the results. The caution displayed in these months still pregnant with inexperience and doubt was much greater than what came later, when violence sharply increased. Constant Central Committee and political commission meetings made it seem like the Shining Path leadership was virtually in permanent session. As was the custom, the meetings were full of conflict, but this time conflict was spontaneous, not provoked.

On May 29, at least two weeks after the insurrection had begun, a meeting of the "Expanded Political Bureau" began. The objective was to assess "the balance of actions" carried out up to that moment. According to its count, ninety-eight actions had been carried out and they had formed "the first detachments. . . . these detachments were, as Lenin said, armed groups without arms, to lead the masses."[24]

The overall conclusion was that "the party, the leadership, the cadres, and the grass roots are following through." With an overstatement that would later become typical, the Shining Path perceived a "great embrace by the masses." Despite the "great success of the start of actions," it concluded that "more and better things could be done."[25]

The next steps were to adjust the plan to intensify activity over the following three months, until the beginning of February. Each action should involve weapons or be partially armed "mobilizations," "harvests," and the continuing "election boycott." Tactical planning and the coordination of individual attacks should be made at the "subzone" level. Above all, actions should be carried out keeping in mind the need to train new detachments and vigorously hone their "structure, leadership, and composition." On the issue of leadership, the classic Communist structure of a double command was stressed: both political and military, without forgetting that both were part of the process of "militarizing the party."

Addressing the methodology of attacks, the meeting defined the five steps that would later be converted into essential components of Shining Path tactical doctrine: (1) the decision on the plan or concrete action; (2) human and material strength and means; (3) preparation (including reconnaissance); (4) the execution of the action (including an immediate report on it); and (5) a review, with a detailed examination of every part of the action, including the leadership's performance. The conclusions of each review were sent to party leadership and put to use to plan the next operation.[26]

By the end of May, the Shining Path's problem was not a scarcity of volunteers, but rather their inexperience and lack of training. "We have fighters, (but the) problem is the building of an armed force: ideological-political formation and organizational formation . . . to establish a double leadership, strengthen discipline, military watchfulness." Even as he repeated that the forging of ideology was fundamental, Guzmán underscored the need to train his "detachments" in "shooting, ambushes, assaults." As each action was executed, leaders had to keep in mind that "audacity is the genius's most beautiful calculation."

The meeting ended on June 5 with a new slogan, presented along with the familiar ones: "Against the reactionary new government." And the saying was appropriately hyperbolic: "We have arrived at the peak where the new flag was placed, we have unfurled it, and we march to the guerrilla war."

Immediately afterward, the San Martín municipal offices were burned and, a little later, the Ayrabamba ranch was attacked, together with dozens of other smaller actions.

The meeting of the Expanded Central Committee (including several militants without official posts) began on August 8. The purpose was to review the first part of the plan to begin armed struggle, to conclude it, and to begin the second part, "On to the guerrilla war!" lasting until year's end.

The quotations from Lenin and Mao that Guzmán had read at the meeting's start, as always carefully selected for the occasion, emphasized the revolutionary virtue of practical learning: "As is natural, a lot of people accused us of having stirred our hands in these matters without knowing how to carry them through until the end," Lenin recalled. Mao asserted that "to fight, fail, fight again, fail again, return to the fight, and in that way gain victory: this is the people's logic."

Reports on activity during the first stage came from a considerable number of local, zonal, and regional committees. Their mere presence was a sign of Shining Path strength and distribution in the insurrection's early months and shows that their organization was much larger and more spread out than anyone guessed then and even later.

Reporting were the Cangallo subzone of the Andahuaylas-Cangallo Zonal Committee (where Dr. Eduardo Mata had been active), part of the Principal Regional Committee (Ayacucho, Huancavelica, Apurímac); the Metropolitan Committee (Lima and nearby urban areas); the Andahuaylas subzone; the Huancavelica Zonal Committee; the Central Regional Committee (Junín, Huánuco, Cerro de Pasco); the Cusco-Puno Regional Committee; the Arequipa-Tacna Regional Committee; the Chiclayo Local Committee; and the Huancayo Local Committee. While it is clear that some regional and zonal committees were very weak, at the very least all had a basic organization that functioned. And all had been active in some way. The organization that had just opened fire wasn't by any stretch of the imagination small and easily dismissed, but was cautiously making the transition to war.

Once the reports were finished and a debate began on a review of the actions, Guzmán had to confront an internal questioning that partially escaped his control. A group of five leaders, some belonging to the Political Bureau and others to the Central Committee, called into question action planning based solely on questions of ideological or doctrinal purity. The argument had begun during the May–June meeting, and Guzmán had managed to control the disagreement by terming it a form of rightism, a move by the "bourgeois military line." But now, the five Shining Path leaders accused Guzmán of a serious deviation from ideological purity, "Hoxhism." The party's actions, they pointed out, did not only put the same emphasis on the city as the countryside, but even appeared to be giving more importance to the former to the detriment of the latter. This was identified with the heresy of the renegade Enver Hoxha.[27]

The accusation shocked those present, and Guzmán found himself on the defensive. It was an unexpectedly fragile moment in his consolidation of power as supreme leader, and none of his retrospective writings omits mention of it, although all are conveniently touched up.[28]

With a chart of completed actions in hand, Guzmán tried to explain that the quantity and quality of these actions didn't show that the city had overshadowed the countryside. Any confusion, he added, stemmed from the fact that "reactionary propaganda gave big headlines to urban sabotage and minimized rural actions."[29] Therefore, the five inquisitors based their accusations on "bourgeois propaganda," not Marxist analysis.

Nevertheless, Guzmán pointed out, armed struggle in Peru had unique characteristics. "A particularity of the popular war in Peru is to make the countryside the principal theater of actions and the cities a necessary complement."[30] This represented a distancing from orthodox Maoism (though not necessarily from how it has been put into practice historically), angling toward the more pragmatic insurrectional doctrine of the Vietnamese. So this was something Shining Path cadres could understand as "development" and not a heresy.

The importance of this discussion is clear. Contrary to what poorly informed analysts of the Shining Path maintained in 1987 and 1988 (that this organization was just beginning to emphasize urban actions at the expense of rural ones), the fact is that activity in the cities—and, above all, Lima—had been more important since the insurrection's beginning. Between 1982 and 1987, there were trimesters when the number of seditious actions in Lima numbered more than those in Ayacucho. Nevertheless, for Guzmán, the countryside never ceased being perceived as the arena for the strategic accumulation of forces and the conflict's final resolution. What is clear is that—perhaps in part because of that accusation of "Hoxhism"—to a large degree the Shining Path left aside its semilegal work in the cities starting in September 1980 until 1986. The MOTC, the urban standard-bearer during those first months, was silently pushed to the side.

Once Guzmán found the most effective line of argument, he had no difficulty overcoming the accusation of "Hoxhism." At these heights, the fact that his strategic methodology had heterodox elements when compared with a dogmatic Maoist vision was abundantly clear. But like Mao, Ho, and Tito in their time, Guzmán presented the difference in method and strategy as a fundamental development of the dogma and not a rupture with it.

With a critical review of their activities in each zone over the previous months completed ("vivisection," according to the language of this meeting, alluding to the attitude of implacable objectivity they aspired to instill), they began on an action plan for the remainder of the year, "To the Beginning of Guerrilla War," the leap into the tumult, and the "overflow" to open insurrection.

The action plan approved during this session, and in a Central Committee meeting immediately afterward (which took place from September 8 to 9, 1980), included a radical intensification of attack, which could take six forms: agitation, mobilization, sabotage, assaults, the reaping of harvests, armed clashes. Each regional committee, and within these each zone and subzone, had to carry out all or part of the plan. Weaker regional committees, for example, should necessarily limit themselves to agitation, mobilization, and sabotage. Stronger ones, like the Principal Regional Committee and the Metropolitan Committee (the latter excluding crop confiscation) had to employ all six forms of struggle, intensifying those that gave better results: assaults, harvests, armed clashes.

These actions were contained within the "Beginning of the Guerrilla War" plan, which would take place between October and December 1980, taking advantage of the moment created by previous actions. To prepare cadres for strategic and tactical difficulties, various texts on guerrilla war and counterinsurgency tactics were distributed, read, and commented upon, from Robert Taber's 1960s classic *The War of the Flea*[31] to the Peruvian army's doctrinaire texts on subversion and counterrevolutionary war.

The basic points that should govern the application of the plan to "begin the guerrilla war" also numbered six: (1) to spur on the "class war" in the countryside, to agitate with actions; (2) to focus on the countryside as the principal theater, with property takeovers as a fundamental action; (3) to focus on the city as complementary, by supporting mobilizations and strikes with armed actions; (4) to apply the six forms of struggle and five steps to each action (see earlier comments about both); (5) to "phase in" the plan between October and December; (6) to maintain a centralized and "objective" plan so that "subjective matters cannot pull it off course" or, in other words, to avoid distortion as the plan unfolds while at the same time stimulating "application with initiative."

The plan also tried to come to terms with one of the most difficult points raised by the transition to war: the partial transformation of a clandestine political party into an efficient military organization. It wasn't an easy task. An organization made up strictly of cells, for example, could not maintain its rigid structure if an attempt were made to create numerous groups, even for a short period. How to come together and disperse efficiently without, at the same time, making cadre and militants more vulnerable to informants and identification was the problem that they then tried to resolve. There was no perfect solution, and the Shining Path chose a course of action borrowed from the Asian insurrectionary model: to accept

Play on words on humans

high casualties as long as they remained inferior to the number of new recruits and as long as most casualties were grass-roots militants or midlevel cadres. In contrast, the leadership had to protect itself at all costs. But it was also necessary to prevent a break in the chain of command after the loss of many militants.

The directives that were part of the "Begin the Guerrilla War" plan defined the methods the Shining Path would use over the following years. Regional committees—and, above all, the Principal Regional Committee—should grapple with the "development of the construction of the armed force." This supposed that they would form platoons drawn from their detachments and simultaneously organize "militias" in areas they already controlled.

Once a military force has been organized on the Asian model of insurrection, three fundamental categories exist: the "principal force," the "regional force," and local guerrillas. Local guerrillas are the first step in the ladder and the initial form of insurgent military organization. This is the guerrilla who remains in a village or hamlet, during the day leading an apparently normal life while at night switching tools for weapons. The second step is the regional force, guerrillas chosen from the local village but better trained and armed and with a range of action covering one or several provinces. Finally, the "principal force" guerrillas come from regional groups and are more experienced, trained, and have better weapons. This is the basic structure of the insurgent army, which at a given moment in its growth stops being a guerrilla force and begins to conduct operations in a conventional war.

In almost all Asian insurrections, neither the regional force nor the principal force is in permanent combat or maneuvers. Most of its time is dedicated to propaganda work, agricultural work (based on the Maoist dictum that an insurgency should not be a burden on peasants), and training. The relationship between these forces and the party organizations at their level is complementary. Local guerrillas provide precise information, a flawless knowledge of the terrain, and, through the party government committees, control over the population. For their part, the regional and principal forces can concentrate a strength that the local guerrillas will never have at their disposal. The design isn't overly complicated but, in order to function well, requires a very disciplined and diligent party organization.

This is what the Shining Path threw itself into building. The raw materials were the already organized detachments. One of the plan directives was to immediately create "special detachments" that depended directly on regional committees and, in a few cases, on the Shining Path leadership. These detachments would not be tied down geographically. In the future, they would be used primarily in so-called annihilation, which is to say murder.

Another plan directive was meant to assure the chain of command even when part of the insurgent apparatus was swept away by police. A "second network" was ordered organized, parallel to the principal one, functioning as a reserve. When the first was taken apart, the second would begin to function. This type of organization would also have another consequence in the future, that of confusing the police and causing more than one interior minister deep embarrassment when it was announced (and with reason) that all of those who had committed a series of attacks had been captured, declarations that, nevertheless, would be followed by blackouts, dynamite blasts, and terrorist attacks.

Finally, together with all of these military measures aimed at the destruction of the state and society, orders were given to take advantage of these very entities. The Shining Path would promote and encourage campaigns for the "freeing of detainees, against repression, and for democratic freedoms and rights." If cynicism were converted into a virtue worthy of canonization, Guzmán would be its first saint.

At a low ebb in August and September, the number of Shining Path actions rose in the first days of October. In Ayacucho, a stick of dynamite thrown at the Civil Guard post on October 2 in Huancasancos, in southern Ayacucho and the capital of the province of the same name, opened the offensive.

On October 8, dynamite exploded near another Ayacucho police post. On October 10, there was an explosion in the Huancapi central square, and a red flag was raised. The Huanta power plant was sabotaged on October 13. On October 20, the "Voice of Huamanga" radio station was attacked. For four minutes, a Shining Path harangue was broadcast. The following day, there were five attacks in Ayacucho and Huanta, the most serious being the attack with stones and Molotov cocktails on a Civil Guard squad car in Ayacucho. On October 23, the squad car carrying the commander of the local army base was attacked with dynamite. On November 5, the Vischongo central square was occupied temporarily by a group that raised a red flag and chanted slogans in praise of armed struggle while firing shots in the air. The offices of the Subprefecture and Electoral Registry were dynamited on November 10. That same day, the Huancapi police headquarters and Popular Action office were attacked with dynamite while explosions were set off near the local prison.[32]

These attacks were not confined to Ayacucho. Across the country, the noise of explosions announced the Shining Path mobilization. In Andahuaylas, the Provincial Council door was dynamited on October 20 and police managed to defuse a package filled with dynamite placed near their post in Talavera. In December, the municipal councils in Talavera, Ongoy, and Chincheros were attacked.

In Arequipa, an electrical tower was dynamited on October 16 and a bigger attack on November 18 left part of the city in darkness. In December, a pickup truck belonging to the Investigative Police was dynamited.

On October 16, the PIP headquarters in Huancavelica was dynamited. As in the rest of the country, these attacks were carried out with small quantities of explosives. On October 20, a high-tension tower that was part of the Mantaro hydroelectric system was also sabotaged with explosives. And in December, there were two other acts of sabotage of increasing importance to the electrical power system. In Junín, attacks occurred almost every day, especially in the La Oroya mining center. On October 20, for the first time part of the track belonging to the country's central railway was dynamited. On December 9, several simultaneous acts of sabotage were carried out against high-tension towers, and there were several attacks a day within the department up to Christmas. In Lambayeque, on Peru's northern coast, constant attacks were carried out—particularly with Molotov cocktails, as in neighboring La Libertad—and on October 15, twenty-seven homemade bombs exploded in the Central Square. In Cerro de Pasco, attacks were more serious, especially sabotage with dynamite.

Meanwhile, in Lima, a mob of about 100 people attacked, looted, and burned a Rímac supermarket. On October 23, the Comas municipal offices were set afire beneath a veritable hailstorm of Molotov cocktails. Over the following days, lesser attacks continued almost daily. On December 15, bombs exploded in seven branches of different banks while a final one, stronger, was set in front of the now hated Embassy of the People's Republic of China.

Dynamite, the essential raw material for Shining Path attacks, now flowed permanently from widely separated and unprotected mining camps and their solitary explosives caches to this clandestine organization's stockpiles. From examining the type of attacks carried out in each region, one can see that the Shining Path had yet to develop a way to ship explosives from one part of Peru to another (in regions with no mining, Molotov cocktails were generally used while dynamite was saved for the others).

Dynamite thefts had yet to reach the exorbitant levels of later years, although they were already considerable. On October 5, an attack on the Chayapa mine, in the Lima province of Huarochirí, netted fifty sticks of dynamite and thirty detonators for the Shining Path arsenal. On October 27, close to 35,000 fuses were robbed from a Huaraz mine (there were two other important robberies of dynamite in the same department before the year ended). On November 15, another attack on a mine on the outskirts of Lima ended with the robbery of twenty sticks of dynamite and 500 fuses. Before the end of the year, two more attacks in Lima added seventy sticks of dynamite and fifty fuses to the total. In contrast, in Puno, the dynamite harvest was even greater: in one attack carried out on a Transportation and Communications Ministry office, the Shining Path managed to acquire three cases of dynamite and 1,500 meters of fuse. The blasting caps were no problem: two days earlier, they had stolen 29,000 from the Pomperia mine.

Dynamite stick by dynamite stick, the Shining Path was providing weapons (dynamite, vital for several years) to its militants, who had been essentially un-armed. And with each incremental increase in violence, they moved from the venial flouting of the law into open armed insurrection.

The Balaguer Case

The results of these attacks were not the same everywhere. In Parliament, several Popular Action senators presented a bill to impose drastic sentences on those convicted of terrorist acts. But the bill did not win majority support even from Popular Action representatives and was eventually tabled in committee. Guiding himself in good measure on the information and analysis he received from his police experts, Interior Minister De la Jara made statements meant to calm fears but which, contrasted with news of the attacks, produced the opposite effect.

After assuming the post of interior minister, De la Jara's principal problem wasn't the Shining Path—from his perspective, something sporadic and controllable—but rather imposing his authority over his police chiefs. His appearance and im-age helped little with officers used to associating leadership with an intimidating presence.

His relationship with General Juan Balaguer, Civil Guard head, was fraught from the very first day. Balaguer, who had held ministerial rank during the last years of military rule, didn't appear resigned to subordinating himself to De la Jara, much less allowing himself to be put at the same level as the chiefs of the investigative police and Republican Guard. When Héctor López Martínez sent Balaguer an official document, Balaguer replied that the vice-minister should not be addressing him directly "because he didn't have his rank."[33] Later, after attending with the minister the first weekly meetings with Belaunde (the minister was accompanied by his vice-minister and the three police chiefs), Balaguer formally asked to attend the meetings alone, without other police chiefs or even the minister himself.

Copies of the request made the rounds of other Civil Guard offices and provoked fervent solidarity with Balaguer, above all among "institutionalist" officers. This group of mid- and high-level officers felt, and not without reason, that their institu-tion had been mistreated and diminished. They wanted to convert it into some-thing powerful and respected. Under Morales Bermúdez, they had managed to win equal standing with the military at the expense of some equipment and budget. Afterward, during the Constitutional Assembly, they had succeeded in redefining themselves not as an "auxiliary force," but as a "police force." A danger-filled quest for legitimacy had been won. Despite resistance from some intransigents, they had also won admittance to the association of generals, where active-duty and retired generals congregated. However, neither the investigative police nor the Republican

Guard had been admitted, which didn't anger the Civil Guard since they treated these policemen like Cinderellas.

Some arguments made by the "institutionalists" were justified, above all protests against the weakening of the Civil Guard at the hands of the military. But other complaints were mere expressions of the feudal mentality imbedded within the institution, that insistence on having exclusive areas and privileges, those sovereign prerogatives that have done so much damage and stifled the country's social and political growth.

On the other hand, the institutionalists did not have a great captain in Balaguer. Vain, overly concerned with the symbols, rituals, and trappings of authority, Balaguer's reasons for confronting the minister had more to do with status and protocol than his officers' "institutional objectives."

The conflict was unleashed at the end of August. During ceremonies held on August 30 to commemorate the anniversary of the Civil Guard's creation, Balaguer gave a speech that was "insolent in its content and form, phrased as a Civil Guard demand."[34] De la Jara did not respond, inhibited by his difficulties in expressing himself in public, which made Balaguer more audacious. At the classic "Civil Guard" horse race at the Monterrico track, Balaguer snubbed the minister. De la Jara, who left the racetrack alone, decided that day "that it's him or me."[35]

It wasn't necessary to wait. Soon afterward, Balaguer made public statements indicating that "the extreme left has a premeditated plan to create upheaval and affect peace with work stoppages, strikes, and subversive acts."[36] He wasn't referring to the Shining Path, but rather the legal left, using the military government's terminology. After reading them, De la Jara ordered López Martínez to draft a public statement distancing himself from Balaguer and expressing his opposition.

Released on September 6, the statement asserted among other things that Balaguer had "lost the interior minister's confidence," yet clarified that this was "in no way meant to question the Civil Guard. Once again it can be said that it is an institution with the complete confidence and respect that it merits as one of the state's tutelary organisms."

On the morning of September 6, the minister and vice-minister found, literally, a police rebellion at their feet. On the fourth floor of the old Córpac building, overlooking the broad patio that once was used by passengers entering and exiting the airport, the minister's office was directly above the third-floor office of the Civil Guard chief. From early on, the patio was filled by a demonstration of Civil Guard officers in support of Balaguer. In Lima as well as other parts of the country, police activity had practically stopped as Civil Guard officers gathered in their stations. The demonstration was not violent, but the air was tense.

De la Jara and López Martínez spent several uncomfortable hours in the narrow ministerial halls as the demonstration boiled below. As the crisis took shape, President Belaunde, attempting to find a diplomatic solution, nevertheless expressed his support for De la Jara. Prime Minister Ulloa joined him. Balaguer and his staff remained in their offices.

The hour came for other police officers to act. Eduardo Ipinze, PIP chief, announced that his institution supported the minister; and the director of the PIP officers' school, Alberto Suárez Caballero, offered to have his cadets march to the ministry (a few blocks away) to protect the minister. Meanwhile, the Republican Guard had already set off, and several buses brought armed officers to the ministry to guard De la Jara. During the two days the crisis lasted, De la Jara and López Martínez slept under PIP and Republican Guard watch.

A few hours into the crisis, it was clear that Civil Guard insubordination had little hope of success. Nevertheless, there was a danger that the officers' massive protest would degenerate into armed violence. Hoping to avoid a larger conflict, Belaunde invited Balaguer and several of his generals to the Government Palace. When they arrived, the president gave his minister his support, but offered Balaguer the post of police attaché in Peru's Washington embassy. Belaunde had created the post that instant.

If Balaguer's fervent followers expected a noble refusal from their chief, they were deceived. He accepted Belaunde's offer immediately. The revolt lost a leader, but the country gained a diplomat.

Nevertheless, tensions remained high for several days. On the street, different branches of the police force traded insults and blows, exposing their paraphernalia to each other. In the police stations, until then divided between the Civil Guard and PIP, the Civil Guard threw the investigators out in a move that became permanent. In the Lima prefecture, shared by the regional chiefs of both branches, there was an interchange of tear gas and shots in the air.

Meanwhile, the Civil Guard was without a head, and the rumors emanating from Balaguer's scheming subordinates was that none would accept the post. Senator Oscar Trelles offered to speak with General Humberto Catter, in the line of succession, and the worried minister and vice-minister encouraged the effort. Catter accepted immediately, and several other generals began to make discreet offers of loyalty.

But there was the problem of taking the oath, an indispensable formality and ritual for accepting institutional leadership. Some weary and recalcitrant officers with smoldering looks and uncharitable comments still remained in the hallways, trying to shame those who had yielded. General Adolfo Palao, one of the first to offer the minister his support, hid the crucifix and carried it from the third to the fourth floor. Catter came up almost as discreetly. But once Catter was in the minister's office, accompanied by two generals and ready to take the oath, it was discovered that there was no Bible upon which to swear it. A search of the fourth floor, at first anxious and then frantic, failed to uncover a single copy.

López Martínez examined the books in his office once again, and found the solution: the Royal Spanish Academy Dictionary, a 1970 edition. "The volume had Spanish leather binding stamped in red. It looked impressive."[37] On it, Catter took his oath. He never learned of the switch.

A few days later, discipline returned to the Civil Guard. Only a few recalcitrants ended up in institutional Siberia, finding little comfort in knowing their leader was in Washington.

The Civil Guard had little luck with its chiefs (like the other two branches of the police). Catter was unquestionably incompetent and led his institution to virtual defeat by the Shining Path in Ayacucho. Without doubt, the responsibility did not lie solely with him, yet by monumentally erroneous decisions (like abandoning police stations in the Ayacucho countryside) he hastened defeat. In 1985, two years after retiring, Catter was included in the case against the drug-trafficking organization directed by Reynaldo Rodríguez López. According to the state's case, Catter's collaboration with him took place while Catter commanded the Civil Guard.

First Blood

The first municipal elections since 1966 were held on November 22, and the results demonstrated that the Belaunde government continued to have majority support. There was something of modest poetic justice in that. Municipal government had been chosen by vote beginning with Belaunde's first government; and his original purpose of stimulating democracy from the grass roots was rescued from a long hiatus under military rule and with the unconditional opening of political democracy. The newspapers confiscated by the military government had been returned to their owners and new newspapers and new television news programs had been started, more than the Lima market could absorb. If silence or the regimented voices that had once dominated the mass communications media during military rule were one extreme of the proverbial pendulum, it now began its opposite swing down a long democratic path, with a spreading cacophony of all types, styles, and origins.

Popular Action's victory in Lima, where it had a solid candidate in Eduardo Orrego, was echoed throughout the country despite a noticeable fall in the number of voters since presidential elections. Second place, however, varied. The Apra continued its downward spiral while the Marxist left, which had decided to unify in August and appeared under the new name of United Left, won second place, revealing a growing popularity.

In Ayacucho, the Popular Action candidate for the Huamanga Provincial Council, Jorge Jáuregui, defeated Germán Medina, of the United Left, in a hard-fought battle. In the provinces where most of the dynamite attacks had occurred, Popular Action also won. Nevertheless, in many districts, the number of blank or spoiled votes was virtually equal to (in Cangallo) or greater than (in Víctor Fajardo) the total number of valid votes.[38] All of these details indicated that the Shining Path's strength in Ayacucho was greater than suspected.

In December, as dynamite attacks intensified,[39] the Shining Path burned its bridges by killing its first victims, delving decidedly into war. Almost simultaneously, on December 26, it left a peculiar message for the new leader of the People's Republic of China.

Several dogs met the morning hung from street lights in central Lima. Tied at the neck, almost without struggling in the still air of Lima dawn, their sad bodies were wrapped in cloth painted with strident characters.

As the streets filled with people, a rumor spread that inside the bundles were not only dogs but explosives. Hours later, several Civil Guard officers climbed the posts and cut down the dogs. The bundles contained no explosives. On the shrouds, the paint was scribbled in furious letters. The words said simply, "Teng Hsiao-ping, son of a bitch."

On December 24, a group of thirty or forty people, apparently led by Eucario Najarro, Víctor Auqui, and Dr. Eduardo Mata, attacked the San Agustín de Ayzarca ranch. Despite the repeated alarms sounded by the ranch owners, there were no police present. The owners and their employees were rapidly captured as a red flag was raised over the chapel. They had been beaten and wounded, some seriously, but they were still alive. Inside the chapel, the owner, Benigno Medina, was first tortured (according to Medina's son, who managed to escape, they cut off his ears), and later they beat him to death. Medina was sixty years old. And as they killed him, they also killed an employee, Ricardo Lizarbe, who was only nineteen.[40]

This was the first blood spilled in the war. The early auguries had all pointed to a coming attack and had been fulfilled. It wasn't the last tragedy to befall the inhabitants of Ayzarca. Over the following years, most of the attackers would die violently, some in combat, others murdered after surrender, just as they had murdered this old farmer and the youth who had just begun to live, their blood required to seal the plan "to go toward a beginning of the guerrilla war." Those dead eyes turned upon a cemetery that for the moment embraced only these two, but would soon fill to overflowing.

7

Guerrillas

The first accurate description of the insurrection published in the Peruvian press appeared in the first days of 1981, under the by-line of journalist Patricio Ricketts.[1] He had traveled to Ayacucho in December. After complex maneuvers to get close to his sources, he interviewed one of the Shining Path's main leaders, at the time living openly in Ayacucho.

It was a unique interview. The etiquette of appearances demanded that the Shining Path leader not openly declare his political affiliation. For his part, Ricketts could not assume it as a given. At first, the answers were phrased as conditionals: "as I understand it, the Communist Party considers that . . ." Little by little, though, his reserve was put aside and the conversation advanced without further circumlocution.

To his attentive and fascinated listener, the Shining Path leader explained that the dynamite attacks were "the simple announcement of the people's war" or, as Ricketts put it, the "exordium to a long speech."[2] It was a substantial exordium. Although concentrated in Ayacucho, the Shining Path was already active throughout virtually the entire country.

But the Shining Path's precise identity and intentions remained a mystery to most Peruvians, including those on the Marxist left. Chants in praise of the Shanghai four and dead dogs wrapped in transoceanic curses against Teng Hsiao-ping not only seemed like political anachronisms, but fringe nuttiness. Usually innocuous nuts crowded Peruvian political folklore. One personality familiar in Lima was Pedro Angel Cordero y Velarde, who from the 1940s through the 1960s proclaimed himself "world emperor" (and, of course, president of the country) and commander in chief of its "earth, sea, air, and core" forces, the epitome of silliness but not by any means its only manifestation. For some, including those on the left, the dead dogs and furious loyalty to Chiang Ching identified the Shining Path as the Marxist version of Cordero y Velarde until December 1980.

But the number and type of attacks stopped them from continuing to describe the Shining Path as political pranksters. Some on the left chose to attribute these attacks to paramilitary groups linked to the Civil Guard, the army, the navy, or the U.S. Central Intelligence Agency (CIA), according to preference. In many cases, these accusations were simply a way to spread disinformation or propaganda. In others, there was sincere, though short-lived, certainty. The left's understanding of the Shining Path, the Shining Path it had seen in Ayacucho university battles and throughout the country, simply did not coincide with the level of discipline, ability, and number of people needed to make the country tremble with dynamite blasts.

In that evening interview, the Shining Path leader did not only confirm the authorship of every action, but he also added several that had not yet been linked to the Shining Path, like the bombing of Velasco's tomb. Ayacucho, he continued, was already in the vanguard of world revolution, and "its leadership" by the Shining Path was inherited directly from Marx, Lenin, and Mao. As far as the rest of the left went, his verbal attacks were already as sharp as they would remain over the following years. United Left senator Enrique Bernales was called the "chief of the Sinchis." The most benevolent term used to describe other leftist parliamentarians was "desk hogs."[3]

It was a strange conversation and, at first glance, improbable. Ricketts was corpulent, full of ceremony, with a gruff voice and face set in the serious expression found more often among suit-and-tie Peruvians from the department of Arequipa than any other group of humans in the world. The speaker, lean and ascetic, without a hint of ostentation, delivered his radical message with a half-ironic, half-condescending smile. Yet they understood each other perfectly. As his inheritance from an intensely radical youth, Ricketts understood Marxist-Leninist categories of thought without any need for translation and was able to distinguish between the coherent development of an argument and the mere parroting of pap. He saw clearly that the Shining Path belonged to the former camp. For his part, his informant sensed a listener able to follow his lead. With surprising detail, he explained how they had organized for the struggle and what they aimed to accomplish in the future.

A little later, on January 26, Ricketts published a short piece where, clearly ahead of any other interpreter of the insurrection, he described the Shining Path's characteristics and intentions:

> Though it may be surprising to say so, these young people with dynamite are not, strictly speaking, terrorists. . . . Whether we want it to or not, Peru has existed in a state of open war for the past six months. A Maoist war, peasant, roughly crafted, and home brewed. . . . But war it is. . . . Whosoever would react to it with disdainful adjectives or would put it all down to a hasty, feverish delirium would be a fool. . . . [Preparation] has gone on for a decade, perhaps fifteen years. What we see today is fruit of great patience, not bewildered improvisation. . . . Long before carrying out the first robbery of dynamite, they had already established a seed bank for revolution and the first "liberated zone" on the heights of Cangallo and Víctor Fajardo. . . . Then they started dynamite attacks and bloody incursions. In synthesis, this is what appears to be the prologue of the envisaged Hundred Years' War.[4]

Within the Marxist left, the article was generally dismissed as Peruvian McCarthyism. Months later, Senator Javier Diez Canseco repeated his accusation that these acts of violence were carried out by the right. "One has to be blind not to see that the right carries out much more complex actions. This latest wave has the right's unmistakable fingerprint."[5] For their part, moderates and those on the right paid little attention. Belaunde, who would later make Ricketts a top adviser and education minister, ended up being particularly impermeable to a dispassionate analysis of the enemy. As 1980 closed, after having described them as "traitors to the motherland," the president began to modify his statements and insinuate that the movement may be directed from the outside, presumably by Cuba, although no one mentioned it by name. Others believed such reticence was unnecessary. Popular Christian Party deputy and leader Celso Sotomarino asserted that "terrorism has its origin in aircraft carriers anchored in the Caribbean."[6]

Even when expressed clearly, the Shining Path's methods and strategy fell on deaf ears within the government, just as they had earlier with the heads of the intelligence services. With the exception of Ricketts and a few others, no one had the minimal intellectual training or absence of prejudice or dispassion necessary to interpret the facts of the matter at hand.

In interviews I had with Shining Path cadres at El Frontón prison in 1982, they told me that, among the bourgeois, Ricketts had been the only one to describe their aims and methods accurately.

On Christmas Eve 1980, a few hours after Benigno was murdered in Aycarza, a Shining Path leader whose prestige had already gone beyond its closed ranks was captured in Ayacucho. She was accused of having attacked with dynamite the

Ayacucho municipal building, the home of the Election Board president, and several other state offices. But other information suggested that her importance went far beyond her role as a leader. She was brought to Lima the next day and kept there for several days as her legal defense mobilized in a successful battle to have her returned to Ayacucho.

Edith Lagos repeated the words her organization had trained all captured cadres to say: "I am innocent and have nothing to do with the accusations the police have made. . . . everything they accuse me of is false. . . . in a society where human rights are respected, freedom is a right and it is a duty to demand it."[7] But there was something about her, perhaps her intensity, the imperious pride with which she carried her small figure in the halls outside the courts, that marked her among her followers and contributed to the legend that would surround her increasingly in what was left of her life.

At the beginning of 1981, the Shining Path had yet to develop the efficient legal defense machinery that became, in later years, the Democratic Association of Lawyers. Although still unsophisticated, there was already a priority on taking maximum advantage of the judicial process.

One model case took place in Cusco between the end of 1980 and the beginning of 1981. On December 22, a Shining Path detachment of about twenty people attacked a farm in Urubamba province. The group's apparent leader, Nora Chirinos, a psychologist and former National System for Social Mobilization (Sinamos) official, was captured soon afterward with seventeen others. A few days later, an investigative judge in the neighboring province of Calca asked for the detainees to be transferred. The police had no alternative but to comply. When the detainees arrived, the judge ordered all released immediately. The case caused a scandal, and the judge was suspended by the Cusco Superior Court and reprimanded.

He was Manuel Febres Flores, a lawyer who had graduated from San Marcos University. Over the following years, he would reappear in Lima as a member of the legal team that defended the Shining Path. After he became one of their most prominent lawyers as counsel for Osmán Morote, captured in 1988, Febres was kidnapped and killed by members of the semiofficial "Rodrigo Franco" death squad on July 28, 1988.

From the first of the year, Shining Path actions intensified in Ayacucho. On January 13, fifteen militants attacked the police station in the town of San José de Secce (also known as San José de Santillana). Attackers found the police completely unprepared. They mounted no resistance. The attackers took two machine guns, two revolvers, an M-1 rifle, and hundreds of munitions.

Thanks to help from townspeople, police sent from Ayacucho the next day managed to capture seven of the attackers and recover the stolen weapons. The others were identified and another woman was captured in Huanta soon afterward.[8]

Information received by police from towns and communities on the outskirts of Cangallo-Huancapi (and sometimes their active cooperation) was still considerable. This had led not only to the arrest of the perpetrators of various attacks, but also the identification of those who had organized and led most of them. One of those arrested in San José de Secce told police that after Edith Lagos's arrest (until then, she had been the Shining Path leader in Ayacucho), a high school student named Carlos Alcántara had taken her place. Alcántara had received the support of those in charge of each of the zones that the Shining Path had created in Ayacucho. His principal lieutenant was a very young woman, who over the following years would acquire a reputation both for bravery and cruelty: Carlota Tello Cuti.[9] Nevertheless, according to the same source, Alcántara took orders from a veteran Shining Path leader, Teresa Durand, whose duty was to oversee activity in Ayacucho city, to transmit ("to send up" in Shining Path terminology) reports from the cells to the leadership, and to "send down" evaluations and new orders.

According to information given by the detainee, most actions had been led and carried out by a relatively small group of people, some known only by their pseudonyms while others used their real names.

Several of the fourteen people arrested because of the attack on the San José de Secce police station had taken part in almost every action carried out previously in Ayacucho and Huanta. Alberto Granados had gone with Carlos Alcántara and three others to seize the "Voice of Huamanga" radio station on October 21, 1980, as well as attack the Ecasa warehouse (the government-run company that bought the rice harvest) that same day. He had also participated in the December 3 attack on the investigative police station and the sabotage of the Entel Peru radio tower on January 7, 1981. In every other attack, the same names reappeared in different combinations: Carlota Tello, Isidoro Choque, Miguel Higa, Willy Esquivel,[10] Gil Arango Huarancca, and some other pseudonyms.[11] The police concentrated on capturing them.

Since the beginning of the year, the sense of urgency among police had been reinforced by the perception that police stations were soon to be converted into the Shining Path's principal target. The day before the attack on the San José de Secce police station, the door to the Canarias police station had been blown off and the telegraph cables cut. On January 15, about fifteen Shining Path guerrillas attacked the Quinua station. The police stationed there reacted and forced the guerrillas to flee. The next day, like a portent of things to come, several Shining Path militants threw homemade explosives at the station.

The same thing was happening all over Peru. Attacks had little impact but were constant. The Shining Path was testing its own forces and tearing down the taboo against assaulting uniformed authority. In Apurímac, there were lesser attacks against Civil Guard stations on January 5 and 29; in Arequipa, explosives were thrown at a Civil Guard station, destroying several doors and cracking the walls. In the department of Cusco, the Sicuani Republican Guard detachment was also attacked with explosives as was the army's "November 27" barracks in the city of Cusco. In Puno, the investigative police station was damaged by a medium-level explosion on January 5.

In all of these areas, suspects were arrested, in many cases the individuals who had carried out attacks. In Ayacucho, for example, after the San José de Secce captures, most of those who had carried out attacks previously were arrested. The identification of Carlos Alcántara and Carlota Tello forced both deep underground. Nevertheless, the captures bought only brief respite. Shortly afterward, dynamite blasts and assaults resumed. The "second network" had been called into action. For the first time during the insurrection, the Shining Path demonstrated its capacity to manage reserves and measure out its forces. This ability reflected not only a larger and more complex organization than what was supposed, but also an ability to plan strategically and tactically that, with the few exceptions noted, no one acknowledged at the time.

"Open Guerrilla Zones"

On January 4, the Shining Path Central Committee began its third plenary session.[12] In contrast to the meetings that had gone on before, this one focused on strategic planning for the insurrection. There were few of the internal shake-ups typical of Shining Path conferences.

Within the context of the insurrection, it was an extremely important meeting. The "Beginning Plan," which Guzmán would later claim as an original contribution to Marxism, was deemed successfully concluded. The country was in turmoil, at war. One milestone (the third in the Shining Path's revolutionary vision) had been reached, and it was entering the fourth and longest stage in the years of blood it had in store for Peru: the "Development of the Guerrilla War."[13]

The objective of the third plenary was to plan and work out the strategy that would carry the Shining Path from these early, sporadic guerrilla actions to a substantial increase, until this activity became decisive. According to Maoist insurrectional strategy (and particularly during the first great stage of "strategic defense"), the purpose of every action (but fundamentally guerrilla ones) is population control and the gradual conquest of territory. Guerrilla attacks were the stick the Shining Path would wield in an organized way to wrest control of basic political organization from the government: the town and district.

Those who attended the meeting were familiar with the steps of Maoist guerrilla methodology. The first actions had opened "operation zones," which is to say areas where guerrillas could go, strike, and retreat. The next step was to open "guerrilla zones" in former operation zones. In guerrilla zones, the insurgency would dispute political power with the government. This did not necessarily mean explicit, visible power, but the real power. Once the insurgent organization prevailed, the next step would be to convert guerrilla zones into "support bases," where the party would then take public political control and begin constructing the organizational foundation of its own state. Progress depended on constant work and expansion, not only to grow but simply to survive. For each guerrilla zone won, new operation zones had to be opened. Each support base had to generate new guerrilla zones, preferably though not necessarily in neighboring areas. Triumph would come, as abrupt and giddy in its final moments as it had been slow and laborious at the beginning, when the whole country was converted into a single support base.

The Central Committee's third plenary session concentrated on determining a strategy to "open guerrilla zones that will create support bases." Along with reports and evaluations of the "second stage of the Beginning Plan," the agenda included a definition of the "development plan for the guerrilla war," the "general political line and unified front," problems in "constructing a (militarized) party in the middle of armed struggle," and, taking an international view, "our revolution within the international class war."

The Central Committee received reports from the Andahuaylas and Cangallo Subzonal Committees (both, as it will be remembered, part of the same Cangallo Zonal Committee), the Central Peru Regional Committee, and regional committees from Jaén, Trujillo, Cajamarca, Cusco-Puno, and Arequipa-Tacna. Also delivered were reports from the Chiclayo Local Committee, the Lima Metropolitan Committee, and the Ayacucho Zonal Committee. This array gives an approximation of the Shining Path's territorial strength, strongly concentrated in Ayacucho and Apurímac, but unmistakable in the country's center and south.

Three fundamental points were raised during the plenary session (and in a meeting held immediately afterward by the Political Bureau, to enact its decisions): how to increase the quantity and impact of insurgent actions in the city; how to plan the growth of insurgent activity in the countryside; and how to organize politically areas in upheaval, taking advantage of the aftermath of armed actions and constructing the rudiments of a rebel state in areas gradually falling under Shining Path control.[14]

How could the Shining Path increase urban violence, especially in Lima? It became clear during the political commission meeting that this question was made up of two problems: how to develop "military work" and the clandestine "second network." A little later, the Political Bureau gave a series of instructions to the person responsible for the metropolitan committee (apparently Laura Zambrano) on the principal areas of work during this next stage. Actions like throwing explosives, fires, and graffiti should be carried out through "action committees" organized by territory. "Higher-level" actions, which is to say sabotage, local disturbances, and political killings, should be carried out by "special detachments" that depended directly on the metropolitan committee. At the same time, the urban organization should carry out "concrete acts of support for guerrillas," which would include both actions that would serve as an echo to peasant actions and the recruitment of militants for rural detachments.

Simultaneously, the metropolitan committee had to concentrate its energy on collecting intelligence. The instructions on this matter were inevitably terse. Collecting "information," the document notes, "implies a relationship with 'special' elements that requires great reserve and discretion." In later years, some cases of Shining Path infiltration in various branches of the civil bureaucracy were discovered, though apparently—judging by the information used by the Shining Path—most of their collaborators were never detected.

However, the most delicate part of espionage and infiltration work was within the "armed and repressive forces." The Shining Path document only directs this work to be "external, through propaganda work, and internal, through the organization of cells and organizations with soldiers, etc." The document underscores that this work was "highly classified" and, of course, a priority.

It is difficult to measure the degree of success the Shining Path enjoyed in this area over the following years. Certainly, circumstantial evidence suggests a degree of infiltration among the lower ranks of the police, as will become evident later on. Nevertheless, only a few cases were apparent or uncovered. In 1981, a private at Ayacucho's "Los Cabitos" barracks was arrested by police when he was discovered to have Shining Path pamphlets and some dynamite sticks in his home. A navy crewman at the Callao navy base deserted, taking with him several rifles. The deserting sailor reappears later in this tale, at the 1983 battle of Sacsamarca.

The metropolitan committee along with the Political Bureau also had to coordinate two specialized tasks: the "protection of structures and people," which was to say the Shining Path leadership, and "administering punishment," which needs no further explanation.

With the city defined as a "necessary complement" to the countryside, the Shining Path still had to define a basic strategy for its urban theater. Until then, actions that provoked rioting and looting had been followed by sabotage and terrorism, which limited their potential for expansion. As long as these remained the central actions, the goal of influencing important sectors of the population could not be won except in a very limited way. The third plenary session began an attempt to sketch out the fundamental areas of a plan that would combine political, trade-union, and association work with military activity.

Deliberations on this theme were only exploratory, not conclusive. Underscored was the desirability of taking over marches, strikes, local and regional work stoppages, and other forms of local protest in order to convert them into violent conflict; or in their words, "with actions, put the party at the head of the people . . . popular resistance with the proletariat as its nucleus and the party leadership imposed on events." Except in some limited cases, this was not achieved over the following years. Only in 1986 did the Shining Path begin to once again emphasize semilegal and open actions, meant to increase their grass-roots support.[15]

Nevertheless, at the stage of "Opening Guerrilla Zones," the fundamental thrust of Shining Path activity remained the countryside. Although the action plan took into account the entire country, it focused on the "principal region," which is to say Ayacucho, Andahuaylas, and Huancavelica. The specific regional plan was designed as "a broad system of actions carried out relatively simultaneously, keeping in mind conditions in each zone." Party committees elsewhere should "develop actions according to their conditions, also simultaneously, as a complementary campaign." Especially in Ayacucho, actions should be designed to undermine prevalent forms of property holding and, above all, "to shake the foundations of the reactionary state," attacking the representatives of state authority at the district level. The orchestrated collection of actions (with sabotage and lightning guerrilla attacks as the principal ones) would transform an important part of Ayacucho into "guerrilla zones."

Most Shining Path cadres had little practical experience. The document makes the point that "not clearly explained are ideas about . . . the two fundamental forms of guerrilla struggle": ambushes and attacks. Adding that such a situation was "understandable" since there was a dearth of firsthand experience, the document emphasized the need to analyze both national and international experience with armed struggle in this regard. Nevertheless, it added, only "with practical experience will we develop a mastery of ambushes and attacks and in no other way."

It is interesting to confirm that as a real guerrilla insurrection began (the previous stage was basically to catalyze the insurrection), the Shining Path was stronger than supposed; at the same time, it suffered weaknesses greater than those suspected. In terms of strengths, the Shining Path was a much larger and more disciplined organization than almost anyone realized then, or afterward: distributed over territory, with a rudimentary, yet functional communications system, and a centralized leadership, which guaranteed unified control over the party apparatus at all times. Yet the Shining Path's preparation in military technique was extremely poor. Its strategic perceptions were well founded, but, at the level of tactical application, ignorance was widespread. At this stage, the Shining Path was generally competent, with committed yet amateur recruits and untrained midlevel leaders.

The plan to "open guerrilla zones" would serve in part to give Shining Path cadres real-life training and, at the same time, begin to organize the insurrectional armed forces. The plan concluded that the problem lay in the "move from disorganized peasant masses to masses organized militarily, like armed forces."

Guzmán had foreseen that the plan would be implemented by technically unprepared cadres. Although this problem was common to various Marxist insurrections in their initial phases, he considered it of paradoxical advantage. The sum of experiences and failures would harden survivors; and as long as the entire organization could take advantage of each action's results, their education would be quick and comprehensive. Simultaneously, strategic planning and the development of a new tactical methodology, where the same steps were prescribed for each action and every campaign, each adjusted to the other, guaranteed that even sloppily executed actions would deliver some results.

After the third plenary session, the Shining Path incorporated the following five-step classification into action and campaign planning:[16] (1) preparation (or preparatory actions); (2) "a forceful answer" (a sharp intensification of actions); (3) the development of the guerrilla war (the action's principal component or the campaign's principal action); (4) the coup de grâce or "earthshaking blow"; and (5) complementary actions. Once these steps were completed, a careful dissection of the action or campaign should take place, to determine correct decisions and errors. Afterward, the cycle would begin again, although supposedly at a higher level of the proverbial dialectic spiral.

The third plenary session concluded that a crucial element in its success or failure was the portioning out of actions over set periods of time. In their words, the "application of the plan" demanded that they "(a) define actions according to regional, local, and zonal circumstances and the moment of execution; (b) allow time for preparation and moving the action forward; (c) a key question is when and how to apply impetus, defining how to confront the reaction's answer. . . . to stir up in order to promote cohesion, readjust in order to rearm and prepare to advance; all in scaled actions spread out over time, with initiative, flexibility, and planning, applying the principle of coming together and dispersing."

Nevertheless, the Shining Path still had doubts about the precise intensity these actions should have. To maintain the dose of attacks that would erode the state's presence and authority without provoking an enormous reaction was an equilibrium that the insurgency needed, but was clearly difficult to attain. "Plans to harass and spread fear with all types of actions and thus foster struggle conditions of a high order, possible, desirable?" the agenda item noted. Despite these doubts, the structure of the discussion underscored the need to prepare for the intervention of the armed forces at any moment. "The police could fence us in and the armed forces delay direct action, but we should be prepared to confront the army at any moment." The eventual entry of the armed forces into the fight would nevertheless have for the Shining Path a beneficial effect as long as guerrillas were able to survive the hostile onslaught. "This would encourage the armed forces to assume greater decisive power, undermining bourgeois democracy . . . for the price of denying the 'Democratic Reconquest' they have crowed about. . . . it implies greater polarization and a deepened struggle with defenders of the bourgeois democracy; all this would further fertilize an armed dispute and the development of popular struggle."

As the insurgency cut away at the state's authority at its district or village roots, the third plenary session emphasized the need to set up immediately the embryo of Shining Path government. Along with traditional Maoist methodology, here they drew on experience accumulated in the years before the war began. Local government organizations controlled by the Shining Path would become "popular committees," and the individuals and groups that formed part of them did so under the Maoist category of "unified front" in the revolution of the "new democracy."

The "unified front" was, in the trinity of "revolutionary instruments" (the other two were the Communist Party and the rebel armed forces), the equivalent of the Holy Ghost: the least concrete of the three, vague in definition and scope, but indispensable.

Within the fiction that the "new democracy" represented, the unified front was the union of economic classes supposedly committed to the insurrection's progress. Following the proletariat's presumed leadership (for its part directed by the Communist Party), peasants and petite bourgeoisie were supposedly enthusiastically grouped within the front, together with strays from the national bourgeoisie. However, not even Shining Path documents dared overstate reality to the extreme of suggesting that either of the bourgeoisie, rich or poor, participated in the "front."

Clearly, however, their absence didn't ruin the design. If there were no bourgeoisie in the "unified front," the party would look after their interests. It mattered little that the historical script guaranteed their eventual liquidation. Each group had to play its role in the historical sacrament. If no one was willing to do it, the Shining Path named itself the executor of its doubtful historical investment.

Despite all, even these fictions played a role. Finding itself close to exercising the duties of a semiopen, clandestine government, the complex bonds of real and ghostly organizations under the Shining Path's centralized control guaranteed that the party would carry out one of the central duties of efficient dictatorship: immerse the great majority of people under its control in an avalanche of separate organizations that not only control every aspect of their daily lives but also, through these multiple affiliations, demand from each individual the completion of duties beyond

Disply contr

the ability of even the most dedicated Shining Path members. In this way, everyone was potentially at fault and was, in consequence, easier to control.

The third plenary session ended when the members of the Central Committee signed the new plan. They also signed the proclamation agreed upon at the time, addressed "to our heroic, fighting people."

Written by Guzmán, the proclamation contained his characteristic prose, frequently vibrant, occasionally edging into hyperbole. He addressed himself to a people who—if we judge by any conceivable poll—wanted nothing more than peace. Yet he set out to convince them that their transcendent interest was better served by blood, destruction, want, and horror converted into a daily occurrence. Like other fiery incitements to violence throughout history, this call to combat resonated with rhythms designed to deafen reason.

> Peruvian people! Today, after twelve years of false revolution and the true reinforcement of your chains under the fascist military regime . . . a new government commands behind the decrepit reactionary bulk of so-called "representative democracy," false democracy, with false rights and freedoms . . . and real oppression.
>
> . . . Your history, people, is of rebellion and combat; . . . In synthesis, people of ours, your history is the heroic and enduring struggle of the masses . . . to create and forge with weapons in hand a new world for your children.

It was prophetic language, rich in conceptual miracle working as it proclaimed the beginning of war, implying new origin and conception myths:

> And today, your best children, flesh of your flesh, steel of your steel . . . today, people of ours, your best and most loyal children have unfurled to the wind the red and blazing banner of rebellion. . . . Today, the children who emerged from your powerful loins hold up their armed actions and their lives as offerings, saluting your heroic struggle and splendid future in this new year.

The proclamation had limited distribution, and few Peruvians were aware of the deeply thought out gift that had been given to them for the coming year. It mattered little to the Shining Path. This type of gift, multiplied exponentially, would overflow in the future. The burning gazes had unleashed their dervishes. The Shining Path's guerrilla war—not the "war of the flea" according to the metaphor Robert Taber made famous,[17] but the war of the ant, multiple, underground, its acts simple but conceptually complex—had begun.

8

The Quota

On April 19, a small Shining Path group made a lightning raid and captured the police garrison in Luricocha, a town located a short distance from Huanta. Only one officer was wounded, Sergeant Artemio Gamboa. No shots were fired. The attackers carried only starters' pistols and stick rifles. As they left, however, they clutched real weapons seized in the assault: two machine guns and two revolvers, along with munitions.

The next day, in the same town, a suspect "who after interrogation admitted having participated in the assault" was arrested.[1] This was all police managed to get from him. The suspect claimed he did not know his accomplices "because they were hooded" or anything about where the stolen weapons were hidden. A little later, he was formally charged by a judge.

He was one of the first people prosecuted under a new antiterrorism law that the government had passed a month earlier, in March. Decree Law 046 had been written and revised by two veteran law professors from San Marcos University, Luis Roy Freyre and Luis Bramont Arias (who only made revisions). It was the first effort of an already anguished government to equip itself with the tools needed to fight the Shining Path. Their concern about striking the balance between the demand for judicial and police action and maintaining the new democratic spirit is revealed in its phrasing. It allowed the police to detain suspects for up to fifteen days. However, the public ministry and local investigative judge had to be notified of the arrest within twenty-four hours. Questioning had to take place with the local prosecutor present. And the investigative phase of the trial could last no longer than six months.

Like so many other laws in Spanish America, this one was observed more through violations of its precepts than by compliance. In practice, judicial investigations lasting less than six months were few and interrogations carried out with a prosecutor present were extremely rare. Despite the youth of the constitution and the democratic regime, appearance and practice were already divorced.

But Decree Law 046 also had crucial conceptual defects. The law was supposed to punish terrorism and defined its scope as "provoking or maintaining a state of fear, alarm, or terror among the population,"[2] which did not accurately define either the Shining Path's methods or its intentions, the capture of power using the many tools of war, only one of them being terror. This fundamental distinction was not understood at the time (or even now), and it lay at the root of distortions not only in how this rebel organization was perceived but also, inevitably, the strategy to combat it.

Perhaps the most important error was the government's failure to have taken into account that its adversaries were not isolated individuals, but an organization with objectives, goals, and plans. Except for incomplete and restrictive ideas related to the intellectual authorship of crimes and "conspiracy in order to commit a crime," the law was designed only to punish those involved and not to confront the organization behind them. To be fair, this defect was common to all the defense mechanisms used by the government against the Shining Path.

Despite its limitations, both inadvertent and self-imposed, the law provoked the immediate, pitched opposition of leftist deputies in Parliament. (The Shining Path would express its opposition shortly afterward, with a small bomb detonated at Roy Freyre's door.) Some protests were aimed at the news cameras, but others were clearly justified.

According to the law, for example, terrorist actions included "destruction or damage to public or private buildings, transportation or communications networks or the transport of fluids or power."[3] Over the following years, some provincial union leaders, whose protests included leading highway blockades, were arrested and prosecuted under the obviously abusive use of this article.[4]

The article of Decree Law 046 that initially caused the most alarm punished the use of the news media to carry out "apology" for terrorism.[5] Opposition to this article—based on its potential to curtail freedom of expression—was widespread.

But in practice, the article was never invoked, not even years later, when *El Diario* fell under the Shining Path's complete control.

At the beginning of the school year on April 1, Shining Path bombers set off dynamite at several Lima schools. Some were damaged enough to close their doors. The impression that these attacks left in Lima, with the memory of the dead dogs hanging from street lights still fresh, was that the Shining Path was not only clearly malevolent, but certifiably demented. It seemed as if its leadership was operating from some Lima psychiatric ward and that the mystery lay in discovering how it had managed to convince anyone to carry out these actions.

Some arrests were made after the school attacks. Pedro Chavarría and Eduardo Palomino Ladrón de Guevara had been captured attempting to bomb another one. The men's appearance, however, did not correspond to members of Marat-Sade's cast. Both typified the image that would later become familiar, when arrests increased: young people, thin, serious, introverted; in general, from poor families, some of which had made efforts to give them a college education; without behavior problems—to the contrary, they were frequently obedient children and siblings, neat, quiet, hard-working, not charismatic enough to awaken strong devotion, but rather a silent appreciation. To see them wrapped in a aura of explosions and an inexplicable ferocity was only the beginning of a much bigger surprise for many families. "I prefer to see him dead," Eduardo Palomino's mother said after his capture.[6] Later, she added, "My baby is incapable of harming anyone." Palomino had studied economics at Huamanga University, but he had returned to Lima over a year earlier, giving no better reason than "mental exhaustion," which, perhaps, was not entirely incorrect.

The legal Marxist left unanimously condemned these attacks, although with varying intensity. Nevertheless, repudiation occupied only a small and grudging portion of its energy. The political parties that made up the United Left and their parliamentarians dedicated themselves to attacking Decree Law 046, thus propelling themselves into a political offensive against the government. They organized or supported marches and aggressive strikes in Lima, and, with great enthusiasm, encouraged a wave of regional work stoppages—organized by regional alliances that ignored their implicit debt to the alliance that had shown them the way: the Alliance for the Defense of Ayacucho.

Using all the tactical resources of agitation at their disposal, the Marxist left asserted, in an increasingly emphatic way, that most attacks had been carried out by the police to provoke more repression and justify the budget increases that De la Jara was already calling for. This ploy was meant to awaken the opposition of the armed forces, permanently suspicious of any increase in police power, especially the Civil Guard.

Given that the government was still controlled by its most progressive wing, this was a suicidal game. In one of his numerous interviews with leftist parliamentarians during these months, an exasperated De la Jara snapped that "during the next military holy week, you are going to be the first ones crucified." Challenged by a landslide of regional work stoppages, many based on impossible demands, the other liberal cabinet member, Labor Minister Alfonso Grados Bertorini, complained that instead of a movement bent on decentralization, he faced one bent on disintegration.

At the time, none of the problems that in the following years, as the Belaunde administration deteriorated, made the work stoppages and protests understandable even existed. In contrast to the military regime, Belaunde's administration displayed notable support for democratic freedoms; and the economy gave signs of sustained growth. Under these circumstances, the left's attitude seemed designed to brandish impatience as an end in itself, circumvent gradual progress in its demand for instantaneous results, and provoke the demise of the progressives and the emergence of the hard-liners. While the left never became the prime instigators of this process, it did contribute to achieving this objective in a relatively short time.

In hindsight, though, it appears almost inevitable that suspicion would reign. Emerging from clandestinity, street brawls, and heated discussions over the best way to conduct an insurrection, most among the Marxist left had entered Parliament with the professed intention of utilizing it as just one more instrument within the panoply of means available to provoke violent conflict. Most of the left's leaders had yet to develop ties binding them to the democratic process, ties that later emerged. Nor did most understand that Parliament should serve for something more than a pulpit for fiery speeches. Many felt that their first duty as parliamentarians was to help, contribute to, and foment "popular uprising," at times in guilty competition with the Shining Path while at others in an openly derogatory way. Goals and strategies varied from group to group—none were particularly clear—but the fundamental impetus and the tactics drawn from it aimed in this direction.

As I suggested in an earlier chapter, the wholesale entry of the Marxist left into electoral politics modified it in a much deeper way than any of its leaders would have guessed in 1980 or 1981. After several years passed, the left would be transformed, perhaps reluctantly but for that reason no less completely, into an important though ignored factor in democratic stability. It wasn't a uniform process, but it was much more generalized than even an optimistic observer would have predicted at the beginning of 1980, after watching societies in Chile, Argentina, Uruguay, and Brazil polarize and hearing eyewitness accounts of those bloody battles.

Deeply rooted stereotypes and profound suspicions on both ends of the political spectrum prevented the democratic assimilation of the left from being clearly perceived and evaluated when it happened. The exception, as always, was the Shining Path. Its analysis, bristling with adjectives, obscured by the use of dogmatic jargon, was nevertheless rigorous. If the paths that the other movements had taken between 1965 and 1980 gave the occasional impression of being parallel, as of 1980 they were not only in opposite directions but in open conflict. The Marxist left would end up defending the society that the Shining Path wanted to dynamite. That stick rifle that Horacio Zeballos brandished at the UNIR rally in 1980 would perhaps end up being fired, but aimed from the opposite side of the barricades, against Shining Path attackers. For the Shining Path, the process that would convert the left into its enemies was itself an unforgivable betrayal. For those who supported democracy, this evolution was a healthy one, although risky, and earned them greater political maturity.

Nevertheless, in 1981, the process was just beginning. The rule remained an ambiguous relationship with the Shining Path and constant conflict with the government. The case of Puno (where in the following years, the legal left and the Shining Path would clash in a bloody fight for control of grass-roots groups and local governments) is especially revealing.

With the election of Jaime Ardiles as provincial mayor in the 1980 municipal elections, the United Left had gained one of its first electoral victories in Puno. The most vociferous opposition came from groups close to the Shining Path and Puka Llacta, whose strength was concentrated in the Technical University of the Altiplano. Once elected, the new mayor and parliamentarians from Puno had to confront—much more intensely than the rest of the country—constant harassment from groups on their left. That's why Puno was especially active when the wave of regional work stoppages took shape.

On March 25, a twenty-four-hour, departmentwide work stoppage began, coordinated by Mayor Ardiles and an ad hoc "unified struggle committee." The "list of demands" adopted by strikers ranged from necessary changes that could be granted immediately to others that bordered on the extravagant.

On April 10, Mayor Ardiles and various others, later joined by even more people, declared themselves on a "hunger strike . . . in support of the list of demands." Three days later, deputy Emeterio Tacuri, a plump Trotskyite, joined the hunger strike in the Lima Parliament building, "demanding that the government solve Puno's problems."

On April 16, the Puno television transmitter was attacked.[7] Wilmer Vásquez, a Republican Guardsman, lost a hand trying to deactivate the dynamite charge. The next day, three notorious radicals on the Marxist left were arrested in a police sweep: Ronald Bustamante, Jawar Orihuela, and Jaime Nina.[8] All three belonged to the "unified struggle committee," with Nina as its president. Police found several sticks of dynamite in a hiding place in Bustamante's house that he had constructed and attempted to hide in. (A member of UNIR, Bustamante would later insist that the dynamite had been planted by police.)

A little later, the detainees were transferred to Lima. Meanwhile, many institutions and organizations in Puno joined the "struggle committee" in calling for their release. On April 18, Puno bishop Jesús Calderón, supported by, among others, Dominican nuns, declared his support for the hunger strike and joined a commission that traveled to Lima to press for the detainees' release. In Lima, the Puno parliamentarians, without the fasting Tacuri, vehemently joined the commission.

Minister De la Jara agreed to release Orihuela and Nina, although he protested bitterly ("every time a suspect is arrested, a parliamentarian appears who demands an unconditional release").[9] Ronald Bustamante, however, remained under arrest and was eventually charged.

The example set in Puno spread elsewhere. While the commission met with De la Jara, a twenty-four-hour work stoppage began in Cusco to demand the release of five construction workers accused of carrying out attacks with dynamite.[10]

Accusations against the legal left for using a double standard when reacting to Shining Path actions were partially justified. Nevertheless, it is necessary to put them in context. Historically, and despite the acrimonious disputes that had erupted, most of these movements had a common origin as well as a shared, instinctive perception of the enemy, though they did not share this perception with the Shining Path: the police, and repressive state entities in particular. With memories of the months shared in prison still fresh, the leftist parliamentarians were convinced that despite their violent differences with the Shining Path, they had a moral imperative (and a political mandate as well) to race to gain the release of people who, although wrong, were still thought to belong to the same team.

Years later, it would be in Puno that the legal left would be slowly carried by events to a completely different position. It was a tortured, painstaking lesson. But bit by bit, the understanding that the Shining Path threatened not only its political survival but also the physical survival of its local cadres emerged. After mourning and burying several of their leaders and activists murdered by the Shining Path, the legal left in Puno took an increasingly combative stance, which would culminate, as will be seen later, in an unavoidable confrontation.

In comparison to previous months, by the beginning of May, the number of dynamite attacks had reached a decidedly alarming level. The extravagant attention to detail shown in some attacks—dogs, tombs, schools—didn't mask either their cumulative effect or the inevitable perception that behind these explosions was not just a small group consumed by bilious schizophrenia, but an organization that covered most of the country in a coordinated manner. Attacks in Ayacucho numbered eighty-three; eighty-one in Lima; forty-eight in Cusco; forty-six in Junín; and twenty in Ancash.[11] Despite this, the Marxist left presented a motion in Parliament to repeal the antiterrorist Law 046. Support for the motion crossed party lines. During the debate, Apra lawyer Javier Valle Riestra, a parliamentarian frequently carried away by oratorical flourishes with little content, asserted that "the terrorists' best weapon is journalistic irresponsibility in magnifying and overemphasizing these events."[12]

Despite an increase in Shining Path activity, it is important to recognize that there remained a tenuous justification to playing down their importance. Until this moment, there were few victims; and the comparison between the number of attacks and casualties gave the latter an almost innocuous appearance, especially if the observer wanted to see it that way. Compared, for example, with the sophistication of the Tupamaros or Montoneros, so recent in memory, the rustic nature of their attacks was not seen as a rebel advantage (broadening their war appeal, removing any elitist taint, and representing a unique experience constructed from the ground up), but rather as evidence of primitivism and impotence.[13]

Nevertheless, the government had to react. Specialized police units (the Civil Guard "Sinchis" and the Republican Guard "Llapan Atic") were sent to Ayacucho and Andahuaylas respectively, to search out and engage the rebels in combat. After carrying out operations more appropriate for a war against Cuba-style guerrillas, both groups still managed to arrest some low-level militants in both areas. In Ayacucho, one farmer was killed and in Andahuaylas an officer was wounded; but neither casualty resulted from combat.

Although they remained tentative, the counterinsurgency forces had already committed several excesses, which would inevitably distort and sabotage their efforts. Georgina Gamboa, a young Ayacucho woman, reported that she was raped by Civil Guard officers. Police denied the charge, but never convincingly. For several months, Gamboa's rape was the symbol that the leftist parliamentarians used to characterize the violent situation in the country.

Almost at the same time, another incident of greater political importance had occurred in Cusco. On May 26, a police unit operating in a Sicuani neighborhood captured two locals and a Lima student: Edmundo Cox Beuzeville. At once, an interrogation began that lasted for close to two days. The suspects confessed belonging to the Shining Path and apparently told them about a hiding place where more than eighty sticks of dynamite were found. Draped in a poncho, Cox was filmed admitting his political allegiance and his participation in several attacks. Weeks later, a portion of the video was shown on Lima television.

However, a poncho had been placed on Cox not to give folkloric color to the scene, but to hide his fractured shoulder. The interrogation had been conducted under torture. Apart from the shoulder, Cox's drawn face in the video gave silent testimony to several days of intense suffering.

Cox was the nephew of Augusto Beuzeville, auxiliary bishop of Lima, who not only went personally to the interior minister to demand an explanation but also galvanized the support of the Catholic Church. The Episcopal Commission of Social Action released a statement demanding that the state "guarantee the physical and moral integrity of the individuals detained."

While De la Jara reacted with caution, ordering an investigation and Cox's transfer to Lima, other prominent members of the government reacted with vehemence. Both the president of the Chamber of Deputies and the Senate, along with the very president of the Republic, sharply responded to the statement and accused those who had signed it—particularly Jesuit bishop Luis Bambarén, commission president—of having supported in silence or openly attacks on human rights committed by the military government.[14] Against this bitter exchange, Cox's legal responsibility for attacks passed to the background.

Over the following years, now married to Shining Path militant Miriam Lezcano, Cox was arrested several more times, in Puno and in Lima, with fake documents and flimsy alibis. In almost every case, he was released by the courts for "lack of evidence." According to police, his importance within the Shining Path grew considerably with time. In 1987, Dircote sources believed he was in charge of the Metropolitan Committee.[15] In that determination, there could have been something of the venerable old tale of sour grapes. Yet the charges against Cox not only ended up being serious, but had started out that way. Nevertheless, resorting to torture put the police in a morally repugnant light and sabotaged beyond repair their own work in this case and so many others. Before the horror of torture, the matter of guilt or innocence became secondary for most people. Nevertheless, as will become clear in this book, the police (and the Peruvian state along with it) did not draw from this experience or the ones that followed it the lessons that any elemental reflection would have made painfully evident.

While politicians and journalists in Lima were enmeshed in disoriented polemics and perceptions of political violence, the Shining Path redoubled the frequency and intensity of attacks.

During the day, the town of Quinua—with its cobbled square, whitewashed walls, pure silence in the pure Andean air, and brilliant light—seemed entirely removed from any threat of violence and the deafening conspiratorial rumor palpable in Ayacucho. A few miles from the departmental capital, joined to it by a paved highway constructed in 1974 by the Venezuelan government to celebrate the 150-year anniversary of the battle of Ayacucho, Quinua appeared to be a quiet backwater at the margins of world events. At one side of the square, along the highway and shaded by trees, there were street vendors who prepared and sold roasted potatoes and chopped meat seasoned with spicy mountain sauces, especially on Sundays.

Visible from the wooden benches and rustic tables was the obelisk on the Quinua plain marking the spot where in 1824 Peruvians led by the Spanish disputed the fate of Latin America with an army of Peruvians, Colombians, and Venezuelans.

Ramiro Flores Sullca, the police chief, was from Ayacucho and knew—especially in the wake of the failed attack in January on the police post—that night brought dangers more real than mythic. Attacks on police posts in San José de Secce and Luricocha had torn apart the fabric of the implicit assumptions upon which police authority rested. These attacks had shattered respect for the uniform—a police officer's best protection in peacetime. And Flores Sullca had known since January that this had instantly changed the way society viewed the police, from protected and almost unassailable to among the most vulnerable.

On the night of August 15, three people wearing Civil Guard uniforms entered the station. Flores Sullca, who had received information warning him of an imminent attack, relaxed his vigilance for a moment. Behind the uniformed men came fifteen or sixteen people. Some carried guns. Flores Sullca had no hope of resisting, but he tried. There was a brief and furious exchange of fire, which ended with Flores Sullca dead and two or three attackers wounded. Meanwhile, Civil Guardsman Rodolfo Manrique, also wounded, managed to flee.[16] With the police station and town in their control, the guerrillas seized two machine guns, two revolvers, and several uniforms before leaving Quinua without haste.

Flores Sullca was the first police officer killed by the Shining Path. With time, he would be joined by hundreds more. The procession of coffins carried by grim-faced officers on their way to the cemetery would become a virtually routine event. But at the time, the Ayacucho police reacted to this violated taboo with vehemence and indignation, realizing at the same time that it was crucial to restore the taboo through actions that would serve as examples.

Almost a month after the attack, on September 7, a combined group of Ayacucho police officers and Sinchis in Huanta province captured two of the most wanted Shining Path leaders: Carlota Tello Cuti, considered the lieutenant of still-fugitive Carlos Alcántara—according to information given by some detainees, the Shining Path leaders responsible for the city of Ayacucho—and Jesús Luján González, who had been captured in January while carrying dynamite, but released soon afterward. Over the following days, there were several more arrests, including that of Dante Cruzat Cárdenas, a member of one of the longtime Ayacucho families that had linked their fate to the Shining Path.[17] Flores Sullca's revolver was recovered and the detainees charged. More arrests followed. Maximiliano Durand, who lived semipublicly in Ayacucho, was arrested. Weeks later, Durand would be formally charged along with the other suspects in connection to the Quinua attack.

Nevertheless, despite the high number of arrests and the detainees' high rank within the Shining Path, violence did not subside. Attacks in Ayacucho and the rest of the country multiplied, increasing not only in number and intensity, but in ferocity.

At the beginning of September, a Shining Path group reached a small village (Túpac) in the province of Goyllariquizga, department of Cerro de Pasco. Without showing their weapons, they called a meeting in the central square. When the officer in charge of the police post, Segundo Paz, drew close to the group, someone supposedly attending the meeting cut him down, with "two shots to the chest."[18]

Almost at the same time, on September 16, a dozen partially masked people attacked the "La Pequeñita" store in Ayacucho city and began looting it. Antonia Carrión de De la Cruz, the owner, tried to stop them and was shot to death. Her son, who fought the attackers in an attempt to save her, was badly wounded.[19]

Abruptly, victims began to accumulate. What had until then been perceived as a quirky uprising became bloody. Most alarming about this new face of violence was the apparent absence of logic for selecting victims. These were humble people. Only with impossible ideological contortions could they be considered guilty of some debt to society. It seemed clear that the Shining Path leadership had thought it necessary to first spill the blood of others.

It was true: the intensification of the war, agreed upon since January, had presumed a change in emphasis to cruel acts. Some were apparently gratuitous. However, the decision to cover the war in blood had been accompanied by another that was much more significant and that would without question shape the character of the war: the decision to promote self-sacrifice, a willingness to die—the quota.

The Quota

Marx, Lenin, and principally Mao Zedong have armed us. They have taught us about the quota and what it means to annihilate in order to preserve. . . . If one is persistent, maintains politics in command, maintains the political strategy, maintains the military strategy, if one has a clear, defined plan, then one advances and one is able to meet any bloodbath. . . . we began planning for the bloodbath in 1980 because we knew it had to come.[20]

When Abimael Guzmán referred to the "bloodbath" in 1988, the insurrection's history was already stained in it. The proverbial meat grinder had processed enough people to make the Shining Path uprising one of Latin America's bloodiest since the 1960s, with clear signs of becoming one of the cruelest wars in the continent's history.

Nevertheless, as of early 1981, extravagance, not violence, was the idiosyncracy of the Shining Path rebellion. As yet, there were few victims and a certain consensus persisted that as long as the Shining Path's fury remained transoceanic (that is, killing dogs and hurling insults at Teng Hsiao-ping and Enver Hoxha), the group's presence in Peru would be basically innocuous. It was, of course, a view as erroneous as it was distorted, although it reflected the low level of violence at the time.

The Shining Path's central committee held its fourth plenary session in May 1981. It is a thinly documented meeting, where in addition to analyzing and refining a plan to "develop the guerrilla war, opening guerrilla fronts as a function of the bases of support," the issue of "the quota" was broached.

This was a principal theme of the meeting and perhaps of those first war years. Not just the subject of heated debate, the quota became a solemn agreement, made with all the ceremony usually accorded rituals. Later, the quota and its practical consequences were mythified and adorned with symbols and metaphors as much by Shining Path commissars as by some leading pundits. Nevertheless, the heart of the debate had eminently practical, military concerns: transform the war into the central preoccupation of all Peruvians through a radical increase in violence, to raise the stakes and turn the blood trickle into a flood. To this end, Shining Path militants had to be convinced of two things: the need to kill in a systematic and depersonalized way as part of an agreed-upon strategy; and, as a necessary premise, not just the willingness but the expectation of giving up their own lives. This second concept is known as "the quota."

In the following years, the quota's very concept and the feverish, fulminating fervor of its expression gave the Shining Path the reputation (and to some degree the appearance) of being a death cult rather than a Marxist party. This charge was repeated from the ranks of the legal left, especially after the 1986 prison massacres. According to these horrified accusations, the Shining Path's inspiration was not found in Marx or Lenin or even Mao, but in Reverend Jones and the Guyana cyanide pail.

In the face of such accusations, the Shining Path reacted with atypical indignation, but without debating the heart of the issue: the relation between war and its costs, especially in blood. To what degree is the latter—in their view—not just the result of the former but its cause, fuel for the blaze? Since 1981, this had been a central issue, and the debate over "the quota" aimed at facing it squarely.

According to the scarce documentation available, the debate was conducted as a rigorous, though fundamentalist development of orthodox Marxism-Leninism-Maoism. Beginning in 1979, in its moment of "defining and deciding," the Shining Path had discussed the struggle's social cost. The essential tension in revolutionary movements between philanthropic intention and objectives and brutal means had been resolved according to Bolshevik and Stalinist tradition. And they had taken up arms. But even though the insurrection had begun, tension had not dissipated nor would it. Abimael Guzmán knew well and understood—as did Stalin in his time—that the conflict would only end when the paradox was driven home and the philanthropists ended their days by serving the commissars, now convinced that to kill gave life, that war brought peace, that the most extreme tyranny brought the greatest freedom. If this twisted thinking once took hold of Europe's most brilliant minds from years between the world wars until the 1960s, why shouldn't it achieve something similar or better in Peru?

Let us first examine the roots of this idea. One of the central themes in the development of orthodox Marxism is to direct violence with dispassionate energy and without hesitation. Marx tackled the problem with characteristic intensity in *The French Civil War*, written immediately after the fall of the Paris Commune.[21] Added to the events of 1848, the Commune's defeat showed Marx that moderation led to catastrophe. "The state apparatus and its structural supports in society cannot simply be conquered; out of necessity, they must be destroyed to be later rebuilt based on revolutionary principles."[22] In the introduction to the 1891 edition, Engels lamented the "reverent attitude" with which the Commune members "stood respectfully at the doors of the Bank of France" while Versailles's troops prepared to retake Paris.[23] In his comments, Lenin further emphasized Marx and Engels's conclusions. Not only was it necessary to destroy the enemy so as not to be destroyed; it was necessary to destroy the state that represented its interests and the social organizations that shored it up. As developed by Lenin and his Soviet cast and later by Mao, Marxist social engineering begins with a demand for general demolition. Sentimentalism, dreams of harmony, and instantaneous justice are, in this school of thought, dangerous weaknesses that have to be constantly fought. In the permanent ethical discussion on valid tactics in a revolutionary struggle, the orthodox Marxist line presents itself as guided by the hardened philanthropy of a surgeon who does not hesitate to cut, to chop off a piece if necessary, to bathe himself in blood if it will save the patient in the long run.

This same hard realism was useful in the design of various strategies for the taking and keeping of power during the reign of orthodox Marxism. The common thread uniting them (Leninism, its Trotskyist variant, the development of the Comintern, and Maoism) is found as much in the emphasis on the demolition of the "bourgeois" state as in the creation of the demolition machine: the Communist Party constructed on a Leninist model (professional revolutionaries, clandestine or semiclandestine, a relatively small core). One cannot forget, however, that in the heart of almost every manager and administrator of destruction, driven to achieve maximum dialectic efficiency and for whom sentimentality is close to pornographic, beats a romantic philanthropy, repressed but intense. The goal was utopia, society built on unparalleled justice: communism. The means to achieve it were supposedly "scientific," and included previous destruction, justified along with about anything else.

The adoption of extreme means for extreme ends, with an apparatus organized to carry those means out methodically, step by step, represented a considerable advantage for Communist parties over their opponents or competitors throughout seventy years of struggle, beginning with the Russian Revolution in 1905. In most cases, Communist parties began their struggle as a weak minority and, as a result, emphasized strategies and tactics that depended on the patient accumulation of strength and its cautious preservation. At the same time, however, Communist parties at war were willing to accept (or induce) dreadful social costs that other organized forces recoiled at or, contemplating them, capitulated before. This was evident, for example, in World War II resistance movements.

As Franz Borkenau has pointed out,[24] communist partisans in Europe during World War II had an incalculable advantage over the non-communist resistance movements, for the former, having a vested interest in social disruption, were prepared to face drastic reprisals, while the latter were constantly restrained in their tactics both by moral considerations and by the desire to avoid extreme civilian losses. The paradox of the Soviet situation lies in the fact that a guerrilla movement enjoying the support of the established government of the country could be used for ruthless, unlimited action.[25]

This was also one of the principal reasons (the others were better organization and strategy) why almost all of the Communist organizations competing or in a clash with a non-Communist movement triumphed. This not only happened in Nazi-occupied Europe but also in China and later Indo-China and Vietnam. Mao's well-known quotations about "the omnipotence of the revolutionary war" and the need to "oppose war with war" arose from one of the armed conflicts that in this century cost most in terms of suffering and human life.

If the acceptance of extreme social costs was part of orthodox Marxism's revolutionary engineering, it took place as part of a permanent tension and search for equilibrium with the principle of gaining and conserving strength. In practical terms, this meant that most losses in various wars were suffered by the noncombatant population.

Nevertheless, the eventual need for self-sacrifice, immolation in the struggle, has been highlighted since the very beginnings of the doctrine of orthodox Marxist insurrection. After criticizing the Paris Commune for not going far enough, Marx applauded its last decision to continue resisting when all hope was lost.[26]

To forge fighting morale, to strengthen militants' commitment, was thus sanctified as sufficient reason to encourage cadres' self-denial, including self-sacrifice. This was reconciled with the principles of preserving strength and the refusal to engage in unfavorable battles if such sacrifices lent more force to the party than was lost. The calculus was a permanent source of fierce internal dispute. But its usefulness was rarely doubted. Again, it was Mao who put this principle in lay terms. "Is it contradictory to fight heroically and then abandon the territory? . . . If one eats first and then defecates, has one eaten in vain?"[27]

This willingness to sacrifice the self has certainly not been a Communist monopoly throughout decades of wars and revolutions. But in comparison with other groups, the Communist parties that emerged victorious were superior not only in strategy and organization, but also in three other areas: patience, willingness to self-sacrifice, and leadership.

Beginning with the Bolshevik Revolution and the subsequent civil war, the struggles fought by Communist parties have been among the most ferocious humankind has lived through. During the Soviet Union's civil war, more than 3 million people died. A few years later, during the convulsions created by massive collectivization and the 1930s purges, there were about 10 million victims. In World War II, the Soviet Union lost 20 million people. In the three and one-half years it took Tito to defeat the Germans and take power, more than 2 million died in Yugoslavia.[28] There are no approximate figures for the number of deaths in China during the endless succession of battles from the 1920s until 1949, but it must have been in the millions. Between 2 and 4 million people were killed in the battles of Indo-China and Vietnam before 1975.

Yet from the ruins of a destruction that would have frightened Tamerlane, the Communist parties emerged—in each of the aforementioned cases—stronger than before the beginning of conflict. They sailed, then drove the tempest. And all of these parties shared the features detailed here. Stalin, Tito, Mao, and Ho directed an astonishingly efficient and devout organization, with lieutenants capable of leading army units with a skill history's great captains would have applauded (among others, Zhukov and Koniev; Lin Piao and Peng Tenhuai; and Giap and Tran Van Tra are prominent figures in any military history) while at the same time following their leaders like adolescents captivated by a severe, wise teacher.

Today, after the fall of the Soviet Union and Eastern Europe's Communist regimes, it is difficult to imagine the spirit and conviction that motivated Communist cadres to carry out and endure some of history's stormiest enterprises. Both the old Bolsheviks whom Stalin ordered shot, yet who died praising his name, as much as the cadres who undertook clandestine tasks in occupied territory knowing that the possibility of survival was minimal acted out of an intense faith in Communist utopia, which they viewed as a scientific possibility yet felt with religious fervor. This secular faith allowed its believers not only to explain self-sacrifice but to desire it, and made crimes and excesses not just understandable but permissible. The concept and use of "the quota" was a central element of orthodox Marxism during its development and domination.[29]

The above digression was meant to lay the groundwork for a fuller understanding of the Shining Path's fourth plenary in May 1981 and its decidedly lethal consequences for Peru. Out of context, the discussion and agreement on the quota appear to be no more than arbitrary homicidal emotion. But in perspective, they should be understood as the entire praxis of the Shining Path—which is to say, a rigorous development of orthodox Marxism.

And it was not merely theoretical, but practical. Against the worldwide consensus formed in the latter part of the 1970s on the excesses of orthodox Marxism— especially under Stalin—Guzmán and his movement not only did not consider the costs excessive, but held up this period as the pinnacle of humankind. They were thinking along the same lines as many of the European and American intelligentsia of the 1920s and 1960s, despite the testimonies that emerged from behind the walls and an abundant and wrenching dissident literature. By the 1980s, the faith and hope in transcendental good that moved so many arms and loyalties, blinded so many eyes, and silenced so many consciences no longer moved anyone in the West or in the Communist world. But it did move Guzmán and his party. In contrast to the great majority of Marxists in the 1970s and 1980s, who looked back with a growing feeling of embarrassment and alienation and at least considered what was done to be excessive, Guzmán and his party insisted that what was done was very good, but did not go far enough.

Peru was to be the place where what went unfinished in other places was completed. Guzmán was well aware that the contagion of fanatical violence takes root slowly in peaceful countries and slower still if they are democratic. Peru was both in 1981. When the fourth plenary met, the insurrection was a year old. Up to then, only one person had died. And Peruvian society, living the diverse possibilities of risk-free expression, of a partial role in government, of the irony and humor pent up after years of military government, was not only impermeable to violence, but refracted it. The almost sweet face of José María de la Jara, the interior minister, his obvious kindness, made building the hate necessary for fanatical violence difficult. Even within Shining Path ranks, a considerable percentage of militants continued to reject killing, the blood threshold, despite the conscious effort made at fostering indignation.

But without blood, the Shining Path's insurrectional strategy was without content. Without hate, it could not shepherd the energy necessary for the immense work of material and moral destruction and then the reconstruction of the alternative world as planned.

Once initial plans for the "Development of the War of Guerrillas" were made, the fourth plenary session agreed to radically intensify violence. The bellicose warm-up had been completed the previous year, and firing up the troops would be easier. An increase in violence was geared to initiate the complicated game of action and reaction, where the goal was to provoke blind, excessive reactions from the state. The greater the success, the easier it would be to transfer the weight of blame to the state—the central objective of war propaganda—and the harder it would be for the regime to maintain a democratic image. Blows laid on indiscriminately would also provoke among those unjustly or disproportionately affected an intense resentment of the government. Most important, however, was that the exaggerated response of the state contribute to the dissolution of peace and help push the nation toward violence.

Escalation presumed a price for the Shining Path. One that could be very high. The party had to be prepared to take crushing blows and not only survive but finally emerge stronger. Measures had already been studied from an organizational and military viewpoint: to establish a double or triple underground network in key locations; to report, analyze, and evaluate each experience, so that the entire organization would learn from actions and a collective memory would emerge; and to concentrate or disperse cadres according to need. The only thing left to be defined was the moral attitude, both personal and in terms of the organization, once this Pandora's box of violence was opened.

As far as we know, during the fourth plenary, Guzmán painted with emphatic strokes the personal consequences of war. Many of those at the plenary, and many party militants, would die, trapped by the same events they set in motion. And they would die in the worst possible ways. Their families would be destroyed, those dear and close to them would be jailed and tortured, others would be killed simply because they were relatives. There was nothing new in this, all of it had already happened in other parts of the world not long ago. But there was very little in Peru's history that prepared it to confront the level of violence that would eventually be unleashed. Dozens, hundreds of thousands of dead. Blood would flow in rivers and the only way to triumph would be by "crossing the river of blood." Guzmán then gave them the choice of deciding if they were determined to persist in the struggle, knowing what the future held. From his point of view, the "people's war" meant a long journey that had to be joined. A bloody Sinai, as inevitable as it was historically necessary. On the other side lay the promised land.

In contrast to other meetings, no direct record of this debate survives. Apparently, opposition was minimal. With predictable solemnity, the Shining Path opted for "the quota": the willingness, indeed the expectation, of offering one's life when the party asked for it. The way in which the decision was taken, as a vote, a vow, took the Shining Path further than other Communist parties, which always attempted to maintain the fiction that self-sacrifice was confined to certain situations.[30]

From then on, preparing for death became a central preoccupation for each militant as well as a way to indoctrinate cadres. After agreeing to the quota, militants no longer owned their lives. Manuscripts read and memorized in meetings, the notes taken in the margins, began to repeat and hammer home this idea. To be prepared for death, to renounce life. A manuscript captured in Lurigancho Prison in 1985 paraphrases Guzmán when it criticizes those who "fear making mistakes": "others are careful, afraid to make mistakes, therefore are not sincere, they make excuses, they try to save their skin, what are they protecting? If you have nothing, if you've given everything to the P[arty], your life is not your own, it belongs to the P[arty]. Too much jeremiad, too much saving your skin."

The same manuscript includes decisions taken during the fiercest months of combat in 1984. After reaffirming the party's actions, it continues: "There is no construction without destruction, these are two sides of the same contradiction." The author accuses the government "of acting worse than the Spaniards who hacked Túpac Amaru to pieces": "The cruel form the war is taking is nothing more than the bloodbath we had proposed and the decision to go with it. We've made the irrevocable decision to cross (the river of blood) and conquer the far shore."

The quota, the ultimate sacrifice, took on even more weight because it was not only offered to the Peruvian revolution but to the cause of world communism, "whose millennium is opening," as Guzmán would say. Another Shining Path manuscript, written in 1985, explains the quota to the faithful: "About the quota: the stamp of commitment to our revolution, to world revolution, with the blood of the people that runs in our country. . . . The quota is a small part of the Peruvian revolution and of world revolution. . . . most [of the deaths] are caused by the reaction [of the state] and fewer by us. They fill lakes while we only soak our handkerchiefs."

Still another document, apparently copied by a midlevel leader in Ayacucho near the end of 1984, summarizes Guzmán: "Blood makes us stronger and if it's this 'bath' that the armed forces have made for us, the blood is flowing, it's not harming us but making us stronger."

As the war became more pitiless, the death vow took different forms. For many Shining Path militants, hunted and anguished, the idea of dying—"snatching laurels from death"—took on the intense attraction of an experience both mystical and sensual. It was the perfect escape from unbearable anxiety, ceaseless work, and the ever imminent threat of capture, with its horrific consequences.

This vision of death as an ardent surrender to the cause, a kind of sublimated sensual possession, opened unknown horizons in each militant's self-love. Combined with a millenarian vision and the personality cult of Guzmán, this created ephemeral, fevered, and mythic forms. Manuel Granados, an anthropologist who has studied the Shining Path, attempted this formula:

- Mao = a spark can *ignite* the meadow.
- A Shining Path militant = I am willing to cross the "*river of blood.*"
- Declaration of the PCP-SL (Communist Party of Peru–Sendero Luminoso) = the leadership is with you at the supreme moment of total release into the *purifying fire* of the A(rmed) S(truggle).
- Shining Path motto = *death* to invent the great subjective myth.
- Blaze-Invincible Fire-River of Blood-Death-*Subjective Myth*-Purifying Fire.[31]

Although its militants fell frequently into the ecstatic death wish anticipation not uncommon in warrior-monk orders, and with the metaphors of bonfires and the flaming forest common to prophetic visions, in general terms the Shining Path tried to maintain its disposition to self-sacrifice within the constraints of political and military utility: "their being is to comply, willing to fight anywhere. There are no restraints and a challenge to death and to snatch laurels from death is forged, war is our daily life, to be willing to die, no one mourns."[32]

Death worship could be paralyzing. But it had the counterbalance of exhausting work, the concrete tasks the Shining Path imposed on its militants. In the end, from those conspirators who combined extreme overwork with the fondling of death fantasies emerged the phrase "holding your life at your fingertips," ready to give it up for the struggle. This expression was repeated by Guzmán in the 1988 interview, and before him in interviews with other Shining Path leaders.

At its core, there was a clear strategic advantage to inducing a disposition to sacrifice: excellent troop control. To be able to do with their lives what war demanded, without protest. To get, for example, what Napoleon achieved, "[that] supreme egoist, who sent hundreds of thousands to their deaths cheering."[33] In Peru, a much greater egoism was needed, which Guzmán certainly did not lack.

But death, and its strange and fascinating attraction, held more sway in the Shining Path's course during a greater number of years than possibly Guzmán even calculated. Written by an anonymous Shining Path militant from the Upper Huallaga Valley in 1984, this mournful ballad ends with a defiant, rebellious rhythm:

On the way out of Aucayacu
there's a body, who could it be
surely it's a peasant who gave his life for the struggle.

. . . Today the quota must be filled
If we have to give our blood for revolution, how good it will be.

The quota's weight changed decisions, arranged events, repeatedly created the conditions for this to become a self-made prophecy. This attitude of suicidal confrontation had already begun to define itself in May 1981, well before the 1986 prison massacre.

9

To Capture Weapons and Means

The individual willingness of Shining Path militants to sacrifice themselves was accompanied by concrete strategic decisions. The Central Committee's fourth plenary session determined that the stage of "opening guerrilla zones as a part of the support bases" had achieved the objective of preparing the way for the spread of armed actions, especially in the "principal region." With the prologue a success, the task now was to expand guerrilla violence. The insurrection's new stage was defined by the Shining Path as "To unfold the guerrilla war." This new stage in the insurrection's growth would last until December 1982 and come to encompass vast regions of the country, especially Ayacucho, spreading with unheard of speed and intensity. Following the Shining Path's insurrectional scheme, "To unfold the guerrilla war" was considered a "fundamental political principle," itself divided in several complementary stages.[1] The first, "To conquer weapons and means," would last from May until December 1981 and is the one that concerns us here.

"To unfold" was clearly a qualitatively more important step than the one immediately before it, "To open guerrilla zones." The latter was in essence only a prologue, a transitional stage between the semiarmed agitation of the first months of struggle and the methodical escalation of violence through predominately guerrilla actions.

When the Shining Path's insurrectional technique is studied in the future, I am sure that the first two years of war, the formulation and continuation of the "Beginning Plan," which grafted the insurrection methodically to Peruvian body politic, will be of central interest. While dogmatic Marxists will frequently argue the dialectical principle of transforming quantity into quality, an axiom no one attempts to really understand, Guzmán not only tried to understand it but also apply it. His undoubtedly superior schematic intellect defined the intermediate objectives along the way and then marked out a detailed route to each one—segment by segment, step by step. In the history of guerrilla rebellions, in few if any did sheer resolve, backed by exhaustive planning, play such a preponderant role. This was an induced insurrection, grafted on, and later nourished by those vulnerable initial moments when the social antibodies rejected it, then were slowly overcome, allowing it to cross the first threshold of weakness.

The Shining Path uprising is not the first rebellion in which a relatively small and militarily inexpert organization has launched itself into armed struggle and managed eventually to grow, consolidate its strength, and, in some cases, triumph. The preliminary stages of insurrections led by Mao, Ho, and Enver Hoxha—all of which would one day triumph—were similar in this way. At the beginning of their uprising, the Yugoslavian Communists led by Tito were like the Shining Path: without weapons, militarily amateur.[2] Yet these groups enjoyed external circumstances that decisively favored their advance: the anticolonial struggle, or the fight against foreign invasion, or a general context of profound, violent social protest. Only in Peru did the plan for insurrection prosper in the absence of any of these factors and, quite to the contrary, when the promise of a democratic opening was unconditional.

By May 1981, Shining Path activity had overcome the state's routine ability to respond or even intentionally look the other way. In spite of itself and blindly, the government began to murmur about an emergency response, just as the Shining Path, several steps ahead in strategic planning and its analysis of the situation, launched an effort to sever the democratic regime's control at the district, provincial, and regional levels and impose its dictatorial control over these dominated areas, marking them with the definitive contradictions of war.

The plan "To unfurl" had ambitious goals for its final stages: eliminate the government's presence in rural Ayacucho and replace it with Shining Path control, a goal it eventually reached. The plan's first stage, however, "To conquer weapons and means," was aimed at providing the organization with the minimum number of weapons necessary to train and motivate its cadres. The actions described in the previous chapter, including the attack on the Luricocha and Quinua police stations and the looting and riots in Ayacucho and Huanta, were part of the first stage.

All of the Shining Path's regional, zonal, and local committees dedicated themselves to stocking up on dynamite and weapons. On April 28, the police station in

La Ramada, in the province of Cutervo, Cajamarca, was attacked. Rebels seized several weapons and uniforms. In Tacna, the "Second Carmen" mine was attacked on June 10, and attackers robbed a large quantity of dynamite, blasting caps, and fuses. Meanwhile, police recovered small quantities of dynamite stolen in Huancayo and Arequipa. At the same time, however, mining camps in Cerro de Pasco (June 22), Huarochirí province (June 28), and Cajatambo (August 1), in Lima province, were attacked, and their dynamite stores cleaned out.

With the discipline of an ant colony, Shining Path followers steadily accumulated their organization's explosives stockpile. And they moved it from one end of the country to the other, patiently, matter-of-factly, but incessantly. There was nothing sophisticated or spectacular in any individual action or in how their logistical apparatus functioned, save for its consistency. It was known that companies providing ground transportation were used to move dynamite after several chance seizures and captures were made. For example, at the end of August, the PIP announced the arrest of María Espinoza, fifty-four, whose apparent shipment of a sack of potatoes contained 300 sticks of dynamite.[3] The suspect claimed that the dynamite did not belong to her. Small quantities of stolen dynamite were seized in Ancash, Huánuco, Piura, Arequipa, and Ayacucho, generally in the luggage of bus passengers or on freight trucks. But only a small percentage of the dynamite taken or stolen at gunpoint from the hundreds of mining warehouses scattered throughout the country was recovered.

Meanwhile, in Ayacucho, at the same time that mobilizations took place in areas it controlled or strongly influenced, small groups of armed Shining Path members began to appear publicly with increasing frequency. These were the "detachments" of the "platoons" belonging to the "first company," still more metaphorical than real in the conventional military sense, but clearly substantial in their political impact. These were groups that materialized, then dispersed with a certain speed. For that reason, the Shining Path seemed not to have the permanence—or the reality—of a regular military organization. But neither did it share those weaknesses.

Still mere seeds, these groups prepared for imminent guerrilla attacks. Of course, they had already carried out several. Notes captured later set out basic guidelines for operations planned at this stage. Between military operations, detachments had to "do rounds" continuously within the targeted region. The objective was not only to harden novice guerrillas, but also to lead acts of agitation, propaganda, and mobilization. Living for short periods among villagers and farmers was a fundamental part of their work. They were an arm of the Shining Path's clandestine government (and received information and eventually orders from the clandestine or semiclandestine Shining Path members in the area) and as a result had to convey the image of an apparently fragile power, but one that had a constant and tenacious presence. At the same time, living together frequently with local people helped them to develop the intimate ties necessary to convert them into fellow countrymen or quasi family members. Strict self-discipline was emphasized from the beginning, and not only included the "Three Rules" and "Eight Warnings" of revolutionary China, but also the order to help farmers with their fields and village chores. As will be seen later, these directives were observed uniformly in areas already under strong influence, while in areas in dispute there were marked differences.[4]

The emphasis on maintaining constant contact with the population was among the party's permanent instructions to its guerrilla cadres. In essence, it was an effort to break with the Latin American tradition of the "errant guerrilla," the memory of which was still very much alive in Ayacucho. In manuscripts containing instructions given during this stage, the party repeatedly warned its cadres to avoid "sticking close to the jungle, so as not to become isolated." The contrast with the Castro-style revolutionaries of 1965 was striking. Between exploiting the jungle's natural protection or immersing themselves in the mountain population, the choice was clear. Eventually, this would change, starting in 1983, among other reasons because in the 1980s the Ayacucho jungle was anything but isolated. But until then, Shining Path actions were concentrated in the mountains.

Conspiracies

Meanwhile, President Belaunde succumbed to the temptation to define the Shining Path as an elaborate conspiracy directed from abroad. After a massive blackout that affected Lima for two days, accompanied by dynamite attacks throughout the city, Belaunde looked for a backdrop to frame his charges. During the celebration of the PIP's institutional anniversary, and using the papal or royal "we" in his remarks, Belaunde declared, "In investigations carried out in a neighboring country, we have been able to prove that certain characteristics of these terrorists are shared with others operating in that nation. That is why we have concluded that this armed plan comes from elsewhere, and is led and financed from elsewhere."[5] At his side, PIP director Eduardo Ipinze gravely concurred, sage as a veteran bloodhound with a nose suffused by the familiar, unmistakable scent of his prey.

The reference was clearly to Colombia, where not long before, President Julio César Turbay had charged that foreign intervention, meaning Cuba, was behind an increase in guerrilla and criminal violence.

While Turbay's charges may have contained a half truth—Cuba's support of some Colombian guerrilla movements, especially the M-19, was beyond doubt, although this failed to explain even a fraction of Colombian rebel violence—the only explanation for Belaunde's insinuation was his own indignant confusion. For Belaunde, builder par excellence, dreamer of great public works to tame the rural expanse, the fact that a Peruvian would dynamite electrical towers or railways or the few road-ways that rode the raucous spine of the Andes was absolutely inconceivable, beyond even the twisted logic of the insane. For a country blessed and afflicted by a rebellious geography, sabotage was a perverse act. It was much easier to explain it away as the work of foreign saboteurs, bent on weakening the country in prepara-tion for an invasion.

Despite his surroundings and the solemnity of the audience, there was much that was pathetic about his charges, repeated endlessly throughout his mandate and at any opportunity. While the reasons that led him to take refuge in this explanation are not only understandable, but moving, the fact is that Belaunde's first obligation as president was to identify properly the nation's problems in order to deal with them appropriately. While it satisfied his moral indignation, the charge that inter-national conspiracy was behind the insurrection did not adjust to reality and led unfailingly to nebulous policies and distorted strategy.

As will become clear with time, and a very short time at that, Belaunde's attitude led his government to attempt to ignore the problem, to bury it in disdainful silence and indirect allusion. One reason was not just the builder's impotent anger, but another important facet of the president's personality, increasingly important dur-ing the second half of his government: his lordly behavior, his courtly manner of speaking, traits that could be traced back to the decisive influence of Nicolás de Piérola, not for nothing called the "Caliph," and through him the culture of colonial Peru, source of patterns of behavior that lived on among Peru's ruling classes, with the clank of tin and a solid dead weight.

Along with the architect, the builder, the tireless traveler, much in Belaunde still spoke of lordlike pretension. Crammed with courtly archaisms, his speeches were frequently an extended metaphor for an elaborate tip of the hat or the twirling of a sequined matador's cape. Without doubt, this helped Belaunde during the election and the first half of his mandate. Although few doubted that he was a man of merit, it later became a permanent source of humor at the Architect's expense.

A little after the ceremony concluded, some reporters asked Ipinze about a possible connection between the Shining Path and drug trafficking. With an ex-pression that an expert poker player would have envied, Ipinze answered that such a connection was highly probable. These groups, he said, were active in neighboring areas, or even the same ones. Both were interested in shattering the state's authority. Standing not far from Ipinze was Reynaldo Rodríguez López, his personal aide, who no doubt agreed with these comments, still four years away from his fall but already one of the country's two most important drug traffickers.

Many believed there was a strategic alliance between the Shining Path and drug traffickers. Naturally, Belaunde was among them, although he would only begin emphasizing it in 1982 and would continue to do so throughout his term on no more evidence than his own stubbornness. When the Shining Path reconquered the Upper Huallaga in 1987 and 1988 and negotiated a coexistence with drug traffickers, who offered no violent resistance, Belaunde felt that reality had vindicated his early accusations and wasted no time in saying so. He was still wrong, but at the time there were problems more serious that a correction of the Architect's analysis.

If there remains anything of interest in this episode before the Investigative Police apart from the president's wrongheaded assessment, the consequences of which would be felt and paid for later, it was the somewhat ironic and curious fact that almost two years later, U.S. ambassador to Colombia Lewis Tambs would begin a campaign supposedly to identify and root out "narcoterrorism," an idea that a Peruvian policeman, indeed General Ipinze himself, had already put forth.

Attacks continued. At dawn on August 31, the U.S. Embassy and the ambassador's residence were pelted with explosives. Damage was minor. With a smile, Ambassador Edwin Corr tried to diminish their importance, but without success.

The conservative press and the Popular Action parliamentarians tied to Javier Alva Orlandini—the majority—intensified their attacks on the interior minister, José María de la Jara. The qualities that had earlier marked his nomination as an example of democratic process and a rupture with the past's repressive habits were now used to illustrate his failings. His cherubic countenance, his obvious goodwill, were mercilessly ridiculed. Among the newspapers, a tabloid called *Ojo* was most inflammatory. "De la Jara is a bonbon" was the first-page headline after the August 31 attacks; afterward, the minister was referred to only as "the Bonbon." The purpose of associating De la Jara with this velvety sweet, half-humorously, half-crudely, was to suggest that what the nation needed was not bonbons, but tiger's milk.

Briefly, De la Jara lost his way and blamed the recent attacks on drug traffickers. He called them reprisals for a recent drug-fighting treaty signed with the United States. In hindsight, it was the saddest moment of his term. Surrounded without realizing it by forces tied to drug trafficking, successfully infiltrated into the highest levels of his ministry, dependent increasingly on the technical advice of mostly corrupt police chiefs, De la Jara's act of blaming drug traffickers was a kind of apotheosis of myopia.

Tied to De la Jara by close personal friendship, Belaunde emphatically underscored his esteem for and confidence in his minister. But this did nothing to halt press ridicule or attacks by parliamentarians controlled by Alva Orlandini. From this moment forward, each Shining Path attack brought with it the direct echo of attacks on "the Bonbon." According to one ministry employee, it was during these weeks that many became convinced that De la Jara carried "shot under his wing." His exit was only a matter of time. The exit was guided by that unchangeable law of Lima politics: all is forgivable, or, better yet, forgettable (shedding blood for no reason, robbery, being poisonously incompetent) except ridicule.

Weekly meetings between De la Jara and Belaunde ceased to be casual get-togethers where two old friends could exchange everything from opinions on party politics to "wedding gossip," according to one frequent participant. Starting in August, hunted and confused, De la Jara worked under increasing tension. Evidence of his anguished vehemence did not escape Belaunde.

At the time, almost all the members of Popular Action were convinced that De la Jara was an important part of the problem, and that he should resign. Even Belaunde, a firm believer in the importance of image in politics, silently searched for De la Jara's successor. "José María is exhausted, stressed out," the president commented to Héctor López Martínez during these difficult weeks.[6]

As De la Jara became increasingly anxious to get concrete results through legal police operations against the Shining Path, his reliance on Ipinze grew. Meanwhile, Ipinze used him to consolidate his control over the Investigative Police.

Ipinze had virtually won his fight with Luque. At the end of the previous year, Luque had made a failed effort to establish a strong position within the PIP. After having improved upon his predecessor's results in State Security, Luque had failed to rise to the rank of lieutenant general. Better luck had befallen Rómulo Alayza, who had graduated with Luque from the Police Academy. Alayza was closely tied to Ipinze and, as it would become clear in later years, with Rodríguez López. After his promotion, Alayza demoted Luque to third-in-command, virtually cutting off any chance he had to assume command. For them, these interior battles were more important than the fight against the Shining Path.

But Luque pulled off one last maneuver. As the third in command of the PIP, he assumed the post of inspector general—that is, the officer whose duty is to uphold the institution's legal and moral rectitude. Luque knew that his position gave him the opportunity to land a potentially fatal blow on Ipinze. If only a fraction of the things murmured about Ipinze turned out to be true, Ipinze would never survive even the inspector general's cursory scrutiny.

In December 1980, Luque managed to get De la Jara to name him PIP inspector general while remaining at the head of State Security. From one moment to the next, he had managed to turn defeat into an important and perhaps decisive victory.

But in the end, he was defeated yet again. Once Ipinze learned of the ministerial appointment and became fully aware of the danger posed, he and his allies reacted quickly and forcefully. It is not clear how many parliamentarians took action or exactly which types of pressure were brought to bear, but De la Jara revoked his order, leaving Luque's nomination as inspector general hanging. Soon afterward, De la Jara "attached" Luque to his office, the bureaucratic euphemism for an institutional kiss of death.

The pressure on De la Jara to deal with Luque was not intimidation, much less threats. If it had been, the pugnacious minister would have reacted in much the same way he did to Balaguer's insubordination. Instead, pressure was exerted on the minister's party loyalty. According to López Martínez, "Luque was accused of being an Aprista."[7] Echoed by a considerable number of influential members of the party in power, this argument was paired with intense pressure by the police chiefs who had backed him during the Balaguer episode, forcing De la Jara's decision.

This was the nadir and shadow over this otherwise worthy minister's work. Luque was not an exceptional policeman.[8] At the very least, however, he was a professional trying to do his duty, unlike his rivals, who drove the PIP to such depths of corruption that their work was not only distorted but entirely perverted. And the first thing to suffer was efficiency. At a time when the Shining Path was at its most vulnerable, when inexperience caused cadres to commit serious errors, and when tenacious and diligent police work could have at least contributed to an effort to suffocate its growth, this inefficiency inflicted more damage on the country than simple negligence was capable of causing. After dismantling society's few, waning defenses, police corruption complemented the Shining Path's agenda and made easier a growth that otherwise would have been fraught with danger.

De la Jara, it must be repeated, was completely innocent of the corruption that ran rampant through his ministry. Pursued from all sides, with the ground giving way beneath his feet, committed to upholding respect for the law and the democratic spirit but without an understanding of or ability to learn about power and how it worked within his domain, De la Jara ended up painfully dependent on his police chiefs, especially Ipinze.

It is tempting to blame De la Jara's generous naiveté for having permitted a notoriously corrupt group of officers to take over his ministry. Nevertheless, none of his successors had better luck. Indeed, when compared with others, De la Jara stands out as one of the most efficient interior ministers to have served Belaunde. Although this isn't saying much, it certainly puts his work in perspective.

But Lajarita (as his friends and enemies, when they forgot to call him "Bonbon," referred to him) carried, in effect, a piece of shot under the wing. Criticism accumulated, not just of his impotence in preventing Shining Path attacks, but also for frequently improper and occasionally chaotic police conduct.

After the clashes that took place during Balaguer's insubordination, incidents between different branches of the police continued. They usually began casually: an attempt to arrest a drunk driver or an out-of-control killer who turned out to be a member of a rival institution. Dozens of armed officers would converge on the spot, followed by insults, shoves, shots into the air, and a fragile armed standoff witnessed by television cameras and gasping reporters. A little later, adrenaline spilled and sweated out, some colonel or general on each side would take uncertain command over the men, and a cautious attempt to untangle gazes, positions, and patrol cars would begin. On the nightly news, after broadcasting scenes of a clash, which became almost obscenely ridiculous as each hour passed, a statement from the interior minister, usually written by López Martínez, would be read, announcing solemn investigations of what had happened and promising decisive punishment if similar incidents continued. And, of course, they did.

Within each institution, those who had taken part in these duels of gazes and exhibitions of paraphernalia were treated as the defenders of institutional honor. They had cut off the institutional enemy, whose "institutional objectives," according to the pseudostrategic jargon I heard from so many officers, presupposed the elimination or at least the domination of their own institution. Civil Guard against Republican Guard and PIP—yet these latter two betrayed no particular intimacy with each other. Each branch with its own traditions, its own folklore, and the fierce, although contradictory loyalty of its members.

Meanwhile, two years after the military had relinquished power, the armed forces had managed to refurbish an image tarnished over their last years in government. In part, this was due to the sorry performance of the police. But it also stemmed from events unconnected to the Shining Path war (at least as it was conceived then), but rather to another, more defined, conventional, and, above all, successful war.

In the mountainous, desolate jungle of the Condor Range, Peruvian and Ecuadoran troops had exchanged fire, at first sporadically and then, after a rapid escalation of hostilities, in an open confrontation, with the full firepower of the military machinery that both countries could mobilize. The Peruvian and Ecuadoran armed forces deployed along the border between the nations, along the ocean, the desert coast, the mountains, and the jungle, preparing for the imminent declaration of war.

On the knife edge of a complete explosion of hostilities, some prudence prevailed, and the war was confined to its initial starting point on the Condor Range. Along the rest of the border, a quiet, armed watchfulness reigned.

After a brief, initial confusion within the Peruvian high command in the eastern Amazon, there was a rapid reorganization followed by the launch of an offensive. Efficiently coordinating the use of the air force with the army's armed helicopters and the infantry, Peruvian troops forced the Ecuadorans to retreat to the other side of the border. Once they had regained their original territory, the Peruvians suspended their advance.

It was a unique little war. Victorious for Peru and frustrating for Ecuador, it allowed both to avoid paying the price of a larger conflict. Beyond an old border dispute that had provoked a war forty years earlier, nothing immediately justified it. It was also strange because it violated the generally accepted rule among political scientists that democracies don't fight among themselves. That was not the case here. But what did turn out to be true was that both democratic regimes contained the war's spread and began to negotiate once the bloody jousting in the forested heights of the Condor had concluded.

In terms of popular support, this was perhaps the high point of Belaunde's presidency, victorious enthusiasm paired with optimism before the implicit possibilities that this triumph opened to the nation, demonstrating as it did efficiency, heroism, and victorious behavior; and also because it was the moment in which the open wounds made by Velasco's 1968 military coup seemed healed.

Belaunde himself appeared in the press as a living example of this triumph, standing in a position seized from the enemy during the reconquest of the mountain range, solemn yet radiant, rebaptized, demonstrating the mapping intricacies that he knew better than anyone to show where the Ecuadoran troops had hurriedly abandoned their posts. At his side was General Rafael Hoyos Rubio, who thirteen years earlier, on October 3, 1968, had arrested him at dawn in the Government Palace to start the military takeover, and now had led this offensive with efficient energy as head of the Peruvian armed forces. Before assuming power, Belaunde had agreed to have Hoyos Rubio take the post of army head, but many had interpreted this decision as a grudging one, motivated by the desire to avoid decisions that would harm the transfer of power or democratic stability, and maintained that Belaunde's allergy to the coup generals made a working dialogue with Hoyos Rubio almost impossible.

Nevertheless, there was the president, surrounded by officers in battle dress who had fought bravely and victoriously, giving them the inevitable lecture on Amazon geography, then praising them with some of the most elegant, graceful flourishes in his oratorical repertoire before extending his hand to an obviously emotional Hoyos Rubio. This handshake appeared filled with the promise of reconciliation and progress for Peru.

No one expected this euphoria to be permanent, but they did expect optimism to last. The economy grew, a war had been won with glory, and the nation's institutions seemed to be maturing. However, all came to naught. Before two years had passed, these expectations were, one by one, crushed.

Hoyos Rubio survived victory only a short time. Months later, the helicopter that carried him and several generals on a base inspection in the north crashed in a desolate spot. There were no survivors.

The Peruvian north and Ecuadoran south, momentarily divided by war, once again united under the solid weight of misfortune. A catastrophic flood, covering provinces and entire departments, collapsed the Peruvian economy's growth and, together with other factors, set it on a steady downward spiral that would continue until the Belaunde administration's last days in power. Hope for efficient government and national solidarity were also devastated by the flood; it was here that Belaunde's government definitively lost the respect and confidence of most of the population. In summary, things went from bad to worse.

Only the armed forces kept a certain prestige won so stylishly in the Condor. When, a little later, Peruvian soldiers took extraordinary and barely concealed measures to help the Argentine war effort during the Malvinas/Falkland War, the pathetic disgrace of the Argentine junta's subsequent defeat did not stain the Peruvian soldiers, but added to their glory. In it, people saw a generous effort to assist free of any expectation of gain or treachery, an effort that gave the Argentines the decisive support that helped them achieve their greatest success, in the air war.

It is important to remember this in order to understand the opinion the armed forces had of themselves and other government institutions, and people in general, during the time when the Shining Path was first growing.

This intense, spreading atmosphere of police disgrace explained many of the Shining Path's successes, which took place thanks to police defects and not their own abilities. With a few exceptions, this was the shared opinion among politicians belonging to almost every party, most soldiers, and even some among the police. At each new report of police misconduct, calls for the armed forces to engage in this internal war and end it quickly and definitively grew more strident. The soldiers who had defeated well-trained and supplied troops and fought in the countryside under supremely difficult conditions had to be able to defeat a group like the Shining Path, badly armed and trained and lacking in any experience, with ease. Luis Bedoya Reyes, head of the Popular Christian Party, asserted that the army had to deal with this problem, which it had been trained to do, an opinion many shared. The police, he said, were fat, pot-bellied, and couldn't climb hills. For some of the country's leaders, the war against the Shining Path (which, it should be noted, was not yet considered a war) seemed to be a question of, in essence, athletic training.

The military, above all the group of officers promoted after Hoyos Rubio's death, seemed to share this opinion. Fascinated by the then recent counterinsurgency experience in Argentina (as well as those in Brazil, Uruguay, and Chile) while repelled by the Velasco regime, this group of soldiers, whose most influential spokesman would be the future war minister General Luis Cisneros Vizquerra, saw the Shining Path insurrection in purely military terms. They compared it with defeated uprisings like those of the Argentine Montoneros, People's Revolutionary Army (ERP), and Uruguayan Tupamaros, and found it embryonic and underdeveloped. Then, they compared the abilities of the Peruvian armed forces that they led with those of the countries that had defeated these insurrections, and found they had nothing to envy, either in officer training, organizational efficiency, or courage. And they concluded that the suppression of the Shining Path uprising would be a minor task, far below their level, but something they would be able to finish up quickly and with only a minor investment of their significant capacity for destruction.

It was from this vantage point that the military viewed the increasing number of police misadventures, not bothering to mask their disdain, but with the contented satisfaction that a professional or master craftsperson would feel when faced with the upstart who has copied his technique but who meets inevitable failure when the time comes to demonstrate similar abilities. The elderly Adgoen generals (Association of Generals), who spent their bittersweet retirement years at attention and watchful of their domain, roundly rejected attempts by the Investigative Police generals to join their institution. Already, in a move many felt was an excessive concession, they had admitted Civil Guard generals. Not another step would be permitted.

Later on, we will examine the military doctrine and assumptions that underlay this attitude. For the moment, however, these observations must suffice, the ones that, in countless dinner parties, cocktail gatherings, and other more formal meetings, indirectly fed the parliamentarians and other political leaders who vehemently demanded the military's immediate entry into the war with a "hard hand," like a purgative, disagreeable but quick, to finish off an insurrection that only police ineptitude had allowed to grow.

New Democracy

An extraordinary issue of *New Democracy*,[1] the Shining Path's theoretical publication, appeared in July 1981. It was the first since the insurrection's start; academic disquisitions were now stamped with the seal of real events. But outside a circle of the faithful, converts, and a few analysts, the document—mimeographed with cramped type—was little read.

If it had been read with the care that the situation demanded, it is possible that some keys to the Shining Path insurrection would have been understood, or at least perceived, at a relatively early stage. Although the atmosphere continued to be dismissive, an early warning about links between events that were apparently humble when considered separately but as a whole important to the insurrection, as well as the elaborate and ambitious theoretical discussion distributed openly by the Shining Path, would have at least demonstrated that what was at issue was not a fanatic, though obtuse organization, but one with the ability to transform ideology into politics and from there into strategy. In the best of all worlds, it would have been possible to distinguish the areas of growth planned by the insurgent organization and the way it proposed to accomplish its goals. If the simple workmanship implicit in these individual actions had been understood as a stage in a developing strategy, intricate and ambitious, it is possible that the trees would not have blocked the view of the forest. That blindfold, the overabundance of derision aimed at the Shining Path, would have been replaced by an attitude more adjusted to the approach of imminent danger.

The purpose of this edition of *New Democracy* was to back up actions with ideology (in the first two articles) and ideology with actions (in the last one). Of the three articles (the fourth is a reprint of texts from "China Reconstructs" and "Report from Peking"), two focused on Peru's situation ("New Government and a General Economic, Political, and Class Struggle Perspective" and " 'Democratization' or a Revolution of New Democracy?") and one on international events ("On the Unity of the International Communist Movement and the Joint Declaration of 13 Marxist-Leninist Organizations and Parties"). The language used is surprisingly unemotional, in contrast to the pamphlets and proclamations made around the same time and given that most of the articles were written after violence had already unfolded. The explanation is clear. Guzmán—the probable author of the original articles—was writing for history, not the moment, and wanted any future exegesis to interpret his actions as a creative, yet rigorous adaptation of Marxism.

In the narrow play between a vision of the world and a concrete decision, orthodox Marxism involuntarily resurrects the platonic ideal of the philosopher-king. So long as the legitimacy of a leader (or an activist on his or her way to becoming a leader) rests in good part on a "correct" interpretation of Marxist philosophy, his or her philosophical credentials will in turn depend on their record as an activist and strategist. Because the relationship between the general laws of history and the actions of individuals or human groups requires a deep understanding of the former in order to synchronize them with the latter, philosophical knowledge is not an abstract luxury but a concrete necessity. To know how to read the stars and draw from them not only one's destiny but the exact route to arrive there is the final test before the supreme chiefs of the party and revolution can be anointed.

This process follows a definite hierarchy. Leaders have to be able to read and interpret correctly the historical principles governing their nations. In turn, their close collaborators have to read their leaders and acknowledge that their interpretation and no other is the only correct one. But above all of them reigns the universal geniuses of revolution, whose knowledge was not just national in scope but international: rooted in time, yet universal. These were not mere kings, but emperor-philosophers, and they identified the great threads that would later be followed by national leaders. Lenin was first to unify a government of people and philosophies. Later to take his place—less outstanding, perhaps, but with a debating style that was, without doubt, decisive—was Stalin.[2] Mao followed, but ruled a divided kingdom, where the formerly minor satraps (Korea's Kim Il Sung, Rumania's Nicolae Ceausescu, and Albania's Enver Hoxha) were developing designs on the rulership of the heavens.

The government of philosopher-kings is not, by its very nature, hereditary (except for the lone and lowly regarded example of North Korea). In orthodox Marxism, national government and the scholastic throne has been, in practice, open to competition. Who would succeed Mao? The author of that "extraordinary number" of *New Democracy* appeared to know.

In the article "New Government and a General Economic, Political, and Class Struggle Perspective," Guzmán maintained that the Belaunde government was nothing more than the continuation of the military regime in the shape of a "crude falsification of the bourgeois democracy that reigned until 1968." This was the military government's desperate answer to the "revolutionary situation that—after maintaining stability in the face of the 1968 coup d'état—began to show itself publicly as a developing revolutionary situation beginning in 1975."[3] Even several years later, Guzmán would maintain this grudging homage to Velasco, considered the most dangerous enemy to the development of a "revolutionary situation."

The "falsification" of "bourgeois" democracy was expressed, among other ways, by the fact that "the fascist regime" had proved unable to "revive" the old political parties, "intimately linked to the definitive bankruptcy of formal bourgeois democracy in this country." The Apra fights between Armando Villanueva and Andrés Townsend and minor splits within the PPC were cited as evidence.

His reasoning—essential for the Shining Path to be able to justify its contention that taking up arms was the only possible solution—was elaborated a bit later. During the 1960s, "confronted with the widespread development of mass popular struggle and the definitive bankruptcy of formal bourgeois democracy in this country, the dominant classes fell back on fascist methods."[4] Nevertheless, this move had "exacerbated" the "revolutionary situation," forcing those in power to fall back on a "falsification" of formal democracy in order to escape a situation fast slipping from their control. To support his argument in this all-encompassing review of the new decade, Guzmán cited the "reactionary magazine" *Perú Económico*, underscoring the magazine's assertion that "Peru will not bear the absence of a definite national strategy for much longer. . . . The next five-year period could be, therefore, the final stage of a process of collective frustration or the beginning of a new era of integration and synthesis."[5]

To summarize, according to Guzmán's own words, the bourgeois "bureaucratic faction" had not lost control of the state. To the contrary, it remained in power. That was why the true status of the governing political parties, Popular Action and the Popular Christian Party (PPC), was "that of being under the leadership of the bureaucratic faction represented by the armed forces."[6]

This was why even the most vehement outbursts from Popular Action spokespeople about measures imposed by the military government were interpreted as tactical discrepancies, not fundamental ones. And even measures openly divorced from the Velasco era, like the Agricultural Promotion and Development Law, were attacked from one side for permitting "a greater concentration of lands in feudal estates," yet were also said to result in "nothing more than the continuation and deepening of (measures) imposed by the fascist regime."[7]

The next arguments were more serious, though already familiar: the marked decrease in real wages for most Peruvians during the years of military government and the persistence of an unequal distribution of wealth, with only the names changed. Continuing, Guzmán accused Belaunde's until then cautious and extremely tolerant government of "attempting to drown the legitimate struggles of the masses in blood and fire," masses capable, he wrote floridly, of "revolutionary violence." It was a baseless accusation, even within his dogmatic argument, only justified in this context because Belaunde had been identified as subject to the "fascist regime."

In addition, however, the repression he writes about was not only invited, but provoked. A quote from Engels, taken from *Revolution and Counterrevolution in Germany*, laid out not only the Shining Path's analysis but its methodology: if all revolution gives voice to a "social need" unsatisfied under the existing regime, repressive violence is frequently necessary in order for this voice to define itself, take shape, and develop.

According to Guzmán's summary, the country was living "a revolutionary situation in development," where the "objective" conditions were clearly present and favored the advance of violent insurrection. To support his thesis about the impending disintegration of the state and peace, Guzmán quoted the economist Guido Pennano—always described as "reactionary"—who, months earlier, had written that in the May 1980 elections, "the people . . . have played their last card of nonviolence. . . . Belaunde has a historic obligation not to fail."[8]

The most intricate insult was reserved, however, for the Marxist left in Parliament. Faced by a revolutionary situation that, Guzmán argued, was even recognized by that "reactionary Pennano," the parliamentary left chose to "defend democracy." Quoting a speech by Senator Enrique Bernales, who Guzmán described as the "well-known and grandiloquent starlet of parliamentary cretinism," in which the senator called on the legal left to defend and perfect democracy, Guzmán concluded that the Marxist left had placed itself at the service of "the grand bourgeoisie" and not only denied that a revolutionary situation existed, but was attempting to thwart it.

It was with this point that the second article, " 'Democratization' or a Revolution of New Democracy?," began. Although the legal left spoke of defending democracy, Guzmán asserted that it was merely defending the "definitive construction of a corporate state" and fostering "the broadening of a fascist social foundation to better put its plans to work."[9] As Guzmán repeated emphatically, formal democracy no longer existed. In its place was a "crude falsification" of what had existed before. Those on the Marxist left "are nothing more than opportunists, bourgeois agents infiltrated in the breast of the workers' movement, the best champions that the bourgeoisie can ever hope for."[10]

In what must be taken in part as an involuntary homage to the power of the very word and concept of democracy, Guzmán wrote that the "democratic path" did not pass through Parliament but rather the "National-Democratic Revolution," necessarily bloody, inherently prolonged, and peasant by nature.

Continuing, Guzmán began to justify the need to take the way of violence, under the guise of "drawing a clear dividing line . . . with revisionism." As it had been elsewhere, Lenin's *State and Revolution*, stuffed with appropriate quotations, was the main text used. According to Lenin, the state is imposed by force and represents the interests of the dominant economic and political class. And its fundamental instruments of force are the army and police.

As a consequence, Guzmán noted, the only way in which the "people" could seize power was "to destroy the old state machinery that the reaction uses to repress them." At the same time, "to destroy the old state, it is necessary to break its spine, which is: the armed forces, and this can only be achieved by constructing the people's armed forces in the course of waging armed struggle."[11]

The Shining Path's policies, program, and method are expressed succinctly in this quotation.

Guzmán continued by launching an unconditional attack on the legal left. Following the basic arguments laid out by Lenin in his attacks on Marxist revisionism—which each new generation of orthodox Communists had attempted to imitate and recreate—the Shining Path chief accused these legal Marxists precisely of this: changing the dogma along the lines drawn out first by Bernstein, Kautsky, and all the old enemies of orthodoxy. Imitating Lenin's direct, pedestrian, inelegant, but nevertheless incisive style, Guzmán literally repeated the insults from yesterday for today's circumstances. These "opportunistic gentlemen" were reviving, according to Guzmán, "the old revisionist argument to win the majority through elections carried out under the old power, of conquering democracy and from there marching toward socialism."[12]

In language meant to be sardonic, but which—like many of Lenin's written arguments—evokes a barely contained exasperation, Guzmán accused the "parliamentary cretins" of convincing people that it is possible "to bring democracy to the state of the great bourgeois and feudal landlords," forgetting, he added, "that power, as Mariátegui taught us, is conquered with violence and is maintained through dictatorship."[13]

What was necessary, he continued, his rough attempt at irony momentarily revealing a strident tone, was an attack on all fronts. The insults left no doubt about who Guzmán considered to be the party's principal enemies, the "opportunists" who were "servants of the reaction . . . these miserable ones. . . . What great swindlers! What zealous guardians of the order established to dominate the people!" They did not speak but rather "cackled," and tied their fortunes to a defense of the "bourgeois" order. For the moment, as in earlier years, the argumentative virulence was merely verbal. It would not remain so in the future, which, in light of the Shining Path's positions, should not have surprised anyone.

In attacking the legal Marxist left, Guzmán spent little time on arguments inspired by current events. His reasoning, which sought to show that it was impossible to "democratize society," "carve out space," "combine forces," or even improve the "people's" lot through elections, was based almost entirely on quotes lifted from Marxism's sacred texts and fundamental defenses: "as Lenin teaches us," "as Marx points out," "Engels shows us," "as President Mao says."

The "great bourgeois and landlord" state, Guzmán continued, will never obediently surrender its power through votes. The distinction made by the legal left between civil and military government was false, since "both represent and defend the same classes that oppress you." "Constructive" opposition from Parliament was equal to a defense of the established order—precisely what Guzmán accused the left of being, of having become the enemy, of being the enemy.

His reasoning was not new. It had been used by Lenin in his fiery debates with the leaders and theoreticians of the Second International, and had supported the bitter fury with which the Communist parties throughout Europe had attacked the social democrats, considered the "principal enemies of the working class" until the very dawn of the fascist grab for power, which ended up sweeping both away. The central argument was the same, yesterday and today: a peaceful or violent quest for power, and what that meant for choosing between gradual and sudden change, negotiation or imposition, reform or revolution. Lenin had underscored the difference in his attack on Kautsky, and Guzmán would repeat it almost a century later: "Truth has now been driven home: what is at stake is the difference between peaceful revolution and violent revolution."[14]

And in effect, if one single characteristic could be said to distinguish orthodox Marxism, it would be the conviction that it is impossible to gain the power necessary to carry out socialist revolution without armed insurrection. In this sense—and it is not redundant to underscore it—Guzmán and his party's theory and praxis should be understood as a rigorously orthodox development of Marxist-Leninism.

Clearly, the concept of orthodoxy in Marxist ideology is difficult to identify precisely, given that it defines itself as a "scientific" system whose criteria of authenticity, individual and historical praxis, foresee the possibility of self-renewal in tune with real-life conditions.

However, an orthodox interpretation, in Marxism or any other axiomatic system, "reads" reality with the interpretive tools determined by the system. The system itself rests on a foundation of principles, truths considered absolute, without which it would make no sense. From this beginning, the development of the ideas involved is necessarily scholastic, which doesn't always mean mere intellectual entropy. To the contrary, this intellectual growth frequently has been and continues to be strikingly dynamic and complex. But, in order to remain true to the fundamentals, forcing events to conform to principles when necessary, intellectual reasoning creates its own language, a conceptual reality that is only comprehensible in context. There is a potentially infinite ideological intermarriage, often incomprehensible from the outside and whose development is frequently divorced from the reality outside dogma, although it retains its own internal consistency.

The secular character of dogmatic Marxism (although at times unclear), its "scientific" aura, and, finally, its permanent reading of reality, gives it great dynamism. Its adaptation to diverse historical situations and social conditions was doubtlessly profound and often successful, although it has also frequently suffered repeated and bloody failures. Of course, orthodox Marxism's ability to adapt itself to the demands posed by different eras and circumstances is also the same quality that, seen in perspective, gives the impression that it has definitively left behind its roots. The Bolshevik Revolution had little to do with Marx's forecasts just as the Chinese Revolution had little to do with the doctrine laid down by the Comintern.

But as adaptable as the system was, the historical unity of orthodox Marxism was maintained by its principles. One was to defend the necessity, indeed the historical inevitability of violent socialist revolution. Beginning with the era of Khrushchev, when several Communist parties renounced the use of violence to gain power, they did not modify the principles of orthodox Marxism, but left them completely behind. Whether they admitted it or not, they broke their connection to Leninism and joined the current begun by the Second International. The subsequent evolution to political positions indistinguishable from those identified with social democrats was grudging and slow, but inevitable. It would culminate eventually in the rejection of Marxism as fundamental doctrine.

This process, natural and understandable as it may be for dispassionate observers, was nevertheless heresy for those who remained within the orthodoxy. If any change in the system's basic principles threatens its very existence and if the system itself is based on the idea of a transcendental conflict, in the clash between them and us, analytical reasoning becomes confused with the demands of loyalty. Anyone who questions the system's foundation betrays it. They become the enemy and act, by definition, as a fifth column. Does this switch stem from innumerable historical and social changes? Are the principles forged from the experience and thought of the eighteenth and nineteenth centuries woefully inadequate to interpret or explain the twentieth century, much less the twenty-first? Change reality before touching the system! Make events crush together a bit, discuss them before mock courts and not in seminars, combine propaganda with bullets, and reality can still be made to reflect the system.

This was Guzmán's position when he attacked the Marxist left. And when these leftists focused their opposition to Belaunde's government on denouncing a supposed "civilian dictatorship" and, as a consequence, "a danger to democracy," Guzmán answered them by denying that any democracy existed in Peru, denying that there was any real difference between the military and civilian government, and asking with rhetorical disdain: "What democracy do they refer to? Democracy for which class?" He continued:

> And what is the meaning of the scandal they construct against this "new dictatorship"? . . . What do they mean to say? That if Parliament exists, there is no dictatorship! . . . What does Marxism teach us about this last point? First, that the Parliament—which has a role in capitalist society, which does not exist in our country, which is semifeudal and semicolonial—is a bourgeois state organ, an organ of the bourgeois dictatorship. . . . Gentlemen revisionists, the problem is not that those who govern us wear uniforms and boots, or white shirts and ties, or that they wear beards and tie their pants with rope,[15] because none of these details absolves them of being reactionary or makes them revolutionary. This is not a matter of civilian or military dictatorship. What is at stake is a class dictatorship. . . . What else could this sniveling before dictatorship in general mean? Is it not clear that power is conquered through violence and maintained through dictatorship, that "the revolution is an act in which a part of the population imposes its will on the remaining part with guns, bayonets, and cannon . . . and where the victorious party must necessarily maintain its domination with the fear that its weapons inspire among the reactionaries," as Engels shows?[16]

Political democracy, Guzmán emphasized, was subordinate to the need to impose and maintain with violence "the dictatorship of the proletariat." A quote from Lenin's debate with Kautsky fortified his position: "The state of the exploited must be completely different, it must be a democracy of the exploited with the demolition of the exploiters, and the demolition of a class means that it suffers from inequality, its exclusion from democracy." Marxism's true fight was not, Guzmán insisted, the fight for democracy, but the struggle for dictatorship. To try to get "the people" to defend democracy was equivalent to getting the "proletariat and revolutionaries to renounce their dictatorship over the exploiters . . . to refuse to exclude their class enemies from democracy, and, therefore, to use their state to repress and crush any resistance."[17] Truly, Guzmán can be accused of many things, but not of failing to speak clearly.

Nevertheless, even within these orthodox parameters, those on the Marxist left had an undeniable argument and this was their growth as an electoral force. In addition, legality, the left argued, had not been awarded to them, but rather conquered by them. The palpable "accumulation of forces" they had gained marked the way: each election would lift the left closer to becoming an alternative government.

Guzmán's aggressive response reaffirmed dogma at the expense of events. No legality had been conquered since no legality existed. What passed for it was a lie. Also, Peru was a semifeudal, semicolonial country, where, as President Mao had written, "we have no Parliament to use or legal right to organize workers to carry out strikes." In other words, the Parliament functioning in the Plaza Bolívar and the right to strike recognized by Peruvian law were also false. Hadn't Mariátegui said that "democratic and liberal institutions cannot prosper or even function on the foundation of a semifeudal economy"? Therefore, Guzmán concluded triumphantly, "since feudal oppression, not democracy, exists in our country, we have no Parliament or legality to use."[18]

With these assertions refuted to the satisfaction of dogma, the only road left was "armed struggle and the creation of revolutionary support bases to feed it." And this was the reasoning for which people had already died and for which so many more would die in the days, the years to come.

The International Organization

As of 1980, the Shining Path had resumed contact with several organizations that were close ideologically, even though, preoccupied with the insurrection's final preparation and launch, the unification of the Maoist organizations that survived had not been a priority. Nevertheless, at the beginning of 1981, the Shining Path was already taking part in debate on the formation of a new "Communist International Movement."

There was very little in common between the Shining Path's real international ties and the fantasy of a conspiracy run from "an aircraft carrier anchored in the Caribbean," as PPC leader Celso Sotomarino had asserted, reinforced in a less specific way a little later by President Belaunde.

After ties with China had been harshly and definitively cut in the wake of the coup d'état by Teng Hsiao-ping[19] and the fall of the "Shanghai Four," the purist Maoist organizations had converged on Albania, the last apparent staging ground of orthodoxy. Nevertheless, Hoxha's attacks on Mao and the attempt this signified to redefine substantially orthodox Marxism forced the Maoists whose faith remained undimmed and whose organizations remained united to break with Hoxha as well.

So, since 1978 or 1979, depending on the country, the orthodox Marxist organizations scattered throughout the globe lacked a geographical and spiritual center, a guiding country, for the first time since the October Revolution of 1917.[20] Swept by historical tempests, anguished not only by the fall of their red Jerusalem, but also because of the bloody failure of some insurrections, several of the surviving Maoist organizations searched each other out and, once a sympathetic spirit was found, began efforts to coordinate and unify internationally.

In 1980, thirteen Maoist groups of different capabilities met in London, Marxism's original source. Both small and minuscule groups were represented, from Ceylon (Sri Lanka), India, Chile, New Zealand, Italy, Spain, France, Denmark, the United States (the "Revolutionary Communist Party"), Senegal, and the Dominican Republic. After the conference, these movements released their first "Joint Declaration" to reaffirm their adhesion to "Mao Tse-tung thought" and call for the "International Communist Movement" to reorganize on this foundation.

Yesterday at the gates of heaven, today dispersed and defeated. There was much that was pathetic about the persistence of these feeble groups, on the margins, lashed to an orthodoxy that had been jettisoned all around them, yet convinced that their loyalty would one day be rewarded with victory. Even though there appeared to be no light illuminating the future. They had lost China to Deng's counterrevolution, Albania to Hoxha's megalomania. Vietnam had definitively resumed Soviet-style "social imperialism." The Malaysian insurrection was defeated. The Indonesian uprising was crushed. The Naxalite insurrection in India was also suffocated while Colombia's Popular Liberation Army (EPL) was stymied, disconnected, obviously imploding. In Iran, where Khomeini landed brutal blows on the secular opposition, the Union of Iranian Communists (Sarbedaran), which took no part in the conference, was preparing for the insurrection that would begin in 1981 and be completely annihilated by 1982. In Peru, nevertheless, a relatively small group had begun a modest insurrection, barely mentioned at the time, even in the most radical circles. But this group felt it had the authority to speak and be heard.

New Democracy included an extensive article on the meeting, penned in Guzmán's characteristic style, that expressed the Shining Path's position "On the Unity of the International Communist Movement and the Joint Declaration of 13 Marxist-Leninist Organizations and Parties."

The article had been written for history, to form part of a future "Selected Works." It began on a note of historical optimism: no split in the history of the International Communist Movement had "been able to stop its uncontainable advance. . . . Unity, struggle, and even division and new unities on a new foundation." If that had been the case since the struggles of Marx and Engels against Bakunin, Proudhon, and Lasalle, or even Mao against Khrushchev and Brezhnev, "why do the results of the current struggle against the revisionism of Teng Hsiao-ping and Enver Hoxha have to be any different?"[21] Above all if efforts at a new union brought together "the deepest and purest among its followers on the foundation of Marxism–Leninism–Mao Tse-tung thought."[22]

The first detail that calls attention to itself is the terminology used. In 1981, the Shining Path continued to use the phrase "Mao Tse-tung thought" to refer to his contributions to what was called "the treasure trove of Marxist-Leninism." This was an extremely important point in the intellectual debate and, as will be seen later, carried important practical consequences.[23] To include "Mao Tse-tung thought" with Marxist-Leninism equaled an affirmation of its transcendental global importance, although the use of the phrase "Mao thought" instead of "Maoism" implied a recognition that the contributions of the leader of the Chinese Revolution were not yet completed and as yet did not match the caliber or the rocklike solidity of either Marx or Lenin's work.

This was a point of controversy within the international Maoist movement, and would sharpen as the opposing groups consolidated their positions. The importance was not simply one of words, as the simple minds of the uninitiated might assume, but, as any diligent student would realize, of foremost importance for the future of communism.

Guzmán's first reservation about the joint declaration was precisely regarding this theme. On the one hand, he recognized that the joint declaration demonstrated "a great advance for having taken on the defense of Mao Tse-tung thought, not only in terms of its foundation in Marxist-Leninism, but also because it represents a '*new stage* in the development of Marxist-Leninism.' "[24] But he added that the declaration erred in failing to recognize the true dimension of this new stage. Instead of considering it a third stage, inaugurating a new era in Marxist development, the declaration implied that although "Mao Tse-tung thought" was an important development, it remained within the boundaries of Leninism. Therefore, the Leninist era continued.

For Guzmán, this was a "very important question of principles." Having retreated from considering Mao thought as Marxism's third stage, concessions had "deliberately" been made to "Hoxha's anti-Marxist campaign." According to Guzmán, this meant a failure to understand the very concept of "Marxism developing by stages" expounded by Stalin in 1924 upon proclaiming the "Leninist era." Even as the Georgian ex-seminarian made this concept into a primary weapon in the vicious fight for power that was then unfolding in the Soviet Union, its consequences were deeply imprinted on the minds of other Communists.

In the same way that Leninism had been the Marxism of the "imperialist era,"

Mao Tse-tung thought had solved problems "that neither Lenin nor Stalin could have resolved, for instance how to carry forward revolution in a colony or semi-colonial country or how to continue the revolution under the dictatorship of the proletariat."[25] Mao had not only pushed the central tenets of Marxism forward, Guzmán maintained, but his analysis "allowed the International Communist Movement to establish its general political line."[26]

The fact that this had not been understood, said Guzmán, explained the deviations from Mao thought evident throughout the declaration. One of the main ones was whether or not to use legal means of struggle. The declaration affirmed that revolutionaries should take advantage of "legal possibilities . . . without falling in the trap of creating or promoting illusions within bourgeois democracy." Guzmán retorted that while "bourgeois democracy" could be used in capitalist countries (meaning developed nations), it was "only and exclusively for the purposes of propaganda and agitation; in contrast it is incorrect to assert that the same should be done in colonial or semicolonial countries given that there, instead of a bourgeois democracy, there exists feudal oppression, although varnished over in a thousand ways."[27]

In the same way, Guzmán, the unbreakable maximalist, showed that the lack of precision in the evaluation of Mao thought in the declaration led to a weak and incomplete defense of the Cultural Revolution. Guzmán added that Mao's genius lay in recognizing not only that class struggle continued after socialism had been installed, but that the bourgeoisie, conspiratorial, bent on reform, would survive and place itself within the Communist Party and among its leaders. As a consequence, the process of beheading had to be constant and cultural revolutions had to succeed one another. Mao's great merit in "discovering" the methodology of the Cultural Revolution lay in that fact that "it resolves the problem of how to ward off the capitalist restoration and how to continue revolution under the dictatorship of the proletariat."[28]

This section also clearly reflects Guzmán's view of the use of power (and what could be expected of him once he conquered it). It would eventually appear, more refined and systematized, as part of the "guiding thought" over the following years. And it should be understood as a fundamental part of Guzmán's political thinking, which has remained exhaustingly coherent over the years. The Stalinist roots of his training, overlapping with Maoism's Jacobin period, come together in a vision of power as a succession of periodic purges, lynching, "cultural revolutions" without end. If in some moment Guzmán had read Quevedo's admonition on tyranny ("Never begin to be a tyrant or never stop being one"), his choice would have been to never stop.

There was one point on which Guzmán was in virtually complete agreement with the declaration. This was the attack on Hoxha as the new source of anti-

Marxist revisionism. Nevertheless, Guzmán believed that attacks on Hoxha should intensify because he represented the danger of an "unclear revisionist." In contrast to other sources of revisionism (the Soviet Union, Teng Hsiao-ping), Hoxha had not been denounced by Mao since he had waited for Mao's death to begin his attack. And, as has been said, in orthodox Marxism, the geopolitical insignificance of this or that tinpot leader is not important. As in any theology, these ideas had their own power; however, this was not in the context of a romantic view of the spirit, but a medieval one.

Guzmán's critique of the declaration was much more emphatic and tough in its evaluation of world politics, the threat of a global war, and the probability of revolution. These thirteen parties had drawn on their own experience to conclude that "the followers of Marxist-Leninism" (which is to say, them) were in great crisis. And despite the continuing development of the revolutionary situation in the world, the "subjective conditions" for it were seriously delayed. For Guzmán, this was unforgivable defeatism. In the first place, he answered, the current retreat had to be viewed in its dialectical context. The strategic offensive of world revolution was just beginning. Over the next 50 to 100 years (the final date was 2,062, a hundred years after Mao's announcement), it would culminate with the "sweeping away" of all of the world's bourgeoisie and revisionists. And the way to begin this process, he added, was not by complaining about the disparity between the revolutionary situation and the capacity of the parties, but by getting to work, "seizing firmly the new task that the revolutionary situation demands, and, as deeds are accomplished, advance."[29]

That was the first long-distance conversation held by the Shining Path with the incipient Maoist international. Over the following years, they would draw closer, although differences would remain. Different groups and their sympathizers would launch enthusiastic propaganda campaigns in various latitudes and languages to benefit the Shining Path. When this and other groups formed the Revolutionary International Movement in 1984, their new magazine, *A World to Win* (edited competently and published simultaneously in several languages), became the Shining Path's platform worldwide. However, a certain distance was maintained, reflecting these initial differences. The Shining Path became part of the movement even as it maintained itself as a "faction" with its own political line. What this meant was something that the old Maoists living in London had no need to ask of Saturnino Paredes, to know or to fear.

11

Tambo

No rumor warned of an attack on the Tambo police station. Despite what had happened at Quinua, no one saw it as an augury or took measures to protect other stations. Did anyone suspect, for example, that the few policemen assigned to Quinua had made the attack possible? Some of the attackers had been caught. Perhaps it was believed that the Shining Path's ability to mount new attacks had been frustrated. Possible. In all probability, however, given that many other police stations in dangerous areas would also be taken by surprise, negligence was the leading cause.

On Sunday, October 11, only three policemen were on duty at the Tambo station. Near dusk, the Sunday market, which each week filled the central square with the colorful presence of people from nearby districts and even distant provinces, was ending. Tambo was a relatively small city, yet strategically important. The gateway to La Mar province and the jungle around San Francisco, it was also the hub for several of the surrounding communities, villages, and hamlets on the Huanta heights.

At half past eight that night, officer Porfirio Díaz took statements from a couple reporting a minor theft and the person accused of committing it (according to the young couple, Jesús Torres and Elena Vivanco, at the station with her one-year-old son, a fourteen-year-old girl, Efigenia C., had robbed a pair of shoes from their stand).[1]

"Seven Lives" was the shoe brand involved. At that moment, there were seven people in the waiting room, gathered around the green baize-covered table supporting the registry book with its blue-lined paper. It was the same green baize and same paper found in hundreds of police stations across Peru.

A man and woman entered. Behind them came many more, their strident shouts punctuated by slogans and the sharp report of revolvers and sweeps of a machine gun. A few seconds later, the police station was captured.

Although police barely fought back, a kind of spasmodic battle—more an overflow of the attackers' nervous energy than any resistance from their prisoners—lasted for almost fifteen minutes within the station and in the area immediately surrounding it. About twenty people had taken part in the assault, and several more had taken up positions outside. Some attackers, their faces covered by ski masks, ran through the central square shouting "Death to Belaunde" and praise for armed struggle, forcing people to barricade their doors. The entire town realized almost immediately that the station had been seized. Some imagined the noise of a massacre, amplified by their terror. Civil guardsman Pedro Villaverde—a local boy, like most of the other officers at the station—was visiting his brother some distance away when the attackers struck, and he realized that pure chance had saved him. Together with Officer Díaz and Officer Jorge Vivanco Vizcarra, the attackers had shouted his name over their shots and an explosion. Far from the station, Villaverde hid in silence.

Inside, almost all of the seven people were on the waiting room floor. Elena Vivanco was wounded in the hand. Her son, shot six times, died instantly. Her husband was also dead. Officer Jorge Vivanco Vizcarra agonized nearby. Efigenia C., the teenager, breathed with difficulty, a bullet in her chest. Officer Díaz, who had pleaded for his life, had two bullets in his shoulder and an arc of machine gun bullets in his leg. With blood streaming from the back of his neck, Sergeant Porfirio Páucar wandered blindly as he attempted to wash from his face the sulfuric acid an attacker had thrown at him.

Only after fifteen minutes did the attackers manage to exercise some self-control. They gathered up the weapons and munitions (two machine guns, two carbines, hundreds of bullets), freed the five survivors, and improvised a brief rally in the central square. Then, they retreated behind the church, some on foot, the rest in two pickup trucks.

Minutes later, as the terrorized staff of the health clinic refused to help Officer Vivanco—terrified by the possible return of the attackers to finish him off, as his family reported later—he died.

The next day, Interior Minister José María de la Jara and Vice-Minister Héctor López Martínez attended their weekly meeting with Belaunde. They arrived with information about the previous day's attack and, in the case of Minister De la Jara, the exasperated conviction that they had no choice but to declare a state of emergency.

Over the previous days, each new Shining Path action had spawned new attacks on De la Jara. The caricature of him as a hapless weakling, goofy and ridiculous, had caught fire in Lima. Now, every Shining Path petard was attributed directly to his impotence, his feebleness, his aura of a tragic "Bonbon." A few days earlier, after three explosives had been found at Lima's Channel Four television station, the owners broadcast an editorial proclaiming, "Terrorism advances, and the government does nothing to stop it. Enough blundering! We demand action!" This would only be possible "when the interior minister pays more attention to what is happening."[2] So it looked as if the Shining Path advance was due only to De la Jara's laziness or lack of concentration. Once a sufficiently hard-nosed politician was appointed in his place, it was assumed, subversion would be controlled.

The campaign to unseat De la Jara was waged openly. Clearly, among its most dedicated members were people within his own political party, Popular Action, especially Javier Alva Orlandini, then consolidating his control over the party apparatus and government with growing success.

Alva Orlandini, then Senate president, made increasingly emphatic public statements about problems raised by this new violence. Along with his reputation as the consummate party apparatchik, he had been interior minister (called government minister at the time) during Belaunde's first government and was remembered as a tough but efficient bureaucrat. In statements made a week before the Tambo attack, Alva Orlandini had said that "now, no doubt exists that foreign terrorists are operating in Peru."[3] For him, it was the only explanation for what was happening. At the time, the national psyche, then widely shared, held that anything imported had to be better; the only ones capable of such efficient violence had to be foreigners.

Reeling, under siege, De la Jara boiled with indignation, but didn't know how to respond. Penned in by the cult of "propriety" then so prevalent within the Belaunde regime, the veteran journalist was prevented from writing passionate broadsides in his own defense. And going to Parliament to confront the hostile majority within his own party was out of the question because of his own painful oratorical limitations.

In their meeting with Belaunde, De la Jara and López Martínez convinced the president without difficulty to take emergency measures in Ayacucho. All that was left was to determine its severity. The new Constitution gave them a range of options, calibrated to the seriousness of the situation. Belaunde chose a middle way: "the suspension of certain constitutional guarantees, a curfew, and intensive police operations."[4]

On Monday afternoon, Belaunde presided over a National Defense Council meeting and, shortly afterward, a special cabinet meeting. Not a voice rose against him, and Belaunde received unanimous support.

The Supreme Decree had been written hurriedly by López Martínez that morning.[5] Some inconsistencies in the draft were not corrected. Nevertheless, the democratic government's first state of emergency was marked by a reluctance to adopt measures of force, true to their determination to establish and uphold civil liberties vigorously. Shining Path militants were termed "misled elements." The state's "obligation" to maintain public order led it to decree extreme measures. The state of emergency declaration was valid for sixty days in five provinces in Ayacucho department: Huanta, La Mar, Huamanga, Cangallo, and Víctor Fajardo.[6] Led by the interior minister, police were charged with reestablishing peace.

That same Monday morning, October 12, two *Caretas* journalists, Sonia Goldenberg and Oscar Medrano, arrived in Tambo. A pair of Civil Guard intelligence service agents, who intercepted them, were already there, attempting to reconstruct the attack. Partially recovered from the night's events, Officer Villaverde showed them the place where he said he fired on the attackers.[7]

In the damaged station, a scene of paralyzed devastation followed the brief, frenetic killing: the walls blackened, blood stains on the floor, furniture broken and overturned. Grief and mourning converged at the health clinic, where a silent Andean chorus squeezed into the entryway, spectators today, victims tomorrow. Within the small building, Elena Vivanco, with minor injuries, was separated from the corpses of her husband and son by a thin divider. Within the charged atmosphere pressing on the closed windows "floated the odor of an autopsy . . . in the room next to where she lies, the nurses are performing the autopsy (on Elena Vivanco's son). The infant was shot six times. . . . A group of local teachers enters the room and delivers to Mrs. Vivanco the proceeds from a collection taken up among themselves. They give her the money hurriedly and then comfort her. 'Yes, well, ma'am. What are we to do! Take strength!' "[8]

If they had been able see into the future, they would have realized that what they said to Mrs. Vivanco could have been repeated to the nation, to Peru. Mrs. Vivanco, slim, almost fragile, lived that catastrophe with admirable stoicism. Yet in the room next to her, the rigorously stupid bureaucracy filled the clinic's tormented air with the smell of the completely pointless autopsy of her infant ("required by law," nonetheless), as incapable of fulfilling its duty to assist as it was stuck to the letter of the law that mandated this useless, though formally required task. And nothing, no one, faced the true dimension of the misfortune that was unfolding or began to confront future ones, except this group of teachers, who placed a bit of gauze on a heart split in two with the delivery of their hasty collection. "Yes, well, ma'am. What are we to do!" The nation would soon follow that early victim's path, painful yet inescapable.

How did the Shining Path organize the attack that shook the government and forced the decision to adopt emergency measures? Days later, the state of emergency in effect, a minor, María Antonieta G., was arrested in Huanta. Several more arrests followed. Two weeks after the attack on the Tambo station, the police had managed to collect testimony that allowed them to identify almost all of those who had taken part.

The attack was a demonstration of the Shining Path's tactical ability to mount an operation at this stage in its development. According to the police report, the first preparations for the attack had begun two days earlier, on October 9. That morning, María Antonieta G. had met with a group of eight people at the crossroads between Huanta and La Quinua. Among them was Johny Cruzat Cárdenas and Marcelino Huamaní García. That afternoon, they had headed on foot for Tambo, crossing the heights above Quinua. They arrived at 10 P.M. on October 9 and slept in an empty house owned by a woman they knew.

They remained in the house throughout the following day and the next, until dusk. Only at midday had one of the group leaders explained to them why they had been summoned. According to police,[9] the group was told that it would attack the local police station within a few hours. Two machine guns and three revolvers were distributed to the higher-ranking Shining Path members.

At 6:30 P.M., nine people left the house and walked to the city's outskirts. On a nearby hill, they met twenty more people, most from the town of San Miguel. A small group came from the city of Tambo itself. This group had two machine guns and a few revolvers.

There, the groups joined. Within a few minutes, they had subdivided into three detachments: most joined the attack group while the rest divided between control, to prevent an improbable counterattack, and retreat, where the youngest and least experienced members of the contingent were concentrated. According to the report mentioned, Johny Cruzat and Elizabeth Cárdenas led the attack.

The attack began at 8:30 that night, from several directions at once. Cruzat and Cárdenas were the first to enter the station. The attack group followed. The entire operation lasted fifteen minutes, except for the time spent in the rally outside the conquered station, where Cruzat, Cárdenas, and two other Shining Path members spoke, repeating the slogans of the moment.

After leaving town, one of the Shining Path members commented, "I think Vizcarra died." He was referring to Officer Jorge Vivanco Vizcarra, who had been targeted shortly before the attack as one of their main objectives (the others were Officers Díaz and Villaverde). The reply of another Shining Path member was one that party doctrine would make typical in such cases: "Let the miserable ones die."[10]

The Shining Path band suffered only one minor injury. The group dispersed rapidly, in two small pickup trucks and a motorcycle. The attackers were left in the highway and returned to their towns after walking through the night.

As is evident, the Shining Path technique at this stage put more emphasis on internal security than on the detailed preparation and tactical training of cadres. Available weapons barely covered the minimum necessary to badly equip half of the attackers. However, massive participation, including the involvement of people who were obviously unprepared, was considered crucial. Under these conditions, it is surprising that Shining Path cadres did not suffer more injuries caused by their own fire and their obvious inexperience. Nevertheless, the seizure of the station and destruction of any resistance were inevitable. Their superiority in numbers (about twenty attackers against three officers) paired with the element of surprise, which was total, made any other outcome virtually impossible. Finally, the attackers took full advantage of the police's need to keep the station open and accessible to the local population. Numerical inferiority at the strategic level, numerical superiority at the tactical level: the Maoist model was strictly applied.

Nevertheless, before the month was out, two-thirds of the attackers had been identified, and a good number of them arrested. But this took place within the frame of a police counteroffensive, temporarily successful, which permitted the democratic government to briefly nurture a hope for victory over violence.

12

The Emergency

At 5 P.M. on Monday, October 12, Civil Guard general Carlos Barreto Bretoneche, chief of the Huancayo subregion, received a telephone call from General Humberto Catter, Civil Guard commander. He was told to travel to Lima, according to military jargon, "with all due haste."

Barreto, a relatively young general (he was forty-nine, and had just been promoted that January), realized immediately what was at stake. The order had arrived at a bad moment. He was suffering from severe stomach upset, the type of affliction, unfortunately, that was less than mentionable under the circumstances. Nevertheless, soon after receiving the call, Barreto traveled to Lima accompanied by a police doctor and his intelligence director. He arrived at 4 A.M. and headed for the offices of the Second Police Region, at the Lima Prefecture. There, the head of the Second Region, General Jorge Monge, told him about the state of emergency declaration. Monge also told him that as the chief of the Huancayo subregion, he, Barreto, was to take command of the new emergency zone. He had to travel to Ayacucho within three hours. Written orders would be delivered to him in the airport, as he boarded his airplane.[1]

At 7 A.M., Barreto found himself at Air Force Base No. Eight with Monge and his assistant, General Héctor Rivera Hurtado. A Sinchi battalion of police trained for special operations was boarding an Air Force Hercules. Logistics officers supervised the loading of equipment. Still pale from the night's vigil and his inopportune rumblings, Barreto received his written orders. Under the general title "Instruction List" and signed by Minister De la Jara, the orders avoided any hint of military jargon and conferred a decidedly civilian mind-set on the operation.

Only during the brief flight to Ayacucho could Barreto read them for the first time and begin to familiarize himself with the mission he had been assigned and the means he had been given to carry it out.

In the Ayacucho airport, Barreto, already recovering from his illness (no doubt spurred by the seriousness of the responsibility placed on his shoulders), was received by departmental authorities and Ayacucho's three police chiefs.

A little later, Barreto led the first emergency meeting in the Ninth Station, which included, along with the police chiefs, the departmental prefect, Marciano Cavero; the Huamanga mayor, Jorge Jáuregui Mejía; and the commander of Ayacucho's "Los Cabitos" army base. Although Barreto had been given authority only over security matters, for all intents and purposes Prefect Cavero ceded to him all political authority in the area.

Barreto's "Instruction List" indicated that he would receive weapons, transportation, and communications assistance from the armed forces. The army would provide light automatic rifles (FAL) and Unimog trucks to transport troops. The navy would supply radio sets. The air force would lend helicopters. In fact, and only after a delay, the army delivered the trucks, but not the guns. The police were forced to train their own drivers. In contrast, radio sets were handed over with no fuss.[2] As far as the helicopters went, two were put at Barreto's disposal during the first days of his command. Nevertheless, the interior minister was expected to pay rent for their use, in cash. The air force upheld this rule without exception, even, as it will be seen, after one of their former chiefs, General José Gagliardi, was named interior minister.

The Vivanco Plan

Despite its rushed beginning, the emergency zone plan achieved several goals. Clearly marking a police high point in the fight against the Shining Path, it engaged their best abilities with results that, although insufficient, were not inconsiderable.

The first positive decision was General Barreto's appointment to command the emergency zone, a move largely due to chance. At the time, Barreto was chief of the Huancayo subregion, which included territorial responsibility over Ayacucho. Nevertheless, more than one of Barreto's many determined Civil Guard rivals saw in this assignment a Trojan horse that would unleash the forces that would eventually ruin his career.

On the surface, Barreto did not appear to be the best man for the job. He was an administrator first and foremost, not a warrior. He had little experience in counterinsurgency war (along with attending the customary "revolutionary war" course during officers training, he had been chief of operations in the campaign against a small guerrilla insurgency in the area around Jaén and San Ignacio, Cajamarca, in 1972). Under the military government, he had worked in the Economy Ministry's budget office. Afterward, the Civil Guard had taken advantage of his expertise in its annual review of its own budget and allocations.

Paradoxically, this training was his greatest advantage. Barreto didn't fit the official stereotype of a counterinsurgency officer transmitted in the doctrine taught to Latin American police and soldiers and later distorted in practice. Yet his training corresponded almost exactly to that considered desirable by one of the most illustrious expositors of counterinsurgency technique. Sir Robert Thompson, for example, believed that counterinsurgency wars were won or lost on the battleground of administrative efficiency.[3] He would have found Barreto to be singularly qualified for this mission.

Intellectually flexible, used to working with civilians, a good resources administrator, with a good eye for anticipating logistical needs, Barreto had, as a policeman, another important virtue: he was an officer with a reputation for honesty and pride in his work, ready to defend his authority if he felt it was warranted without first considering the consequences to his career. Barreto did not precisely belong to the mixed group of young Turks, the "institutionalists,"[4] whose members would, with great differences according to personal circumstances, follow a common path of frustration over the following years. He had kept himself, and would continue to keep himself, some distance from the institutional cliques—some formed around graduation classes or some commander—that were determined to fight for power within the institution. At the same time, he lacked charisma, generally expressed with the gruff voice and haughty manner that so many young officers, motivated by unfocused yet fervent desires for institutional revindication, searched for in the belief that these traits marked the hidden leader, the one chosen to rescue trampled authority, unfurl and give luster to lost banners, and conquer the glory and respect denied, in the best tradition of feudal mythology. Nevertheless, in his own way, Barreto surprised them all when he assumed command, as we will see as we examine the insurrection's course in 1986.

The "Instruction List"

Given the circumstances, the mission entrusted to Barreto was extremely ambitious. Written in inevitable bureaucratic jargon, it was to "viabilize the reestablishment and maintenance of public order, in view of the serious alterations which have generated a state of exception decreed by the supreme government."[5] Peace had to be established within sixty days, a testament to Interior Ministry optimism about the abilities of the police special forces and the operative superiority gained by adopting military criteria to fight the rebel Shining Path. Barreto was in command, and with the help of his personal staff, made up of midlevel officers, he coordinated the campaign that included the three field commanders in the emergency zone: the colonels at the head of the Civil Guard, the PIP, and the Republican Guard. Later, a Joint Chiefs of Staff was established at the Ninth Station. There, tactical planning and operations control was concentrated. The area declared in emergency included five provinces within the department of Ayacucho (Huamanga, Huanta, La Mar, Víctor Fajardo, and Cangallo) and covered 7,166 square miles, with a population of half a million people.[6] It should be remembered that this area includes extremely rugged terrain: mountains, gorges, high moors and plains, high jungle. There were no more than thirty miles of paved highway. The rest were maintained or semimaintained dirt roads, in varying stages of endemic deterioration. Seasonal rains usually began in November and occasionally lasted until March or April. During this period, air travel, especially by helicopter, was extremely restricted, above all if it was necessary to cross a mountain range. Barreto had to assume that weather would ground the two helicopters assigned to him during a good part of the sixty-day emergency.[7]

Barreto arrived in Ayacucho with police reinforcements from different areas (or command groups) within the Civil Guard, the Investigative Police, and the Republican Guard. The largest group was made up of Civil Guardsmen from Lima. The Sinchis, the special forces group within the Civil Guard, numbered 40 men. All together, initial reinforcements totaled 193 policemen, including 32 officers.[8] These men were added to the 677 men, divided among the existing police forces, already in Ayacucho (of these, 466 were Civil Guardsmen). In October, additional policemen were sent to Ayacucho, raising the total number of reinforcements to 392.[9] This meant that a little more than 1,000 men had to cover the extensive, rugged area within the emergency zone.

In practice, the number of available helicopters was reduced to one. Troops were transported with a varied fleet of vehicles, including ten trucks borrowed from the army, three pickups from the Transportation Ministry, one from the Education Ministry, and eight of their own smaller vehicles.

The weapons available were also varied, predominately machine pistols and hand weapons, both appropriate only for close combat. In some stations, and among the Sinchi squads, the most powerful weapons were ZB-30 machine guns, true relics of the post–World War I years (the Allies discontinued them in large part in the 1930s) yet still in good working order.[10]

With these tools, Barreto had to reestablish order and maintain peace. The most important actions that his "Instruction List" ordered him to take were "to apply measures to restrict the exercise of certain liberties. . . . Curfew. . . . To carry out sweeps and incursions using the surprise factor to the maximum . . . identify and capture leaders . . . with the necessary probative evidence."[11] Immediately, Barreto was ordered to "detect, neutralize, and/or destroy the elements that prepare or carry out subversive acts."[12] All in sixty days, with one thousand men, less than twenty vehicles, poor intelligence, and flawed doctrine.

The list ordered Barreto "to subject yourself to the measures included in the Political Constitution of Peru, in its pertinent sections." This was a euphemistic way of prohibiting excesses and revealed De la Jara's permanent interest in keeping his term as minister uncontaminated with cases of torture or the "concrete pajamas and dynamite suppositories" demanded by certain critics who supported what they understood to be a "hard hand."[13]

Embracing his task with enthusiasm, Barreto rapidly mobilized the resources put at his disposal. By October 13, reinforcements had already been distributed among the five provinces declared in emergency, and the Joint Chiefs of Staff, functioning since the previous day, had prepared the first "Operations Order." Its name, "Vivanco," was in honor of the Civil Guardsman killed in the attack on the Tambo station.

With "Operation Vivanco" planned by a coordinated staff that believed in its ability to counterattack and eventually dismantle the Shining Path, police morale lifted noticeably. Neither before nor afterward did the police achieve the same level of energy and enthusiasm as during the latter half of 1981.

Morale was carefully shored up by Barreto, who tried to transmit equally to all three forces a sense of participation and mission, the conviction that success depended on internal unity. This was their moment to demonstrate, especially to the military, what the police forces were capable of when they operated under a single command and cooperated, and did not mutually sabotage each other.

Barreto's first order gave the "Joint Command of the Police Forces"[14] authority over the emergency zone. The invocation of the same title used by the country's highest military authority was for many police officers the closest they could get to bliss. It was their emergence from the sad routine of imitating the military: their insignia, their gestures, the way they wore their gold braid. Without losing their own institutional identity in the process, the police had achieved the military's stature.

Predictably, the military considered Barreto's choice of title a trespass. The immediate and appropriately brusque protest made by the army's commander in chief, General Francisco Miranda Vargas, and the armed forces joint command translated into hurried calls to Barreto from the head of the Civil Guard, General Catter. In the end, a compromise was reached. The name was changed to "Joint Operative Command of the Emergency Zone." Barreto's title became "chief of the zone in a state of emergency."

As frivolous as this episode appears, one cannot ignore its importance to the protagonists. From the institution's feudal point of view, names and formalities were closely linked to hierarchy and authority. And if one is defined in great measure by belonging to an institution, occupying a role condemned to secondary status contributes little to the self-assurance and confidence necessary to win a war. By affirming shared ties between the three police forces and mirroring the military hierarchy's highest realms, Barreto strengthened the police's ability to operate in a coordinated manner and lifted their morale in the region. From that point on, and until the state of emergency ended, the police forces in Ayacucho cooperated without further bickering.

Under "Joint Operations Order Vivanco," the police took the initiative beginning the night of October 13. Police detachments had occupied the University Residences building by surprise, capturing the fifty people staying there. Most, though not all, were students. Among the prisoners was the veteran activist Nelly Carhuas. University president Enrique Moya protested the police incursion, but after Barreto spoke with him and promised to free students who were not implicated, tension ebbed. Meanwhile, with the curfew in force in urban Ayacucho[15] and with the Shining Path in obvious retreat, attacks stopped completely.

The police plan divided the emergency zone into five sectors that corresponded to the five provinces, with one exception: the fourth sector included Víctor Fajardo province and parts of Cangallo while the fifth sector included only Vilcashuamán, then a part of Cangallo.

Six field teams took responsibility for actions, each backed by reserves and an intelligence unit. Each group was further divided into patrols assigned certain territories. For example, Huamanga province had six patrols;[16] Huanta had ten; La Mar had seven; Vilcashuamán had six; and Cangallo-Víctor Fajardo had five.

The area covered by these field teams was vast. In almost every case, it was also difficult and rugged. For example, the La Mar group had to cover an area from the Tambo heights to the Llochehua jungle. Each patrol had to comb its area, carrying out "incursions, house searches, seizures, arrests of those responsible for subversive actions, sabotage, and terrorism either directly or as support according to the circumstances."[17] In addition, they had to carry out regular police functions. One task in particular leaps to the forefront. Each patrol had to carry out "a review of foreigners or people without proper documents, focusing on Chileans, Ecuadorans, Cubans, Russians, Colombians, and Argentines."[18]

Even at this level, the search for international conspiracy continued. According to Congressman Sotomarino, anyone from Argentine Montoneros to supposed agents from the mythic "aircraft carrier anchored in the Caribbean" were leading the Shining Path. The order seemed to reflect the overwhelming lack of information about the Shining Path that afflicted the security forces in general. But there was something more. It was a concession to the basic assumptions that supported the counterinsurgency doctrine practiced by the Peruvian security forces as well as the political parties in power. They had made it clear that they believed in a foreign conspiracy. The natural inclination of the police was, as much as possible, to make their findings match these opinions.

The first patrols had to operate from October 13 until October 23. Each group's leader had a list of seventy people wanted for questioning: all were locals, not a single one was a foreigner.

Surprisingly, the list was headed by Carlos Alcántara Chávez, the high school student considered the head of the Shining Path in urban Ayacucho.[19] Under his command, Alcántara had many of the Shining Path's veteran militants. Very few of them appeared on the list, which did include figures like Víctor Quintanilla and Nelly Carhuas, already captured.

By the end of October, results seemed promising for police. The 400 policemen who had taken part in the patrols had carried out a total of 113 operations, encountering no resistance. They had arrested 185 people, seized close to 200 sticks of dynamite, 330 feet of fuse, some blasting caps, and literature. Although not astonishing results, notable was the complete halt to Shining Path actions within the emergency zone boundaries.[20]

Even more important was the progress made in investigating earlier attacks. Having retaken the tactical initiative, and with the Shining Path in retreat, the police didn't have to worry about solving new cases and could concentrate on investigating the ones they had.

As has been noted, the San José de Secce assailants had been captured by locals the day after the attack. Another six people, five identified only by their pseudonyms, remained at large.

With the capture of almost all of the participants, among them Carlota Tello Cuti, Jesús Luján González, and Dante Cruzat Cárdenas, the case of the Quinua police station attack was practically closed. Only two of the attackers identified remained at large.

Almost all of those who had attacked the "La Pequeñita" store had been identified, and many arrested. And, finally, most of those who had attacked the Tambo police station had been arrested.

Police patrols continued searching towns and hamlets, looking for armed bands but also individuals wanted for arrest or simply questioning. With between ten and twelve operations a day, their rhythm remained intense. Not a single patrol achieved what was then its more fervent desire: to find the enemy and force it to engage in combat. However, arrests remained constant. In some cases, veteran militants or activists were captured, especially in Vilcashuamán. But in other cases, those arrested had little if anything to do with the insurgents. The search for foreign agents delivered results that were pathetic at best. Instead of those implausible "Cuban, Russian, Colombian, and Argentine" conspirators, the police arrested a young French tourist on October 19, Therese Jacqueline Marie. The French Embassy quickly intervened and, after arranging her release, bustled her out of the country. In the airport, her face reflected the anguish of the sudden arrest and the mistreatment that followed. Only a threat in her case, carried out in the cases of other detainees.

Despite the recommendations contained in the "Instruction List" and Barreto's direct orders, the treatment by police of detainees as well as the population at large had become the source of serious problems.

Police belonging to the Sinchi Battalion of the Civil Guard's 48th Division were in good measure wrapped up in the black legend that over the following months would convert their name into a synonym for brutality for many of Ayacucho's residents and the country as a whole. At the same time, however, as the unit with the best combat training, the Sinchis spearheaded the police advance. For that reason, they were considered both an irreplaceable part of police strategy and an important element in the Civil Guard's sense of honor and institutional power.

More conspicuously than other units, the Sinchis embodied the limitations of counterinsurgency strategy and the doctrine behind it. While their reason for being was counterinsurgency, within a few months of being partially deployed in the Ayacucho theater of operations the Sinchis were already weighed down by accusations of routine intimidation and occasional brutal excesses without being able to point to concrete results in the fight against the Shining Path.

In reality, the fundamental defects of the Sinchis lay in their very formation. The Sinchis had been created in the mid-1960s, before the insurgent wave that followed the Cuban Revolution finally subsided. For the purposes of this volume, it is enough to point out that Peru was considered to have the potential to become one of the most important backdrops for the guerrilla tempest that blew through Latin America that decade. First the peasant land takeovers, then Hugo Blanco's activity in La Convención and the spasmodic attempts to complement it with guerrilla operations, and finally the MIR and National Liberation Army (ELN) insurrections in 1965—across the political spectrum, all were understood as unequivocal symptoms of a revolutionary situation.

While the Cuban government concentrated its energy on trying to foment guerrilla outbreaks in Latin America, the United States—whose foreign policy at the time was directed toward fighting "small wars" of leftist orientation throughout the world, the beginning of what would later be called the "counterinsurgency era"—substantially increased its antiguerrilla presence in Latin America.

In addition to its usual intelligence work, the United States Central Intelligence Agency (CIA) was responsible for coordinating the U.S. government's counterinsurgency efforts in Latin America. Between 1960 and 1965, its Western Hemisphere Division grew by 40 percent.[21] Other American agencies, especially the Agency for International Development (AID) and the Defense Department, "provided coverage and additional resources" to the CIA.[22] As in Vietnam, the CIA's cooperation with the U.S. Army's Special Forces was especially close. This unit sent personnel who, under CIA control, concentrated on organizing and training units specializing in counterinsurgency throughout Latin America. According to Marchetti and Marks, more than 600 "mobile training groups" were sent from Fort Gulick to the rest of Latin America.[23]

"In the wake of the Bay of Pigs,"[24] this effort reached its height in Peru with the formation of the Sinchi counterinsurgency battalion in the then remote jungle settlement of Mazamari. Having foreseen the spread of pro-Castro guerrillas, American counterinsurgency functionaries concentrated on setting up and training a special forces unit, modeled on their American counterparts, to confront and defeat guerrillas in their own element. Mazamari was built as a self-sufficient jungle base for the training and housing of special forces. Training was given by the "Green Berets and trainers from the CIA's Special Operations Division."[25] All equipment, from uniforms to parachutes, was financed by the United States government.

Meanwhile, however, the guerrillas were eliminated by the armed forces, just as the Sinchis received their best equipment and training. As of that moment, their existence provoked open resentment from military leaders, especially the army. Army pressure prohibited the Sinchis from parading in Lima.[26] Clashes, above all the eternal struggle to establish hierarchies and staffs, sharpened to the point of open conflict. As was inevitable, the army prevailed.[27]

Afterward, when Velasco Alvarado's military government ended military cooperation with the United States, the Sinchis entered a kind of temporal bubble. With the American trainers and equippers gone, the Mazamari base remained just as they had left it, changed only by the passage of time. Most of the founding officers remained, aging along with the equipment. They hoarded their memories, their immutable techniques, skydiving each year with the same, increasingly venerable parachutes (in 1982, Gagliardi managed to change them)[28] and prepared their small units to fight fierce battles with uniformed guerrillas, like the ones they had prepared to confront in the 1960s.

Isolated, they continued—perhaps to a greater degree than other Latin American military and police units—the process of distorting a doctrine that had arrived already distorted. Although they would toss around some hollow phrases about the importance of politics in counterinsurgency war and occasionally considered some "civic action" (a little hair cutting or free tooth pulling, for example), their training to operate in small units and carry out aggressive actions in combat came to be considered the core of counterinsurgency. Given the importance in this type of combat of surprise, ambush, rapid reflexes, aggressiveness, and even ferocity, these qualities also came to be considered primordial. Instead of being viewed as an essentially political conflict, the counterinsurgency war was seen as the sum of tactical events. War would be won by physical conditioning, harsh ferocity, and the ability to play dirty.

After the first police clashes, the police high command presented the Sinchis as a panacea. "The Civil Guard itself presented them as saviors," López Martínez remembers, "but Sinchis only bring problems."[29]

Most Sinchis were good fighters. Save some exceptions, their record in the few times they were able to fight under the circumstances for which they had been trained was adequate. But in a different war, where these abilities were usually of little use and most of their blows were lost in thin air, the exasperation that resulted only accentuated their tendency to bully the population and try to inspire terror. They were feared, but also hated. And the Sinchis, poorly informed and looking for an enemy that did not set ambushes in isolated spots but in the middle of the population, frequently treated the entire population as suspect. And they did it in their special way, with the predictable results handily exploited by the Shining Path.

On October 23, I accompanied a Sinchi contingent in their most ambitious operation to date. Four Sinchi "squadrons" led by Major Javier Mariús prepared to converge on the pass leading to the Apurímac River jungle, hoping to cut off the retreat of a suspected Shining Path column that, according to their intelligence, was meeting on the heights of La Mar province and planned to later fall back into the river canyon. The initial preparation and execution of the first stage of the operation was accomplished with palpable efficiency despite the fact that they had at their disposal only one helicopter to transport the squadrons. Nevertheless, by midmorning, already gathered in the silent provincial capital of San Miguel, the Sinchis clearly were confused. The information that had led to the operation was not, apparently, correct. Viewed in perspective, it seems probable that the maneuver had been more or less illusory, designed to take advantage of the Sinchis' particular abilities in the hopes that the enemy would be gracious enough to play its assigned role. As in other instances, this did not happen. The operation continued, thanks to Mariús's improvisational ability, but converted into a simple patrol.[30]

The night before, I had attempted to interview Maximiliano Durand in the PIP's departmental headquarters in Ayacucho. Two days earlier, the Shining Path leader had been taken from Lima in order to stand trial in Ayacucho. He was one of the Shining Path's highest ranking leaders. Although his position in the organizational hierarchy was almost public, his arrest has certainly annulled any direct participation. I saw a "pale and weary" Durand little disposed to an interview, which, taking into account the circumstances and his apparent defense strategy, was understandable. The little he said formed a part of it. He claimed "to be outside of party politics and blamed the accusations against him on academic rivalries and provincial intrigues."[31] It was, as will become clear, an effective strategy.

This was my first visit to Ayacucho. The city was also living its first weeks under a state of emergency. The transition to the atmosphere of primordial violence that would later dominate its days had already begun, although few recognized it as yet. In the depthless Andean night, the streets were deserted. The only ones about were a few police patrols. Meanwhile, their colleagues prepared for their nocturnal incursions, to kick down doors and make arrests.

During the day, this city seeded with churches and chapels still offered up striking tableaus, at time ominous, at times enchanting. Mestizo and Indian, baroque and melancholy. The expressions of a people used to the intense, pure light of the clear Andean sky, to high, barren mountains, poor soil, poor lives, artistic genius, endemic suffering. People walked free of the asphyxiating violence that would one day strangle their dreams and waking hours. It was still a time of alarm mixed with a certain titillation. It was possible to perceive in some a certain local pride, paradoxical and perverse, in the face of the Shining Path's first blows in this war of shadows.

I had already had several interviews with General Barreto. In those first days of the state of emergency, Barreto was staying in the Tourist Hotel. After work, there was plenty of time to chat. Once the first week of maneuvers had ended, Barreto was optimistic. The arrests had penetrated the Shining Path organization. The terrorists were in retreat. The police were on the verge of solving all of the previous attacks and capturing all of the perpetrators. From the point of view of combat efficiency, the Shining Path guerrillas, he said, didn't amount to much. Attacking isolated police outposts didn't compare to confronting the Sinchis.

Because the Sinchis had already been accused of committing excesses, I asked Barreto a question that I would in the future have to repeat numerous times. "Do you believe that it is possible to carry this campaign to a victorious conclusion while respecting basic human rights?" His response was immediate. "I have very clear orders," he told me, "and if I catch anyone mistreating or torturing some prisoner, I will begin an immediate investigation. I don't beat around the bush, and my people know it. On the other hand," he added, "I can't be everywhere. The Sinchis are tough. And as far as the PIP go, you know how they are."

Submarines in the Mountains

The next day, I went with photographer Oscar Medrano to the PIP's departmental headquarters. It was a building filled with plainclothes policemen, armed with an array of weapons and expressions that were far from friendly. We were told that Colonel José Salas Cornejo, the PIP chief, was busy, but would receive us shortly.

People came and went, so—after the usual inquiries—we ceased to be of interest. We wandered to a stairway that went down to cells and the prisoners held in them. Climbing the stairs was a young man in handcuffs, accompanied by two policemen who appeared barely out of their teens. The prisoner didn't seem to be more than seventeen or eighteen. He had the fair complexion common in parts of Huamanga and Cangallo. His face was terribly swollen. More recent blows seemed to have been landed over older bruises. He appeared gripped by overwhelming fear and anxiety, yet was making a supreme effort to avoid being totally submerged by these feelings. In contrast, his keepers had tranquil expressions.

I approached him, asked his name and why he had been so badly mistreated. He murmured some reply, staring fixedly and with an almost savage intensity at a point that appeared to be deep inside himself. He said nothing more. It was clear that all of his energy, all of his force, was centered on not breaking, and that the horror that awaited him, not his memory of it, tormented him most.

It was Dante Johny Cruzat,[32] one of his keepers said. But just as Oscar Medrano tried to take a picture, an adult policeman came forward, shouting that photographs were not allowed, and took the prisoner away.

Medrano and I took advantage of the chaotic movement of people to go down the stairs and head toward the cells. There, in the patio that fronted them, several policemen were engaged in a very loose interpretation of what it meant to stand guard duty. Most were very young, with the almost beardless faces of recent academy graduates. In the patio's center, seated on a lonely chair, a woman ate from a metal plate.

Medrano drew close and began to take photographs. Startled, she tried to hide her face. For the young policemen, the scene became suddenly entertaining. Several approached the chair where she sat. "This is Nélida Laura, the little terrorist," one of them told me.

The others urged her to lift her face, "your little face, your sweet little face," and she seemed more embarrassed than afraid. The policemen spoke to her with ironic tenderness, as if they shared secrets. It was a brief scene, but the sexual undertone to these juvenile jokes gave them a particularly obscene cast, above all because their festive spirit seemed to feed from her desperation.

She wore a pullover and brown moccasins, without laces. For another moment, she did not lift her face. When I asked her why she would not talk to us, she answered, half hiding herself, half looking, "because journalists are liars." It was not the moment to debate the level of truth or falseness in her statement, so instead I asked if she had been mistreated.

She raised her face and looked at me. It was an attractive face, that of a handsome Ayacucho woman. But her eyes seemed to look out at me from a well of sadness, distant, profound, with her drowned in it. And perhaps the very fact that there were no outward signs of violence on her gave a tragic force to her gaze. A soul in torment, youth squandered, all at once. "They arrested me for taking part in a meeting,"[33] she said, "they say it was a terrorist meeting, but it's not true. . . . I left early."

"Have you been mistreated?" I repeated.

She briefly looked to either side, where the boys still looked at her, with sparkling eyes and improperly close. She then looked at me and, with an anguish that I had witnessed but few times until that moment, slowly said, "All that I can tell you is that until my arrest, I believed that Hell only existed in the afterlife."

I looked at her in silence. I asked nothing more. Medrano, a veteran reporter who had seen much, lowered his camera and took no more photographs.

"What are you doing there?" an older officer shouted, approaching rapidly from the stairs. "Don't you know that this is a restricted area?" He was a commander who had just been alerted to our presence.

"Do we torture?" asked the PIP chief with a bitter and tired gesture, yet making a visible effort to contain his anger. "No. No, we don't torture."

How then did he explain Cruzat's swollen face, the woman's statement?

"Listen," he said, dragging out his words, each one angrier. "This is not torture. This is interrogation. We don't damage anyone. We don't mutilate. We must interrogate."

"This is what you call interrogation? This is not legal and you know it."

"I am going to tell you what I know," he said, clearly exasperated. "I know that these people kill, these people torture! Why aren't you concerned with what these people do? We have to grab them before they get any bigger! Do you understand me!"

"And that's why you use torture?"

"We don't torture! I'll tell you what we do. We'll hit them some, or hang them up, or give them the submarine, but this isn't torture."

"Sir, that is torture."

"Listen. We don't do them any harm. They all get a medical exam. When the doctor examines them, everything is OK. And they tell us what we need to know. And so we can, so we save lives. These people kill, did you know that? What side are we on, huh?"

Is it necessary to say that the sea is superfluous to this indoor submarine? Generally, a small basin was sufficient. With the hands tied behind the back, the victim is submerged again and again, each time to the point of drowning. It was a preferred method since it left no marks and rapidly broke the captive's spirit. According to what I was told, the PIP employed submarine specialists. I was told specifically of a lieutenant colonel who was a veritable master of the technique. With only one glance, he could determine precisely how long each prisoner would last. Apparently, no one had died at his hands in the course of his damp and tiring career.

That afternoon, we spoke about some of what had happened with local journalists. One of them, *Oscar Mendoza*, asked us if we wanted to interview a woman who had been tortured. When we told him that we were interested, he agreed to guide us that night.

A few hours later, *Mendoza* returned. As we headed out, he told us about who we were going to see. Her name was Yori Luz Sáenz Huamán, a Huamanga high school student who had been arrested two weeks earlier in connection with the attack on the "La Pequeñita" store. After the subsequent interrogation, she had apparently confessed not only to having taken part in the looting, but also in the store owner's murder. But the judge who had arraigned her had ordered her release. She was sixteen, and there was no place to hold juveniles in Ayacucho.

We asked if she was a known Shining Path sympathizer. Neither *Mendoza* nor the other Ayacuchan journalist who accompanied us was entirely sure. They were more familiar with her elder brother, a robust adolescent nicknamed "The Greek," apparently because of his well-developed physique, which—within the limits of poverty and the poor nutrition that existed in Ayacucho—had been cultivated out of his enthusiasm for body-building. He had disappeared from view months earlier, and it was assumed that he was deep underground or in the countryside, together with the Shining Path's first guerrilla units.

We hailed a taxi in the central square, an old Ford that took us uphill into the slums that encircle Ayacucho. After a hard-fought climb for the venerable old motor, past unlit and solitary streets where the headlights seemed to perforate a precarious and shifting tunnel in the huge darkness, we arrived at a small level spot, where the vehicle stopped. It would go no further. We paid, got out, and began to walk. *Mendoza* turned on his flashlight and guided the small group. Only while walking was it possible to see behind some windows—covered with rough cloth— the flickering lights of candles or kerosene lanterns. Now that the noise of the engine in gear and happily headed downhill receded, the silence was deeper and more clear. It was just possible to hear the uncertain and hesitating sound of our footsteps on the rocky street, the occasional scrape. To our left, far below, the lights of central Ayacucho appeared distant and appealing.

It began to rain. We hurried our steps, turned to a narrow street heading down. Before long, we paused before a partially unhinged door. This was the house.

The door was opened by an aged woman, thin and nervous, but not fragile.

Mendoza spoke with her in the soft cadences of the local Quechua dialect. It was Yori Luz's mother, who spoke little Spanish, so Medrano and *Mendoza* conversed with her in Quechua. Her hair was arranged in traditional Andean style: two long braids, a hat. Her hair was almost entirely white and her face, narrow, emaciated, was creased with wrinkles.

It was a humble house, but not badly made. Two or perhaps three rooms were roofed. One section had a cement floor. The rest was hardened dirt. A hall between the rooms and a small patio behind had no roof.

We sat around a small table in a room with three walls, an unintended terrace. The roof was tin. The rain grew more intense, and the tape recorder registered the background noise of the rain against the tin, at times drowning out our voices.

Two girls, holding each other by the hand, entered the room. They were probably between six and eight years old, wore clothing that was truly in tatters, and were shoeless and obviously not very clean. But both possessed that instantaneous charm shared by most children. They remained close together, moving as children both timid yet curious will do, poised to exit running or remain paralyzed in place, already accustomed to life's disadvantages; forced already to hide their innate tendency to discovery and light under premature coverings of fear and pain. Yet these qualities were alive and glowing in the shade, undefeated, attempting timidly to reach the surface.

"Are these your grandchildren?" I asked the woman. No, she answered in Quechua as Medrano translated, as if asking for forgiveness, they were her daughters, the youngest. So she was younger than she looked. Life's cycles tend to be so different depending on one's fortunes!

She then began to tell us how the family was being harassed constantly by the police, especially after her daughter had been freed. The Sinchis had entered her house two, three times, she said, climbing the patio wall, screaming, shooting. Not always in the air. And she shined a light against the wall near the point where, a little above eye-level, the tangential trajectory of a bullet was clearly visible.

It wasn't only this. The last time they had come, she continued to say in Quechua as she pointed to the dark patio, her dog, the mother of this puppy—and she placed her hand on a small and nervous mutt—had barked, and they had shot it to death. The little girls, their eyes wide open, listened and watched. And as they did, their mother repeated the words the Sinchis, according to her, had used to say goodbye. "Now this one, and next time the other dog."

Yori Luz entered the room, walking with difficulty. She had the bloated face and smell, so common in the Andes, of raw wool and sweat and someone who had recently woken. She was a heavy woman, with long and thick black hair that was unbrushed and rather greasy. As she spoke and emphasized parts of her story, her gums would show, but not when she smiled. She wore a skirt that was dirty, with a pair of holes near the hem. By no stretch of the imagination could anyone describe her appearance as pulled together or even clean. Neither did she seem to be a particularly nice person. There was an angle in her, difficult to pinpoint exactly but clearly not promising; an impression of potential malevolence, of cruelty. But she spoke now of her memories of pain and suffering, just as they had been experienced by a sixteen-year-old, and this not only gave her story an air of sincerity, but also helped to express some of those essential truths that only suffering and, to a lesser degree, adolescent intensity can bring.

She told us of her arrest and the subsequent interrogation. It was an injustice from the beginning, she said. Only curiosity had drawn her to the murder scene and that's why she had been arrested. But her story was improbable. Later information tended to confirm that she had taken part in the terrorist attack.

But her story moved to the interrogation. They had hung her up, she told us, with her arms tied behind her back, until she was suspended in the air, screaming or moaning when they beat her with wet towels or grabbed her by the legs and jerked her downward. And afterward, the submarine, silent agony, the most tormented howls converted into just a rush of bubbles.

Even now, she could not touch her hands behind her back, and it was clear that her shoulders remained painful.

We all listened, the three of us, the mother, the girls. The tape recorder absorbed her voice and the rain's metallic impact. Medrano worked with a flash. The explosions of light, white, brief, made the shadows more real. The sound of the electric motor in Medrano's camera was recorded on the tape, with the voice, the rain, but without the darkness that surrounded us, the eyes of the girls, the blackened lantern, our silence.

We left the house after speaking with Yori Luz for perhaps another thirty minutes. The next day, we returned to Lima and became absorbed in the frenzy that precedes the close of the week's issue. The editor in chief, Enrique Zileri, did not doubt for a moment the need to publish the story. The article appeared with a full-page photograph of a seated Nélida Laura, speaking of Hell and surrounded by young policemen. There was another, smaller photograph of Yori Luz, recounting her version of the abyss. And there was, of course, information on the state of emergency.

At some point during the closing, the editor in chief told me that another journalist who had been in Ayacucho a week earlier had brought him a tape obtained from a friend who was a policeman. It was brief, and seemed to have been recorded secretly. On it, two voices were audible, although it was possible to feel the presence of others. One voice belonged to a mature man, playful, who spoke in a light falsetto and pretended to be an old teacher reprimanding a badly behaved student. The other voice was spasmodic, anguished, breathing rapidly, noisily, desperately. The first voice said, "Ah, no, no. You aren't telling the truth, you're telling these little lies!" Murmurs, broken breathing. The first voice again. "Ah, no, no. That's not the case. Ducks to the water, to the water, ducks!" Watery noises and, after a moment, a sound that was in part an explosive intake of breath, in part a guttural expression of pure suffering. And then, sobbing, a voice that implores.

It wasn't possible to use the tape. The other journalist said that to do so would expose his source and he remained firmly opposed.

Once the article was published, Barreto made his disapproval of such behavior clear. Among those affected was Colonel Salas, the PIP's departmental chief, who felt unjustly punished. He made me aware of this when we met shortly afterward. In 1989, Salas, promoted now to general, was the head of Dircote in Lima.

Nélida Laura was sent to prison in Lima, her collaboration with the Shining Path apparently confirmed.

I heard about Yori Luz again a year later. It was through a report filed by our correspondent in Huamanga, accompanied with photographs. Yori Luz's little sisters appeared in two of them, together, holding hands, eyes open and afraid, with the serious expressions of children who have seen everything there is to see and yet more. In the other photograph was Yori Luz, stretched out on a concrete table in the morgue, barefoot, wearing the same stained skirt, that expression of emphasis frozen on her face.

They had finally arrived for her, climbing the patio walls. But they weren't police, but Shining Path guerrillas. According to the information we received, the Shining Path had finally concluded that Yori Luz had broken during interrogation and had begun to name other militants. The intruders took her little sisters to another room while Yori Luz was told to kneel and look at the floor. One of the guerrillas approached her and fired two bullets into the base of her neck. When we received the information, the cadaver was still unclaimed and nothing was known about the mother's whereabouts. The girls were alone. Yori Luz was seventeen.

But then, in October 1981, at the war's beginning, all that had happened so far was simply a pale sampling of the calamities to come. Nélida Laura's stifled desperation and the pain saturating Yori Luz represented only the tragedy of youth deceived. Inflamed by the words of fanatics, the sellers of that philosophical snake oil, their youth had been hurled into the fire. But it wasn't the anticipated epiphany of struggle, dawn, and light, but the torturer's basement. A half-filled basin, where agony and desperation floated, waiting.

De la Jara's Exit

On October 23, in Cusco, Aprista student Antonio Ayerbe died as a result of a police beating after being detained as he took part in a protest of increased bus fares.

No extenuating circumstances excused the crime committed by the police officers who detained Ayerbe. The interior minister immediately took the predictable measures of dismissal and prosecution.

At the same time, the incident resolved the conflict about De la Jara's Interior Ministry tenure. Despite the declaration of a state of emergency in Ayacucho and the virtual halt to Shining Path activity, the campaign of attacks against De la Jara had not diminished in intensity. "Bonbon" continued to be a treat for the tabloid *Ojo*. The majority of Alva supporters within Popular Action drew together to demand that he appear in the Chamber of Deputies. Dagoberto Lainez, one of Javier Alva's close collaborators, openly collected the signatures of parliamentarians to obligate De la Jara to speak to the Chamber. De la Jara's timidity about public debate was a fact openly manipulated by the groups in conflict. Some wanted him humiliated, and De la Jara was determined to deny them that satisfaction. On the other hand, the group opposed to Alva Orlandini's hegemony found De la Jara indefensible, and even Belaunde harbored no doubts about the need to replace him.

Yet De la Jara wasn't convinced that this was the right time to resign. He feared it would leave the impression that he was ceding to the Alvistas. But here, too, he found himself alone. Two days after Ayerbe's death, after a long dinner in the La Pizzeria restaurant, Manuel Ulloa and Javier Arias Stella persuaded De la Jara to resign.[34]

Beaten down, and without the spirit to do it himself, De la Jara asked López Martínez to draft his resignation letter. The letter alluded to Ayerbe's death as an incident that "offends my democratic conscience" and made it impossible for him to remain in office. López Martínez himself took it to Belaunde, who underscored to him the need to "change the image" of the interior minister.[35]

Once his resignation was made public, several opposition parliamentarians and some members of Popular Action praised his intentions, his moral courage, and the final gesture of his resignation.

With De la Jara's exit, the initial period of the Belaunde regime embodied by this small and rotund minister ended, as did a democratic reform of the mechanisms of state security, force based on legitimacy and tolerance.

There is little doubt that De la Jara did not have the experience necessary for the job, the ability to lead complex institutions in conflict, or an understanding of the ways in which corruption exists and camouflages itself. To these flaws was added an insurrection, making the internal battles and finally failure a foregone conclusion.

Nevertheless, after reviewing both the good and bad aspects of his term, De la Jara emerges as one of the best interior ministers to serve Belaunde. This isn't a capricious statement: few times since then has the Shining Path suffered the arrest of so many top leaders. Never again did Ayacucho experience two months of tranquillity like those between October and December 1981. No other minister imposed civil authority like De la Jara, as he did when confronted with Balaguer's insubordination. No other minister shared De la Jara's concern for supporting democracy, the protection offered by law, and the human rights of the governed.

Although it was then interpreted as just another symptom of his foolish weakness, it was on this last point that his real strength rested. Today, when ten years of fighting and the consistent failure of "hard-hand" policies have forced even the most myopic among us to see that democratic legitimacy is not an obstacle, but rather an important weapon in the counterinsurgency war—as long as it is supported by a realistic strategy implemented by capable people—Lajarita's tenure appears, in perspective, equipped with a fundamental consistency that none of those who followed him achieved. With time, the supposedly tough politicians along with the supposedly hard soldiers ended their careers more defeated than that poignant, honest, and steadfast "bonbon."

13

Illusions

Contrary to what some expected, De la Jara's exit did not mean that Interior Ministry control passed to Alva Orlandini's faction. The president had already chosen the person to whom he would entrust public tranquillity.

José Gagliardi Schiaffino, an air force lieutenant general, was a recently retired veteran of aviation when Belaunde offered him the Aeronautics Ministry in 1980. Earlier, he had been labor minister under the 1962 military junta; commanding general of the air force in 1966; and aeronautics minister throughout Belaunde's last four cabinets, from 1967 until the 1968 military coup. After the coup, Gagliardi requested retirement and formally ended his friendship with General Juan Velasco Alvarado. For the next twelve years of military rule, he was in bittersweet retirement. With Belaunde's return, Gagliardi had once again been offered the Aeronautics Ministry. Initially, he had been fearful of accepting the duty. "So much time has passed, I'm out of touch," he told Belaunde when offered the post, after the election victory. "Get up to date between now and July 28," Belaunde responded.[1] And so he had.

Once De la Jara resigned, Gagliardi was called to the Government Palace. Awaiting him with Belaunde was Prime Minister Ulloa. Without preamble, Gagliardi was offered the post of interior minister. "What terrible thing have I done to merit being sent to Interior?" Gagliardi asked in jest.[2]

He asked for time to consider. They granted it. Gagliardi immediately met with his family, and they agreed that he should accept the post. However, he had yet to make up his mind when he saw that the television news programs were announcing his appointment. He immediately called Ulloa to ask what had happened. "Look," Ulloa said, "we can't wait any longer . . . if you want to create a ministerial crisis, hand in your resignation."[3] Gagliardi accepted the post.

The decision to name Gagliardi had been made exclusively by Belaunde, a person alert like few others to the value of image and convinced in this case that "image would produce success."[4] What was needed was someone who, with his mere presence, would underscore severity, the energy of an organized force—an upright soldier who would meet all the requisite ideals of gallantry, honor, and elegance in conduct that Belaunde admired in military men. For the president, Gagliardi was an exemplar of each of these qualities.

To some degree, Belaunde's impression was true. Gagliardi was a man formed on a foundation of strict discipline, which—in contrast to so many other military men—had stayed with him throughout his life and not just during his training years.

He was from the province of Cañete, and his biography made him seem as old as history itself. He had been educated in a strict boarding school where he learned carpentry and cabinetry, trades that would occupy his free time in the future along with the riskier pastime of fishing. He had been a cadet in the Caserta flying academy during the final years of Italian fascism, at a time when Abimael Guzmán was just learning to walk. He managed to extricate himself from the initial tangle of World War II with luck and by sea. Later, he was a fighter pilot, flying radial engine Curtiss Hawks. He didn't get to fly the first jet planes because when they arrived, around the Korean War, he was too old to fly.

Despite his age, Gagliardi remained vigorous and lucid. He arrived at the Interior Ministry with admirable optimism, and believed that, with the proper dedication and discipline, consistent and perhaps definitive results could be won in the short term in the battle against terrorism.

To his credit, there were certain other traits that gave the appointment of this veteran aviator a certain air of anachronism. His honesty was beyond suspicion (when I interviewed him in 1987, Gagliardi continued to drive an automobile made in 1967, and it was clear that, although he maintained himself with dignity, it was on a fixed income), and he assumed that everyone around him operated exactly as he did. And now he was about to enter a forum where honesty was, definitively, the exception. He was a man entirely lacking in malice, in a medium where malice ruled. He believed that discipline, top-down rule, and other military attributes could be applied through a simple order, in a place where people were used to moving on several levels and using several versions of reality and idioms at the same time. His concept of severity was paternal and protective, in an atmosphere of badly sustained appearances, of police whose commanding officers were corrupt to the core. He was, in summary, a man of integrity who was ingenuous. He had been a good aeronautics minister. There, industry without malice was a useful attribute and survived relatively unscathed. However, there was no chance that this would be the case in the Interior Ministry.

His arrival at Córpac was met with some fear, heightened when, just after arrival, he requested Ipinze's resignation. Many thought that Gagliardi had information about who was doing what within the Interior Ministry and feared an internal purge. Ipinze's exit was decided in part by Gagliardi, but it was above all because Controller Miguel Angel Cussianovich had insisted. "So I called Ipinze to my office and told him that I had an order from the comptroller, who requested his resignation, which I had already approved."[5] PIP general Rómulo Alayza was named to replace Ipinze.

Speedily, the Interior Ministry's official police and civilian bureaucracy captured Gagliardi's essential bonhomie and developed the corresponding measures to neutralize it efficiently. By overemphasizing the external display of adhering to directives and discipline, they managed to convince Gagliardi that his orders were being followed both in letter and spirit, something that certainly did not happen.

With time, Gagliardi began to realize what was going on, thanks in great measure to the advice of Héctor López Martínez, who continued on as vice-minister until Gagliardi left his post. But even then, Gagliardi was unsure of what to do. ("I thought that I could improve the infrastructure. And I also understood this as ability to act.")[6] He concentrated on doing what he did best: trying to improve the equipment provided to the police force, its organization and effectiveness as an institution. Later, fearing the social cost of using the armed forces to fight the Shining Path, he tried to improve the police force's ability to act in the counterinsurgency war, despite his own realization that it was also prone to committing excesses, to going too far, and lacked discipline. ("[The Sinchis] lack the concept of protecting the population in the sense of making friends; instead, they raze everything and believe themselves all-powerful. . . . It seems that there were too many abuses and violations in Ayacucho.")[7]

In the end, and despite differences in appearance, training, and style, there was much that Gagliardi and De la Jara shared. And while the press didn't stick Gagliardi with any of the saccharine nicknames bequeathed to De la Jara, within the Interior Ministry halls he became known by the affectionate name of "Nono," or "Nonino," the little grandfather. And I would hurriedly add that this similarity in the perception I have of both men's goodness, honesty, and even ingenuousness, far from being a drawback, elevates both and even ennobles their failure—above all when they are compared with the shysters who then and now swarm through those halls, living as parasites off of power and the country itself.

Rasuhuillca

During the month of November, the police force maintained an undisputed initiative throughout the emergency zone. Complementing the presence of local police detachments (in stations and interconnected command posts with the incessant deployment of Sinchi patrols, the police dominated the entire theater of operations. They took advantage of the lack of opposition to concentrate on the districts where, according to intelligence reports, the Shining Path had set up a relatively influential organization. Carrying with them lists of people wanted for questioning, police combed the provincial capitals, towns, and villages. At the beginning of November, central command distributed a list of fifty-two fugitives.[8] By the end of the month, a high percentage had been captured. Although some names were included in error, most were Shining Path members. And some were high-level.

Taking into account the low quality of intelligence information in police hands at the emergency's beginning, it is clear that within a month, it had visibly improved, the result as much of Barreto's efforts to get the three branches working together as the fact that each branch—especially the Civil Guard—had sent some of their best intelligence specialists to Ayacucho. It was then possible to integrate and develop information gathered from existing files, new reports of activity, and field operations and mine them all fully.

For all practical purposes, there is no doubt that the police inflicted serious damage on the Shining Path. At the time, these advances were more important than anyone calculated. Many of the leaders later freed during the 1982 attack on the Huamanga prison were captured then. As a result, the Shining Path was forced to retreat for a longer period of time than expected and called into action its "second network." And organizing it took time. Meanwhile, the police took advantage of the impetus won by their initiative.

Nevertheless, the police command did not fail to recognize that their achievements were relative, especially when the amount and quality of the intelligence they received improved. They began to see that they had only begun to glimpse the tip of the iceberg of insurrection. Although they had yet to perceive the enemy's true nature, at least they did not overlook the fact that they were far from victory. So on November 1, the Joint Chiefs of Staff indicated that, "while it is certain that the Joint Operative actions have allowed us to momentarily neutralize terrorist actions in the emergency zone, it is abundantly clear that if we do not manage to capture all of those implicated along with the intellectual authors and the principal leaders of the PCP-'SL,' subversive attacks will continue. So long as they obey their strategy for struggle, they will be in retreat so that they can later continue with greater aggressiveness."[9]

With the end of the state of emergency imminent, just as those in the police high command realized among themselves that the Shining Path had not been substantially hobbled, they began to receive information about an approaching reaction by the seditious organization. For this reason, in their "Summary" dated November 27, the Joint Chiefs of Staff recommended that "the state of emergency and the suspension of constitutional guarantees in the five provinces of Ayacucho department continue for thirty days longer."[10] Barreto himself asked Belaunde on December 3 to prolong the state of emergency for thirty more days despite the fact that he had been asked by both GC chief Lieutenant General Humberto Catter and GC Region II chief Lieutenant Jorge Monge to suggest that the emergency be lifted. Belaunde answered Barreto's request by indicating that it wasn't convenient to prolong the emergency declaration "for political reasons."[11]

With only a few days left before the end of the state of emergency, Barreto and his staff allowed themselves to be seduced by a dream shared by every counterinsurgency soldier: to locate and surround the enemy, shut off all escape, and force it to fight or surrender.

On December 8, acting on the basis of unconfirmed information suggesting that "on the heights of and/or around Rasuhuillca-Huanta can be found a command center of the so-called PCP-SL Special Group,"[12] the police command mounted its most important operation since the insurrection's beginning. Departing from Ayacucho and San Miguel, five operative groups (Alpha, Beta, Gamma, Delta, and Omega) converged at once and from different directions on Mount Rasuhuillca. Each of the five patrols was made up of thirteen men (an officer in charge, nine Civil Guardsmen, three PIP officers), and all were assisted by the only helicopter then operating in Ayacucho. The operation went according to plan, but did not locate a command center or a single member of the "PCP-SL Special Group."

And so, on December 12, with the state of emergency lifted, Barreto left Ayacucho. Without doubt, the immediate results of his command were positive. With limited means—men, equipment, and, above all, intelligence—he had managed to calm the area. During the two months that he led the counterinsurgency effort, the guerrillas had failed to mount a single attack. Only on December 10, after a lunch given in the Tourist Hotel to celebrate Barreto's birthday, did a bomb explode outside the hotel, causing minor damage. It is a record unmatched to this day.

Clearly, another impressive achievement was that he had managed to control the area in two months without anyone being killed. The "social cost," in other words, had been negligible. This was another achievement that was not repeated then or afterward. Much is owed to then ex-minister De la Jara, whose dogged insistence on respect for human rights for the detained and the civilian population subjected to police actions had been transferred—as it never had before or would be afterward—to actual orders issued in the field. With a basis in fact, the police command could assert that it had "the recognition and support of the population because police operations were being carried out according to the Constitution, standing orders, and the Declaration of Human Rights."[13]

While De la Jara could be said to have insisted on handling the emergency politically, Barreto was the one who actually applied these policies on the ground. Even with these limitations, he achieved much better results than any other police or military commander in the emergency zone. It was a complicated task and not completely successful, as was evident with the publication of reports of torture in *Caretas*. Nevertheless, in contrast to what almost any other police or military commander would have done in his post, Barreto punished the officers who permitted torture. In doing so, he sent an unequivocal message to the men under his command, that they—despite the twisted nature of their training and professional behavior—understood perfectly. For López Martínez, Barreto "was the best there was."[14]

I believe it to be true. Nevertheless, as I have written, his achievements have to be understood in relation to the limitations inherent in the means he was given and the failure of those who went before and came after him. Because once the state of emergency was over, so too were the dreams of pacification. On the day the state of emergency ended, December 12, a contingent of twenty Shining Path guerrillas seized the Civil Guard post in Totos, in Cangallo, and took weapons (including machine guns) and uniforms.[15]

Far from ending, the war had just begun. And now the counterattack would take flight.

14

A City Dominated
A Blow Is Struck in Ayacucho

As of January 1982, the police force lost the initiative against the Shining Path in the emergency zone. It was an uneven process, punctuated by steps backward and moments of respite accentuated in the countryside and gradual in the city. But before the year's end, the inescapable reality was that the Shining Path would emerge victorious in Ayacucho.

On January 6, the Shining Path seized the town of San José de Secce for the third time. On two earlier occasions, the Civil Guardsmen had been overpowered. They were yet again. The attackers arrived on horseback just as night was falling. While the larger group surrounded the Civil Guard post, another detachment searched out the local appointed governor, Alberto La Rosa Quintanilla, to kill him. A year earlier, after the January 11 attack, La Rosa had convinced a group of townspeople to follow the Shining Path attackers as they left, captured several members, and delivered them to the police.

Between the dense darkness, the rain, and the confusion created by gunshots and explosions near the police station, La Rosa managed to escape. Meanwhile, resistance in the police station conformed to the strictest interpretation of brevity possible. Minutes after the station had been surrounded, the policemen surrendered. Relieved of their uniforms, shoes, and weapons (two machine guns, a carbine, two revolvers, and four boxes of recently confiscated dynamite), the men were kept as prisoners during the entire attack. The station was completely destroyed with dynamite.

Days later, a police patrol arrived in San José to assess damage. Almost all of the local authorities and a good number of the families there offered to rebuild the destroyed station and asked that the number of officers posted there be increased.

However, Civil Guard command in Lima had decided to withdraw from San José and other threatened towns. The decision to "retreat the stations" (as the measure was termed) was in essence to abandon the countryside, a concession of territory to the Shining Path. The importance of this implicit first defeat was perceived throughout the hamlets, towns, and peasant communities of Ayacucho. Civil authorities quickly learned that the only way to survive was to escape or submit to the Shining Path. In towns as different as Chuschi and San José, Ayacuchans who had banded together to chase after the first Shining Path bands understood the same message as their local officials: to oppose the Shining Path was to invite death. The abandoned stations, the Civil Guard emblems ripped from the walls, and the vague promises to return made by departing policemen reinforced this message with the same eloquence as the anonymous letters slipped by night under the door and the surprise, preemptory incursions made ever more frequently by the Shining Path.

Attacks were not confined to the countryside. On the same day as the seizure of San José de Secce, there were two attacks in Ayacucho city. In the first, a Civil Guardsman was wounded and robbed of his machine gun and revolver. In the second, Republican Guard Adrián Ramos Flores was killed—and his weapons stolen—on the hill known as Acuchimay. When he was a student, Ramos Flores had been a drummer in the "Mariscal Cáceres" High School. It was not improbable that some of his killers may have been former schoolmates.

Meanwhile, the Shining Path was confronting several problems. A significant number of its operative cadres had been arrested. People like Hildebrando Pérez Huarancca, Edith Lagos, Carlos Alcántara, Eucario Najarro, Amílcar Urbay. Maximiliano Durand remained in custody, and the Shining Path devoted considerable energy to winning his freedom. Intelligently handled, the effort to gain Durand's release assumed a low profile. Through an international campaign of letters to the Peruvian government, the Shining Path maintained that Durand was simply a scientist dedicated to researching alternative energy sources and their use in Peru. His world, it was suggested, went no further than biogas ovens, windmills, and solar heaters. One letter, for example, published in *Caretas* on January 18, was sent from Paris and signed by nearly 600 people, led by writer Julio Cortázar. The letter maintained that "Dr. Durán's [*sic*] academic career is well known in Peru and abroad. . . . His constant concern for putting his scientific knowledge at the service of independent alternative technology development in Peru has made him . . . into a specialist with international fame in the scientific community."

At the same time, the letter demanded the release of over "eighty-six peasants" jailed "as a consequence of the application of DL 046, which violates the most fundamental rights of the Peruvian people."

A few days later, Durand was ordered released by an Ayacucho court. After remaining in Peru for a brief period, he left for France, where his "constant concern" over the following years would be to organize an international support network for the Shining Path.

While other leaders also fought to obtain their freedom legally, wherever possible the Shining Path also employed the tactic of planning and carrying out escapes. Everyone was needed for the radical intensification of insurrection that was planned for the following months.

Due to a lack of either coordination or good-faith efforts, attempts to win releases continued even as escapes were planned. For instance, at the beginning of March, *Caretas* received a letter from the mother of Isabel Sánchez Cobarrubias, arrested as a suspected terrorist in Arequipa. The letter asked for her release "because it has not been proved that she has taken part in any illegal acts." And the letter ended with unusual intensity: "I beg you to listen to the anguished entreaty of a desperate mother and an innocent child who is only five years old, my granddaughter, who needs her mother, whose life has been made impossible in that place that claims to be the Women's Readaptation Center but which is nothing of the sort."[1]

The letter was written on February 23. On March 1, Isabel Sánchez Cobarrubias and another prisoner charged with terrorism, Nelly Chávez Díaz,[2] escaped from prison with help from the outside after fatally shooting Republican Guard private Luciano Puma Sierra.

On February 28, a massive escape attempt from the Ayacucho prison was cruelly put down. Four Shining Path prisoners died in the attempt,[3] and another two, Eucario Najarro and Amílcar Urbay, were seriously wounded and sent to the Huamanga regional hospital.

Other Shining Path members had been admitted to the hospital earlier, among them Carlos Alcántara, diagnosed with osteomyletis, and Russel Wensjoe, a young Liman from a relatively well-off family who had cast his lot with the Shining Path. Nevertheless, Wensjoe had been found not guilty by the courts and had won a verdict granting his freedom.

Insistent rumors indicating that this attempt had only been a bloody practice run for the real thing circulated over the next several hours. On March 1, the intelligence service of the Republican Guard in Lima received information about an imminent armed attack on the Huamanga prison, communicated to Gagliardi.

He acted on it immediately. "I took this information seriously. I not only warned the police, but I also sent them twenty reinforcements."[4] He also ordered that a warning be sent over the radio to the departmental head of the Republican Guard, Commander Víctor De La Cruz. At the same time, staff from the Republican Guard headquarters in Lima called the head of the detachment at the Huamanga prison, noncommissioned officer Herbert Rosemberg, to underscore the warning.

When the reinforcements arrived, however, Commander De la Cruz decided that it wasn't worth wearying them since the information received didn't specify a date. Meanwhile, prison guards took no special precautions. Only seven guards were on duty, a third of the twenty officers who should have been working under normal circumstances. As night fell on March 2, the twenty Republican Guard reinforcements rested or slept in their incongruous barracks, a building that had formerly housed a restaurant specializing in fish and was still known as "The Golden Gills."

The other police chiefs, Civil Guard colonel Carlos Delgado Matallana and Investigative Police colonel Andrés Morales Vega, had not received clear information about a possible attack. There was no special alert. A party was beginning in the Tourist Hotel and lasted until almost midnight.

In Lima, Gagliardi accompanied his family to a gathering and turned off his car radio. López Martínez kept his on.

At seven o'clock that night in Ayacucho, three people wearing the uniforms of Civil Guard officers appeared at the home of truck driver Melquiades Acosta and asked to borrow his vehicle to transport some personnel. Acosta declined, absolutely correctly since he was drunk, and he reminded them that the police had their own vehicles, "to which the pseudo officials responded that indeed they did have vehicles to carry small numbers of people, but they repeated their request, obliging the owner to obey and conduct his truck to the reservoir located in the Mariscal Cáceres Housing Development, taking with him his assistant, Medardo Acosta Vásquez, twenty-five years old."[5]

Upon arriving at the reservoir, the Acostas were put under the gun, bound, and threatened. Dozens of people began to emerge from hiding places "and began to divide themselves strategically and offensively throughout the city in an authentic Commando Type Operation [*sic*] with specific instructions to attack the Civil Guard, Republican Guard, and PIP stations as well as the homes of the departmental prefect and the president of Ayacucho's Superior Court . . . with the goal of impeding the forces of order from foiling the massive escape they planned from the Ayacucho Prison . . . which would be attacked as their main objective."[6]

Over the next three hours, the Shining Path attackers silently assembled at their appointed places. The truck had been parked near the rear of the prison. At 11:45

P.M., the operation began. Republican Guard Florencio Aronés, the only policeman on duty in the tower overlooking the rear of the prison, was cut down by sharpshooters. Immediately, Shining Path guerrillas climbed the prison walls with rope ladders. With explosives, they blew open a pathway through the gates and walls that separated one area from another. The Shining Path prisoners were waiting. Already organized, they joined the attackers.

Meanwhile, the most intense attack had been launched against the prison's main entrance, where most of the Republican Guards were concentrated. A hail of bullets and explosions destroyed a roof, a wall, several doors, and windows. In those first moments, Republican Guard José Rea Conde was killed. From that moment on, the remaining Republican Guards abandoned any pretense of fighting, "protecting themselves and hiding themselves in the different cubicles within the office of the Penal Center, because of the overwhelming number of subversive elements with weapons, firepower, and fighters."[7]

At the same time, small groups of sharpshooters had opened fire on the Civil Guard, PIP, and Republican Guard stations. The first bullets had been seconded by dynamite explosions. When some officers were wounded, the rest blockaded themselves within their barracks as best they could. In every case, they found themselves boxed in.

On Ayacucho's streets, mobile Shining Path teams dedicated themselves to hunting down the isolated policemen serving as sentries. After the officer protecting the house of Prefect Marciano Cavero was wounded and the offices of the Superior Court were riddled with bullets, the streets emptied of police. In less than thirty minutes, the Shining Path had established complete control over Ayacucho.

In Lima, López Martínez was in his house when he was informed of a generalized Shining Path attack on the capital of Ayacucho. Only a few questions were necessary to establish that the police were barely in control of their own stations. When the vice-minister made direct radio contact with Ayacucho, he could hear the desperation in the messages from the barracks under attack. Screams and hysterical insults mixed with the out-of-control chatter of the machine guns and the rotund blasts of dynamite. López Martínez called Belaunde and reported what appeared to be an imminent disaster. At once, Belaunde called the war minister, army general Luis Cisneros Vizquerra, and asked for an immediate analysis of the situation. Should the soldiers at the "Los Cabitos" barracks save the police and retake the city?

Meanwhile, López Martínez received increasingly anguished messages. With desperation in his voice, PIP colonel Andrés Morales Vega asked for the help of the troops at "Los Cabitos." Otherwise, he said, the Shining Path would make mincemeat of the police.[8] A loss of morale and the complete surprise of the attack were audible in both Morales Vega's voice and the background noises.

In the Civil Guard's Ninth Station, the situation was only slightly better. A larger number of Shining Path fighters had surrounded it, and hostile fire was fiercer than in other locations. For more than thirty minutes, none of the policemen risked making any coordinated counterattack, remaining immobile within their station. Only after Colonel Delgado Matallana managed to take control of the perimeter around his barracks and organize a group of Sinchis, under the command of Captain Guillermo Linares Bay, did anyone head toward the prison, where the Shining Path had clearly mounted its most important attack.[9]

From the Republican Guard barracks, Commander De la Cruz—as he explained later—had ordered a captain to go to the prison with reinforcements. However, he added, this officer, under attack, had remained barricaded in the station until the assault ended. Nevertheless, none of the large windows of "The Golden Gills" were broken. Neither were there bullet holes in the walls.[10] At the PIP barracks, only one bullet hole was visible in a cornice.[11]

Meanwhile, López Martínez was again in touch with Belaunde, who said "he had spoken with Cisneros. The 'little cadets' had told him that the police were unable to respond, that they had dug in, that he [Cisneros] believed that the arrival of the 'little cadets' could cause greater chaos since the Shining Path was already falling back."[12]

Without even attempting to close off the highways leading out of Huamanga, the army command refrained from acting when to do so would have meant an important change in the results of the Shining Path assault.

At this point, the prison escape had already ended. Lords of the area, the Shining Path fighters had freed all of their prisoners. Along with 78 of those accused and convicted of terrorism, another 169 people held for common crimes also escaped. While the escapees organized themselves and some boarded the truck, the battle began anew.

After exchanging fire and forcing the Shining Path fighters attacking in the Civil Guard first sector to fall back, Captain Linares Bay and his Sinchis had continued to advance until they were close to the prison. There, they confronted the Shining Path's principal containment force. During the brief, fierce exchange of fire, almost at point-blank range, Linares Bay and two other Sinchis were wounded and the rest of the group was forced to retreat. The Shining Path also suffered important casualties in the skirmish. Among them, grasping an old Star machine gun seized from a policeman in an earlier assault, was Doctor Eduardo Mata Mendoza, in death unveiling his political affiliation.

The exchange of fire with Linares Bay's men showed the Shining Path that it was in an increasingly precarious situation. The surprise factor, which up to that moment had won excellent results, was becoming diluted. The operation now risked disaster. The subsequent evacuation of the city was so rushed that, contrary to their custom, those escaping didn't collect the bodies of Shining Path cadres cut down in battle. Furthermore, several weapons were abandoned, weapons that the Shining Path would have normally made greater sacrifices to keep.[13]

In their haste to leave the city, their plans to free the Shining Path cadres in the hospital were also abandoned.

Most Shining Path members left in the truck seized from the Acostas. On the outskirts of the city, they stopped at a gasoline station and filled the tank. Later, as they passed the police checkpoint on the Via de los Libertadores highway, they peppered it with bullets, encountering no resistance. They vanished on the road to Huancavelica.

In the hospital, concern had mounted since the gunfire had begun. Located near the Republican Guard barracks, the hospital rang with the sound of close combat. Later, near midnight, while the city was still under Shining Path control, private cars began to arrive with wounded policemen. Jesús Huasasquiche, the night doorman, registered their arrival hurriedly. When the shooting stopped close to 1 A.M., a period of relative silence lasted almost an hour. At some point, a rumor circulated that the Shining Path was coming, and this sparked hope in a few, fear in most. Starting at 2 A.M., Huasasquiche recorded a series of entries:

2:00. A Civil Guard car enters through emergency.
2:02. A Republican Guard car with a lieutenant colonel enters to receive information.
2:21. A Republican Guard car enters with personnel.

Close to a dozen Republican Guards, among them noncommissioned officer Rosemberg, entered the hospital. They were "drunk on defeat" and had decided to take revenge on the sick and wounded Shining Path members in the hospital. An armed mob, among them a Civil Guardsman, split between the central corridor and surgery.

Shooting in the hallways, the police screamed at the hospital employees to go into the rooms. They found the rooms where leading Shining Path members Russel Wensjoe, Carlos Alcántara, and Amílcar Urbay were held, and forced them out with blows. The Republican Guardsmen on hospital guard duty, who minutes earlier had feared for their own lives, let their prisoners be taken away.

Eucario Najarro, shot several times during the February 28 escape attempt and at that moment awaiting delayed surgery, had an oxygen mask over his face and was connected through an intravenous tube to a bottle of liquid. Several policemen hit him, tore the oxygen mask from his face, and pulled out the tube. One of the guardsmen began to strangle him with his bare hands. When Najarro didn't immediately succumb, the policeman took the intravenous tube, slipped it around his neck, and with another guard pulling from the other side strangled Najarro until his body ceased to move.

Meanwhile, Urbay, Alcántara, and Wensjoe were taken from the hospital. Víctor Melgar, a nurses' aide, reproached the policemen, but they threatened him with their weapons and forced him into a room. Nearby, several nurses and patients rescued Filipina Palomino from the police who were attempting to take her. Another prisoner's guards saved him with difficulty, explaining to the lynch mob that he was not a terrorist but a common criminal.

Nurse Julia Huayhualla entered Najarro's room just as the policemen were leaving with their victims. Najarro's face was covered with a blanket, and he was motionless. Huayhualla replaced his oxygen mask and the intravenous tube. Najarro took a breath, bit by bit showing signs of returning to life.

At almost the same time, Wensjoe, Urbay, and Alcántara were shot to death outside the hospital.

Najarro would live another four years. On June 18, 1986, when the Shining Path rioted in Lima's prisons, Najarro was among the rioters in El Frontón. Before nightfall on June 19, he died together with dozens of other Shining Path guerrillas who fell during two days of riots, battle, and killing.

At dawn the next day, many things had irrevocably changed. The most visible difference were the open and empty cells in the Huamanga prison. And despite the fear and hysteria of the previous night, the relatively untouched facades of the police stations, especially the PIP and the Republican Guard, underscored the almost obscene contrast. Across the city, family members and officials gathered bodies and piled them in the morgue, some wrapped in woolen blankets, others naked.

On Wednesday, as the first grammatically coherent messages from Ayacucho were received, it became evident that the defeat had been aggravated by the crimes committed in the hospital. Gagliardi, whose decision to send reinforcements the previous day had been thwarted by the Republican Guard commander in Ayacucho, vacillated between indignation and an inability to comprehend what had happened. A rule-abiding militarist to the core, Gagliardi ordered the police chiefs to prosecute those who, out of negligence or ineptitude, had permitted a disaster that could have been completely avoided. "There was negligence on the part of Republican Guard chief De la Cruz, who not only did nothing, but took no special measures in the prison. The order I gave was that the directors in chief complete the investigations and hand these individuals over for prosecution."[14]

Once the order was issued, the minister believed it would be carried out. Nevertheless, Commander De la Cruz would not only survive Gagliardi within the institution, but would also overcome the ire of General Noel the following year. Transferred to Lima, he was sent off from the airport by his men with guitars and teary embraces. Obviously, De la Cruz was incompetent, but he was also well liked by his men. His superiors made an effort to protect him from Gagliardi's gaze until things had blown over. "Perhaps our greatest failing," admits López Martínez, "was not having better control inside the police, in seeing that these people were removed. Responsibility for following through was passed off onto subordinates, which for Gagliardi was normal."[15]

On Thursday, March 4, what had happened in the hospital was already clear. Nevertheless, the first official report on the night's events, prepared by Civil Guard general Walter Andrade, included the hospital victims among the "ten civilian casualties, all terrorists . . . as a result of the subversive attack described previously."[16] As a way of salvaging personal responsibility, it was noted without explanation that some were hospital patients.

Disgusted and horrified, Gagliardi asked López Martínez to prepare the text of his resignation. López Martínez persuaded him not to resign, and instead to prepare a statement and order an investigation. Gagliardi accepted.

The statement was made public the day after the Council of Ministers meeting on March 5,[17] when the gloomy news was presented. The text, midway between cautious and confused, announced an investigative commission and promised to leave no stone unturned "in properly clarifying the way in which these deaths occurred with the purpose of issuing exemplary punishment, as the law provides, to those found responsible."[18]

The commission set up by the Interior Ministry, chaired by lawyer Nicolás de Piérola y Balta, and the commission set up by the Justice Ministry, directed by Vice-Minister Federico Tovar, cleared up what was left to be cleared up. Some Republican Guardsmen, led by noncommissioned officer Herbert Rosemberg, were prosecuted for the murders.

On Friday, March 5, several funeral processions converged on the Huamanga cemetery. The largest followed the cadaver of Carlos Alcántara, dead at twenty years of age, an important Shining Path cadre despite his youth. A crowd chanted Shining Path slogans as he was buried. A little later, another funeral procession began to bury the remains of Republican Guardsman Florencio Aronés, a bit older than Alcántara, in the same cemetery and amid speeches and mute pain.

In Lima, reactions to the attack covered the spectrum between the understandable and the surreal. Popular Christian Party deputy Celso Sotomarino charged once again that terrorism was imported from Cuba and urged the nation to break relations with Fidel Castro. President Belaunde trotted out another familiar theme. The incident had to do, he declared, with the perennial alliance between terrorists and drug traffickers, between "vice and violence."[19]

The following week, Lima was left partially dark after an electrical tower connected to the Mantaro Dam was blown up. Several attacks followed. For the first time, explosives were thrown at the Government Palace. They weren't powerful bombs, so their effect was more symbolic than real. Nevertheless, the Council of Ministers formally discussed whether the armed forces should intervene in the fight against the Shining Path. Belaunde was inclined to keep the counterinsurgency effort at the level of the police.

Within the Marxist left, the reaction to the Shining Path's incursion in Ayacucho was surprise and, among some, a shot of energy. Organizations relatively close to the Shining Path, like Puka Llacta, began to lose their reservations about pledging themselves to the path of violence. Puka Llacta's newspaper announced that the events in Ayacucho, "the assault on the prison and the freeing of prisoners from the dungeons," had shaken elements of the "election-mongering pseudoleft . . . in their comfortable easy chairs, which give them bourgeois legality."[20] But more important than its diatribes against the United Left was its position on the Shining Path. Puka Llacta recognized that it was a "revolutionary organization, the ally closest to our party," and that it had assumed armed struggle "seriously, with forcefulness and audacity." It added that "we support the Shining Path and we will back up their actions with concrete political and military actions." The "theoretical and political discrepancies that we have with the Shining Path are secondary and will continue to contrast and be resolved in the concrete terrain of actual revolution."[21] Puka Llacta's incorporation would considerably strengthen the Shining Path, especially in the central highlands.

The Shining Path celebrated its Ayacucho incursion with elation. In the main document published during the first years of the insurrection, *Let Us Develop the Guerrilla War!*, the "assault on the Ayacucho Public Prison" is described with grand hyperbole as a "heroic action, marking a historic milestone . . . it pulled our comrades and combatants from the dungeons of the Peruvian reactionary state. . . . our guerrilla war, with the audacity, effort, and blood of the people's soldiers, has been strengthened and has completed a great leap in its development."[22] Referring to the hospital murders, the document recognizes the three victims as Shining Path militants, "our valiant comrades," and denounces their deaths as an "execrable murder," the result of "abject, miserable cowardice." And they vowed vengeance "no matter how many years pass between the crime and the just punishment we will impose."[23] It is perhaps beside the point to note that murders committed by the Shining Path, aggravated by having been committed in cold blood, were celebrated as "resounding actions that shake the state's semifeudal foundations."

Leaving aside the hyperbole, what is certain is that the Shining Path attack on the Huamanga prison was a rude awakening for the state and Peruvian society. At this moment as in no other, there was a clear understanding that the Shining Path had been poorly measured and fought blindly, and that its real dimension, surely greater than that supposed, was as yet unknown.

For the Shining Path, the assault on Huamanga and the prison escape was also the moment at which the "First Company" of the embryonic rebel army was formed, twenty-three months after the decision had been made to "forge it with deeds" at the Beginning of Armed Struggle.[24]

At the same time, following the Shining Path's insurrectional scheme, the incursion constituted the "finishing off" within the "second moment" ("To shake up the countryside") of the plan "To unfold the guerrilla war." The next step, to intensify actions and begin to set up their own way of governing through "popular committees" in controlled areas, should immediately follow.

From a purely military point of view, the Shining Path attack was a typical case of the overwhelming effect of surprise on ill-prepared troops, also badly led and poorly disciplined. At the tactical level, the crushing effect that the intelligent use of explosives could have on the combat morale of troops barricaded in their quarters was a clear lesson. Unfortunately, this lesson, along with others, was not used to improve tactics and procedures. Over the following months and a series of defeats, they would have to be relearned and freshly forgotten.

15

Let Us Develop the Guerrilla War

Liberty – Normality – Discipline

Let Us Develop the Guerrilla War! was written by Abimael Guzmán during the final weeks of March, and printed and distributed secretly shortly afterward. It was the first time that the Communist Party (Shining Path) as such had made its position on the insurrection public.

Let Us Develop the Guerrilla War! is a short pamphlet, fewer than thirty pages, divided in four sections:

1. Armed struggle burns victoriously.
2. Counterrevolution stirs up our struggle.
3. The crisis of the reactionary order is accentuated and the people clamor for armed revolution.
4. Let us develop the guerrilla war.

Although the document frequently reveals itself as nothing more than an extended proclamation and repetitious hyperbole ("the unconquerable and growing flames of armed struggle . . . which on our earth, sooner rather than later, will become a roaring armed hurricane"), it doesn't stop at just exalted self-worship and an unconditional diatribe against the government.

Let Us Develop the Guerrilla War! proclaimed that the Shining Path had carried out 2,900 actions over twenty-one months of struggle. It claimed responsibility for acts of sabotage "which struck at and undermined the ruling economic and social system of exploitation"; the seizure of farms and the murders of their owners, "resounding actions that shake the state's semifeudal foundations"; attacks against "Yankee imperialism, the main imperialist dominator on our lands"; and an attack against "the Chinese embassy, sinister lair of the revisionist Teng." Above all, it claimed the authorship of "vital and transcendent" actions against the state, including attacks on Popular Action offices, municipal buildings, and voter registration centers. Murders were presented as "admonitory actions against known repressive agents . . . and against landowner tyrants and little tyrants." The robbery of weapons from the Callao Naval Air Base with the help of a naval officer who deserted[1] was "the important incursion into the Callao Naval Air Base, which they have tried in vain to hide." The list included the Ayacucho prison escape and the dynamite explosions at the Government Palace on March 10.

According to Guzmán, these actions were evidence of four Shining Path conquests: the tempering of the party and its cadres; the formation of an armed force through guerrilla actions; the increase in the quality and quantity of actions; and the rise and development of guerrilla zones, the future locations of support bases.[2]

The reaction of the Belaunde government to the insurrection was described with a thick cluster of invective. After mentioning Decree Law 046, the warlike language, reeling with praise for blood and destruction, is momentarily transformed into legalistic jargon ("In this way, the so-called autonomous judiciary . . . using falsified evidence, rushing through procedural requests, twisting laws, and selling off principles . . . reveals more deeply its counterrevolutionary essence and highlighted are dark bowels of the legal system and the sacrosanct judiciary"). Although the Association of Democratic Lawyers had yet to emerge as an institution specialized in taking efficient advantage of the legal fringes, the tactic of wrapping dynamite charges in the paper reserved for official documents was clear from the very beginning.

Referring to the counterinsurgency, *Let Us Develop the Guerrilla War!* qualified it as "a resounding failure," especially the declaration of a state of emergency in October 1981, and rejected the government's characterization of them as "terrorists." At the same time, Guzmán indignantly rejected any suggestion that the Shining Path had ties to the Soviet Union. The revolution, he sustained, "cannot be in any way united to the most sinister center of contemporary revisionism, which has made the motherland of Lenin and Stalin into today's hegemonic superpower."

This statement was followed by a multiple diatribe against the pro-Soviet Communist Party, "the old sellers of workers at the service of collusion and the fight between social imperialism and Yankee imperialism"; and against the pro-Chinese "Red Homeland" party, "yesterday's 'enemies' of Teng Hsiao-ping and today his adorers can do no less than attack us for combating the Yankee social imperialism of their new master and, more seriously, for applying the Marxism-Leninism-Maoism that they invoked yesterday and today renounce." Both of these groups and all of the other parties on the Marxist legal left were defined as "this dirty, rotted spume that floats according to the whim of the waves, acting as fragile sustenance for union bureaucratism and false proletarian parties."

This description of the political and social situation didn't linger over occasional contradictions. State companies, for example, went in a single sentence from being "a great weight" put on "the people's backs" to "a succulent offering to the insatiable jaws of grand capital, especially North American" with only a single comma of separation.

In its evaluation of the enemy state, the Belaunde government became the clear expression of the "transitory nature of the demo-bourgeois order." The other powers of the democratic state were equally obsolete and useless. Real power, affirmed *Let Us Develop the Guerrilla War!,* lay in the armed forces, yet it was unnecessary to fear them excessively, since "we will never forget that in essence, strategically, an armed force has only the force of the society that it defends no matter how much it is tactically armed to the teeth."

The actual situation, Guzmán affirmed, could only be solved through war, for which the Peruvian people were prepared by their long history of peasant rebellions. With the conceptual spell-casting he so often used, Guzmán and his organization were transformed into "our heroic people" who, hurled into violence, understood that struggle "tunes, mobilizes, organizes, politicizes, arms, and prepares us for the great contests to come." That's why the Communist Party, "the organized vanguard of the proletariat," had thrown itself into the struggle and since January 1981, "in agreement with the Central Committee," had developed the guerrilla war, the most arduous and prolonged part of "the people's war."

Proclaiming themselves autarkic, "dedicated practitioners of the principle of supporting ourselves with our own efforts," Guzmán emphasized, nevertheless, that they were also "followers of consequence of proletarian internationalism" under the banners of "Marxism, Leninism, Maoism . . . and fighting for revolution in our motherland, we also serve the world revolution that combats and will combat until communism shines over the face of the earth."

The document suffered from a rushed composition and is poorly argued, abundant in adjectives, and repetitious. In contrast, the final paragraph, written in quarrelsome, sonorous language, gives a striking portrait of Guzmán's passionate belligerence: "Peruvian people! Like enraged thunder, your hardy voice begins to express itself in the vibrant, purifying tongue of revolutionary violence, of armed struggle and guerrilla attacks, in the guerrilla war you shape milestones in your new history, your definitive history. The great journey is begun, it will be long and difficult, but decisive victory, well, 'Other than Power, all is illusion!' "

This conviction in the pursuit of the absolute end of history would mean that this year and during those that followed, dozens and hundreds of young people would tremble with millenarian fevers and with gusto comply with the demand to destroy their flesh and pulverize their lives, to further stoke the blaze.

The Mountain and the Sunflower

Between April and May, the seventh plenary of the Shining Path's Central Committee met to prepare the most important party meeting since 1979, National Conference II, held that May.

Once National Conference II had ended, the first plenary of the Central Committee met to implement the agreements. Several meetings of all the regional and zonal committees were also held to achieve the same goal and lasted through August. The combination of these events shook the Shining Path to its very core.

Predictably, the first meetings were self-congratulatory. The attack on the Huamanga prison had made the country tremble. "We are in a very favorable situation. We have an excellent position."[3] The waves of discontent their actions had caused within other parties on the Marxist left were underscored. "Revolutionism[4] has renounced revolutionary violence: this has created problems with their bases." At the same time, at the strategic level, they had managed to get "the four Regions to act together as a unit." Coordination needed to be improved so that in the future, "the country is considered only one battlefield; a single plan for the country."

With the scenario established, they went on to an examination of the "principal action" (the assault on the Ayacucho prison) and several others that had been planned in coordination. The picture that emerged was surprising.

The original plan for the attack on the Huamanga prison had been drafted by the Shining Path Central Committee, with Guzmán's decisive intervention. It was essentially the same plan executed on March 2, especially as the attack began. "An extremely audacious plan, in command of surprise, our action's power. The plan's brilliant proposition: to contain the enemy in its own nest. Annihilated."

Nevertheless, the original idea was to make a frontal assault on the prison. The guards were to be defeated and eliminated even though this might provoke a high number of casualties. ("The party was ready to make a payment of up to thirty comrades.") The entire operation was to last no more than five minutes. The objective was to free cadres for the "reorganization of the party, annihilation of the enemy's forces, and provoke the First Repression."

The initial plan had been scheduled for February 28. Orders had been communicated to prisoners within the prison, and the appointed hour had been set for ten o'clock that night, to coincide with a riot. Throughout the rest of the country, other regional committees had been told to prepare parallel escapes for imprisoned Shining Path members. In Arequipa, as was mentioned, a bloody escape was carried out on March 1. In Jaén, the plan for a prison attack had been aborted by the individual responsible for the northern regional committee.[5]

In Ayacucho, the plan misfired from the very beginning. When the appointed hour arrived, "there were no weapons and we had other problems. . . . At 10:10 P.M., the comrades inside began the action." As described in the preceding chapter, this action failed. In the attempt, four Shining Path members were killed and five were badly wounded. The report concludes ominously that "there is a blood debt with the comrades responsible for the action."

Why had the operation failed? According to the report, the Principal Regional Committee was itself responsible for distorting and mutilating the plan. "It was twisted as being too extreme." Opposition had provoked a lack of coordination. At the last moment, the committee's political chief, "César," had assumed military leadership. Most criticism was directed against him. "C. César does not concern himself with the operation, he only wants the glory, to be a great general." Worse, the report noted, after the attempt on February 28 failed and a new plan was put forward for March 2 "on the insistence of the masses," those in the regional leadership drafted a "Proposal Plan" that was seen as "opposition to the Central Committee's plan. . . . what they wanted was to make it appear as if the action depended on them alone."

The modified plan replaced the assault on the prison's main entrance with a deployment to hold off a police counterattack. The shift was harshly condemned by Guzmán, who said "they don't want to annihilate the enemy force, a betrayal of a basic principle of war." And while it was certainly true that the final result was successful, the action itself had been plagued with errors. The action lasted an hour inside the jail while those on the outside had only planned to hold off police for twenty-five or thirty minutes. Essentially, César was responsible for it all. Nevertheless, "when he reports, it is clear that he presents himself as the savior, a gentleman rescuing damsels in distress. C. Héctor gives a completely different report: a parade of heroes mounted on stick horses."

In contrast, no one claimed responsibility for the hospital disaster; and here Guzmán directed his heaviest artillery against those responsible for the Ayacucho Regional Committee. "César makes a parallel plan for getting the comrades out of the hospital. He drapes himself with the party's actions, making a public display that C. 'Héctor' was the one responsible and that César deserves all the glory." For Guzmán, this attitude went far beyond trying to co-opt the glories of others:

conspiracy lay at their root. "The matter is that he wanted to topple the leadership, pull down the secretary-general and change the direction of the party. He was like a feudal lord, owner of the Principal Regional. . . . he is in it for personal power."

The time for a beheading had arrived. The hero of an hour earlier was now a moral pariah. All that was left to see was if this first manifestation of Bonapartism in the Shining Path had been isolated or was part of a broader conspiracy. Guzmán quickly cleared away any doubt: " 'Héctor' also displayed his disconformity with the secretary-general's plan, and is responsible for the deaths that took place during the squad's retreat. For concurring, 'Clara' shares responsibility." However, blame was not contained within Ayacucho. There was complicity in the Northern Regional Committee. "The comrades 'Alberto' and 'Isabel' also opted for a position in accord with comrades 'César,' 'Héctor,' and 'Clara.' "

The charges against the Shining Path commanders were made between May 5 and 6. On May 10, after messages from the "bases" indicated that two-thirds of the Shining Path were for "the defense of the party and its principles," Guzmán announced that the debate had reached a point of internal crisis and that it was now indispensable to take a position. This was not a personal matter, he emphasized, but a problem that had to do with the correct political line: "a struggle with the people's full support or an antagonistic struggle." On May 15, the accused leaders were allowed to present their position. Afterward, the Central Committee met "on the two-line struggle and . . . the problems of each comrade." On May 16 and 17, they continued by "destroying the points of conflict." After an intense "criticism and self-criticism," a breath of air was allowed the tormented Ayacuchan leaders. Meanwhile, most of the pressure was directed against the leader responsible for the Regional Committee of the North, "Alberto," and his lieutenant, "Isabel."

"Alberto" could not even claim the dubious glory of a completed action. Both he and "Isabel" shared "responsibility for the failed escape attempt of the Jaén prisoners, but principally 'Alberto.' " The attack against the man in charge of the Regional Committee of the North, made by another member of the Central Committee, was ferocious: "he lies to the Central Committee . . . he goes to meetings with preconceived notions, an individualist, petulant, a speculator, he speaks in a language different from that of the party, he has not completely subjected himself to the Central Committee . . . his criticisms are without spark, without conviction. . . . He speaks like a landowner. . . . He tried to paint the Northern Regional black, saying that the conditions to shake up the north did not exist."

On May 21 and 22, Guzmán made the decisive intervention. At this level, the majority—including the five victims—awaited a demolition. Guzmán didn't disappoint anyone.

"There have been more than twenty days of meetings," he pointed out, "and there has been entanglement. I am patient on purpose, no one will doubt that there is a leadership that directs the armed struggle. . . . The reactionaries rant against the party and its guiding thought, and these four idiots do the same. The party has no fear of making this struggle more antagonistic, we must sweep away rightism, conciliation."

On the contrary, the reinforcement of discipline and a centralized leadership was indispensable. "We must impose discipline with rigor no matter what the cost; the slightest weakness means death and hunger. To act with implacable severity, whosoever does not act in this way is a traitor. . . . Lenin foresaw the cost of millions."

Guzmán added that these five members of the Central Committee had expressed resentment for having been so ferociously attacked. This clearly revealed their deviation. "There is a right, obligation, and responsibility to combat mistakes. . . . Armed struggle is two years old, it must be understood that the party carries it forward, it has its head, its leadership . . . the party has not sprung from nothing. . . . We cannot permit a conspirator to try and destroy the party; either we are Communists or conspirators."

The "conspirators" felt hurt, he added, which simply demonstrated "where their separation from the general line, the principles, leads. . . . nothing impossible has been asked of them, they have made it impossible. . . . they think that their contributions are not recognized . . . they obstructed the strike, they acted in a ridiculous manner, they even revealed their discontent when they served a cup of coffee; they seek to antagonize because they want to take flight in other ways . . . they want to make noise so that they can factionalize, they cannot hope for more."

Those with "a rightist position" had failed; "they want to go against the secretary-general, but . . . the reality is that here the majority is on the left. . . . we are ready to confront the attempt to create factions. . . . If some return to their bases and form factions, they are traitors."

There was not the least danger of a schism. The overwhelming majority of delegates competed to condemn this unfortunate quintet in the most vibrant and explosive way. After the remaining vestiges of resistance were crushed, buried, and exhumed to be crushed again, Guzmán concluded that they had achieved "a great victory against the right. . . . All that is left is to define the position of the comrades."

Defeated and dazed, the five leaders began the painful process of self-criticism: the admission of error, describing their mistakes in the harshest terms, implacably lashing themselves, thanking others for having attacked them, declaring that their subjection to the party, its guiding thought and general line, slogans, plans, and programs, was complete, absolute.

Four of these self-criticisms were accepted conditionally, with a strong admonition, while the fifth was rejected, because it "failed to break or draw clear lines" with previous behavior, persisting in a "crafty, treacherous position."

After the torment engineered by Guzmán subsided, order was reestablished.

Guzmán pointed out that "the two-line struggle has been the deepest and most intense of all of our events." Yet its result was optimal. "Ninety percent of the party has united . . . it is impossible to unite 100 percent. In this way, we have sealed the party's great unity."

The time for celebrating had ended. They had also achieved something else: to drive home Guzmán's physical and metaphysical dominance. As one leader said, "In the end, the problem is one of a single Leader. . . . each time the party has strayed from its guiding thought, it has failed." And the only way to maintain an unwavering and true point of reference in the inevitable struggle of contrary opinions, in the permanent two-line struggle, was to "enthrone the guiding thought of comrade Gonzalo." This preemptory dialectical necessity had not yet been sufficiently understood nor obeyed by the individualistic deviations within the party. For that reason, matters had degenerated into a "rightist plot" against the leadership.

The annihilation had not completely finished. Immediately after Conference II, the Shining Path Central Committee met in a plenary session to evaluate its agreements. In the first meeting, given that the criticized and self-criticized quintet had not as yet demonstrated the requisite docility, Guzmán attacked them. "Stop playing around with these whimperings and laments in your self-criticisms. . . . The point is that they want to go against the agreements made at the National Conference II." And he warned that "they aren't going to examine their militancy . . . agreements won't be revoked here: they will be expelled immediately. Here, the problem is that they are disgusted with their punishment. . . . what is ridiculous is that they are standing in an individualistic mudhole. . . . We must have confidence and fight mistakes, to not do so is treason. Some . . . what they are is a personification of a gang . . . they have no right to entrap armed struggle. . . . There has always been the two-line struggle within the party, it is an elemental norm within the Communist line, whoever negotiates betrays this norm."

The verdict against the quintet was drastic: "These comrades have been fists against the mission given to them by the party, they have betrayed it. They have an obligation: go to their bases and undo the injustices they have done. They will have to self-criticize, vivisect themselves, have a genuine change of attitude and not secret problems."

This was degradation, a return to their bases. And it supposed a reorganization, with the help of the comrades being punished, of the clandestine party's structure. The National Reorganization Committee was created, to direct the purges that would take place in the midst of armed struggle.

At lower levels within the Shining Path, a veritable fever of criticism and self-criticism shook the regional and zonal committees as reports on the events of Conference II were circulated. The Shining Path's radical wing launched itself against more moderate cadres. For example, in the Regional Committee of the

North, the sacramental rites were carried out true to the exigencies of the form. It is worthwhile to reproduce here a portion of the final criticisms and self-criticisms:

Arturo: We have been able to observe that agreements of high importance have been reached. . . . I declare my complete agreement with the National Conference. . . . Guiding thought has been proved in the heat of battle. . . . The punishment and measures imposed are fair. To condemn rightist positions, the maneuvers of the cadres responsible for the principal action to twist the plan pointed out by C. Gonzalo. . . . I reject their black positions, they aim at planting mines beneath party unity by claiming C. Gonzalo is an extremist. . . . I want to break with those who harbor these ideas, to repudiate and condemn. . . . My self-criticism because of disconformity with the agitprop campaign . . . I have been stupidly boring, I reject the attitude I have had.

Felipe: . . . I accept my mistake of failing to direct myself to C. Gonzalo as the party leader, of being irresolute, I condemn my black attitude; I support with fervor the furthering of what C. Gonzalo has said; I am for sweeping away with this, ready to deliver over my life.

Hernán: . . . With mastery, C. Gonzalo has directed the contradictions that have occurred . . . the masterful attitude of C. Gonzalo has swept away these positions. . . . C. Gonzalo has been accused of being an extremist; they have twisted the plan for the principal action. . . . I agree with all of the agreements made by the Second National Conference. . . . My decision to accept what C. Gonzalo punishes . . . we hold up his image and semblance . . . no one but C. Gonzalo will lead our struggle.

Antonio: When we must take a position, to do so in a firm and resounding way. . . . C. Arturo . . . has only gone in circles without addressing the fundamental issue . . . it serves to disorient the other comrades. C. Misael . . . has problems with revolutionary violence and does not declare if he is willing to deliver over his life.

Arturo: I take responsibility for my self-criticism. I erase my attitude . . . these are petit bourgeois holdovers. . . . I want to crown the guiding thought.

Misael: My intervention . . . is an old-world attitude. . . . self-critically, I take responsibility for breaking with it and sweeping it away . . . my willingness to give the blood quota and enthrone the guiding thought.

Andrés: C. Arturo has not taken a position on the core issue . . . and C. Misael has said nothing here. . . . He has problems with revolutionary violence, fear of the reaction.

Felipe: I believe that C. Arturo should firmly express his willingness . . . to carry out this plan. . . . C. Misael doesn't take to heart what has been put before him.

Santos: Arturo and Misael don't go to the principal issue, always going for its branches. . . . Where is their submission? They should clearly and concretely self-criticize.

Arturo: The left is alert to the problems of rightism that my person has expressed. . . . I thank my comrades for helping me with their criticism. . . . I declare my submission to the guiding thought and I am ready to learn from C. Gonzalo.

Misael: The comrades have shown me my attitudes . . . that express fear of the reaction, old-world attitudes. . . . I self-criticize myself for all of these mistakes and rotten criteria that don't help. I am ready to do anything I am told. I am convinced that with revolutionary violence we will win all.

In hindsight, it is interesting to compare the fates that befell the leaders of the forces that battled in Ayacucho that night of March 2. The commander of the successful guerrilla attack, "César," was demoted after an implacable series of attacks against him. The victorious leader of the operation in March had by May been completely pulverized as a leader. In his case and those of his lieutenants, victory was the prologue to disgrace.

In contrast, the head of the Huamanga police barracks remained at his post. While certainly Colonel Delgado Matallana relinquished his duties for brief intervals as other police generals arrived, then hurriedly returned to Lima, in the end he once again took command of the city and the department. Until the final moments of the police defeat, he propped himself up with the bitter determination of courage devoid of good fortune.

Only Commander De la Cruz was removed, as was noted earlier, because of pressure from the interior minister. His farewell in the Ayacucho airport was complete with his officers' toasts and the strums of their guitars.

Once the dust settled, the message that victory is a disgrace and defeat brings a certain stability was clear to every commander on both sides of the battle. At that moment, the figure of Guzmán beheading his best military leaders and a government rusted with inertia and incompetence gave the impression of achieving the same result.

It was not so. The purge of five members of the Central Committee was closely related to a total reorganization of the movement, affecting it at every level, from doctrine to tactics. Its effects were felt markedly until 1986, and that is why it is worthwhile to linger a bit longer over the agreements made at the Second National Conference, their reason for being, and their consequences.

"One Must Be a Philosopher to Make War"

The most important motive for the purge of leaders was Guzmán's need to maintain absolute control over the war's course. But the inertial force of modest success conspired against his authority. In practice, the division of strategic centralization and tactical decentralization was difficult to maintain. For the leaders of some regional committees, like the Principal Committee in Ayacucho, direct control over party machinery and sharing the risks and the construction of victory made absolute submission to a distant leader difficult.

Neither was their relation to Guzmán (at least in the case of the veterans) that of the faithful to their prophet. For them, Guzmán was, without doubt, the most admired among many, the party's driver, but he was still human, still fallible.

When Guzmán decreed escape attempts in all of the nation's prisons where there were Shining Path prisoners, maintaining Ayacucho as the center of the action, it is certain that he had in mind what the reintroduction of liberated cadres would mean, as a way of counterbalancing the bloodbath of a future purge.

But when he sent a detailed action plan to the Ayacucho Regional Committee, and it rejected a portion of it, the decision to carry out a true cultural revolution in the midst of struggle appears to have been taken.

For Guzmán, avoiding casualties among his own ranks at all cost at this point in the war did not demonstrate military efficiency but political stupidity. As he pointed out months later, in an explanatory pamphlet entitled *Military Thought of the Party*, "To make war, one must be a philosopher. C. Gonzalo poses battles politically, not technically."[6]

One of the most important demands of insurrection at this moment for Guzmán was to multiply the effect of upheaval. This went against not only the natural tendency of any military commander to protect his forces, but also an individual's instinct for self-preservation and a repugnance for killing if it could be avoided. Save for some exceptions, the Shining Path's attacks up to this point had not been systematically sanguinary.

A strange situation, that of a party chief occupying the most radical position, coldly ferocious, while his captains fought to maintain a more moderate course and tried to soften his orders.

Once the situation was defined, Guzmán provoked the National Conference II crisis. The objective was to increase the level of violence in the war exponentially and impose absolute authority over the organization—to make the Shining Path more lethal, to literally exert the power of life and death over his own.

To inflame war was not an end in itself, but rather had specific strategic and political objectives. Before looking at them, it is better to examine the radical change National Conference II brought to the Shining Path.

Taking place at the same time as the "beheadings" and purges, National Conference II was held to evaluate the state of the insurrection, define plans for action, and present advances in party doctrine. This dual plan was a clear expression of Guzmán's talent for running the party: how to carry out a comprehensive purge without paralyzing the organization, how to link this purge to the war's progress.

The evaluation of the insurrection was optimistic. "The party has carried out more than 3,500 actions during two years of armed struggle; more or less five actions a day." In January 1981, the long stage of "Developing the Guerrilla War" had begun, and would last until just before they achieved strategic equilibrium. Each segment of this stage had to be organized into hierarchical plans, so that each political or military act would be part of a planned effort and would contribute to it. Otherwise, the action would be wasted or, worse, would be counterproductive.

"The 'Development' has contributed a great deal," Guzmán noted in Conference II, "so today the problem is not to begin, but to win, to triumph." To achieve this, the party had to readjust its mechanisms, overcome inadequacies. The party's growth and the insurrection were fruit of the disciplined application of the correct method, the "guiding thought." For the purposes of the conference—if not for the most elated apologists—" 'guiding thought' is Marxism-Leninism-Maoism applied to our circumstances . . . as shown in the two-line struggle, the military line, and specific lines."

Until this moment, the "guiding thought" had been the exhaustive adaptation of "Mao Tse-tung thought" to the Peruvian situation; during Conference II, it emerged as a separate conceptual entity, not as a tool of "Mao thought." From this point forward, "guiding thought" came to be what "Mao thought" was during the Chinese Revolution: a young tree growing in the shade of those two venerable oaks, Marx and Lenin, eventually gaining their stature.

In order for "guiding thought" to take the place of historic "Mao thought," it was necessary to canonize Mao, to put him at the same level as Marx and Lenin. While until 1981, the Shining Path had continued to refer to "Mao Tse-tung thought" as a development of Marxist-Leninism,[7] in 1982, in *Let Us Develop the Guerrilla War!*, it spoke of "Marxism-Leninism-Maoism." Of course, this shift didn't go unnoticed in Peru or in international Maoist circles.[8] In treating Maoism as the third stage of Marxism, the Shining Path presented two simultaneous and audacious affirmations to Marxist-Leninist scholars. The first was explicit: the development of Maoism had become a fundamental part of the system. The second was implicit. If Maoism was now a finished concept, completed, then "guiding thought" was beginning to take its first young steps as the next stage of Marxist "development," filling in the prints left behind. This was the background to Conference II.[9]

The purge of the five Central Committee leaders was sharpened, therefore, when they were accused not only of having failed to follow "guiding thought," but also of attacking it. How else could they explain having discarded Comrade Gonzalo's plans and labeled him an "extremist"? If Guzmán was an extremist, then "guiding thought," his creation, was also extremist; and what these leaders proposed to do was throw it away. Maoism against Mao? "Guiding thought" against Guzmán? Only conspirators could dream up such a thing!

The reaction against the "conspirators" created an atmosphere ripe for the exaggerated reaffirmation of "guiding thought." Conference II "authorized" the need to "enthrone the guiding thought of C. Gonzalo" and also approved the party slogan of "Learn from C. Gonzalo . . . because he is support, is leadership . . . because he has firm principles, maintains the course, and brings it into being."

From that moment forward, an essential part of revolutionary commitment would consist of a declaration of "absolute submission to C. Gonzalo and to guiding thought" without discussion or criticism. Already during Conference II, the personality cult had acquired messianic trimmings. "We must think in a single way, this is not to shackle other people's thought, the problem is that guiding thought gives support to all of our activity . . . key is to enthrone guiding thought."

The importance given to the "correct" ideology took on a more specific aspect. Correct ideology was now the Second Coming under construction. "We have the most elevated ideology. . . . The key is gathering around guiding thought and the principle policies. We have the will to make all difficulties yield because we have the guiding thought and this is the key." One of the principle conclusions of Conference II sounds like a vow: "Two years of armed struggle have given us a great conquest: guiding thought, fusion of Marxist Leninism, Maoism in our Revolution; with it we rebuild the party, with it we begin armed struggle, with it we conquer bases, and with it we will triumph."

That was one of Guzmán's most important triumphs within the party. In the future, his voice would be the decisive one and his vote final. And the throne in which he and his cogitations had been exalted was not temporary, but rather one that had been prophesied. Now he could not be toppled by a vote, only by exorcism. And this would not be easy.

With the sunflower heads at his feet, the Jacobin prophet turned immediately to drawing out the strategic principles that would be applied henceforth, and to lay out their immediate plans.

The struggle was now to conquer power. And each aspect of struggle should be directed at the following "four matters on power":

1. Struggle for power for the party and for the people, and not for power for people, individuals, or bosses. (This was to prevent other outbreaks of Bonapartism; as far as Guzmán was concerned, the implicit paraphrasing was "I am the party.")
2. The basic principle of war: annihilate the enemy's basic force and preserve our own. We do not support absolute preservation, since this is tied to the problem of the quota.[10]
3. Strike: the immediate link to conquering support bases.
4. Establish support bases, that is [sic] the core of the popular war.

The second "matter" was that frigid mountain breeze, the consequences of which would persist until the 1986 prison massacre. To summarize, Guzmán maintained that it was necessary not only to fight for the revolution, but also to die for it. Blood was necessary to feed the flames, sacrifice to amass hate.

"We people with a plethora of faith . . . during the fourth plenary session, we promised to face down the bloodbath. . . . there is no one who fails to feel the blood shed by the people's children. . . . the quota is necessary; they have not died, their hearts live and beat within us."

Beyond the boundary of party jargon, Guzmán had clearly understood, and from the beginning, that a common trait shared by all the Communist guerrilla insurrections that had been successful was the high social cost of war. In Yugoslavia, China, and Vietnam (and the Soviet rearguard occupied by the Nazis), Communist guerrillas had consistently confounded their enemy's calculations because of their willingness to accept enormous sacrifice, even provoking reprisals with the goal of irreversibly polarizing the war. The way in which Guzmán understood the principle of the preservation of force had nothing to do with the numerical calculation of a military technician, but rather an evaluation of the political and military effect that a given sacrifice would produce as opposed to the advantage of survival for future actions. A complex calculation, to say the least, which Guzmán manipulated with imperturbable aloofness.

Commenting on the war's cost for the Shining Path, in December 1982, *Military Thought of the Party* mentions the advantage of sacrifice: "This is nothing but a good start, a fruitful beginning watered with good blood . . . this is nothing but a preview. . . . While yesterday, before the BAS [Beginning of the Armed Struggle], we did not know what it meant to lose lives in armed actions in our country, today we know it. This blood steels us . . . it makes us . . . more willing to ford any river, to cross hell, and to assault the heavens . . . the cost, in the end, is small."[11]

Soon after Conference II, a Regional Committee of the North leader interpreted, in simpler language, what was required: "Our struggle is a single one: deliver our lives. . . . We must sacrifice ourselves and obey."

The ruins of El Frontón were still four years away.

To Strike!

The same spirit of radicalization of war guided the drafting of the plan "To strike to advance to the support bases!" "To strike!" was the last stage of the plan "To unfurl the guerrilla war." Its purpose was to serve as a link to the future "Great Plan: To Conquer Bases," which would begin in January 1983 (and would last until December 1986). "To strike!" had a particular importance. The purpose was to increase pressure on the countryside and consolidate the offensive, with the goal of ending the state's presence in guerrilla zones and setting up the first "popular committees," the organs of the Shining Path government, embryo of future "support bases."

"To strike!" encompassed two campaigns and a brief rounding off. The slogans were simple: the plan had to be carried out simultaneously in every region, but centered on the "Principal Region." In the countryside, the slogan was unequivocal: "To raze." In the city, it was more nuanced: "To mobilize, undermine, assist." Primary importance was given to the countryside.

The Principal Region would act as a spearhead, with the other committees "in emulation." The task was "to disconnect the power of the large landowners, disrupt the power of the authorities, and hit the enemy's living forces." It had a simple territorial criteria: "Clean the zone, leave bare ground." In the city, actions were to be centered "principally against production," by entering "the very site of production." In addition, they were to begin actions termed "selective terrorism."

As the Shining Path document directly noted: "In To strike!, the key is to raze. And to raze means to leave nothing behind."

16

The Offer of Asylum to Guzmán

One of the strangest episodes in this strange war took place between May and July 1982. For a brief moment, the government believed it had won and acted as if it were simply negotiating victory. When the illusion vanished, the government attempted, more out of embarrassment than reasons of national security, to keep the details of this story secret.

On April 28, 1982, the head of State Security, General Guillermo Rivarola, informed Vice-Minister López Martínez that his agents had a lead that could change the war's course. In hiding, Abimael Guzmán appeared to be seriously ill and was deteriorating. The situation was so serious that, according to Rivarola's information, some of his closest collaborators and family members were trying to initiate negotiations with the government to get him out of the country.

López Martínez asked for more precise details. Rivarola supplied them. That day, in the "Marko" snack bar, an interview had taken place between a journalist and one of Guzmán's confidants. The confidant had asked the journalist "to intercede with President Belaúnde to get him out of the country because he suffered from acute anemia, and so the government would get rid of this headache." At the same time, according to the report, Guzmán's confidant had asked the journalist to interview "the number two in command, Osmán Morote."

190 OFFER OF ASYLUM

Perhaps the heady hopes aroused by this information helped cover up any trace of fraud. The thrill of a big chase seized the Interior Ministry. Rivarola received eager orders to broaden his investigation.

On May 5, López Martínez received a note from Rivarola indicating that a *Caretas* journalist was interviewing Guzmán at that moment. López Martínez ordered the journalist located immediately. Hours later, Rivarola reported that his agents had been unsuccessful in their efforts to find him. The police had only been able to confirm from the magazine that the journalist had left early with a photographer.

I was that journalist. I had not been doing an interview with Guzmán, but rather a daylong report on the Civil Guard's training schools, arranged weeks earlier. Few times had I been surrounded by as many police officers as during that day. López Martínez found out about this one or two days later,[1] and at that moment probably glimpsed the true dimension of police confusion. But how could he pass up this thrill, especially when victory seemed within his grasp?

Near the end of June, Rivarola arrived at the Interior Ministry visibly excited: his prey was within sight. His sources had let him know that Guzmán had arrived in Lima very ill and was staying, together with Augusta, his wife, in the home of his parents-in-law at Pershing 550, Jesús María. The house was surrounded by his detectives. They could make an arrest at any moment.

Accompanied by Rivarola, López Martínez went to Gagliardi's office and briefed him on the apparently final denouement. During the meeting, Rivarola received a call and went to the vice-minister's office to answer it.

When he returned, he brought another piece of news that electrified the minister and vice-minister. Rivarola had just been informed that the La Torre family had established contact with his people in State Security to begin negotiating Guzmán's surrender. They asked for guarantees that he wouldn't be killed and asked for him to be admitted into a clinic because he was suffering from an advanced stage of "kidney cancer" and needed almost constant dialysis.

All seemed to converge: the information on April 28 had indicated that Guzmán suffered from "acute anemia," caused, apparently, by kidney cancer. There was no time to lose. Gagliardi and López Martínez warned President Belaunde that they had to inform him about something of vital urgency, and headed for the Government Palace.

The minister and vice-minister told the president about the latest news. Although it was true that Guzmán had not been seen entering his father-in-law's house, all of their information indicated that he was there, practically on his deathbed. Was he guarded by his own people? Perhaps. It was possible that he would attempt to resist a violent arrest.

Belaunde did not display much enthusiasm for the news. After meditating on it for several moments, he said he did not want Guzmán to be captured under these circumstances. He thought the Shining Path chief wanted to die like a kamikaze, turning his death in a final attack on the government. If he were arrested and died in the process or later in police custody, Belaunde and his government would be accused of having murdered him and he would become a martyr. Belaunde did not want a martyr, much less one whose death would be laid at his government's door.

Gagliardi and López Martínez, that dialectic pair whose partnership inspired inevitable literary analogies, were for a moment overwhelmed by the same paradox. After bending over backward to capture Guzmán and other Shining Path leaders, it was now no longer appropriate to do so. Politics at the highest level, it must be admitted, shared the kingdom of paradox with Zen Buddhism.

What, then, to do? They arrived at what seemed the best solution: if Guzmán's days were numbered, let him die free, outside of government custody. They would guarantee that he would not be arrested if he chose to admit himself into a clinic or—and this was the best option—he would be given a immediate safe conduct if he chose to leave the country.

For the offer to have any effect, Guzmán had to harbor no doubt of its seriousness. If he received it via a police intermediary, he would consider it a trap. It was essential for the offer to be made publicly, through an authorized government spokesperson.

That same day, Minister Gagliardi made a public statement about internal security. Terrorism, he said, was practically under control. And, in harmony with this democracy's tolerant and generous principles and given that the government knew that Doctor Guzmán was "in ill health," he wanted to let Dr. Guzmán and his family know that the government would guarantee his safety if he admitted himself into any of the country's clinics or hospitals, and he should not fear arrest; or, if he preferred it, they were prepared to offer any assistance necessary for him to leave the country "with the family members he wishes to bring with him."[2] As López Martínez remembers, the intention was "to load him on an airplane and send him away."[3]

Meanwhile, following the spirit if not the letter of the president's instructions, "the operation to locate and stake out [Guzmán's whereabouts] was deactivated,"[4] avoiding any hint of a trick or trap in the offer made. The police officers posted around Carlos La Torre's house were withdrawn. Within the Interior Ministry, the anxious wait for a message from Guzmán or his family began.

Over the eventful weeks that followed, the rush of developments barely gave Gagliardi and López Martínez time to reflect on this confused episode. With the order to withdraw the police from Carlos La Torre's house, the police could rightfully claim that their hands had been tied and Guzmán had been allowed to escape. While this was certainly true, on the other hand, if he was so sick, how could he have escaped? Why had he not turned himself in? Why had he not taken advantage of the government's offer? Police informants had their own answers: according to some, Guzmán had died and Osmán Morote had taken over the Shining Path leadership. According to others, he continued to be in serious condition, a virtual prisoner of the Shining Path's hard-line leaders, who considered any negotiation with the government a betrayal. "So," López Martínez says, "it was never possible to determine if we could have captured him or not."[5]

Nevertheless, everything seems to indicate that the information Rivarola took to López Martínez was wrong. And the basic premise on which it rested, that Guzmán was ill, was never verified.

The "acute anemia" and "kidney cancer" attributed to the supposedly agonizing Guzmán seem to have originated in a diffuse recollection of the illnesses he suffered during the 1970s. At that time, it was common knowledge in Ayacucho that Guzmán had a "blood disease" (a detail that was included in some of the most insulting broadsides distributed by opposing groups). But Guzmán's sanguineous illnesses were very different from the ones detailed in police reports that aroused such hope and unintentionally revealing decisions, as sudden as they were unfounded.

Guzmán's Illnesses

Until 1972, Guzmán did not appear to have any significant health problem. On doctor's orders, he took a week off from work in September 1971, apparently to recover from a cold. But on June 5, 1972, Guzmán asked for leave from the university to undergo medical treatment in Lima. Permission was granted on June 20. On June 22, Guzmán submitted the paperwork "that proves treatment was received" and announced that he was reassuming his university duties.

On October 19, Guzmán asked for a leave of ten days, "because of illness, agreeing to support my request with the relevant paperwork." On October 23, he turned in a medical certificate, signed by Percy Cáceres Medina, which certified that Abimael Guzmán had been treated for "rheumatoid arthritis" and "blood irregularities."

On October 24, Guzmán gave a formal request for medical leave to university president Ishikawa "because of illness (the same one I have been suffering from since June of this year)." Together with the medical certificate, he attached a report from the National Institute of Cancerous Diseases, later returned to him. Nevertheless, the fact that Guzmán was treated in a place dedicated to cancer treatment filtered through to his enemies: the antifascist Federation of Revolutionary Students (FER), the Confederation of Revolutionary Workers (CTR), and the FUE, which, in the habitual war of paper insults slung back and forth in this period, drew grotesque caricatures over the caption "the cancerous one."

In November, Guzmán had to travel "urgently to the city of Lima . . . for personal health reasons," as he himself reported in a request for salary payment. Attached to the request was a certificate from a university doctor, Miguel Mariscal Llerena, reporting that Guzmán suffered from a "hematic reaction to high altitude" which required "specialized medical attention." After making his formal request, the university granted him time off for treatment.

On December 14, 1972, Percy Cáceres Medina certified that he was carrying out "extensive tests" on Guzmán, "to determine the factors that cause symptoms of a temporary lack of adaptation to high altitude." On December 19, Guzmán returned to Ayacucho and delivered written proof of treatment received, later returned to him.

In April 1973, Guzmán requested a monthlong leave, "including time for a medical checkup." Once the leave was over, on May 16 Guzmán requested an additional month off "because of illness." "As the authorities are aware," Guzmán wrote, "for at least a year, I have been suffering from polycythemia. Despite the treatment received, I have as yet not fully recovered." In the inevitable attached medical certificate, Percy Cáceres declared that he had been treating Guzmán from "October of 1972 to date, for polycythemia (polyglobulin), produced by his lack of adaptation to high altitude." Cáceres prescribed "thirty additional days at sea level . . . except in the case of complications."

In June, Guzmán asked for his leave to be extended for another thirty days. Finally, he returned to the university—where, meanwhile, the Shining Path had been the target of unprecedented attacks—only at the beginning of August 1973, after an absence of over three months.

The paperwork submitted by Guzmán at the time describes his health and its development. A blood test taken in the Miraflores Health Center on May 15, 1973, showed a hemoglobin level of 15.8 gm/dL with a hematocrit value of 42.5 percent. Repeated on June 16, the same analysis revealed a hemoglobin level of 15.5 gm/dL and a hematocrit value of 38 percent. An April 24 Schilling hematogram measured 5.2 million red blood cells and 9,700 leukocytes. Reevaluated on July 20, the same exam showed 4.2 million red blood cells and 5,400 leukocytes. On the surface, it wasn't a serious case, and it was clear that he enjoyed the usual recovery of those suffering from polycythemia upon his return to sea level.

Nevertheless, it was no longer possible for Guzmán to reside permanently in Ayacucho or any other mountain location. Any prolonged period at high altitude would result in a progressive deterioration—with the symptoms and risks inherent with polycythemia—which, nevertheless, would be reversed once he returned to sea level.

On September 24, 1973, Guzmán was confirmed as associate professor "for the term allowed by law." Nevertheless, that same day, the University Executive Council agreed to offer him a fellowship "at 75 percent salary" for the period of one year, once they received a proposal for a research project.

The project, "The Work of Mariátegui," was finished the following month, in Lima. Guzmán would never again live in Ayacucho for prolonged periods.

A year later, when the fellowship and leave had ended, Guzmán sent a memorandum to the university president from the Lima offices of San Cristóbal de Huamanga National University. He explained that it was impossible to return to Ayacucho since "only tomorrow will I be able to see the doctor who is treating me, who has been abroad."[6]

This time, the treatment was given by a dermatologist with the "Daniel A. Carrión" Tropical Medicine Institute at San Marcos University. This is the first time Guzmán reports being treated for psoriasis. However, his prescription suggests that it wasn't a serious case.

Guzmán rejoined San Cristóbal de Huamanga National University on October 31, 1974. Nevertheless, he reiterated his request for a leave on December 30 of the same year, because he was "suffering from an illness that requires special treatment."

In 1975, Guzmán's numerous sick leaves became just one more argument in the rancorous battle between Shining Path professors and their increasingly strong opposition.

On July 11, 1975, after the university began disciplinary proceedings as a result of the Huamán Poma de Ayala dispute,[7] Guzmán wrote to the university president from Lima explaining that he had had to leave Ayacucho urgently "for health reasons," which is why "until today I have not been able to submit the relevant paperwork." He asked that the president "take note of the state of my health as well as my need to request leave because of my illness." He also asked that "the charges in the process against me be forwarded to me, since it is not possible for me to be present in Ayacucho for the reasons I have noted."[8]

On July 15, Guzmán sent an additional request to President Ishikawa, emphasizing that his urgent trip to Lima had been due, "as has been informed in previous petitions, to the fact that I have been suffering from polycythemia for some time" and explaining that he could not have earlier explained his situation because "since I have been obligated to rest, it has not been possible for me to present the corresponding documentation any earlier."[9]

The request for a thirty-day sick leave that Guzmán had submitted met with hostility from the authorities who controlled the university, now enmeshed in open confrontation with Guzmán. Edilberto Lara, director of personnel, ordered an investigation of the medical certificate's authenticity and combed it for any bureaucratic error. Had it been endorsed correctly in one area of health care and not another? Should it have been included in this request or in a previous one? Why wasn't the medical certificate accompanied by laboratory reports? The implicit assumption of these inquiries was that Guzmán was lying; or, more likely, that it could be bureaucratically proved that he was lying.

On August 15, 1975, Guzmán directed himself, in a lengthy letter, to the university president and gave a detailed explanation of his health problems. Attaching thirty documents, Guzmán wrote that "in 1972, I began to suffer blood alterations, which even some medical colleagues in the university are aware of. . . . you can also see that I have gone for consultations to several Medical Centers like the National Institute for Cancerous Diseases, the Investigative Center of the Tropical Medicine Institute of San Marcos, the Anglo American Clinic, the Miraflores Health Center, and several doctors."

> All of this is due to the fact . . . that my body produced an initial multiplication of damaging elements of undetermined origin; later, polycythemia developed, from my body's overreaction to high altitude; later, I developed psoriasis; and finally, my polycythemia persists and has grown worse. I ask that you pay special attention to how rapidly my presence in Ayacucho dangerously elevates, in terms of my health, the hematocrit value and hemoglobin percentages, which could produce future repercussions or unexpected and damaging alterations. At the same time, I ask that the percentages referred to over the years be compared and it will become evident that from November 1974 to May 1975 they have increased more than in previous years. And that, in addition, let it be kept in mind that my body's reaction to high altitude is not due to the height [*sic*] of Ayacucho; although I have lived in this city since 1962, I only began to suffer from polycythemia beginning in 1972.[10]

Guzmán added that "as is known, polycythemia demands a life at sea level and adequate medical supervision; today, this is more pressing for my health than in previous occasions, so that I can recover and normalize my sanguineous formula and determine . . . if it will be possible for me or not, physically speaking, to return immediately to live at a high altitude like that of Ayacucho." After this detailed and apparently straightforward explanation, Guzmán asked for an additional leave of three months for reasons of illness, "with rights to a salary."[11] The leave was granted, but his salary was progressively reduced by a fourth with each passing month.

Guzmán never returned to Ayacucho as a university professor. On January 26, 1976, he resigned his professorship.

Seen in perspective, Guzmán's illnesses had an important impact on internal battles within the university; and his forced absences coincided with a decline in Shining Path hegemony. With Guzmán far away, university authorities, until then intimidated by Guzmán's Stalinist proclivities and the cold authority with which he managed the contest for power, were increasingly audacious in confronting the Shining Path.

In more general terms, Guzmán's illness forced organizational readjustments within the Shining Path. Increasingly, Guzmán had to delegate daily decision making for the party in Ayacucho and its different apparatuses beginning in 1973. As of that year and more so thereafter, his place of residence—and, consequently, the Shining Path headquarters—was in Lima and La Cantuta, with short trips to Ayacucho and other mountain destinations only for specific events. The effect this had on Guzmán's character—his irascibility, the barely contained tension, the increasingly imperious, biting content of his decisions—seems to mirror the effect his condition had on his health: the rapid increase in blood density in particularly rebellious moments of tension or frustration, which forced rapid descents to Lima and near immobility until his blood "thinned out" again.

But it would be wrong to extract too many conclusions from these episodes. Guzmán was no invalid. After a period of adaptation to the limits imposed by his illness, he adjusted the organization, party control, and his own work to these new conditions. At the very least, polycythemia played an important role in spurring Guzmán to speed up the organization's conversion to clandestinity, to move around cadres and prepare for the insurrection.

There is something of a cruel paradox—or perhaps poetic justice—in the fact that Guzmán shared an important trait with another rebel leader whom he so belittled and railed against: Che Guevara. Guevara lived with the constant fear of a sudden ambush of asthma, the surprise strangulation of his bronchial cavities. For his part, Guzmán suffered the inevitable migraines, the sensation of the progressive solidification of his blood due to polycythemia, the disagreeable peelings and scaling of psoriasis. In both cases, the obligatory resignation to illness simultaneously spurred action, the desire to mobilize men and loyalties, cut through delays toward the realization of a goal. The difference lies in the fact that Guzmán was the better planner and a superior strategist.

Was there anything, then, to the information that mobilized General Rivarola in 1982? All seems to indicate that it was a flawed conjecture based on Guzmán's medical history, not a concrete fact. Obviously, the "acute anemia" alleged by the first report was the last of the problems that would afflict Guzmán. "Kidney cancer" appears to be an erroneous interpretation of the problems he had with his blood and the insults of "the cancerous one" that persisted in collective memory. That Guzmán may have been immobilized is, of course, believable; but this did not suggest any imminent expiration, but rather a recent return—after too long a stay— in the mountains. But it is improbable that Guzmán, a person who took pains to preserve his safety in clandestinity, would have engaged in the imprudence of staying in his parents-in-law's house, where he had been last arrested in 1979.

Other factors also lead me to believe that the information was false: soon after this episode, the La Torre family left the country voluntarily and traveled to exile in

Sweden. And a few months later, after the fall of Vilcashuamán, a bag with Guzmán's personal documents was found near the destroyed police headquarters. At the time, widely different interpretations were made of this strange discovery. But, considering the circumstances that surrounded this attack on the police barracks,[12] the public invocation made by Minister Gagliardi to the supposedly agonizing Guzmán, and the importance that this attack has been given in the Shining Path pantheon, my impression is that Guzmán was there, and that his documents were a kind of calling card directed at Belaunde and Gagliardi. This dialogue with obvious symbols—the monosyllabic rumble of explosions after the premature declarations of triumph made by some minister, the darkness of the "pope-out" power cuts as an answer to John Paul II's calls for peace—had become habit for the Shining Path. I could be wrong, but I don't see a better interpretation.

The other fact that does seem clear is that wherever Guzmán habitually stays, it is certainly not the mountains. Since the war began, his presence in the mountains seems only to have been relatively brief. Out of necessity, the Shining Path *incahuasi*[13] is probably located in the country's large cities or in the jungle, not in the Andean range.

17

The Colloquium of the Blind
The Intelligence War

After the embarrassing episode of the asylum offer to Guzmán and the stepped-up Shining Path offensive, the demand for reliable information about the Shining Path and its leadership reached levels of near desperation within the Interior Ministry.

Information should have been plentiful. There were so many intelligence services that, even if each one could only get a little information, the combination of forces should have provided an intimate portrait of the Shining Path. And they attempted to do just that. Vice-Minister López Martínez held regular meetings with each of the chiefs of the armed forces intelligence services. For their part, the intelligence heads of the police forces coordinated the exchange of information with their military counterparts in periodic meetings in the ministry, presided over by the chief of the National Intelligence Service (SIN).[1]

In theory, the SIN was at the top of the hierarchy within the "intelligence system." Within the distribution of functions of a supposedly harmonic pyramid, the SIN—whose responsibilities lay within the realm of "strategic intelligence"—was basically in charge of analyzing information collected by the other services, and distributing their conclusions according to the type and scope of the information. In practice, as is true across the globe although with particular variations, the diverse intelligence organizations held back or denied information, dedicating much of their energy to watching each other—or people who made their chiefs uncomfort-able—and celebrating other services' failures. From this point of view, the last several years had been an endless party. At the same time, the different services shared, at times without knowing it, informers and analysts. So the intelligence community's incestuous character was one of the problems that influenced its ability to get and identify fresh and useful information. But it wasn't the only problem. During part of 1982, the SIN was led by army general Ludwig Essenwanger. Despite his name, General Essenwanger was not only a Peruvian, but a provincial one, from Cañete. Minister Gagliardi, also from Cañete, initially thought that Essenwanger's presence would result in a fluid interchange of information. "I have had long conversations with my fellow Cañetan Essenwanger, Cañetan to Cañetan. I have asked of him: Listen to me, help me with this. . . . of course, I asked for help from the air force, but there was nothing definite."[2]

Over its troubled history, the SIN has been more often in need of help than able to give it. Under Velasco Alvarado, the SIN's position was ambiguous. On the one hand, preference was clearly given to the army's intelligence service. On the other hand, the SIN was no bureaucratic boneyard, but an office of power. With the exceptions of General Eduardo Segura, whose star was extinguished during the final leg of his career, and General Rudecindo Zavaleta—who years later would resurface, tied to Rodríguez López—the other chiefs named by Velasco were soldiers who had his trust and occupied, both then and afterward, important positions: Generals Pedro Richter, Enrique Gallegos, Rafael Hoyos Rubio.

Under the Morales Bermúdez administration, the attempt to take apart the SIN seems to have been more determined. With Peru's economy devastated, its budget remained constant (which automatically meant cuts proportional to inflation). As one veteran employee noted, "it was considered a residual byproduct of the army. They only sent spineless generals or colonels with no future."[3] With resources in critical short supply, the SIN had agreed to employ officers sent by their institutions for a year's service, if they were lucky. But most affected by these conditions was the network of informers that, in any intelligence service engaged in internal sur-veillance, formed the central vertebrae in the process of acquiring information.

According to sources within the institution, the number of paid informants working for the SIN numbered 300 at the beginning of the Morales Bermúdez administration. A significant number had been "seeded" in Andahuaylas and nearby areas after the 1973 land takeovers. Over the following years, they began to pay them per report, then later reduced their overall number. After a time, the number of informers was reduced to thirty. By the time Morales Bermúdez left office, only a handful were left.

Languishing, the SIN experienced a partial recovery between 1976 and 1978, under the leadership of General Juan Schroth Carlín. Schroth was a serious soldier, who some SIN employees considered the best intelligence chief they had under military rule. "He tried to closely follow the formation of subversive groups. . . . To a degree, the Shining Path organization and groups close to it were followed."[4] Others thought of him as a hard worker, dedicated and disciplined, but of limited intelligence. "He was alright, but had a limited grasp."[5]

In any case, Schroth had two basic limitations: his relationship with the military president, Morales Bermúdez, was not good and he was a rabid anti-Communist, blind to important differences between leftist groups.

In addition, under the Schroth administration, the final stage of the bloody war against guerrilla and terrorist movements in the Southern Cone took place. To a great degree, the attention of the intelligence services was occupied with observing the development of the conflict, and interchanges between the homologous services in the affected countries were constant and intense. In the case of Peru, the most fluid relationship was with the Argentines, but it wasn't the only one. "It was possible to have cases where diplomatic relations were poor, but intelligence agreements continued to function. Agreements existed with Ecuador and even Chile."[6]

Only with difficulty could the SIN's cooperation with Argentine intelligence have been greater throughout the dirty war. In several documented cases, Argentines tied to the Montoneros were arrested in Lima by mixed groups of Argentine police and SIN agents, interrogated under torture in Peru, and later delivered—generally, at the Bolivian border—to the Argentines. The arrest of Noemí Gianotti de Molfino ended in a strange and sinister way: detained in Peru and delivered to Argentine intelligence, Molfino later was found dead in a Madrid apartment.[7]

The practical consequences of this cooperation were multiple and, in almost all cases, adverse. The Velasco-era model was completely abandoned, without even saving its best lessons. The true north of efficiency was now thought to be the way in which the Brazilian, Uruguayan, and Chilean militaries had done away with armed insurrection and even the militant opposition within their countries. There was not only a sense of solidarity with the Argentine soldiers responsible for the dirty war, but also admiration and respect for the combination of systematic cunning, organization, and brutality employed by their armed forces to pulverize the Montoneros and ERP.

From this vantage point, the intelligence services, and especially the SIN, dedicated themselves to finding the national equivalents of the Tupamaros, Montoneros, or ERP in Peru, or their precursors in the social tumult. Blind to context, awaiting the repetition of the insurrectional recipe concocted in the Southern Cone so that they could apply the same counterinsurgency antidote, they did not waste time on substantial differences in history and so did not collect any of the details that daily reality offered up. Under Schroth, where many of those who led the intelligence efforts in the war against the Shining Path worked, this essential limitation was in great measure shared by the armed forces in general and filtered into the counterinsurgency strategies carried out over the following years.

A little before the military government's exit and the civilian return, Morales Bermúdez removed Schroth from the SIN and replaced him with General Mario Villavicencio Alcázar. It was Villavicencio's luck to be the last SIN chief under military rule and the first under the democratic regime. His legacy was quite poor, although there is a difference of opinion as to why. According to one version, Villavicencio directed the dismantling of the SIN under orders from the Morales Bermúdez government, but was also motivated by personal interest.[8] According to others, Villavicencio was bound by a thankless mission: the dismantling of the SIN with the added restriction of limited access to Belaunde. "These were six months of difficult work. Belaunde almost physically spurned the intelligence service. Villavicencio had a difficult time with access. They would make him wait for up to two hours." Yet the same person admits that, in any case, Villavicencio did not bring high-quality information. "Fears were limited to Red Homeland, to Hugo Blanco."[9]

At the end of 1980, when Villavicencio was transferred, his replacement was General Essenwanger, who remained at the head of the SIN in 1981 and 1982. A consensus exists in qualifying his tenure as extremely poor. In 1982, then deputy Alan García publicly claimed that Essenwanger's brother, Walter, was in custody and charged with terrorism—which was true. In García's judgment, this disqualified Essenwanger from acting as the chief of, theoretically, the country's most important intelligence apparatus. Walter Essenwanger was freed by judicial order that same year, but Ludwig Essenwanger resigned his post at the head of the SIN in September 1982.

During these years of deep depression, Essenwanger's family relations were the least of the SIN's problems. Without valuable sources of information, its few available resources badly administered, the SIN analysts dedicated themselves simply to surviving. "These were years of vegetating. We lived off of only what other agencies gave us."[10]

When put up against the demand to produce intelligence, this informative desert created an especially ingenious bureaucracy that depended on secondhand information and the mirroring of information. This process infected every level of intelligence gathering, but it achieved an especially artistic expression within the SIN. There, the best analysts had created their own fabric of contacts with other intelligence services, especially those with the greatest operative capacity. These were informal relationships of mutual convenience, since the other services sought to take advantage of the SIN specialists' analytical abilities to interpret or simply "clothe" their facts. For instance, *Rogelio Ramírez* was accustomed to filling out his reports "with snippets of articles published in newspapers and magazines, a couple of visits, and the knowledge of how the left operates. The writing was done in intelligence jargon, and the cake was baked. Four or five hours of work per week was enough to turn in a report that would frequently prompt the SIN chief immediately to order his car and go to the Government Palace to inform the president of this latest, urgent discovery. I could dedicate the rest of the week to the things that interested me."[11]

In this demoralized atmosphere, it was inevitable that the experienced analysts—shared, as it has been noted, among most of the agencies—would come to an informal agreement on how to feed information or, more frequently, the appearance of information to their bosses and how much to dole out. They harbored no desire to sabotage, but merely to survive within the bureaucracy. It was the cunning of malnutrition: how to make food last as long as possible, how to fool hunger with mere flavor, how to improve appearance with leavening agents. It is perhaps mere idleness to add that this was no esoteric game, but rather something perceived with more or less clarity at all levels of government. But so long as the appearance of movement supplanted movement itself, bureaucratic beheadings could be delayed indefinitely, careers could be topped off with comfortable retirements, and for a time these state offices could be converted into the private property of whomever was at their head.

Examples of this process were, naturally, a theme of great interest among the informal community of analysts during their infrequent meetings. These civil employees in an apparatus controlled by soldiers, inferior institutionally, were called "nobodies" in Lima slang, in some cases by pedantic or incompetent bosses. Yet they achieved secret satisfaction in their intellectual superiority, taking pleasure in knowing more things about their bosses than these men could possible suspect, including the relationship between changes in official bank accounts and the personal accounts of their bosses.

Even then, some of the uses to which the intelligence system was put scandalized even these hidebound sensibilities. This was the case, for example, of the son of a SIN director who loved to race cars. While his father headed the SIN, the boy took part in almost every race—driving SIN cars. "What's worse is that he was a terrible driver. He didn't win a single race and destroyed, literally destroyed, what remained of our fleet of official cars. . . . instead of being used in something that even vaguely resembled a work-related task, the cars we used for surveillance and to follow suspects who were far behind the race leaders at some point on the highway between Chalhuanca and Cusco."[12]

The anguished demand for information or actions that would locate or neutralize the Shining Path leadership, especially Abimael Guzmán, inspired the SIN to carry out some operations. The first was in 1982–83; the second—to refer to it pushes forward this story's narrative thread—was in 1984. This latter one had a suggestive, though not original name: "Scorpio."

Both were costly and had the same result: zero. "The only difference," comments one of the analysts, "was that after these operations, some of the chiefs built houses. It seems that these operations have a special relationship with the level of private construction."

If the situation was desolate at the pyramid's peak (where, at least theoretically, the SIN could be found), then each of the other intelligence services had defects and limitations that were equally significant. The police intelligence services—whose efficiency was literally a question of life or death for emergency zone officers—were clearly among the most troubled.

The Civil Guard intelligence chief during 1981 and part of 1982 was Colonel Juan Zárate Gambini. Zárate was a relatively young officer, energetic and self-assured; he had both training and talent in tactics. However, his duties only touched this area tangentially.

In the torturous and frequently pathetic battles for promotions and first place within each rank, Zárate had played his cards handily up to then, but not so well as to have avoided bitter enemies and rivalries within his institution. During Balaguer's insubordination, Zárate had thrown in his lot with Catter and the new command almost from the first. This clearly gave Zárate's career a tremendous boost, while that of his eternal rival, GC colonel Félix Tumay, had been paralyzed. At the same time, the "institutionalists" allied with Balaguer viewed Zárate with hostility paired with an implicit vow to engage in future acts of vengeance.

In lashing his fortune to the inept commander Catter, Zárate had taken on a heavy, inert load. Yet it was clear, on the other hand, that for a young and ambitious colonel there was no alternative.

Civil Guard intelligence had been one of the most valuable services in providing reports about the Shining Path as the insurrection was being prepared. Far from surprising, this was due to the broad territorial coverage of Civil Guard posts. That had also been why the Shining Path had led mass mobilizations to force them out of critical areas.

Nevertheless, the clarity and finally the quality of information collected was directly related to the training and perceptiveness of the officers at each post, generally quite limited. The Lima analysts, who received raw information, were often incapable of winnowing value from the chaff that surrounded it; and the few times they succeeded, their efforts were ignored by the military government.

In 1981, Zárate brought together a staff of young officers with some initial training in the field and tried to take advantage of the information in his files and to exploit to the fullest whatever came in. In perspective, the results were not bad. A not insignificant number of Shining Path leaders were captured between 1981 and March 1982, so many that the Shining Path made a priority out of setting them free. As Héctor López Martínez notes, even in this calamitous tune, there were some redemptive notes: "The attack on the Ayacucho prison can be seen in a positive light. . . . a significant number of important Shining Path elements had been captured. Some were prominent at the highest levels within the organization. These captures had been made basically in 1981. Barreto made many arrests."[13]

But even in its best moments, the GC intelligence service was far from perceiving the depth and breadth of the Shining Path organization, or grasping the speed and rhythm of its attacks. Its relative successes fell well within the Shining Path leadership's own calculation of losses deemed inevitable in the stage of "To strike the countryside" and "To unfurl the guerrilla war." Limitations were many and stretched from the progressive erosion of sources as police posts in threatened areas were lost or closed to the inability of police analysts to comprehend—through the use of structured reasoning—the Shining Path's complex revolutionary system. As has been noted, Zárate's special talent was for tactical operations. At this level, he enjoyed good results, especially within the city of Ayacucho. But beyond this, one enters a level of blindness which—it must be said—the Civil Guard shared with the rest of the country.

Other factors that had a direct influence on results were less excusable. The ferocious jealousies between different police agencies and their combined attitude toward the military resulted in the interchange of little information (except, of course, the routine garbage), a poor coordination of operations, and an emphasis on the failure of others in order to mitigate one's own.

In this sad game, Zárate had before him—despite his willingness to carry out his duties—insuperable limitations. To this was added the incident that led to his exit. In the meetings of the "intelligence community" that had taken place routinely since the end of 1981, the energetic and quarrelsome colonel let his opinions be known in a way that the other directors, especially Essenwanger, found increasingly difficult to bear. Insult was added to injury when the Civil Guard captured Essenwanger's brother. Soon afterward, after some meetings during which Zárate was more belligerent that usual, the directors of military intelligence and the SIN declared him, with sublime snobbishness, "persona non grata" in the "intelligence community" and informed Gagliardi of their solemn accord.

Zárate had to leave his post as intelligence director, having won himself new and important enemies. Nevertheless, the principal one, Essenwanger, had more important things to worry about soon afterward when Deputy Alan García received "from a reliable source" information about his brother, Walter. As is evident, the Byzantine wars raged and the real war was forgotten.

Over the following years, Zárate managed, against all predictions, to survive changes in command and, above all, Balaguer's return to the Civil Guard. After having kept himself just out of Balaguer's reach in posts that depended directly on the interior minister, he was named second-in-command of the GC antidrug police in 1984. In 1985, after the Rodríguez López scandal, he became its commander. His tactical efficiency then found almost unlimited possibility. Numerous operations, daring and cunning, had the personal stamp of Zárate, now a general and apparently free of any institutional vulnerability. Of course, repeated on this new front was the same dynamic that characterized his work in intelligence in 1981 and 1982: because they always fell short of the true dimension of the problem, these regularly successful operations only served to illustrate the magnitude of his strategic defeat.

In 1981, the Investigative Police intelligence service was led by recently promoted PIP general José Jorge Zárate. As has been explained, Zárate was a key person in the drug-trafficking organization within the PIP command headed by Reynaldo Rodríguez López and had been connected to it since 1975. The deteriorating situation created ideal conditions for the gang to camouflage its activity within the covert actions and secret polls that were supposed to form part of counterinsurgency intelligence gathering.[14] With the backing of the institution's command structure, the intelligence leadership was in a strategic position to control police chiefs disgusted with the exponential increase in corruption and who were tempted to launch their own investigations. The fight between Luque and Ipinze was still too recent to be easily forgotten. By exploiting his position, Jorge began to be feared by his equals and even by those who outranked him in tenure and experience.

Certainly, Jorge was not an enemy to be taken lightly. Within the PIP, he was known as very intelligent and especially good at establishing beneficial social relationships (which, within the PIP, had always been important). He was the valedictorian, designated by the title "sword of honor," of his graduating class, and was destined to command his institution. What to outside observers would have been perceived as Jorge's greatest defect, that he was an almost compulsive gambler, was within the PIP frequently considered a virtue: gambling permitted him to establish advantageous social relationships within the intense and complicated crucible of chance. Debts, loans, obligations, secrets, desperation: wasn't this a field where police talents flourish? But whatever Jorge's talents were, they were never applied to the fight against the Shining Path. It is impossible to give a detailed description here of Rodríguez López's organization. It is enough to note that as far as the functioning of the intelligence services was concerned, PIP corruption was so pronounced during that critical period that it effectively paralyzed vital areas within the institution.

When Jorge left the directorship of PIP intelligence, his post was occupied by PIP general Teófilo Aliaga. At the time, there was speculation within the PIP that the history of the organization over the following years would be dominated by the fight for command between Jorge and Aliaga. In good measure, it was, although both ended up losing. Somewhat older than Jorge, Aliaga was also the "sword of honor" of his graduating class. Since his time as a cadet, under Manuel Prado's second administration, he had excelled within the investigative police. At the time, discrimination against the future investigators by the Civil Guard, the dominant institution with the most social prestige and which controlled the only police academy, was crushing.

During a visit to the academy made by Government Minister Ricardo Elías Aparicio (minister between 1960–62), Cadet Teófilo Aliaga, ignoring possible reprisals, spoke publicly to the minister to protest the discrimination and mistreatment the investigators suffered and asked that the investigators be made independent of the Civil Guard. The minister was deeply impressed, independence was granted, and for a time Aliaga was an institutional hero. Yet his status did not place him beyond the reach of the laws that govern the rise and fall of careers within the police department.

Under Schroth, during the second part of the military government, Aliaga was assigned to the SIN. As with almost all of the officers serving at the time, the distortion of the Argentine prism affected his understanding of the Shining Path insurrection.

In any case, when Aliaga took command of PIP intelligence, the level of neglect from central command was such that only a performance bordering on the miraculous could have resuscitated it. In contrast with Jorge, Aliaga could not count on other PIP commanders' favor. Although, over the following years, he did his best not to antagonize them, his position as an outsider was a clear disadvantage.

As director of intelligence, Aliaga lasted a few months. Afterward, he managed to be transferred to the migrations office, where his direct dependence on the Interior Ministry gave him protection from the PIP leaders. Nevertheless, Aliaga was not completely cut off. Months after having left the intelligence service, Aliaga, together with the then GC colonel Félix Tumay and Director of Government José Terry, tried to form an ad hoc intelligence group that depended directly on the interior minister (in shorthand, called Coamin). The group met several times before being dissolved by Minister Gagliardi. During the Belaunde years, Aliaga was a cautious careerist, attempting to keep alive any chance he had to take command of his institution. When the Apra triumphed in 1985, it seemed that his patiently cultivated relationships would at last bear definitive fruit. The crumbling of the Rodríguez López organization spelled the end of Jorge, and it seemed as if all obstacles to his gaining command of the PIP had been removed. Nevertheless, the Apristas who took over the Interior Ministry had other plans, and Aliaga was also "invited" to retire.

Beginning in 1982, an operative group within the PIP obtained the best results. The "Dicote" (later rebaptized as the "Dircote," the Counterterrorism Headquarters) had not had a promising start. Organized as an operative division within State Security, its creation was, apparently, a response to continuing acts of terrorism and sabotage by the Shining Path in Lima. However, its bureaucratic reason for being had another, more important inspiration. State Security has been one of Ipinze's main worries ever since PIP general Edgar Luque Freyre had decided, in the words of López Martínez, to "show his hand" and offer the new Popular Action administration his experience in the security field. To Ipinze's great alarm, after the poor showing of another police chief, Luque was named director of State Security in 1981. In order to neutralize him, Ipinze set up Dicote, placing at its head an officer who was particularly addicted to him, PIP colonel Héctor Agurto Cisneros.

Agurto not only was godfather to Ipinze's children, but owed him his institutional resurrection. In effect, Agurto had been relieved of his PIP duties just before Ipinze assumed command, because of accusations related to his private life. Under normal circumstances, once an officer has been relieved of duties, return to the institution is just short of impossible. That he had not only returned, but had been given command of a division of vital importance, clearly showed just how much he owed Ipinze and what Ipinze expected of him.[15]

With such an unpromising beginning, the Dicote would seem to have been destined to no role other than that of hampering the work of State Security. Initially, it operated as a PIP station in Miraflores's Porta Street, in an old and neglected house obviously unsuited to police work and with the look, seen from the outside, of having suffered an abrupt humiliation.

In August 1981, I interviewed Agurto there. The colonel had a resonant voice and a studied, almost unctuous manner. He was obviously astute, and his most eye-catching inconsistencies were frequently masked by his effort to appear worldly. But it was clear that together with this image—the image he would, without doubt, want to be remembered for and presented with before God the Father—there was another, much less presentable one, which revealed itself again and again and permitted a much better interpretation of the many vicissitudes of his fate.

Even then, Dicote managed to make some important captures in the latter half of 1981. However, given the demands of the situation, the balance of his productivity was negative.

In 1982, Agurto was "invited" to retire, and this time his exit was definitive. State Security had gained a new chief, PIP general Guillermo Rivarola. Dicote was moved to a State Security office in the Prefecture, and PIP colonel Víctor Gastelú was named as its new head.

Over the following months (and to a great degree, over the following years), State Security was converted, through the Dicote office, into the state's only defense unit that delivered regular and consistent results in the fight against the Shining Path. From the police point of view, there were moments in which all of the important cases in Lima were resolved. Of course, this was not enough to stop all Shining Path actions in Lima—much less in the rest of the country—since the Shining Path only used in its campaigns elements within the organization that could be replaced, since it assumed that operatives would probably be caught. Nevertheless, within the limitations of police work, Dicote braked the Shining Path's advance in Lima.

Over the first months of 1982, Rivarola maintained effective control over State Security. With a frame predisposed to excess weight and an affable style that tended to turn pompous in formal situations, at first glance Rivarola didn't appear to be the right person to head State Security. The results he produced, however, were superior to those of all of his predecessors. And both Gagliardi and López Martínez highly valued his commitment: "I believe that the best [State Security chief] has been Rivarola. Both for the results and the example he set for his subordinates."[16]

Since Dicote did most of the work, it was natural for the relations between Rivarola and Dicote chief Víctor Gastelú to become increasingly tense week by week, case by case. There was both a clash of styles and bureaucratic jealousies. In addition, and this was perhaps the fundamental reason, Gastelú was a stubborn cop, tenacious, a hard worker, who believed he had a clear vision of what to do in Lima about the Shining Path and he was sure that he was the most able to direct police operations.

In many aspects, Gastelú was not a typical police officer. While most officers had been trained in the Officers' School, Gastelú had begun his career in 1949 among the lower ranks, as an auxiliary policeman attached to the then Investigative and Vigilance Corps. Only after several years of work and repeated attempts had he been admitted into Officers' School. As an officer, his promotions had been, for the most part, arduous and long delayed. The difficulties of his career were in part explained by his family's affiliation to the Apra. Gastelú was the godson of Haya de la Torre, and his police career had swayed in good measure to the beat of the Apra's political ups and downs. From 1980 to 1985, now in the critical stage of his career, Gastelú used only his first name: Víctor. In 1985, after Alan García's victory, his full name, Víctor Raúl (which in itself in Peru constitutes a political declaration), was proudly unfurled, perhaps for the first time. The problem then was that there were too many Víctor Raúls or their equivalents.

Gastelú had spent most of his career in State Security. Because of this, he was able to bring with him to Dicote several of the best officers who had formerly served with him or who had been his students in courses he gave for future officers. Some of them had served under Agurto and so could provide a certain continuity.

Under Gastelú's leadership, Dicote began to operate almost from ground zero. Considering the obvious seriousness that Shining Path attacks had already assumed, the conditions under which they worked are an eloquent testimony to the astonishing ineptitude with which the Peruvian state confronted the Shining Path war.

While the offices belonging to any of the numerous PIP generals, even those of the most redundant ones, were spacious, had at least one direct telephone line, and had an amazing abundance—kitschy, but no less real—of office equipment, the entire Dicote was housed in only three rooms at the rear of the Prefecture. For several months, it had just one telephone extension, not a single radio, and not even a vehicle. In the first weeks, neither did it have its own files. In addition to having to depend on the little collected by State Security, their deficiencies necessarily determined their operational style.

Without previous intelligence on Shining Path actions, Gastelú persuaded Rivarola to scatter patrols in places where there was the greatest likelihood of attacks. The first arrests were blind, but Dicote began to open individual files on suspects (it eventually had more than 5,000 files). After a few weeks, its intelligence was increasingly accurate and police operations more specific. They could not follow suspects, as much for a lack of personnel as poor communications. Operative teams would normally take part only in predetermined missions. Dicote came to have seven operative groups, each with four men.

Even a slightly elevated number of arrests would make the State Security offices creak. Detainees were grouped in two of the three Dicote rooms. A police officer, always hooded, was assigned to each one to keep the prisoner incommunicado. Under these conditions, which were abusive by definition, other outrages occurred, which, if not inevitable, were certainly difficult to prevent.

Was torture the Dicote's normal form of interrogation? Although the existence of cases of torture during interrogation—despite Gastelú's vehement denials the numerous times I interviewed him—lie beyond any reasonable doubt, and seemed to me to be frequent, I believe that their intensity during the first three months of war was less than that experienced in other Investigative Police units. I can't explain this lesser incidence, but it is possible that if one exists, it is related as much to the greater complexity of the investigations as well as the specialization of most Dicote officers.

To serve in State Security was one of the least coveted fates within the PIP since the beginning of the Shining Path insurrection. The reason was simple: no one got rich in Security. While behind every appointment to the narcotics or white-collar crime divisions lay furious competition, the opposite was the case in Security. For many police officers, to be sent meant exile from their true professional destiny. For this reason, the officers that remained in Security year after year owed their fates to either very powerful enemies or a real commitment to their work. With few exceptions, these latter officers were among the most intelligent within their institution, and one of Gastelú's smartest moves was to surround himself with a good number of them.

In perspective, it is curious to see how, in more than one way, the work conditions within Dicote constituted a mirror image of those within the Shining Path. On both sides, the competitors waged a war of the poor. The Shining Path had, literally, converted this need into a virtue, and the Dicote detectives weren't far behind. For example, the few police officers who engaged in following suspects and needed to get in touch with the office had to find a public telephone wherever one could be found, call the PIP switchboard, and ask the always overburdened operator to transfer the call to the extension, usually busy, of the boss. In that very office, conditions were sometimes so incredibly clogged and unsecured, with detainees being held within, that during the frequent power blackouts, each detective was assigned one or more detainees to watch over personally. As long as the blackout lasted, the detective had to hold on. It may be redundant to point out that they had no emergency generator or anything of the sort.

Even under these conditions, this unit's productivity outstripped that of any other group. With truly miserable salaries, especially since they risked their lives every day, the officers and some of the support staff frequently put in ten- to fifteen-hour days for days on end. Officers like then commander Javier Palacios had several artists making drawings of the Shining Path organization and mode of operation, directed the analysts who read seized manuscripts, grilled other officers on the precise meaning of Shining Path terminology, and took part in planning new operations. Aside from the sins and excesses common to police work in Peru, the Dicote's dedication during this period was notable. To compare it to the attitude of other units, lazy and corrupt, is instructive. It seems to confirm a strange and somewhat disquieting constant in our institutional history: the poorly equipped group, yet the one with a capable and motivated leadership, has always achieved the best results.[17]

In the relative terms of Peruvian reality, success created new problems. Rivarola had been transformed into the only bearer of good tidings that the government could count on. Gagliardi and López Martínez tried to have ever more frequent contact with him, underscoring his new status to the PIP chief.

New alliances were inevitable. Just as Rodolfo Ballesteros assumed command of the PIP (his predecessor, Rómulo Alayza, left on January 17, 1983, months after being publicly reprimanded by the attorney general for passing on false information in the most important drug-trafficking case up to that time, the case against Carlos Langberg), he began to maneuver to cut off Dicote from State Security. Gastelú, who expected to benefit from this change, supported the initiative with enthusiasm.

Through the usual bureaucratic maneuvering, Dicote gained the category of headquarters, the same level as State Security. As a consequence, its name changed to Dircote. Over the following weeks, it was sent pickup trucks and given new offices at the rear of the Prefecture. For Gastelú, nevertheless, the change was the beginning of a comic opera of office politics that continued even as this book was being written. Its central plot was his prolonged and always frustrated attempt to assume the Dircote command (and later that of the institution), imbued with that combination of almost fulfilled hope and sudden failure that Sylvester the Cat and Wiley Coyote know so well.

Once Dircote was formed, Ballesteros let Gastelú know that a mere colonel could not command a head office, and offered to make him a general in six months if he remained patient. Meanwhile, PIP general Agurio Saldívar, who had just finished a term in Ayacucho, assumed the Dircote command. But Agurio didn't bring the best portents for Gastelú. When it came time for promotions, Gastelú's was postponed and another member of his graduating class, Fernando Reyes Roca, who would be united with him in an all-encompassing rivalry over the following years, was promoted to general and, soon afterward, named Dircote chief. Gastelú continued to play second violin, registering successes of regular importance while consistently losing bureaucratic battles. Aside from anything involuntarily comic about these misadventures within the special logic of the police world, to understand them is important in order to grasp the comprehensive progress of the war. The energies dedicated to waging the pathetic battles to keep oneself afloat and sink one's competitors were, without any exaggeration, greater than those put into action against the Shining Path.

The arrests Dicote managed to carry out were, as has been noted, insufficient when compared with the Shining Path's progress throughout Peru in 1982, including in Lima. The reason was partly due to the fact that Dicote only acted after a crime had been committed. Its identity as a purely operative group imposed drastic limitations on the quality and depth of the intelligence it could gather. For this reason, only with difficulty could arrests reach beyond the organization's middle levels. As long as high-level Shining Path cadres could continue to recruit more grass-roots militants than they lost, they would always remain one or two steps ahead of Dicote, which in effect is what happened.

So the Dicote did not satisfy the troubled Interior Ministry's anguished demand for intelligence, for precise information. When it attempted to supply it (as in the case of Guzmán's supposed illness and imminent capture), results had been embarrassing. On the other hand, none of the other measures taken by Gagliardi to improve the collection of intelligence had delivered or would deliver results.

The Interior Ministry had also requested information from the CIA station chief based in Lima. In 1982, the station chief was Peter Morton Palmer. Faced with López Martínez's constant requests, Palmer delivered what, according to him, was all the information held by the CIA on Guzmán up to that moment.

Guzmán's file consisted of fewer than two pages of telex and was filled with errors. "A Peruvian named Abimal Guzmán-Reynoso, born on December 3, 1934, in Arequipa, Peru, to Chilean parents. . . . In October of 1966, he traveled to Russia, returning on November 11, 1966." The final paragraph is a good sample of the document's bureaucratic style and lack of clarity. "According to a Peruvian magazine, Guzmán is a member of the Political Bureau of the Shining Path, considered the most important entity within the Shining Path leadership. Guzmán is also a member of the Shining Path's Central Committee and operates using the pseudonyms 'Alvaro,' 'Alvaro I,' 'Alvaro II,' and 'Gonzalo.'" The report also listed Guzmán's voting card and passport numbers and the exact dates of his exits and reentries into the country, which only served to indicate the CIA's possible sources of information within the Peruvian security forces, without providing any of the intelligence so desperately needed by the interior minister.

Relations with intelligence contacts in the Soviet Embassy were less fluid than those with the CIA, at least at the level of the Interior Ministry leadership. The intelligence links kept by the Soviets, especially the KGB, with the different armed forces and police varied widely. Among them, the navy was most unwilling to maintain relations of any sort with the Soviets. But the army and the air force, which had both stocked up heavily on Soviet weaponry in the 1970s, had constant contact because they needed to maintain their equipment and train officers and technical personnel.

At one particular moment, cooperation in terms of intelligence and the training of police became extensive. That the Soviets put a great deal of importance on this relationship can be deduced by the position of the person who led the Soviets in the first renegotiation of the Peruvian military debt: Yuri Andropov, who lent his decisive support to a refinancing of the military debt for an additional period of ten years. This renegotiation was considered so favorable for Peru that in 1978, the then SIN head, Juan Schroth Carlín, awarded Andropov, still KGB head, the Peruvian medal of military merit during a trip to Moscow. The award was more than simple recognition from the Peruvians. Even completely anti-Communist soldiers like Schroth saw no problem in continuing to cooperate on technical matters with the Soviets, whose talents in the combined arts of intelligence and police work were the object of admiration.

During the military government and until 1982, dozens of army and police officers received scholarships from the Soviet government for police and intelligence courses in the Soviet Union. At the same time, the SIN maintained fluid contact with the Soviet Embassy's intelligence chief. This lasted until Essenwanger left in 1982. Afterward, when two naval officers assumed successive command of the SIN (rear admirals Edgardo Colunge and Javier Rocha, in 1983 and 1984), the relationship was cut off for all practical purposes. Nevertheless, since 1986, when

General Edwin Díaz took over the SIN, there was a rapprochement with the Soviets.

Starting at the end of 1982, but above all from the beginning of 1983, the Shining Path accused the Soviet Union of active collaboration with the counterinsurgency efforts of the armed forces and police, "supplying approximately 50 percent of the military and police equipment and hundreds of 'military advisers.'" In one document, the Shining Path accused the Soviet Union of providing the helicopters and advice for use in operations in Ayacucho. As will be seen, these accusations were followed by several attacks, some bloody.

While most of the Shining Path accusations were exaggerated (for example, the helicopters used in Ayacucho were not Soviet-made), it is also true that some police and military commanders who served in the emergency zone had received KGB training in the Soviet Union during the military government. Nevertheless, the knowledge received in these courses did not produce a single change in the war's course.

Within this abundance of institutions dedicated in theory to intelligence gathering, with foreign service operatives also populating and complicating the picture, and despite the desperate urgency with which information was sought, what is clear is that in these critical months no authentic light illuminated the informational twilight. And the dialogue of those who governed with their spies continued to be a colloquium of the blind.

18

The Fall of Vilcashuamán

In the wake of the attack on the Ayacucho prison, clashes continued. To the pressure exerted by Gagliardi and López Martínez on the police to take the offensive and deliver results, it responded with isolated measures and ephemeral eruptions of activity.

On March 4, GC general Walter Andrade assumed emergency zone command. Over the following days, he dispatched Sinchi patrols to attempt to recapture the Ayacucho prison escapees. The results were not satisfying. On March 7, a Sinchi patrol captured a wounded Jesús Luján González in Julcamarca.[1] He arrived at the Ayacucho hospital close to death and died three days later. The only other person recaptured that month was Félix Quispe Palomino, also caught wounded in Ongoy, Andahuaylas, on March 21. In the same operation, another escapee was killed: Carlos Flores Cerna.

The other escaped prisoners were invisible to the police search.[2] What this meant in terms of the dimension of an organization able to maintain deep clandestinity for so many people at a time was not perceived clearly.

Without allowing police to take a breath, the Shining Path intensified attacks. On March 9, sharpshooters harassed the Quinua station. The next day, the police checkpoint on the Los Libertadores highway just outside Ayacucho was attacked.

At dawn on March 18, the police post at the Canarias mine, located in Víctor Fajardo province, was attacked. Rumors of an imminent attack had become insistent over the previous days. GC colonel Carlos Delgado Matallana, who had been there just days before, responded to the mineowners' anxiety by sending them three police officers. Nevertheless, their police detachment was—even counting the reinforcements—markedly smaller than the one in place during the 1980 labor troubles.[3]

The guerrilla attack took place at dawn.[4] Surprised as they slept, the police were vanquished before they could resist.[5] The only one with a bullet wound was mine security chief Adolfo Pickman. In a dawn assembly, a "popular trial" was held—Pickman was brought before it bound and with his eyes blindfolded—and he was pardoned. Given the high tension between management and workers that had reigned in the mining settlement for two years, the guerrilla group's conduct in this instance was relatively benign. Pickman and the police were loaded into one of the mine's dump trucks and released a mile from the mine.

The Shining Path arsenal increased with the weapons and explosives seized: four Star machine guns and four Smith and Wesson revolvers. It would have been a relatively thin harvest without counting in the 5,600 sticks of dynamite seized from the mine's stores.[6]

On March 19, as the ministers awaited the weekly Council of Ministers meeting, the dominant theme was the new confrontation. However, Belaunde didn't touch on it even during a later session with the Council of Defense. Its silencing was a sure sign of Belaunde's growing irritation and indignation. He had learned the technique of ominous silence, of studious avoidance, from Peru's nineteenth-century leader and boss, Nicolás de Piérola. This was in contrast to Peru's other president of the past century, José Balta, whose legendary furies provoked fleeting hurricanes in Lima's halls of power. Piérola chose the method of deliberately ignoring bothersome matters along with especially irritating or offensive people. For Lima, where courtesy was highly valued, the interpretation of who was in or out of the "Caliph's" favor (such was Piérola's nickname to his followers) was an important skill honed by those in power. Belaunde had studiously copied his master's tactic. However, the problem in 1982, as it had been in 1881 when Piérola led the Peruvian government from a capital surrounded by invading Chilean troops, was that people neither wanted nor needed august sphinxes to decode, but rather leaders who could interpret problems for them, explain them clearly, and point out concrete ways to resolve them.

The same day that the Council of Ministers recognized the importance of the seditious violence by overwhelming it with its silence, a Shining Path band assaulted the Providencia farm, in the province of Andahuaylas, Apurímac. The owner, Alfredo Echegaray Trelles, was murdered. Since the attack was evidence that the Shining Path's scope of action had reached beyond the Ayacucho emergency zone, the government, following Gagliardi's suggestion, immediately declared Andahuaylas in a state of emergency.[7]

On March 26, the Shining Path intensified the campaign "to strike" the district of Vilcashuamán.

One canyon over from the towns of Parcco and Pomatambo—four years away from their own hour of tragedy—the Ayzarca farm had continued to operate after the December 24, 1980, incursion. After the murder of its owner, Benigno Medina Zea, his daughter, Marina, had run the farm with her husband, Andrés Gutiérrez, a retired civilian pilot. They knew that their mere presence at the farm was a challenge to the Shining Path. Nevertheless, they continued to live in the main house with their two- and four-year-old children. Eight policemen, connected to Huamanga by radio, had been stationed at the farm, and the family itself had acquired some weapons.

A little before six in the morning, the sentries sounded the alarm. About eighty people had taken up positions around the farm. One of the sentries, GC officer Silvano Añanca, exchanged fire with the first wave and was killed just as the attack began. Those that remained barricaded themselves on the second floor of the house as best they could and returned fire. The defenders were armed with four machine guns, five .38-caliber revolvers, three .22 revolvers, and two old carbines. Their munitions were limited (no more than two cartridges per machine gun). However, the attackers also appeared to be poorly armed.

The difference—a factor that again and again would tip the scales in a sudden and decisive way over the following months—lay with dynamite. Narrowing the distance from their target, taking cover as close as possible, the Shining Path attackers launched explosives at a constant rate. These were primitive grenades, made of dynamite sticks. Yet they were effective. Some were as powerful as regulation grenades. If combat had been restricted to bullets, projectiles traveling in straight lines, the police would probably have been able to fight off these sieges. But they had no way to fend off the parabolic arcs of the explosives. Hurled against the usually weak roofs common in the mountains, the grenades converted this shelter into a trap. Normally, the mere reverberation of the explosions and the crash of the roof caving in would end any resistance. In this case, while the defenders made desperate radio calls to Ayacucho, the resistance continued.

The Shining Path attackers closed in,[8] throwing dynamite from a chapel only about 100 feet from the house. They then set to work lighting the house afire. It was only then that the Gutiérrez family and police surrendered. From the partially ruined structure, they waved sheets like flags of surrender.

Marina Medina was left in the house with her children while her husband and the police were taken away. The last Marina Medina heard were her husband's protests as he was beaten.

At 4:30 that afternoon, the police returned. Exhausted, barely clothed, beaten, defeated. But alive. Andrés Gutiérrez did not return with them. His wife would wait for him for several more weeks before having to look at decomposed human remains and reconstruct, on the basis of details still visible among the rotting materials, her husband's identity. This would soon be the fate of dozens of Aya- cucho families on both sides of the conflict or, more frequently, in between. Marina Medina was one of the first to live it.

At 5:30, a helicopter arrived with a contingent of eight Sinchis. Not far away, still on the banks of the Pampas River, the attackers could still be seen. The survivors, guarded by the Sinchis, took refuge until they could be evacuated to Huamanga.

That night, the entire country was plunged into darkness. In Lima, a general blackout was followed by attacks on malls in the Lince and Miraflores districts. Groups of Shining Path militants armed with Molotov cocktails and plastic bags filled with gasoline started several fires and a generalized panic. Some were cap- tured, especially in Lince. GC policeman Washington Falcón suffered first-degree burns in the fire at the Arenales mall in Lima.

On March 30, an armed Shining Path group entered Concepción, in Cangallo province. A post office employee and Popular Action militant, Grimaldo Castillo, was captured and murdered in a barely disguised act of "popular justice." Accused of providing the police with information, Castillo was first beaten, then shot. His body was tied to a light post and hung with insults—"This is the way snitches die," a message that would rest on so many still-warm chests. According to reports, his body was then mutilated.[9]

A photograph taken at the beginning of April 1982 at the Ayacucho airport shows the arrival of Castillo's remains in a helicopter. Three women and a girl follow the Sinchis who, at a trot, carry Castillo's cadaver in a blanket. The three women weep with open desperation. And the little girl cries with terror and pain, clutching one of the women as if to protect her. The Sinchis, impassive, keep moving. That poor child. For the Shining Path, Castillo was just one of the victims, partly chosen by chance; it needed to break the government's hold on the countryside and impose its own control. For the little girl, Castillo was half the universe.

Death rituals would once again become the center of life in Ayacucho. Solemn funereal rites would be inscribed on the memory of the place while the explosions of pain would be forgotten.

Some weeks later, still in April, a group of Popular Action members from Miraf- lores made a singular gesture that I don't think could have been made before or repeated later. They traveled by land from Lima to Concepción in Ayacucho to hold a moment of silence on the spot where Castillo had been murdered. Then they returned to Lima. The trip had much in common with what the government did, especially Belaunde: a gesture, which went no further than symbolism.

On March 31, the police post at Vilcashuamán had a premonition of an immi-

218 THE FALL OF VILCASHUAMÁN

nent attack. Vilcashuamán was an administrative center, commanded by an officer in charge of several detachments and smaller posts. The number of police there had steadily increased as more distant outposts had been abandoned. About twenty policemen were assigned to Vilcashuamán, but their combat morale was poor since these men had been subjected to the Shining Path's systematic intimidation at their previous posts. In addition, they had few munitions and less faith in the efficiency of their weapons, machine guns and revolvers, against the vastness of the mountain landscape. At night—with the town submerged in darkness ever since the Shining Path had dynamited the electric generator a year earlier—all of the policemen took refuge in the station.

That night, after an entire day of persistent rumors, moving lights appeared on the gentle hill that overlooks Vilcashuamán. In the frigid night, shouts and threats reached the station. The police machine guns responded nervously to the darkness. Radio calls to Ayacucho became increasingly desperate. At 7:30, a policeman was wounded, although it was never clear if the cause was accidental.

In Ayacucho's Ninth Station, GC general Jorge Monge Llanos, head of Region II of the police, which included Lima and Ayacucho, asked by radio for calm and concrete information. Monge had just arrived from Lima where an exasperated Gagliardi had pressured him to go on the offensive, to keep a foothold in the countryside. As far as personal courage went, Monge needed no one to push him. A general of humble origin, he had started his career as a beat officer and had risen with determination. Although born on the coast, in Chincha, his nickname was "The Cholo," used in Peru to mean brown-skinned mountain dweller. His wiry crew-cut and features matched his nickname precisely. He was also one of the few generals respected by his subordinates, whose well-being was of genuine interest to him. And that night, hearing over the radio the Vilcashuamán officer's growing anguish and fearing an imminent collapse, no better alternative occurred to him than to grab a machine gun, load up a military Unimog truck with policemen, and begin a night journey to Vilcashuamán. Almost every curve in the long road was perfect for the ambush of a solitary truck. If only half of what was being transmitted from Vilcashuamán turned out to be true, the Unimog would be ambushed several times. Valiant, Cholo Monge did not linger over risks. This was his greatest virtue.

Radio traffic between Ayacucho's Ninth Station and the Vilcashuamán command center had been followed by the interior minister in Lima with growing anxiety. Constant failure in Ayacucho throughout March had begun to foment a feeling of desperation within the ministry, not only because of the Shining Path's seeming strength, but also the police's apparent weakness. According to Héctor López Martínez, "These were months of clash after clash, and there was no consolation other than what was done in Lima."[10]

When, about nine that evening, Gagliardi told Belaunde the news, including details about the wounded policeman, Monge's journey, and the latest twist, the abrupt cutoff of radio communication, the president surprised Gagliardi by saying that he too would travel to Vilcashuamán at first light, to lend moral support to the besieged station.

After failing to dissuade the president of the Republic, the honorable Gagliardi made the necessary trip arrangements. With the first rays of dawn, the presidential airplane took off from the Callao air force base, with Belaunde, Gagliardi, the commander general of the army, Francisco Miranda Vargas, and the aeronautics minister, José García Calderón, aboard.

Forty minutes later, they landed in Ayacucho, where an air force helicopter was warming its engines. The few hours between the decision and the trip had been enough to roust the city's leaders. All were lined up at the airport when the presidential airplane taxied to the parking area.

But when Belaunde emerged from the airplane, the first person to run to him was Marina Medina. Weeping, the Ayzarca survivor embraced him and begged him to help her find her husband. The terrorists had already made her an orphan, she told him, and now they would kill her husband.

Perhaps at this moment, and during the rest of the day, fate tempted Belaunde to seize victory. On the cover of that week's *Caretas*, as Marina Medina wept on his chest and he embraced her, his face was fixed in an expression of severity and energy, that of a man confronting a grand collective task, not the customary softness that increasingly became the target of caricature (drawn on a cloud as he uttered his favorite word, "gallant"). With the image still fresh of the president raising the country's flag at the Paquisha military outpost after the 1981 border clashes with Ecuador, a high percentage of the public saw Belaunde as someone who could galvanize its collective energy, the person able to channel and direct it.

In the next moment, Belaunde, Miranda, Gagliardi, and García Calderón had boarded the helicopter and crossed Cangallo, flying toward Vilcashuamán. Marina Medina remained in Huamanga, soon to know that she was not only an orphan, but a widow.

What had motivated Belaunde to abandon his studied silence, go from ignoring the Shining Path to this impulsive act?

Vilcashuamán touched a sensitive cord within Belaunde. In his personal biography and political doctrine, in everything that had justified his national political prominence over the past four decades, Vilcashuamán, the "Sacred Hawk," was one of the main sanctuaries.

Vilcashuamán had been the administrative center of Peru's first empire, and later melancholy testament to its disappearance and oblivion. Nothing spoke more eloquently of defeated grandeur, of power vanquished, than Vilcashuamán, and this was the source of its intense fascination for erudite Peruvian travelers. When he was still a candidate, Belaunde had visited Vilcashuamán equipped with books like *Peruvian Landscapes* by Riva Agüero[11] and *Coast, Mountains, and Jungle* by Aurelio Miró Quesada.[12]

Riva Agüero—an exceptional writer and historian as well as a politician who, over the course of too long an intellectual career, went from the positivist fervor of his youth to the pathetic and bitter fascism of his waning years—had arrived in Vilcashuamán in the middle of a leisurely journey through the Peruvian Andes in 1912, in search of signs of that city that chroniclers had described as both a sacred spot and a principle imperial administrative center populated by 4,000 inhabitants. The empire's main roads converged on Vilcashuamán, considered by the Incas to be the precise geographic center of Tahuantinsuyo. Apart from the primitive Pokra shrines, the Inca Pachacútec had erected a temple to the Sun, guarded by 50 men and next to a "acjllahuasi." There, according to the chroniclers, 500 virgins and 500 of the Inca's women were housed. On top of the temples, beneath the gaze of the Sun and Moon, sat stone thrones that dominated the mountainous landscape.

Spanish domination, and specifically the foundation of Ayacucho, had meant the rapid decline of Vilcashuamán, which did not slow under the Republic. Riva Agüero saw "the prostrated Vilcas, forgotten on every map, reduced to the decrepit and miserable village that I viewed with grief in the brilliant sadness of a June afternoon."[13] Riva Agüero's description of Vilcashuamán was a pained funereal lament that Belaunde had very much in mind when he arrived years later.

> I had never before felt such a piercing and heartrending sensation of decadence. The village's silence was deep, because almost all of those who dwelled there were still in their fields. The warble of birds, the humble noise of the animal pens, the cackle of hens, and the footfalls of a mule train disturbed the solitude that had once listened to songs of adoration to the Sun and frenetic praise for the Inca. . . . Remains of a great historic shipwreck under the light of the setting sun, one could say that the ruins of Vilcas encompassed a desperate melody, more destitute and anguished than the music of the native panpipes. Extinct and plaintive opulence, legendary sorrow, two notes that hold the soul of the Peruvian Andes.[14]

Riva Agüero's elegy to the Incas' wilted glory was made even more painful when he compared it with the image of how the place must have looked in its past splendor:

> the clean footpaths of pebbles strewn with flowers, the army of 30,000 Indian warriors with lances, axes, *macanas*, breast plates, and metal armor . . . the copper *champis*, the shields, and the shirts of woven gold of the privileged Inca militias, "that shone strangely," according to the phrase of Pedro Pizarro: the litters for the idols; the hammocks of the important chiefs; and in a tower that today

lies in ruins, the Inca with his collar of pearls and emeralds and the regal cloak clasped at his breast, his forehead bound beneath the loose and bloody *mascapaycha*, gold and scarlet, and the striped turban.[15]

Was it even conceivable that Belaunde, proponent of a return to imperial sources to recover past grandeur for the future, could have avoided a pilgrimage to Vilcashuamán when he was a candidate? Certainly, his architect's pragmatic mind had very different perceptions than those of Riva Agüero. Where Riva Agüero remembers having traveled vertiginous paths ("Then the path twists, grasping the hills on the right and descending in fearsome switchbacks, which appear like balconies over the chasm"),[16] Belaunde had seen another monumental message from the wisdom of the past: "Where the wheel did not exist (among the Inca) they could fall back on endless stairs to gain the heights, taking advantage of the places where there would be no landslides to obstruct the way. Near Vilcashuamán, there are thousands of these steps, the longest staircase in the world."[17]

This was Belaunde's tie to Vilcashuamán and what it symbolized for him. And that explained his dawn journey to the town under siege.

Still early that morning, when the sun had wiped the ghosts from the air, the helicopter descended to Vilcashuamán. Belaunde was the first to descend, and he walked toward the central square, followed by Gagliardi, Miranda, and García Calderón. Their arrival was so unexpected that no one went to meet them. The police were concentrating on General Monge, who had arrived a little earlier.

Minutes later, the national flag was raised in the central square and the police detachment, now energetic and alert, was standing at attention around the perimeter. Belaunde, joined by the officer in charge, reviewed the troops, whose warlike demeanor appeared restored. After the review, Belaunde met briefly with some local people at the entrance to the ruins of the temple of the Sun. There, raising a glass of *chicha*, the president saluted the people who surrounded him.

> They told me that there was alarm the night before in Vilcashuamán. That the town was in darkness—its electrical generator blown up by terrorists a year ago—and that these elements took advantage of the shadows to attack once again with sharpshooters, skilled in marksmanship, quick to escape. I could not resist the impulse to come and see them without delay to tell them that I am with them and those who defend order.[18]

Later, the gesture made, or, in the language of the bull ring that so accurately expressed it, the *desplante*, the pass that leaves the bull blinking in enraged confusion as the bull fighter turns his back on it to receive thundering applause, Belaunde returned to the helicopter and went back to Ayacucho. There, he visited the market—where he was applauded—and the Civil Guard, Investigative Police, and

Republican Guard stations. When he spoke to them, Belaunde demanded a firmer attitude toward "the enemies of the Constitution and peace." And from the Republican Guard, he emphasized "serenity." In his language, this was a reference to and a reproach for the Ayacucho hospital murders.

As the day ended, the president found himself once again in the Government Palace and a waning light fell over the mountains around Vilcashuamán. The gesture had been made. And for Belaunde, especially for Belaunde in his later period, the gesture, the form, was almost all there was. Thus the allusions to the bull ring (where form is the essence, and the actual event, the bull's death, is an accident that the team of horses glosses over rapidly) appeared ever more frequently in his conversation and speeches.

While he was a candidate or during certain moments in his previous administrations, the gesture would have served Belaunde well. It corresponded to Belaunde the political fighter as opposed to Belaunde the builder. The fighter met battle like a bull fighter, not a warrior. Borricaud had already noticed this when he described another incident—whose drama appears copied from the bull ring—in Cuzco, on May 21, 1962.

> A stone was launched from this group, or more precisely several stones, and one struck Belaunde in the middle of his forehead. With his face bloodied, the orator returns to the platform and declares: "What does it matter that a drop of my blood falls in Cuzco's central square, where the forefather of our independence, Túpac Amaru, was killed! As far as I am concerned, I want the people to know that I am not only willing to shed some drops of blood from an unimportant wound, but also to give my life to underscore the lies of the Apristas and the Communists in Cuzco!" The game is won. His followers lift the candidate on a litter and bring him to his hotel. The lesson to be learned from this episode is the architect's ability to transform any event in his life into a historic moment or, if you prefer, a defining moment. General Odría, who suffered a similar incident in Huancayo, was struck dumb, while the architect invokes Túpac Amaru. . . . In the Cuzco episode, the challenge is converted into triumph; this time, the architect defeats his adversaries through the beauty of his gesture. But can a successful political position be circumscribed by the symbolic efficiency of a gesture?[19]

In the case of Vilcashuamán, the challenge was accepted. The glove thrown down by Belaunde at the temple to the Sun was taken up by silent hands in the night. The answer was pondered over by people who lacked even the compunctions of a wild bull.

On April 3, guerrillas struck Ocros. First, they assaulted and destroyed the "La Colpa" farm outbuildings. Then they caught a community member named Arcadio

Pillaca, accused him of collaborating with the farm's owner, and killed him. Two days later, a group of reporters arrived at the miserable house where his neighbors, "grief-stricken and drunk," attended Pillaca's wake, the body stretched out on a table with the head destroyed by "a bullet in the temple that had popped his eyeballs."

After La Colpa, the guerrillas entered Chumbes. There, they looted Pastor García's store and forced him "with shoves and blows" outside. Other guerrillas entered the farm of Leoncio Kajatt, whom they accused of collaborating with police for having served them in his restaurant. García and Kajatt were taken outside town and shot at the foot of a precipice. García survived. Badly wounded, he crawled back to his house. Only two days later did one of his children take him to the Ayacucho hospital. Such incredible histories of survival would become frequent over the following years. These were hard people, accustomed to extreme privation and long suffering.

In contrast, the red flag emblazoned with the hammer and sickle continued to wave over Leoncio Kajatt's house a week after his murder. No one in his family dared take it down and the police had yet to present themselves.

On April 4, General Walter Andrade went to Lima. After four days of bureaucratic battling in the capital, he returned to Ayacucho. But this time he was only chief of staff for the new commander: GC general Héctor Rivera Hurtado, a policeman specialized in the control of street disturbances. Andrade would remain in Ayacucho until the beginning of May, when he would travel to Huancayo to assume command of the subregion. He appears once again in this history, in 1985, connected to the Rodríguez López case. Rivera remained in Ayacucho until June 14. Medical problems were the apparent cause of his return to Lima, where—in a more benign climate—he recovered and assumed command of the Civil Guard training facility. At that time, GC colonel Carlos Delgado Matallana once again took command of the emergency zone while dozens of generals in Lima squabbled over the space allotted to their small offices, their redundant duties. At the very least, Belaunde's visit provoked a flood of government activity. In three days, three ministers visited Ayacucho—among them, War Minister General Luis Cisneros. Afterward came calm, abandonment. After a few weeks, Delgado Matallana would once again find himself alone, trying desperately to stick his fingers into the dikes that were disintegrating.

Nevertheless, during the weeks that Rivera Hurtado remained in Ayacucho, there were police actions. Since the middle of April, police had been provided with a small number of Hechler and Koch rifles and combat uniforms. Some police reinforcements also arrived.

It was then that a search operation with the grandiloquent name of "Hawk II" began. About 200 policemen stirred up the districts of Ocros and Vilcashuamán for several days. No battle ensued. In contrast, several arrests were made in Ayacucho city, including that of the longtime leader of the Defense Front, Máximo Cárdenas. Police also captured another prison escapee.

Meanwhile, violence had intensified in other parts of the country, especially Lima. On April 24, mineowner Luis Jäger was ambushed and killed on his way to the mountains around Huarochirí, outside Lima.[20] His mine had been seized and looted a few hours earlier.

On May 15, the Shining Path again attacked and held the city of Tambo for several hours. They met no opposition since a few days earlier the police officers sent there had retreated to the provincial capital. The same thing began to happen throughout Ayacucho. In an attempt to increase their defensive ability, the police continued to abandon posts and command centers in order to concentrate themselves in a few fortified locations. The occupation of Tambo was relatively prolonged and obviously benefited the Shining Path.

As the fragile standoff was beginning to fall apart, one of the three air force helicopters stationed in Huamanga was withdrawn. The air force demanded an hourly fee from the interior minister for its use. The iron laws of commerce could not even be bent for Gagliardi, a former air force general.

At the beginning of July, Shining Path actions intensified. In Ayacucho, the Ayrabamba farm was attacked and burned, and several machines were dynamited. In the neighboring province of Andahuaylas, the Occobamba police station was attacked. Civil Guardsman Augusto Buleje died in the brief battle.

On July 5, the Ñaña Civil Guard post just outside Lima was attacked by a group of ten Shining Path guerrillas. The attack on the poorly defended post was a complete surprise. Seconds after it began, two officers were dead. The remaining two, however, did not surrender. In the fierce gun battle, waged at close range, another officer was mortally wounded and two of the attackers were cut down. The surviving officer, Gerardo Lozada, whose practice of sleeping with his revolver under the pillow had saved his life, wounded two more attackers and forced the rest to retreat. Two Shining Path guerrillas, Roberto Herrera and Luis Torres Cherres, were lying on the ground, beside the three policemen. Based on their arrest, the Dircote would severely limit the Shining Path's activity east of Lima.

The increase in Shining Path activity was generalized across the country. In Peru's northern Andes, the town of Angasmarca in the department of La Libertad was attacked on July 11. Civil Guard rookie José Goñaz was cut down in combat, and the police station, along with the town, was seized by the Shining Path.

That same week, armed Shining Path bands continued to force local authorities to flee the Ayacucho countryside. Zenón Palomino, Calliara's appointed governor, and Hermenegildo Retamozo, former Huancaraylla mayor and a member of the local Popular Action committee, were murdered in their towns.

On July 20, Tambo was attacked yet again by the Shining Path. This time, the attackers came up against a police detachment reinforced by a small group of Sinchis. Civil Guard command had forced them to return after witnessing the indignation that followed the seizure of the city on May 15. In an intense exchange of fire, which took place primarily at night, the attackers were forced back. Two police officers were wounded and one guerrilla was killed.

Almost at the same time, an attack of hallucinatory proportions took place. Allpachaka, an experimental and peasant training farm run by the University of Huamanga, was occupied by armed Shining Path guerrillas. Despite all, Allpachaka had been one of the university's showcases. There, agronomists and their students experimented with Andean crops and agroindustry and bred improved strains of cattle. Even during stormy times, Allpachaka continued to represent the university's first efforts to place itself at the forefront of local progress. When the guerrillas retreated, this was the scene journalists described: "Twenty-five Brown Swiss cows dead. Four breeding bulls with their throats cut. Twenty-five cattle stolen. The training center dynamited, the seed bank, bedrooms, tool shed, cafeteria, cheese-making room, the milk-processing area. Destruction of the pesticide warehouse, the wine warehouse, medicines for the animals, files, administrative documents. The burning of the hayloft . . ."[21]

The incursion caused a commotion in the university, even among Shining Path sympathizers. A diverse group, including the former university president Efraín Morote, suggested or stated that the attack had been carried out by paramilitary groups tied to the government whose hatred of the university knew no bounds. The image of a guerrilla slitting the throat of a stud bull seemed to many sincere people a pornographic distortion of the very concept of the fighter armed to win a better world. Soon, conspiracy theories of all types began to flourish on the left, some spun with political objectives or, more frequently, out of conviction.

But the clear light of reality did not delay long. Soon after the incursion, professors and university students traveled to Allpachaka in two buses, to help begin the almost hopeless task of reconstruction. Outside Ayacucho, the buses were stopped by armed guerrillas, who claimed responsibility for the attack. They called the Allpachaka program a center of imperialist penetration and reformist illusions, and prohibited any attempt to rebuild. By then, the time of open discussion and even physical confrontation on campus had passed. The volunteers returned, crestfallen, to Ayacucho.

More than any other attack that year, the Allpachaka incident fed the Shining Path's reputation as a Pol Pot–type insurgency, which in later years would become so difficult to contradict. In perspective, it is clear that the Shining Path's most violent and radical wing, guided by Guzmán, had been in control since 1982. In Ayacucho, the Jacobins were already in control of the group's actions, and they made the department feel their heavy and ferocious presence. Over the following months, it would provoke tragedies much greater than Allpachaka. If what was at stake was broadening the war, making the countryside shake, and replacing one government for another at the local level, the Shining Path leaders in Ayacucho were well on their way. Only after several years did the more moderate wing again make itself heard, when these excesses were combined with oppression and tyranny over dominated communities that began to strike back and hand the Shining Path dramatic defeats. But by mid-1982, this realization was still far off.

Important acts of sabotage were also being carried out throughout Ayacucho. The Cangallo bridge was seriously damaged. The Tambo electrical plant was put out of service. And, in retrospect an act of great importance, the bridge that linked Vilcashuamán to Vischongo was destroyed.

Other attacks continued. The town of San José de Secce was attacked yet again. The war continued to expand in Andahuaylas, tearing the social and institutional fabric. In Ongoy, a community that had played such an important role in the 1973 land seizures, the Shining Path murdered community member Félix Laura and forced community president Guillermo Olarte to flee for his life. As far as I know, it was the first time in Peru that a Marxist leader had been killed by guerrillas. It would not be the last. The Shining Path's willingness to kill across the entire political spectrum would deliver a mixed bag of results. In Ayacucho and Apurímac, it helped the Shining Path sweep away all opposition to its control of local government. However, the 1987 murder of Zenobio Huarsaya, the Marxist mayor of San Juan de Salinas, Puno, was extremely harmful to it.

The resignations of Ayacucho's governors, lieutenant governors, and mayors reached massive proportions. What else could be expected?

Only in Lima did police investigations deliver palpable results. Based on the evidence collected from the Shining Path guerrillas killed in Ñaña, the police made several arrests. Although differences between State Security head General Guillermo Rivarola and Dircote chief Víctor Gastelú were becoming more pronounced, investigations advanced. By the end of that week, most of the attackers who had survived Ñaña and the murderers of Luis Jäger were in custody. Investigative Police chief Rómulo Alayza stated at the time that 100 percent of the attacks in Lima had resulted in arrests.[22]

The following week, on the night of August 19, the Shining Path dynamited several electrical towers, causing a generalized blackout in Lima. At the same time, groups of saboteurs threw incendiary bombs at several stores scattered throughout Lima. In one case, in La Victoria, one fire blazed out of control for several hours. The Parliament suspended its session for a convincing reason: the building was pitch black. In the city center, one member of a team of saboteurs was engulfed in flames when a Molotov cocktail he held in his hand and was about to throw exploded. He emerged from the store that he had tried to burn into the dark street and advanced into the crowd, a living torch, parting them as he attempted to flee. "He ran without stopping—toward Tacna Avenue—but in silence, without asking for help. In the darkness and in the brilliance of the flames, it appeared like a ghostly fire that diminished little by little in the distance."[23]

It was José Túpac Yupanqui, a student and nephew of a journalist who was then working in the office of the presidency. He only made it to Tacna Avenue. There, he collapsed. He was taken to a hospital, where he quickly died. He was seventeen.

On August 20, the government declared a state of emergency in Lima and Callao. Prime Minister Manuel Ulloa announced the measure, and declared that, "the government believes it is in a position to make an important blow against the terrorist organization that is challenging the country."[24] GC general Jorge Monge was named chief of the police command in the emergency zone.

On August 22, Vilcashuamán fell. At dawn, a Shining Path detachment of between sixty to eighty people silently entered the town and took up combat positions, surrounding the police command center that was located in the Provincial Council, on the central square. Just before the sun broke over the roofs, the shooting began, dispatching almost immediately the two guards standing in the doorway. The other policemen, woken in the middle of gunfire, ran to their stations and began to return fire.

After Belaunde's visit, the Vilcashuamán police detachment had been reinforced with several additional officers, including some Sinchis. The quality of their weapons had also been improved with the addition of Hechler and Koch rifles and some hand grenades. They also had a Thomson radio. In neighboring Vischongo, the police detachment had also been reinforced, and both expected the other to offer mutual support in the case of an attack. Clearly, the sum total of detachments close together was a way to establish a point of police strength in the province. The Vilcashuamán detachment was commanded by a lieutenant named Pereyra, whose second-in-command was Second Lieutenant Alberto Molero.

Nevertheless, if one takes into account the moment they chose for attack, the last moment of dawn, it was obvious that the Shining Path was sure of victory. For them, it was clear that some combat would take place in daylight, and that they were giving up the advantage of a night battle.

Within a few minutes, the gunfire had become intense. From windows shielded by sand bags, the police tried to keep the Shining Path guerrillas at a distance. But the attackers rapidly drew closer. Saving bullets, the guerrillas concentrated on stunning their adversaries with explosives.

As Interior Minister Gagliardi described it before an upset and silent Congress several days later, the Shining Path had manufactured grenades by pressing three or four sticks of dynamite around a stone, "making with all of this a compact mass covered by a sock twisted several times until a very compact and strong ball is formed; and then this is placed in a band used in what are called *guaracas* or slingshots. Launched in this way, the grenade can travel up to 160 to 170 feet, and this is what they did."[25]

The explosions were so strong that sections of the wall began to crumble. Civil Guardsmen Alcio Maraví and Juan Compite had already fallen. Between the gunfire and the explosions, officers Abraham Santillán and Oscar Morales were killed.

As the central square disappeared in smoke, the only helicopter left by the air force in Ayacucho passed high above the city. Despite the obvious destruction caused by the battle, the dust, the crew saw nothing and continued on. As for the radio, it never worked. The batteries were dead. Since the electrical generator had been sabotaged, they hadn't been recharged. The Vischongo garrison could thus explain why it didn't intervene in the fray.

The Shining Path moved in rapidly. The first explosives landed on the roof, perforating it. Then real disaster struck.

Several grenades fell within the council building, destroying walls and the will to fight. According to one version, some of the officers' own grenades detonated as if out of sympathy. It was then that Second Lieutenant Molero and Guardsman Miguel Cárdenas were killed. Apparently, Molero tried to shift position when he was cut down.

Lieutenant Pereyra and some Sinchis escaped from the rear of the building and, hugging the walls, ran quickly and managed to escape.

The rest, five men, surrendered. Before 8 A.M., Vilcashuamán had fallen. In the same square where Riva Agüero had remembered today's abandonment and yesterday's splendor, and where weeks earlier Belaunde had arrived to offer his gesture and issue his challenge, five policemen with their jackets torn and still unsteady from the explosions stood with their hands up, surrounded by the triumphant guerrillas of the Shining Path.

The occupation of Vilcashuamán was brief. Two stores were looted and the foodstuffs divided among the townspeople. There was an obligatory rally in the central square. Afterward—in two trucks they had seized—the guerrillas retreated with their prisoners. When they abandoned the trucks a half mile down the road, they liberated the guardsmen.

Gagliardi arrived in Vilcashuamán the next day. He had traveled from Lima with Catter. Delgado Matallana joined them in Ayacucho. After flying over Vilcashuamán, "We saw the Civil Guard post still smoking from the air. Then I could imagine what had happened the night before. The station was in ruins."[26]

In town, where he was met by a guard of six men hurriedly brought from Vischongo, Gagliardi could see the destruction for himself. "We saw that the spectacle of the post was really out of Dante . . . the rooms within it still smoked, and from within we could see the ferocious manner in which it had been destroyed."[27] A few hours later, the minister returned to Lima, and his presentation to the Parliament had the heightened drama of personal experience.

On August 27, in a meeting of the Council of Ministers, there was intense debate about the possibility of calling for military intervention in Ayacucho. With the exception of those representing the armed forces, most ministers were in favor of immediate intervention. Despite the fact that he was military, Gagliardi was opposed. On this occasion, Belaunde inclined the balance in Gagliardi's favor. But from this moment forward, there was no doubt about the military's inevitable entrance into the war, and the army began to make its plans.

The fall of Vilcashuamán was a hard blow for President Belaunde. "With Vilcashuamán, Belaunde really felt the impact. But, as a man of gestures, he refused to give the enemy any credit. The silence, in this case, was very meaningful."[28] It was a silence that thundered. That year, and especially during those ominous months, news of new murders or—what for him, a builder to the core, was more serious—important acts of sabotage, made him repeatedly lose his composure. "When he would hear of acts of violence, he would slam his hands to the table and grimace. These moments were infrequent and very brief. Afterward, he would 'recompose himself,' to use his bull-fighting expression. He never had these fits of violence against people, only when faced with certain situations."[29]

Over the following months, the Shining Path did not distribute much propaganda among its militants about the seizure of Vilcashuamán. When I was in El Frontón in October, this attack was barely mentioned, while others were emphasized. But in later years, references to Vilcashuamán increased in number and importance in Shining Path literature. In 1985, *A World to Win*, the International Revolutionary Movement magazine (the international organization that backed the Shining Path), published a series of drawings made in prison by Shining Path militants. With the heroic figures common to social realism, almost all of the drawings commemorated the seizure of Vilcashuamán. The caption described the attack as "a key battle at a time when local feudal tyrants were forced out and the first popular committees were established."[30] The drawings were made in Lurigancho and dated October 7, 1984, the anniversary of the foundation of the Communist Party of Peru.

The initial silence followed by the propaganda wave could be related to a little-known event. After the attack, next to the razed police station, a bag was found containing Abimael Guzmán's personal documents: his university identification, issued by the University of Huamanga, two copies of his law degree, and a certificate of conditional freedom, renewed by the police department's Judicial Zone II.[31]

At the time, the discovery raised more questions than answers. But it appears that Guzmán was present during the attack. The president of the Republic's challenge had been returned by the person who would soon leave behind the designation of Comrade Gonzalo in order to become "President" Gonzalo.

While the results of this encounter had a special meaning for those who were engaged in a duel of gestures and symbols, other scenes, frozen in battle or in its aftermath, sent a message about the future of the war and a harbinger of worse times to come. As *Caretas* concluded, "what detail better captures the incredible nature of this situation than the helicopter—the only helicopter—passing high overhead while below they take apart the police station?"[32]

And what scene better describes that violent encounter after centuries of neglect than to see that square that Riva Agüero had imagined beautiful, shining, and filled with thousands worshiping the Inca, him with his brow girded by the "loose and bloody *mascapaycha*, gold and scarlet," submerged in shadow even in the midst of light, alone and arrayed only in private fears and furtive glances. And the scarlet tint was not sacred, but, in that still-smoking building, the blood of two dead guardsmen, humble, hurting, defeated.

Party Military Thought

In December, when the plan "To strike!" was concluding, and on the eve of the beginning of the "Great Plan: To Conquer Bases," the Shining Path distributed for internal use a typewritten document[1] that was about thirty-seven pages long and was meant to set down and standardize "party military thought." The document had been prepared and distributed after the National Conference II shakeup. The goal was to inform midlevel Shining Path cadres about the doctrinal foundation behind military actions; describe in detail the dialectical relationship between tactics, strategy, doctrine, and ideology; and define the uniqueness of its military thought as a qualitative advance of Marxism-Leninism-Maoism.

The document summarizes the Shining Path's military philosophy, the theme of greatest interest. In addition, given the circumstances under which it was written—after the Conference II purges and the decision to "enthrone guiding thought" in the midst of an abrupt radicalization—"party military thought" ends up expressing the Shining Path's core beliefs during the years that war became of supreme value to it.

According to the document, to understand "party military thought" means to join oneself "to a single idea and a single action." That, the document asserts, "will make us invincible" and will carry us "with a firm and sure step to victory."

Military thought is, it states, an important part of "guiding thought," which in turn—the document emphasizes—is "an advance of Maoism." As is natural, the text adds, the creator of "guiding thought" has a vital role in the Shining Path's military thought. "C. Gonzalo is the soul, the torrent of the proletarian military line . . . the very soul of this advance is C. Gonzalo's military thought. We must learn from C. Gonzalo." At the same time, military thought does battle with pseudoscience, "rightist positions that hold within them a bourgeois military line."

According to the document, Shining Path military thought is divided in two parts: before and after the beginning of armed struggle.

The first section begins with the "showing and sketching out of the way" by José Carlos Mariátegui, "later brought to a higher level by Comrade Gonzalo." According to the document, which includes passages from Mariátegui, this thinker affirmed that socialist revolution in Peru would be:

- Violent: "power would be seized through violence and would be held by a dictatorship."
- From the countryside to the city: "antiimperialist and antifeudal."
- Prolonged war, massive, total.
- Clash of masses and nations, not armies: with "a new type" of army.

However, the text makes it clear that "Mariátegui's theses are implicit and the leadership has systematized them. . . . because of C. Gonzalo, we know Mariátegui's military thought, because he systematized it in light of Marxism-Leninism-Maoism."[2] For the same reason, "it is not enough to speak of Mariáteguism. . . . Mariátegui must be interpreted through Marxism-Leninism-Maoism. Comrade Gonzalo has done it, and on doing it, has made an advance."[3]

According to the Shining Path, once Mariátegui had died, the new party leadership "disclaims the insurrection in order to oppose revolution,"[4] and in that way "threw away" the 1930s, "when there was a revolutionary situation and therefore conditions to begin armed struggle."[5]

After several years of party and revolutionary decline, the period of "Party Reconstruction" begins, lasting from 1962 to 1979 and divided into three periods: the "Determination" (1962–69); the "Application" (1969–75); and the "Culmination" (1976–79). During this period, the fundamental points of the Shining Path's military thought are defined:

- The adoption of the party's "general political line," made "the only line."
- The determination of the "path to surround cities from the countryside."
- The construction of the party's "armed forces," beginning in 1964 when "this special task is made concrete in Ayacucho and military work is advanced."[6]
- The party is reorganized, a "party leadership" is adopted, and "the reconstitution is completed and a foundation is laid for the Beginning of Armed Struggle."

The document reiterates the Shining Path thesis that there was a second revolutionary situation in Peru at the beginning of the 1960s. "If, in the wake of Mariátegui's death, the party had continued with the Red Line, we would have been put at the head of the movement. But revisionism took over the leadership."[7] At the same time, it affirms emphatically that only the lucky providence of Guzmán's existence made the insurrection possible. "Marxism-Leninism-Maoism exists in Latin America and only in our party has it been applied, because we have the leadership of C. Gonzalo. . . . The party that Mariátegui founded did not jell. Revisionism usurped the leadership. And it is C. Gonzalo who has given us the party we have today: a combat machine that advances the guerrilla war successfully."[8]

The stage of armed insurrection begins, according to this document, when the Shining Path decides "to break the fifty-year spell" and lend the party machinery to convert it into a warlike organization, "sure that our action would be the beginning of the transformation of our people."[9]

As of this moment, the Shining Path begins a long process "to militarize the party." Assuming that the present period is one of wars that would slowly intensify until reaching the level of global conflict, they assert that "all Communist Parties in the world must militarize. . . . This is C. Gonzalo's great contribution to world revolution."[10]

Despite the accusations made against Guzmán in events that predated the decision to begin the insurrection, the Shining Path's militarization did not mean that the party would cease to be a political organization to become an embryonic army. Save for the overriding goal of taking power, Castro-style revolutionaries rid themselves of their political function and ended up by subordinating politics to their military activity. In contrast, the Shining Path maintained its military function subordinate to politics, a difference that was emphasized and became more pronounced as the insurrection grew. The Shining Path armed forces were, from their earliest stage, only one of the party's political instruments, and also served as a conduit between ideology and action.

For Guzmán, the militarization of the Shining Path did not presume a conversion into an army, but rather the focus of political activity on armed insurrection and restructuring the party so that it could direct the war. Politics concentrated on the war, but did not become subordinate to the military organization charged with waging war. Instead, the military organization was kept under strict control at all levels. The armed forces, small or large, could never become the active arm of party politics or the interpreter or shaper of ideology. Strategy, plans, and insurrectional campaigns were carried out as a result of the party's political objectives and therefore were political actions carried out with military means.

Within the Shining Path's military concept, actions in war only made sense if they served the purpose of slowly gaining power for the party. And the party only served a purpose if it interpreted ideology loyally at every level. For Guzmán, a follower of Leninism and Maoism who pushed them to an extreme, war is a political exercise where the use of military means is integrally controlled by political objectives. This is a fundamental distinction. In practice, it meant and means that the party carries out actions different from conventional military ones, and evaluates their success or failure differently. This is the thinking behind the statement that "in order to make war, one must be a philosopher. C. Gonzalo posits battles politically, not technically."[11]

For this reason, the Shining Path defines "armed struggle" through "principle policies" that center on military matters. These policies cover the entire insurrectional process, which would eventually move through all of the conventional stages: Strategic Defense, Strategic Equilibrium, Strategic Offensive. The document emphasizes that "Strategic Defense," the "longest and most complex" stage, was the current one, and would last for several more years. In comparison, the stages of parity and strategic offensive would be much shorter.

According to the document, advance during the stage of Strategic Defense would be achieved through fixed milestones. Each one would be determined by different types and categories of policies, with the following ones being most important:

- Main Strategic Policy: long distance objectives.
- Main Fundamental Policy: objectives reachable through coordinated and specific plans in the medium term.
- Main Basic Policy: The main objective throughout the first stage of insurrection is "To conquer support bases."

With these main policies, the "party military thought" explains the relationship between these milestones and phases in the war.

- *Definition*: The "Main Policy" in this stage is the "Beginning of the Armed Struggle," which in turn is a "Political Strategy" since "it is above all a political problem."[12]
- *Preparation*: "To take the 'military line' as central," also a strategic policy.
- *Beginning*: It has two stages, defined by its main policies.

"To begin the armed struggle" and "to begin guerrilla war" are united through the "beginning plan," which Guzmán proclaimed as another original contribution to the revolutionary arts.

"To develop the guerrilla war" was both a "main strategic policy" and a milestone in the Shining Path classification. According to them, it would take place over a period of several years. Each one of its main policies represents an advance of the overall plan. Until December 1982, these were:

- *To open guerrilla zones as a function of support bases*: between January and April 1981.
- *To unfurl the guerrilla war*: defined as a "Main Fundamental Policy," covering all of the actions between May 1981 and December 1982, whose main policies were:
  - *To conquer weapons and means*
  - *To stir up the countryside by promoting guerrilla actions*: divided in two plans and a cleanup, with a "principal action": the assault on the Ayacucho prison.
  - *To strike in order to advance the support bases*: divided in two campaigns. The second one should have culminated in January 1983.

Since 1983 and until the end of 1986, the "Main Basic Policy" or the "Great Plan" to conquer support bases would be carried out.

In the second volume of this work, more details will be given on each stage and their relationships with party events and the progress of the war. What is important to have in mind here is the form political action by the Shining Path took when the organization decided to militarize. Although tinted with military means and methods, their short- and medium-term objectives continued to be clearly political. And this was the form, complex and apparently intricate, through which Guzmán tried to resolve the apparent contradiction of militarizing the party without converting it into an army, of committing the party to war without having war control the party.

In "To unfurl the guerrilla war," the Shining Path's growth was revealed by increased action. Because of its nature and the virtually total ignorance among the general populace of Shining Path strategy, some actions were not noticed. The main action of this type was the formation in towns and communities of "grass-roots committees," the semiclandestine organisms of Shining Path rule that were replacing government authorities who had fled or had been killed. The Shining Path's main emphasis during the remainder of 1982 was to cause extensive damage to state authority in districts still beyond its control. It is almost beside the point to add that the purpose of grass-roots committees, especially in these first stages, was essentially to organize volunteers or coerce people into broadening the war.

The control of areas in rapid expansion and the need to mount increasingly important operations hurried the Shining Path's work on organizing the foundation of a permanent army, separated from its territorial networks. After the assault on the Ayacucho prison, the "first company," which remained permanently mobilized, was formed. Now it could equip relatively large groups. Virtually unarmed since the beginning of the insurrection, the Shining Path had seized a not insignificant number of military weapons in violent attacks, and had systematically confiscated civilian weapons in the areas it controlled. By mid-December 1982, according to an accounting kept by the Interior Ministry, the Shining Path had two light machine guns, an assault rifle, fifty-four submachine guns, fifty-two revolvers, and an unknown number of carbines and shotguns. Not a lot, but enough to cause considerable damage, thanks to its active logistical network, which could move weapons from one end of the country to the other according to need.

The Shining Path arsenal suffered no scarcity of dynamite. After systematically seizing dynamite in a multitude of attacks on mining settlements, the Shining Path had thousands of sticks by 1982. And as has been made clear, these were not just used in sabotage, but also as offensive and defensive grenades in assaults, skirmishes, and ambushes.

Since October–November 1981, the Shining Path had expected the army to be called into Ayacucho. Under the current circumstances, Guzmán preferred to delay it. "C. Gonzalo proposes: a police occupation, not a military one, benefits us. It has been said that it is not advisable to carry out grander actions as a complementary plan since this could generate problems. . . . If the army comes, we will avoid it and target the police forces, the enemy's weak spot."[13] Of course, the Shining Path had another year to focus on the "weak spot."

As 1982 ended, the Shining Path had managed to make a substantial advance. "Party military thought" reflects a feeling of success within the rebel organization, but it doesn't hesitate to emphasize the need to push the party "To conquer support bases," the "core of the path to surround cities from the countryside. It is the key to the people's war."[14]

For the Shining Path in that exceptional moment of success without setbacks, which would not repeat itself, the way in which Guzmán manages its sudden and successful growth is revealing: with a tight rein and by consolidating control. The key to success in the stage of "To strike!" he reiterates, is having defined the "center of guiding thought: the Military Thought of C. Gonzalo" and having "enthroned" it. And "enthroning" the thought of the red monarch was, in the end, the supreme goal and master key of success. "To enthrone guiding thought will be a hard and decisive battle. It is the crucial battle between two classes, two paths, and two lines. In the two-line struggle, it is proposed that guiding thought and the military line be enthroned. And the core of the two-line struggle is the military line: proletarian and bourgeois. The military problem can only develop according to guiding thought. Party military thought is the guiding thought of C. Gonzalo."[15] Orwell would have appreciated the complex conceptual journey that concluded by converting Guzmán into an emperor of the spirits and, as a consequence, of lives. But he would have had to have recognized this fanatic's efficiency, unifying and focusing wills through carefully designed plans that demanded people who would first devote their lives and later sacrifice themselves.

The Shining Path literature of this period is one of frank praise for war. It does not describe war as just a deplorable historical necessity but, above all, as a superior way of life, a purification, strengthening, and a way of selecting only the best. In December 1981, the Shining Path published a twenty-four-page pamphlet called *On War: Proverbs and Quotes.* The pamphlet was filled with sayings glorifying war. The pamphlet must have been successful because it was reprinted in January 1982. Together with classic proverbs and quotes were those of extreme militarists, the cultivators of multitudinous butcheries:

War is sacred, a divine institution and one of the world's sacred laws. In men, it sustains all of the great values, like honor, dispassion, virtue, and bravery, and this one word keeps them from falling into the most repugnant materialism. (Moltke)[16]

War is humanity's most invigorating iron cure. (J. P. Richter)[17]

Why was a Marxist quoting the unfettered militarism of Prussian imperialists? In reality, both quotes accurately convey Guzmán's attitude toward war at the time, and in some way express his own thoughts.

The "invigorating iron cure" was just around the corner. On December 30, 1982, the Shining Path declared the plan "To strike!" successfully completed. In a broadside circulated among its cadres, the leadership considered the plan's results "a great success . . . mainly in the Principal Region: Ayacucho, Apurímac, Huancavelica." As a result of this "success," the armed forces had entered less than a week earlier. After evaluating the first clashes, the Shining Path issued its troops their first orders.

The entry of the armed forces should be seen as a "qualitative change" in the political situation. Despite the fact that the party was "prepared to develop in this situation," they recommended that cadres pay attention to the advice of President Mao, to scorn the army's strategic abilities while "acknowledging its tactical ability." The order was to avoid direct confrontation. "Harass, go around, search out weak spots." Nevertheless, clashes that would be much more cruel were in the offing. "Essentially, the armed forces have a sinister plan to massacre . . . to declare a war without quarter. We will also give them a war without quarter."

Cognizant of Belaunde's unwillingness to hand over responsibility for the counterinsurgency war to the army, the document interprets the recent change to a defeat of the president by the armed forces. The document ends by proclaiming that the "people's war" is invincible and the guerrillas' determination to "continue combat." And that was how the two bloodiest years of the war began.

20

The Siege of Ayacucho

Along with the Ayacucho offensive, the Shining Path's other regional committees, especially the recently purged Northern Regional, made an effort to intensify attacks. This smaller organization risked suffering greater setbacks than the Ayacuchans.

On August 24, a Shining Path group that had just assaulted the "Santa Clara" farm in Cutervo, Cajamarca, clashed in Sócota with a Civil Guard contingent and was demolished. Its leader, Isidro Chonlón Gasco, was shot four times before most of the group's members surrendered. Recaptured weapons included two revolvers, a carbine, and a submachine gun, all seized in previous attacks on police stations. Chonlón survived his wounds. "In every battle, there are dead and wounded," he told a *Caretas* photographer hours after his capture, when it was still unclear if he would live or die. In El Frontón, Chonlón would become known as one of the most rigid and vehement cadres. He died in the 1986 prison massacre.

Captured in the same skirmish was a woman with a defiant air. Her identification papers carried the name Sandra Mantilla. It was Nelly Chávez, the same woman who had escaped with Isabel Sánchez Cobarrubias from the Arequipa prison after killing their police guard on March 1.

Over these months, the number of Shining Path women killed or captured was unusually high. At the beginning of April, Catalina Adrianzén had been captured in

Cuzco, after her embryonic organization was taken apart during a pathetic attempt to burn a tractor at an agricultural cooperative. Two militants were captured by the furious peasants and delivered to police. The rest were arrested soon afterward.

A month after her capture, I managed to interview her. The veteran Shining Path leader, wife of the then fugitive Antonio Díaz Martínez, was in bad shape. She had open sores and marks on her wrists caused by being kept for long periods in handcuffs. But most of the damage appeared to be psychological. According to her, she suffered from "mental gaps and amnesia." Soon after entering prison, she had to be transferred to a psychiatric clinic, where she remained in 1987.

In Tacna, the Shining Path militant Rosa Soldevilla was captured in August. The Shining Path had ordered her to move from Huancavelica in October 1980. Attacks in the department had been relatively minor but were testimony to the Shining Path's determination to leave no area untouched.

In Andahuaylas, just as the afternoon was ending on September 3, a group of Republican Guards wearing peasant clothes left town in a pickup truck to try and recapture an escaped prisoner. On their way, they were intercepted by two individuals on the highway. A man and a woman stood next to a pickup truck blocking the road, flanked by the sheer wall and precipice of a spot known as Umaca, between Andahuaylas and Talavera. Both gripped revolvers, and must have assumed that the others were unarmed civilians. Before the pickup carrying the Republican Guards completely stopped, one of the policemen opened fire with a submachine gun. The woman fell. Her companion threw himself into the gorge and its bushes and deepening twilight. The Republican Guards, believing that they might have to fight a larger force, returned immediately to Andahuaylas. When they returned hours later with reinforcements, they found no bodies. Their search of the area finally located the woman's body in a small hut nearby, partially covered with straw.

The next day, Minister Gagliardi arrived in Andahuaylas with War Minister Luis Cisneros Vizquerra. The trip had been planned previously, to coordinate lodging at the local army base for a group of Llapan Atic, Republican Guard special forces, and how the two institutions would cooperate. In Andahuaylas, Gagliardi was told about the previous day's clash and that the female guerrilla's body was in the morgue.

Gagliardi went to the morgue. "I saw a woman lying on a concrete table, wearing blue jeans, a sweater, and beneath the blue jeans wool underwear. She had several bullet wounds. One of them was in her back . . . I looked at her and she looked to me like Edith Lagos."[1] The minister ordered fingerprints to be taken, so he could bring them to Lima. On Saturday night, soon after returning to Lima, the positive identification cleared away any doubt: the body was that of the small and by then legendary guerrilla.

The Interior Minister gave the news personally to President Belaunde. The general feeling within the ministry was that, even though it had been pure chance, her death was a severe blow to the Shining Path, perhaps decisive. With perceptions veiled by the experience and model of Castro-style rebellions, the Shining Path was still analyzed in analogous terms. The effect of the death of a commander whose importance was enhanced by legend was believed to be similar to that in a "focus"-style insurgency: devastating. Nevertheless, for Belaunde, there was no reason to celebrate. This was only one more irrational and incomprehensible tragedy that, along with extinguishing lives, represented what the Architect considered to be the national equivalent of suicide: bombing power lines, destroying highways. Without revealing any reaction, the president told Gagliardi that "she should be given a Christian burial."[2]

Minister Gagliardi ordered the police to notify Edith Lagos's family of her death and to allow her parents to exhume the body without delay if they wished and take it to Ayacucho. Soon afterward, Edith Lagos's father traveled to Andahuaylas, where he identified his daughter's body and began his return to Ayacucho.

Reporter Ilpidio Vargas, one of the profession's more original practitioners in the Andes, accompanied him. The invention of the tape recorder had freed Ilpidio for eternity from the bothersome need to take written notes. His notes were sonorous, and mixed his provincial formality with hurried speech, sustained by the infinity of turns of speech that provincial radio announcers employ. His production of audio cassettes was prodigious: the human comedy in weekly installments. For tense editors, overwhelmed by the demands of closing the weekly issue, to receive from Ilpidio a package at the last minute, which would disgorge with a clatter a flood of plastic audiocassettes, was a fundamental spiritual exercise. The great merit of Ilpidio and his perpetual tape recorder, nevertheless, was that they provided the full, round tones of life without interpretation.

On this occasion, nevertheless, the testimony was of a different nature, spare in sound, yet strange. All along the dusty road, groups of people stopped the funeral procession, grieved over the deceased, and watched her continue her journey.

Well before dying, Edith Lagos had touched the fibers from which myth is woven among certain groups of poor people. The image of the polite rebel, the romantic bandit, that arises from almost any civil conflict was in this case a woman. There was nothing romantic about Guzmán or his old guard. Perhaps because of this, a collective longing for a tragic figure in this rebellion had focused on Edith Lagos.

The small and vehement Shining Path member, who had just reached her nineteenth year, had other characteristics that in Latin America attract the collective imagination and form at times the seed of unique cults and followings. In contrast to her father, a merchant who had become wealthy in a relatively short time, Edith Lagos was a person who exuded the intense and total devotion to the Shining Path rebellion that joins the destinies of so many young and idealistic people to mournful epics: a vision of a society built on transcendent and enduring justice beyond the flames and the sacrifices that the journey to it would imply. Because these features were so pronounced in her, in sharp contrast to the atmosphere of her childhood, Edith Lagos symbolized this generation of young Ayacuchans, clay shaped for sacrifice.

Months before she died, in the Huancayo market, a model for so many markets in other towns, wooden statues of an idealized female guerrilla standing beside a budding tree were sold. It was almost an Andean Diana, Huntress, glazed with the ambiguity of fertility and war.

This vision of Edith Lagos held within it the certainty of a brief life. So it was almost a requirement that she die so the young myth could grow. When her cadaver arrived in Ayacucho and the final rites of the funeral and burial were being prepared, the whole city was caught up in the moment. Once more, the auguries had come true. The solemn and mournful rites called out to the entire population.

When the casket was taken to the street for the procession to the cemetery, thousands awaited it. Some calculate that there were 30,000 people. Although this may be an exaggeration, it is beyond doubt that this was the largest crowd assembled there in a decade. Even Huamanga archbishop Federico Richter Prada, a bitter anti-Communist if there ever was one, presided over the funeral mass as the crowd spilled from the courtyards and filled the streets.

When, just outside the church, the casket was draped with a red flag bearing the hammer and sickle, the collective spirit saw nothing contradictory. To them, it was perhaps more an extension of the liturgy than a clash of faiths.

There are those who swear that Abimael Guzmán accompanied the procession.[3] If so, he was completely safe for as long as it lasted. Colonel Delgado Matallana ordered all police to retreat to their barracks to prevent confrontations with the crowd. The Shining Path banner passed openly, and many of its victims as well as people who would become victims in the near future applauded it.

Even the government's chance victories ended in defeat. The Shining Path's organizational machinery, but above all the myth it took advantage of, transformed the death of Edith Lagos from a defeat into a victory.

What led Edith Lagos to this unfortunate holdup in Umaca? The most consistent story was told by a priest to Nicholas Shakespeare.

Edith Lagos's lover was teaching her to drive. For this, they needed a car, so they got one, but it stopped working with the lesson half over. That was when they saw the pickup round the curve and approach them. They both thought that it was just right to finish their lesson. . . . [The police] opened fire and Lagos was killed. Her companion recovered the body and hid it. A child who saw this told the police when they returned, and the corpse was taken to Andahuaylas.[4]

The myth of Edith Lagos also died in its infancy, a few months after her burial. On the one hand, the war itself, with its increasing spiral of violence and cruelty,

242 THE SIEGE OF AYACUCHO

suffocated it. Afterward, there seemed to be nothing redemptive or romantic in the way people lost their lives. On the other hand, the Shining Path strategy, hard, schematic, overorganized, had room for only one personality cult, that of Guzmán, who embodied the party. Edith Lagos's brief apotheosis galvanized the organization, attracted young admirers, imprinted on the rest the sense of their power and inevitability. She was not needed for more.

Not every member of the Shining Path attended the funerals. That same day, a contingent of twenty Shining Path members occupied the town of Matará, in the district of Acocro, not far from Ayacucho. There was a market in Matará, the weekly market. The guerrillas brought with them a prisoner. It was Fortunato Nieto, captured a few hours earlier in his nearby farmhouse. Now the house was burned, and the cattle—seventy head of Brown Swiss and sixty purebred sheep— had been herded up, to be distributed or more probably sacrificed. Nieto's brother, Filomeno, had just been taken prisoner in Matará. Another brother, Aurelio, had managed to escape at full gallop.

Fortunato Nieto had gone to the farm despite his wife's entreaties, nervous about recent violence. Nieto believed he had no personal enemies. Captured in his house, taken to Matará clad in his underwear, and draped only in a sheet, he saw his house burn and his belongings stolen and, in town, bound in the power of his captors, he saw his brother, Filomeno. And he also saw that the people attending the market stared at him with looks both fascinated and fearful, the kind used for people who are going to die. Nieto's last lesson in life was, as I wrote at the time for *Caretas*, "that in these times in Ayacucho, if someone is considered a 'class enemy,' it's not necessary to take it personally since in any case your fate is sealed." Soon after seeing his brother murdered, Nieto was also killed in the central square, after a simulacrum of a "popular trial."

Beside the corpses was laid a sign that said: "This is how the exploiters and the snitches who are against the people die." Another praised the Shining Path and the guerrilla war. Because no one dared touch it, a flag similar to the one that at that moment covered Edith Lagos's casket remained in the square for more than twenty-four hours. It was only removed when a judge arrived from Ayacucho to "recover" formally the bodies.

The countryside and fear were "struck" at the same time.

El Frontón

After the March attack on the Ayacucho prison and the escape of the Shining Path detainees, the government's first worry was that more escapes would take place. The justice minister, in charge of the prisons, decided to carry out a provisional refurbishment of the island prison of El Frontón so that the government could move all of the Shining Path prisoners there. In a short time, two large cellblocks were built along with one smaller one, and men detained for suspected participation in seditious activities were sent there from across the country.

At the beginning of October, I visited El Frontón with photographer Oscar Medrano. We were the first journalists to visit. We were granted permission to interview one of the prisoners who was not Shining Path, Pastor Anaya. A short time earlier, he had been adopted as a prisoner of conscience by Amnesty International.

The reopening of El Frontón in order to confine there new and unheard-of rebels also resuscitated both a fascinating and sinister part of Peruvian history.

In times past, someone had seen in El Frontón, relatively soft in some things, harsher in others, a Lima equivalent to Devil's Island. The comparison was only partially correct. Visible from Callao on a clear day, the vague outline of the island that emerged between the sun's glare and the persistent mist perfectly suggested the history of cruelty, sadism, and violence that several generations of detainees had either produced or, more often, suffered. But no sensation of the ominous finality of the French penal colony existed there, the virtual certainty of being buried in life. To the contrary, for many Peruvian politicians, a stay at El Frontón was only a stretch of the path that would carry them to power. President Belaunde had been a prisoner there briefly during his years as a fiery candidate. Pedro Beltrán, one of the most controversial and important figures in Peruvian politics after the war, was also a guest. But Armando Villanueva, the Apra's defeated candidate for the presidency in 1980, and many of the Apra and Communist members of Parliament had spent much longer and tougher periods on the island.

Only the mention of the names of some of the places in El Frontón could awaken intense emotion. Seal Point, for example, was that species of punishment cell invaded by the sea just as the tide began to rise, carrying with each curling wave the certainty of a long night of agony. Other places stood out in the folklore of common prisoners. Beaches where legendary duels with knives had settled battles for primacy, where escape attempts began and tended to abort, along with the lives at stake, in the rock-strewn whirlpools of "Camotal."

Along the walkway that fronted the distant coast was the post, where many of those sentenced to death saw their last sunrise. Not far away, another punishment cell, this one dry, seemed so like others in the world's innumerable prisons—yet it was worse. It was so low and narrow that it was impossible to stand, impossible to sit, much less to stretch out; and it was only barely possible to breathe. According to legend, it was common for prisoners to go in tough and come out crazy, especially if the cell was shared with some small, slimy, climbing, or hungry animal. What is certain is that no one left the cell on his feet.

With so many stories of horror and humiliation associated with each building, each cell, and each cave, to close El Frontón had been seen as a rupture with some of the most sordid episodes of the recent past.[5] And it was abandoned. For a time, the island remained deserted. Some cellblocks fell down on their own, or the doors fell or were pulled out. Misery and cruelty moved on to other venues.

But the Shining Path insurrection undermined these good intentions. Faced with the risk of more escapes like in Ayacucho, the government decided to immediately rehabilitate the island and imprison the Shining Path prisoners there. In one case, new buildings took on the name of the blue paint bordering the walls. Another was simply called Beach 1.

The Shining Path prisoners as well as others who did not belong were quickly transferred to El Frontón. As happens invariably in Peruvian prisons, the cellblocks were immediately filled beyond capacity and the already marginal infrastructure was quickly overwhelmed. Poor installation meant the electric generators fell apart; and old structures in the Chaparral, overgrown and abandoned, were once again put into service.

Veteran employees from El Frontón's history returned to take responsibility for this new generation of prisoners. They returned as old soldiers who neither hurried their steps nor became excited as the familiar bugle called, but rather trusted that their long experience would help them carry out their daily duties. Bureaucrats like former El Frontón director Brígido Carbajal escorted us to the island. I supposed that he must have seen almost everything that men and prisoners can do and how they fight back. Yet this old guard now confronted new weapons and tactics, and found that the experience had now been transformed into a deadweight on aged bodies and outlooks.

Immediate needs revived El Frontón. The island's new life lasted four years. From the very beginning, it took on a very different aspect than the bureaucrats who had revived it had foreseen. One or two years after it was reopened, the same functionaries who had reopened it could not figure out how to close it. In El Frontón, the Shining Path became for the government a phantasm that distilled and exaggerated the insurrection's national presence, attacking blind spots, growing uncontrollably.

Although the Shining Path had first objected in principle to the move, it rapidly adapted to the new conditions and fully took advantage of them. While at the beginning it didn't want to come, by the end it would not leave. After discovering the convenience of its main "shining combat trench," it won control inch by inch, until it made the prison into a center for training, internal advancement, planning, and indoctrination.

The conquest of this prison, along with other prisons that would fall under a less absolute control over the following years, was an encapsulated version of what the Shining Path insurrection was trying to achieve throughout the country. For the government, it was not only an uncomfortable reminder of the troubling differences between hurried bureaucratic plans and their consequences, but also a threat, since intelligence officers began to see the prison as the place where the Shining Path leadership really functioned, controlling the threads of the insurrection from the island.

Most troubling about the Shining Path's control of El Frontón was that it communicated a disastrous premonition that eventually came to pass. The elements that tend to be present in the violent disentangling of a conflict—anxiety, desperation, mental confusion, vengeance—swelled to an inevitable explosion. And the Shining Path leadership followed and provoked this denouement with its eyes wide open.

Even then, the conclusion was a surprise to the other actors involved. The Shining Path's El Frontón did not crumble bit by bit over time, but was destroyed in the midst of explosions and screams of combat and death. When the Blue Cellblock fell, the enormity of what had taken place buried the history, the legends, the ghosts of the past. El Frontón then became the backdrop of that fight, that demolition, that massacre. Seal Point, the knife duels, the private epics of stoic prisoners and sadistic guards, were erased in the clamor of that bloody battle.

And once again, this tragic wind swept away comparisons and even memory, and in doing so created an entirely new history.

Once we arrived at El Frontón, we walked with Brígido Carbajal to the area around the Blue Cellblock. It was almost noon, and breakfast was just being served to the prisoners. They were lined up in the patio, taking turns filling their plates with food. Two Shining Path representatives chided a prison employee roundly for the delay.

The 250 men waiting maintained their places with obvious military discipline. The group could have served as a demographic cross section of the country. No single type predominated. As the representatives continued their discussion, the prisoners began to chant slogans. The contrast with other Marxist organizations was clear from the very beginning. Instead of their somewhat spontaneous and disorganized choruses, the Shining Path slogans were shouted with the precise and sharp emphasis of a disciplined and trained group.

At each side of the square patio, a voice shouted the slogan in an ordered manner without interruption. The rest of the group responded immediately. Each slogan was repeated three times before continuing to another, with one exception: each slogan to "Marxism-Leninism-Maoism" (now no one confusedly mentioned "Mao Tse-tung thought") was followed by three to "the guiding thought of Comrade Gonzalo." Recent internal shake-ups within the Shining Path had been abundantly reinforced in El Frontón. Aside from "Gonzalo," the only other person named in the slogans was Edith Lagos. A lone voice called out, "Comrade Edith Lagos." The chorus answered, "Present in the armed struggle." "Who killed her?" "The dog Belaunde." "Who will avenge her death?" "The people in combat." "How will they avenge it?" "With weapons in their hands!"

In a brief moment of silence, Medrano and I passed within the formation of men. The silence continued. While Medrano took photographs, I asked no one in particular if along with slogans they had composed some songs, my tape recorder well in evidence.

They sang for nearly an hour, a precise and solemn chorus. While the tunes were borrowed from their Spanish, Italian, and Soviet Communist forebears, the lyrics were completely original, and the pen, the arrangement—or, at the very least, the supervision—of their leader was evident. "Except for power, all is illusion. Assault the heavens with the force of a gun!"

And it continued:

Communist Party, leads to a new life,
Like smoke doubt, fear, blow away;
We have the force, the future is ours,
Communism is a goal, it will be reality.

Next, with a surprising allegro, the adoration:

And the people who listen closely,
after returning from a day's labor,
It is Gonzalo! the fire sings,
Gonzalo is armed struggle.

Gonzalo! the masses roar
and the Andes shake,
they express the burning passion,
a steeled and sure faith.

At some moment, an annoyed guard in a nearby tower overlooking the patio shot into the air. The men in the formation didn't react, nor did the strength of their voices waver. Months later, after a failed riot attempt, the Republican Guard abandoned the tower and left control of the patio to the Shining Path.

Soon, we passed to the Blue Cellblock, which at the time was entirely under the control of the Shining Path and where prison employees no longer entered. There, I conducted a long interview with various representatives, who took turns speaking depending on the subject at hand. The first thing that came to my attention within the cellblock was the internal order and discipline. Despite crowding, the halls were clean (the walls were decorated with Shining Path iconography) as were the bathrooms. Throughout the interview, many of the prisoners wanted to come close to hear it, but other prisoners, whose disciplinary function was clear, ordered them to step back.

I asked them what they thought about other Marxist parties. They answered that the other groups were not Marxists, that they had "yoked themselves to the cart of the reaction." What was their opinion of groups close to them, like Puka Llacta? They responded that "one must fully understand the policies of the United Front." If the members of these parties or groups wanted to "leave behind their wrong positions," they should self-criticize, dissolve, and request their inclusion in the Shining Path on an individual basis. This was the way the Shining Path understood the operation of the so-called United Front.

How did the Shining Path justify the murders of governors, mayors, small businesspeople? "We kill them because they betray the people's cause. . . . There is no alternative for these individuals but to kill them." A few weeks earlier, a Shining Path detachment had tried to kill the president of the community of Ongoy, Félix Olarte, a member of the UDP in Andahuaylas. Failing to capture him, members of the detachment whipped his wife and shaved her head. I asked if they considered this action fair. "It is fair," they answered, "because they are creating illusions, they were serving the enemy. Well, this is justice; justice has class meaning. That is why we impose justice on these people. This is fair, it is correct, it is necessary. In addition, this is a revolution; and anyone opposed to this revolution will simply be crushed as just one more insect."

What were the contributions of guiding thought to Marxism? One cadre was designated to respond to this specific theme. Guiding thought, he said, was an advance of Marxism-Leninism-Maoism, it was a new stage that was not only valid in Peru, but was universal. Continuing, he mentioned several "magisterial contributions" made to Marxism by "Gonzalo": the synthesis of the dialectical laws into a single one, the law of contradictions; the dialectical unity between the objective and the subjective; the systematization of the five phases of armed struggle (explained in detail in another part of this book); the discovery of the laws of the advance of bureaucratic capitalism on a feudal foundation; the identification of the measures necessary to avoid the regeneration of capitalism once the revolution had triumphed ("to organize ourselves into a triple leadership, as party cadres, military commanders, and statists. And arm the masses. So that if we deviate, they will crush us"). Another contribution was the broadening of the laws of the people's war to the global level. While the cadre recognized that "Gonzalo's" written work remained sparse, nevertheless, he hurriedly added that "Let Us Develop the Guerrilla War" was a "pure expression of Comrade Gonzalo."

Without going into the intellectual content of "Gonzalo's contributions," what was important for these organized, disciplined, and fanatic believers who answered us was not only that they were articles of true faith, but that they were absolutely proved to be true.

Soon afterward, we were taken to Beach 1, where Pastor Anaya was held (he was released soon after the publication of our report). There, prisoners had individual cells, one supposed for those who had asked to be isolated. Nevertheless, except for Anaya, the rest of the prisoners were Shining Path, although most of them seemed to be city dwellers. There, we also saw a demonstration, although somewhat less rigid than in the Blue Cellblock.

Through Anaya, and later other prisoners who were members of the United Left, we received the testimony of how difficult it was for non–Shining Path prisoners to live with them, with constant pressures, routine insults, permanent hostility. Except for Anaya, most of these prisoners had gone to one of El Frontón's older areas, called "the Chaparral," obligated to labor for free for the prison authorities in exchange for not being sent to the Blue Cellblock.

The Chaparral was the last stop on our visit. I knew that Luis Kawata was there and tried to interview him. It was impossible. Between the twists and turns of the semidestroyed cellblocks, evasive replies to our queries, and the stolen glances and hand-signaling I glimpsed among prisoners, it became clear that Kawata was avoiding us. Once we realized this, we pretended to have lost interest in the interview and continued to visit other ruined cells. Suddenly, we returned to the place where we had spotted an improvised grill where prisoners were frying fish. And there was Kawata, frying his lunch among a heterogeneous group of prisoners. I approached him and told him that I wanted an interview. He babbled a no, and withdrew with another prisoner while a third prevented us from following.

Not all of the prisoners in the Chaparral belonged to other Marxist groups. Some were people captured as members of the Shining Path, but who had later had problems with the group and had tried to avoid harassment and the interminable rites of humiliation by transferring themselves to the Chaparral.

Were all of those in the Blue Cellblock confirmed and dedicated Shining Path members? According to one Republican Guard officer with whom I conversed as we awaited the boat that would return us to the mainland, the percentage of dedicated Shining Path members was relatively small, but they dominated the rest through coercion and constant pressure. "They arrive here without training, and they leave expert," he told me. The Shining Path's true leadership was a mystery to most. Meetings were held at night, with ski masks on, to avoid identification. Shining Path sentinels watched the Republican Guards twenty-four hours a day, noting their every movement. It appeared to be a pointless task. It wasn't.

We pushed off when it was already dark. A mixed group (the lawyers and family members of prisoners, Republican Guards, prison employees) filled the small boat.

As we left the pier, only a small part of the Chaparral was visible, and small groups of prisoners walked aimlessly and in no particular order around the area where they had been frying fish. After we rounded one promontory, we crossed in front of the Blue Cellblock, where another coordinated activity was being led in the concrete beehive. A banner recently hung from the cellblock windows proclaimed "Long Live the Development of the Guerrilla War!" A lawyer for Shining Path prisoners, until then unnoticed, turned to the Blue Cellblock and the prisoners who watched the boat leave, then raised his fist in the air to give them a prolonged salute. He later turned to the other passengers and crew in the darkened boat, with a defiant glare that little by little dissolved once again into his formerly expressionless countenance.

In the future, I would have cause to remember again and again that long pause, when the Blue Cellblock was lost in the distance and the darkness, especially after the building's final fate. But it was hours earlier, standing in the midst of that block formation, listening to these mournful songs of war and faith, that I arrived at the conclusion that the country faced in the Shining Path a movement whose discipline, intensity, and fanaticism had no parallel in our history, perhaps in Latin America. In that cellblock, now lost in the darkness, were being fed some of the gales that would batter Peru in the future with a force much greater than what was now being felt.

Under Siege

The Shining Path offensive began in Ayacucho in mid-October. Having already made important strikes against medium-sized police detachments (the last attack had been the destruction of the Mayoc barracks, between Ayacucho and Huancavelica, where grenades, rifles, and some light machine guns had fallen into Shining Path hands) and swept away local police stations, the campaign "to strike" continued to systematically tighten the encirclement of the department capital. The siege had two simultaneous dimensions. One was physical, and consisted of the palpable eradication of government authority in the countryside and its replacement with semiclandestine "grass-roots committees." The second was psychological, to use fear to amplify and multiply the effect of military actions. Seemingly bad-tempered attacks contributed to the Shining Path's most practical objective: to close gaps in the encirclement, brutally submit controlled areas, and chip away at the cities from the inside.

On November 4, Yori Luz was killed. Her body remained for several days in the Ayacucho morgue. No one claimed it. Her two sisters, who used to follow Yori Luz around when their mother was gone, were still doing turns around the morgue two days after the murder. For me, their image remains as the living expression of those unfortunate enough to have been children in Ayacucho during those years. There was no respite for these children of war. Only a generation brutalized from its first breath.

On November 10, a Shining Path band attacked another of the university's experimental farms, Wayllapampa. It was pure looting and destruction. Along with the purebred pigs sacrificed and tools destroyed, the main victims of the day were 182 double-breasted turkeys. The attackers had left Ayacucho city and returned to it after the attack. The route between the city and farm was dotted with feathers and turkey carcasses.

Meanwhile, the Shining Path prohibited local peasants in areas it controlled from planting more than what they needed to survive. Going to markets where they would sell their harvests and possibly supply the city was also banned. With these government-style orders issued in the region, the Shining Path acted like the victor.

In Huancaraylla, where guerrillas had killed a former mayor that June, teacher Aurea Quispe de Huamán was kidnapped and killed by the Shining Path on November 5. In Cangallo that same day, a businessman was liquidated.

Meanwhile, student Alberto Rottier was killed by a drunken Republican Guard in Ayacucho. The owner of one of the discotheques that were popping up all over the city to satisfy police demand was also shot to death. Police morale, never high, not only reflected the generalized decomposition within the institution, but also wartime misadventures in Ayacucho and a growing sensation of impotence in the face of the visible worsening of the situation.

While defeat and decomposition tend to feed one another, in Ayacucho, they strolled hand in hand. Things had gotten so bad that the Ayacucho district attorney had felt compelled to write an emphatic letter to Colonel Delgado Matallana in October.

Pointing out that, despite the fact that they faced "an enemy as dangerous as these terrorists," the police "are dedicating themselves to alcoholic beverages and love affairs with girls," the undaunted official continued to analyze and communicate his recommendations:

> On October 1, in a place where Sinchi police in a drunken state began to challenge each other to a game of Russian-style roulette [sic], and one died in this drunken episode; then yesterday, Sunday the third of the current week, a drunken Civil Guard policeman . . . was shot by members of the Investigative Police who were also drunk. . . . In third place, all of the discotheques in the city should be closed immediately . . . to avoid the terrorist-sex operation, since these places are frequently patronized by police members [sic].[6]

On November 14, the Allpachaka farm was once again attacked by the Shining Path, which finished off whatever had escaped the earlier destruction. That same

Shining Path group continued to a neighboring farm, Nuñuhuayco, killed two workers, and carried off 400 sheep and 70 head of cattle.

On November 16, the town of Pacaycasa, only twelve miles from Ayacucho, was occupied by a Shining Path contingent. The district council building, the post office, the health clinic, stores, and local restaurants were dynamited and set afire. In Huanta, someone who traveled from Lima to attend a family member's funeral was captured and killed by the Shining Path.

Over the following days in November, killings increased. All of the victims were modest people. A post office worker and his daughter in Huancapi, a Canarias mine guard, a cook, a farmer. In some cases, several members of the same family: the Chuchóns and the Palominos, for example, were killed at the same time or in quick succession. In the village of Chajo, a Shining Path group tortured and killed Cipriano Palomino and Filomeno, his son (although it had apparently been looking for someone else). Before the group left, it distributed a list with the names of future victims in the district. There were eleven names, six of them Palominos.

Meanwhile, in Lima, the atmosphere of confusion and pessimism did not let up even after State Security arrested Haydeé Cáceres Hidalgo. For Gagliardi, the sensation that the situation was deteriorating was mixed with a sense of personal failure that this honorable soldier made no effort to hide: "I went in optimistic, with the idea that things weren't so bad. . . . I left with a sense of failure. . . . I am satisfied with what I did in Aeronautics. But in the Interior Ministry, I didn't achieve what I thought could be achieved: diminish terrorism, drug trafficking, and common crime. I didn't manage to decrease any of them. This is why I left the Interior Ministry with such serious doubts."[7] During his final months, Gagliardi had used his powers to the maximum, trying to contain the continual unraveling. Still opposed to the entry of the armed forces in the counterinsurgency war, he feared the social cost that it would entail, the effect on the troops, and other dangers that his ministerial experience of a few hours after the 1969 coup had taught him well. Instead, he believed the alternative lay in substantially improving the output from the intelligence services and issuing proper equipment to police.

He had tried out other ideas as well. After the celebration surrounding the Virgen de las Mercedes, the patron saint of the armed forces, he had publicly offered to engage in a negotiation with the Shining Path in order to find a way to make peace. He offered complete security, even if this meant speaking with masked representatives.

Prime Minister Manuel Ulloa publicly contradicted him almost immediately, announcing that the government would not negotiate with terrorists. Gagliardi did not respond, but the next day, he delivered his resignation to Belaunde in the Government Palace.

The president did not accept it, and he publicly expressed his support for

[handwritten marginalia: Murders or clay, discussed out of context... not attached to who context...]

Gagliardi, although without backing his effort to begin a negotiation. But as a result of this struggle, the cabinet agreed that Gagliardi would only remain as interior minister until the end of December. Over the following weeks, choosing a successor became the object of rancorous infighting between factions within Popular Action.

The first to try to gain the post was Prime Minister Ulloa himself. Aware of his sagging fortunes as economy minister and attempting to move to an area where he could achieve tangible, perhaps spectacular results, Ulloa wanted to shift to the Interior Ministry while remaining president of the cabinet. Ulloa believed that the entry of the armed forces was inevitable, and with his cousin, General Luis Cisneros Vizquerra, as war minister, he was confident of a close collaboration that he could administer at the Interior Ministry and coordinate as prime minister.

Ulloa was convinced (to a large degree by his cousin, Cisneros) that with the military intervention and a well-armed police force, the Shining Path insurrection would be put down in short order. For this reason, the funds and debt authorizations that De la Jara and Gagliardi had fought for so unsuccessfully throughout their terms were granted as the year ended. The amount reached $68 million along with a special credit of $6 million for the Sinchis. Most of the funds would be disbursed the following year, when the new interior minister was in place.

Sure of his success, Ulloa arranged for key people to help him as minister. Héctor López Martínez, among others, would continue as vice-minister.

Once he had decided on a plan of action, Ulloa formally asked Belaunde (for the first time) to name him as the next interior minister. The interview lasted more than three hours, and, in the words of a witness in the waiting room, Ulloa "entered triumphant and exited crestfallen."

Belaunde's irritation with Ulloa had been growing throughout 1982. Starting with apparently unimportant things, like the prime minister's lack of personal discipline and habitual tardiness, distance had grown between them gradually. Later, when Ulloa had been received in China as a head of state, the prime minister's satisfaction had provoked the exact opposite sensation of disgust in the rightful and not a little jealous head of state. Told beforehand of Ulloa's ministerial plans, Belaunde, who as much as Ulloa was aware of the successful example posed by Venezuela's Carlos Andrés Pérez while undoubtedly wishing to avoid imitating Rómulo Betancourt in this case, waited for the prime minister to formally offer his services before turning him down, politely but not for that reason any less firmly. Given that Belaunde already had in mind a new prime minister, Ulloa's continuation in the cabinet was no longer a consideration. As the witness to Ulloa's shock said, "It's that when Belaunde decides to get rid of someone . . . !"

In retrospect, Ulloa was lucky to be turned down. Guided by the imprudence of Cisneros, who "gave the impression that this sedition was of no importance, that for the armed forces it was like playing with amateurs,"[8] Ulloa, like all who went before him and many afterward, was possessed of an optimism born from a profound ignorance about the strength and size of the enemy he proposed to fight. Without meaning to, of course, Belaunde saved him from defeat.

Since the beginning of December, the Shining Path substantially intensified its offensive. It had begun the last campaign of "To strike!" and police resistance in Ayacucho was cracking and beginning to show signs of falling apart.

On December 3, the Shining Path celebrated the exalted Guzmán's birthday. The red prophet was given homage with the most propitious sacrifices. A simultaneous blackout darkened Lima and Ayacucho. On San Cristóbal Hill, which overlooked colonial Lima, and on Ayacucho's La Picota Hill, hundreds of cans with burning material inside drew a fiery hammer and sickle in the blackness.

In Ayacucho a day earlier, a regional work stoppage had paralyzed activity in the department. The Defense Front appeared to be organizing the stoppage, yet several other groups, including the Ayacucho Chamber of Commerce, also supported it. Their list of demands never mentioned the Shining Path, but they did demand the withdrawal of the police special forces and the lifting of the state of emergency. Whoever had not supported the Shining Path ideologically now took part in order to unfurl this metaphor for the white flag of surrender.

During these days, this collective sensation of defeat was expressed in a confidential memo from the Ayacucho district attorney, Guillermo Arce Ramírez, to the attorney general, Gonzalo Ortiz de Zevallos. There, the picturesque yet perceptive attorney, whose "sincerity and moral force that characterizes the undersigned, inspired by his calling to loyally carry out the high purpose of Procedural Law DL No. 52," prompted him to communicate "on the subject of these serious terrorist incidents . . . and the daily progress that these terrorists of the Shining Path Communist Party are obtaining."

The police forces . . . do not want to confront this with the firmness and bravery that they should display, these officers having chosen to concentrate themselves in their barracks, abandoning many Stations . . . making it possible for the terrorists to become the lords of all of the rural areas of the provinces of Huamanga, Huanta, La Mar, Cangallo, and Víctor Fajardo. . . . In the aforementioned provinces, the terrorists have begun for all intents and purposes to govern.

This proselytizing work of the Shining Path is now operating . . . in all of the schools . . . in many incursions made in schools, always noted has been the presence of fifteen- and sixteen-year-old youths . . . without any student or teacher confronting them with a discussion to clarify matters at least, since it is understood that there is fear that they will be executed on the spot. . . . in the "Mariscal Cáceres" National High School . . . two months ago . . . once all of the students had begun to sing our National Anthem, they changed the note and began to sing out loudly the guerrilla songs and hymns, before which situation the school director . . . tried to awaken their prudence, telling them that this was a danger to their lives, when one student spoke out and said: Mr. Director, have no fear, nothing will happen to you if you join our ranks.

. . . As a result of this indoctrination, in rural areas the population . . . is under the control of Shining Path government and even to travel from village to village the people have to request a sort of "visa" or "permission" from the terrorist chief.

The inefficiency of the police forces . . . who more often dedicate themselves to drunkenness and amorous exploits with girls . . . and without confronting the Shining Path, because they never oppose Shining Path incursions, but rather surrender and peacefully hand over their weapons and all of their equipment to the Shining Path . . . who attack these towns sure of victory and without suffering any casualties, except in rare situations. . . . Ayacucho's urban population is left to fend for itself . . . and what this is causing is that merchants, small industrialists, and many citizens are planning to migrate to the Coast . . . which in the long run will convert Ayacucho into a desolate City . . . a painful prospect that should not occur in this corner of the motherland because of its history of liberty and much commented upon social tradition.[9]

"I'd Give My Job to Rommel and Montgomery!"

On December 3, I returned to Ayacucho with other reporters. Three represented *Caretas* (editor Enrique Zileri, photographer Víctor Chacón Vargas, and myself) and were joined by William Montalbano, then with the *Miami Herald.* The paralyzed city and the vehement Colonel Carlos Delgado Matallana received us. A Sinchi founder and one of its first officers, Delgado Matallana's personal bravery was beyond doubt. Unfortunately, this did not translate into success in the theater of war.

Delgado Matallana, hurt by a recent article of mine that described his leadership as incompetent, invited us to his headquarters to explain the situation from his point of view.

"The first thing you must understand," he said, "is that these are not the guerrillas from 1965. The ones in Jaén? Also a small group! These guerrillas have incubated for fourteen years. And most of them are Ayacuchans." Without warning, perhaps spurred on by his lack of sleep, the obvious tension, he erupted with a passionate speech: "After what I have seen of the things they are capable of doing . . . these people are murderers, they are beneath contempt, they have lost their souls!"

With a map of the department covering one the walls in the Joint Chiefs' office, he pointed out that he had under his command 6,800 square miles, "a satanic landscape, with over 500,000 inhabitants scattered everywhere" and less than 1,000 men to guard the population. The only way he had at his disposal to cover these long distances, these trails edging precipices, was a single helicopter, "which only flies during the day and in good weather."

"What would you do?" he asked us, "because with these means, with this support, I'd give my job to Rommel and to Montgomery together, to see what they would do!"

Soon afterward, we managed to interview Máximo Cárdenas Sullca, who, as president of the Defense Front, was the titular organizer of the work stoppage. Without doubt, he was aware that, in this new hierarchy, both he and the Front had only the limited autonomy that the Shining Path deigned to give them.

Short and gaunt, Cárdenas continued to give the impression, in earlier years so deceiving, of fragility. Yet now, this impression was less improbable. After thanking us for our visit formally and with great courtesy, he expressed the hope that the work stoppage would help answer "the demands of the people, to end the secular postponement that they suffer." The old revolutionary went down a list of public works and reforms that the Front was requesting for Ayacucho, all sensible and reasonable, possible to achieve in the short term. If this was all . . . "Do you believe that if these demands are met," we asked him, "the violence will cease, would the Shining Path turn in its weapons?"

It was a question that perhaps Cárdenas would have liked to answer, but he obviously could not. With a part timid, part evasive smile, on a visage that still revealed something of his former iron resolve, he told us, "violence is one of the manifestations of the people because of their poverty." And he let us know that it was not appropriate to discuss the theme further.

At noon, we left for Huanta, in a Civil Guard Land Rover, the only way to get around during the work stoppage. We were looking for a German farmer who, in the tragic language of Ayacucho, had been converted into that proverbial journalistic metaphor of the man who bites the dog.

On the night of November 26, a Shining Path contingent attacked the "El Carmen" farm, owned by Eduardo Spatz and his wife, Huanta-born Adriana Cárdenas. It had been one of the war's most announced attacks, seen in Huanta more as the imposition of a sentence than a surprise attack. But Spatz and his wife fought back. After a furious gunfight, the attackers retreated, leaving in a field a Yenan-style cap "with three stars" and a red flag made of "fine cloth," perhaps a final gift from Adriana Cárdenas's niece, Augusta La Torre, the first to condemn Spatz to death five months earlier.

Two days before our arrival, an Ayacucho radio station had reported Spatz's death, finally cut down by the guerrillas' inexorable reach. In Ayacucho, no one knew anything about his fate, including the police.

When we arrived at the farm's entrance two hours later, the scene would have been bucolic save for the sign at the entrance prohibiting entry, warning of fierce dogs. A skull rounded off the sign, a bullet hole through it. Several other craniums, the harvest of a search through an ancient tomb we were told, crowned the exterior wall, which closed in the hen house, the pig sty, the doghouse, and the Spatzes' residence.

The couple was still alive, although to the rest of Huanta Spatz and his wife were little more than persistent specters. When we arrived, both were preparing for another interminable night of watching and gripping their weapons.

They were an incongruous couple for the role that circumstance and their decision had thrust on them. As she gripped an old bolt-action Mauser rifle, Adriana Cárdenas appeared fragile, although she would later reveal a modest, though unwavering bravery. Cárdenas as well as her husband, both in late midlife (he was fifty-five, and she forty-something), appeared intoxicated with fatigue, uninterrupted insomnia, and sustained themselves with that brittle, nervous energy that shores up extreme efforts.

Spatz was armed with a semiautomatic 12-gauge shotgun, a Lüger pistol, a revolver, and a dagger. Short, pot-bellied, with a German accent so pronounced that in other circumstances it would have been almost a parody, the first impression that Spatz inspired, surrounded by skulls and this harsh, death-worshiping scenery, was involuntarily disagreeable (the *Diario la Marka*, a newspaper, had written that Spatz was a "former Nazi fighter," which, considering his age and after reviewing his biography, seemed improbable).

On the other hand, the detail of this unfortunate scenery was overshadowed by what the Spatz's solitary battle represented: the confrontation of the few against the many, this unique resistance to the tyranny of terror. These were reluctant but courageous fighters, surrounded in a Shining Path sea. They fought on despite the fact that people in Huanta considered them corpses. Even the police were afraid to help them.

The story had begun five years earlier. Augusta La Torre had come to the farm to propose that Spatz, a longtime hunter, sell his weapons. He refused. After a tense argument, Augusta screamed at the portly German, "You are one of the first people we will burn!"

Since March 1982, they had begun to notice that armed people passed near the farm. Adriana's family members and friends warned them that, in fact, "they were to be burned."[10]

When they heard about the general warning against planting more than five acres of crops, Spatz didn't plant a thing. Instead, he cemented in several windows, moved out items of value, put barbed wire on the exterior wall, and stockpiled munitions.

Two months before the attack, they received a Shining Path ultimatum. Leave with what they were wearing. A month later, they came to understand that they would be annihilated.

The attack began before 9 P.M. on November 26, in the midst of a torrential rain and the furious barking of the dogs. After the shouts of "Long live the armed struggle!" the dynamite blasts and shots began. The Spatzes, already in firing position, returned fire. Spatz fired while his wife reloaded. During the twenty minutes that the battle lasted, he used more than 300 bullets and all of his guns.

The Shining Path retreated. The next day, the attackers let it be known that they would return. It was a question of saving face. And for the Spatzes, the mere possibility of sleeping at night became a waking dream. They asked the police for help. The Huanta chief sent two local officers to the farm. But the mother and wife of one of the officers went to Huanta immediately and raised such a scandal that they had to be recalled the next day. No replacements arrived, and the chief told them that he could not guarantee their security. He advised them to move to Huanta, as close as they could to the police station.

The Spatzes tried to move. No one would rent them a house. They were told that the Shining Path had given an order that no one was to buy from them or sell them anything. Friends and family members continued to do business, but only in secret.

When Adriana Cárdenas went to Ayacucho to ask for help from the head of the emergency zone, an officer told her that he could not distract his men by offering the Spatzes protection. But he did suggest that they buy "a pair of walkie-talkies at Sears" so that they could request help during the next attack.

When we left the farm to begin our return to Ayacucho, the Spatzes awaited that night with greater apprehension than those that had already passed. It was the eve of Guzmán's birthday. Without much hope, Spatz asked us to request that the local police command center send two officers for a couple of days. "It is almost for sure that they will attack tonight or tomorrow. . . . I'm exhausted, and my wife can't do this any more."

In contrast to so many other stories, this one did not end badly. The Spatzes had to abandon the "El Carmen" farm, but they saved their lives. The story of their solitary war made the cover of *Caretas*[11] and the first page of the *Miami Herald*. The West German Embassy took an interest, and helped Spatz leave the country. His family stayed in Huanta until he found work in West Germany before joining him. The family did what it could to protect her, and Adriana Cárdenas was able to wait in peace in Huanta. She finally emigrated to West Germany, where her husband had found a job working as a night security guard.

In Ayacucho city, the police were undermined morally, not defeated in battle. Except for occasional incursions in the city and its outskirts, generally carried out by the Sinchis, the police concerned themselves first and foremost with their own protection. Fear of an attack like the one that had taken place in March was intense. Guards and night patrols concentrated in the city center. Few officers dared walk on foot at night—even downtown—for fear of the trembling trigger fingers of their own men. Nevertheless, in a not entirely incomprehensible paradox, the disco-theques were filled to capacity. Armed drunkenness and semipublic eroticism—linked without distinction to victory or defeat, but never to one's own exploits—repeatedly offended the mores and self-respect of a conservative, peaceful city. It was not quite the "sex-terrorist operation" denounced by the good district attorney of Ayacucho to his Lima superior, but its effect varied only slightly. The sight of police officers strutting their plumage in the company of more or less shamefaced young girls, watched with disapproval by older Ayacuchans and fury by Ayacucho's young men, were common. As these etiological rites were performed, what caused special friction was that the dominant male was not the victorious macho, but quite the reverse. I would not dare conjecture about how much sympathy the Shining Path won as a result of these damaged relationships, but I do not doubt that many found in the guerrillas' actions a very private satisfaction and saw them as almost a form of vengeance against the impudence that offended so many in public, in private, or both at the same time.

Meanwhile, Belaunde's government continued to keep the armed forces away from the daily direction of the counterinsurgency war. In the meeting of the Council for National Defense that followed the December 3 blackout and attacks, measures to fortify the police were approved. The then recently promoted general Octavio Herrera Polo was named as the new commander of the emergency zone. And both the money as well as the authorizations to incur debt that Prime Minister Ulloa had freed earlier put into motion the machinery of logistical acquisition and the implacable internal battles between different police branches to control them. The next prime minister, Fernando Schwalb, announced that the armed forces would only give increased logistical support to police without directly intervening in operations. The following week, when the situation had deteriorated further, the government decided to push forward by fifteen days the change of command in Ayacucho, while maintaining its decision to keep the armed forces out of the war.

At another level, the frivolous ignorance about the Shining Path and the insur-rection that persisted among most of the country's leadership elite continued to reveal itself as the situation worsened. At the beginning of December, for example, the head of the Popular Christian Party, Luis Bedoya Reyes, and leader Richard Amiel advised the government to investigate the few Chilean refugees left over from the Allende era who still remained in the country. There, they suggested, lay the secret threads of the insurrection.

On December 9, one of the most important Andean bridges was dynamited, over the Pampas River and linking Ayacucho with Andahuaylas and Cusco. Two smaller bridges, Ocros and Pajonal, were sabotaged at the same time.

The bridge over the Pampas did not actually fall, but it was so damaged that it had to be demolished. For President Belaunde, who considered it pure demented destruction, this was a blow to his most cherished ideals. The next day, he sent his transportation minister, Fernando Chávez Belaunde, to direct and coordinate the installation of a temporary bridge. Two days later, the mayor of Ayacucho and president of the Departmental Development Corporation, Víctor Jáuregui Mejía, was shot after inaugurating a health clinic outside Ayacucho. Two people riding a motorcycle approached Jáuregui as he left the clinic, surrounded by friends but without bodyguards. The passenger shot him several times, at point-blank range. Wounded in the face and temple, Jáuregui collapsed. His attackers sped away and were lost from view.

Jáuregui's companions were left so confused or frightened (the day's celebrations had done their part in clouding their equanimity and ability to react) that they remained standing around the immobile body for ten minutes without doing anything. But when one of them noticed that the mayor was still breathing, a hoarse death rattle, they picked him up and took him to the hospital. Meanwhile, the news had spread throughout Ayacucho.

Jáuregui's family arrived at the hospital almost at the same time that he did. They asked Dr. Germán Medina to take charge of the wounded man. Medina, who as the candidate for the United Left had faced Jáuregui during 1980 municipal elections, agreed immediately, but several of Jáuregui's friends disagreed and kept the doctor from touching him. One of them shouted, "This doctor is red. He can't be trusted. He's going to finish him off." Nevertheless, the family insisted and prevailed. In the midst of this tremendous tension, Medina did what he could to stabilize the weak vital signs of a man with two bullets in his head. Hours later, when the immediate danger had been enchanted away, the exhausted Medina opened the door to his car. On the driver's seat, he found a written note: "The people have a thousand eyes, a thousand ears. The best medical attention for the miserable ones, and for the people only to get rich."[12]

While Jáuregui was cared for in the Ayacucho hospital, news of the attack was given to Belaunde. He ordered the presidential plane to fly immediately to Ayacucho with an emergency surgical team aboard, to bring Jáuregui to Lima. The Parliament, deeply shaken, declared a recess.

Operated on in Lima on the following day by the country's finest neurosurgeons, Jáuregui survived and managed, after several months, a partial recovery. He later returned to Ayacucho, where he remained retired from political life. No one bothered him further.

Meanwhile, the city of Huamanguilla was occupied briefly by a Shining Path contingent. Mayor Artemio Palomino and Councilman Juan Huamán were murdered in the central square. A peasant who had been shot died three days later.

Rumors of a bloody attack on Ayacucho for Christmas circulated with growing force. Emigration by airplane, already marked since the attack on Jáuregui, overwhelmed the normal capacity of the airlines.

As the rush to leave threatened to turn into a panic, the military and police intelligence service gave credence to the rumors of an imminent Shining Path attack on Ayacucho. And despite the fact that police reinforcements had arrived over the previous days, few people believed the police could fend off a serious Shining Path attempt.

Their doubts were settled in two days. On December 20, Huamanga subprefect César del Solar was wounded by four shots just 200 yards from police headquarters. The next day, two Shining Path militants entered the office of the regional director of the National Institute of Culture, Walter Wong, and shot him. Afterward, they walked slowly away, their faces uncovered, among institute employees paralyzed by fear.

Wong died in the Ayacucho airport, as doctors tried to evacuate him to Lima. Hours later, during a ceremony in the Naval College, Belaunde received the news, and made the immediate decision to entrust the pacification of the emergency zone to the armed forces.

At noon, Héctor López Martínez received a call from the president, who asked him to draft the executive order that would approve the entry of the armed forces into the war and bring it to the Government Palace without waiting for Gagliardi. The minister was in the beach resort of San Bartolo, attending the closing ceremonies of classes for Civil Guard women. Belaunde probably wanted to save his interior minister from having to witness the unpleasant moment when he would sign the order that would make official the police failure and cede control of the fight to the armed forces.

When López Martínez arrived at the palace, he encountered there the military ministers, the heads of the armed forces, and Foreign Minister Arias Stella. After reading the draft of the executive order, Belaunde ordered the term "sabo-terrorism," which fascinated López Martínez, to be removed. In the short time it took to recopy the document, War Minister Cisneros Vizquerra made a speech about the

THE SIEGE OF AYACUCHO 261

situation. He, like the other soldiers, "were just as one would have supposed, thinking that they had the situation in hand. . . . At that moment, the impression that I got was of the assured smile of people who thought it was an easy matter. Very assured."[13] In contrast, Belaunde's expression was serious and concerned throughout the afternoon.

The executive decree ordered the armed forces to assume control of internal order in the emergency zone.[14] None of those present in this meeting thought that the military campaign would last more than a couple of weeks. The most pessimistic among them calculated a few months.

Two days later, pushing forward the military entry by a week in order to prevent the suspected Christmas attack by the Shining Path, soldiers from the infantry's Division II, headquartered in Huancayo, and the Airwing Division from Lima arrived in Ayacucho. Trucks loaded with troops, on their way to "Los Cabitos," crossed paths with the funeral procession that carried the remains of Walter Wong to the cemetery. It was the first of many similar encounters.

A long stage of the insurrection had reached its end. The democratic government had failed to put it down with the normal means of control at the disposal of civilian government. Upon entrusting the war to the armed forces, in a country where the limitations of civil control over the military apparatus were and continue to be evident, few doubted that this region in turmoil would be subjected to a regime very different from that in the rest of the nation. And that, for a brief and violent time, much blood would flow. Except for the matter of how long it would last, on this last point no one made any error.

Notes

The Arrest

1. File No. 019-DSE-PE, January 7, 1979. For his part, Ricardo Letts managed to elude capture.
2. Ibid. In the chapter "The Fall of Vilcashuamán," there is additional information on Guzmán's missing documents.
3. Interview with noncommissioned officer *Pablo Aguirre*, January 29, 1987.
4. Ibid.
5. Interview with Laura Caller, September 7, 1987.
6. Interview with NCO *Pablo Aguirre*, January 29, 1987.
7. File No. 022-DSE, January 11, 1979.

Chapter 1

1. *Caretas*, January 4, 1980.
2. In 1982, his last year of service, growth was registered at 0.9 percent. The following year, the economy shrank by 12 percent.
3. *Caretas*, January 4, 1980.
4. Among the dozens of articles that the magazine *Caretas* dedicated to the Langberg case, see the following: "Esa vez en Ayacucho," *Caretas*, no. 684, February 8, 1982 (the first article on the case); "Sí, Villa Mercedes es de Langberg," *Caretas*, no. 685; "El caso se profundiza," *Caretas*, no. 687, March 1, 1982 (Langberg's arrest); and "Entrevista el la Maison de Santé," *Caretas*, no. 811, August 6, 1984.
5. Interview with Juan Granda, August 22, 1987.
6. During the student battles of 1972–76, an attempt was made to blow up the door to Carlos Tapia's house with explosives.
7. The FUE was the largest student political group at San Cristóbal de Huamanga National University (the others were the CTR and Antifascist FER). The FUE managed to end for a time (in 1974) the Shining Path's hegemonic control over the Ayacucho student movement.
8. Interview with Juan Granda, August 22, 1987.
9. Ibid.
10. Interview with *Victor Suero*.
11. In February 1980, Alfonso Barrantes, who over the following years was to become the left's largest vote-getter and strongest coalition candidate, removed himself from the UDP's candidate list.
12. Fernando Tuesta Soldevilla, *Perú político en cifras* (Lima: Fundación Friedrich Ebert, 1987); Alvaro Rojas Samanez, *Partidos Políticos en el Perú* (Lima: Centro de Documentación e Información Andina,), pp. 217–36; Piedad Pareja Pflucker, *Terrorismo y Sindicalismo en*

Ayacucho (Lima, 1981), pp. 23–25. My percentage totals of the votes won by the Marxist left differ somewhat from those of Rafael Roncagliolo (cited in Piedad Pareja's book) because I don't include Frenatraca among what he terms the "grass-roots parties" and he does not mention the Socialist Party.

Chapter 2

1. Interview with *Víctor Suero*.
2. Interview by *Elba Carrasco* with Quispillacta authorities, 1985.
3. Ibid.
4. According to law, the armed forces are responsible for guaranteeing election security.
5. *Panorama*, a news magazine show, May 21, 1980. In Piedad Pareja Pflucker, *Terrorismo y Sindicalismo en Ayacucho* (Lima, 1981), p. 91.
6. The main Chuschi study is a book written by Billie Jean Isbell, *To Defend Ourselves* (Austin: University of Texas Press, 1978). Later the director of the Latin American Studies Program at Cornell University, Isbell lived for long periods in the community between 1967 and 1975. David Scott Palmer studied the effects of the agrarian reform in Chuschi, among other locations, in his doctoral dissertation: "Revolution from Above: Military Government and Popular Participation in Peru, 1968–1972." Also of interest is Antonio Díaz Martínez, *Ayacucho: Hambre y Esperanza* (1969; Lima: Mosca Azul, 1985), especially pp. 100–105, which is written from the Shining Path perspective.
7. Palmer, "Revolution from Above," p. 220.
8. Isbell, *To Defend Ourselves*, p. 49.
9. Ibid.
10. Ibid., p. 65.
11. Palmer, "Revolution from Above," pp. 221–23. Isbell, *To Defend Ourselves*, pp. 192–93, 238.
12. Interview by *Elba Carrasco* with Chuschi's Protestant pastor, 1985.
13. Isbell, *To Defend Ourselves*, p. 226.
14. Ibid.
15. Ibid., p. 237.

Chapter 3

1. Among the available notes, I have guided myself by a typed version prepared in 1981 by the Ayacucho chief of police office. "Long Live the Armed Struggle!" was based on captured notes and notebooks.
2. The quotation, with some changes in the transcription, comes from the letter to Ludwig Kugelmann, April 17, 1871. In *C. Marx, F. Engels, Obras Escogidas* (Moscow: Editorial Progreso), pp. 705–6.
3. This transcription reflects idiomatic mistakes made in the original.
4. A brief, sanitized version of the incident exists, seen from a Shining Path point of view, in "Bases de Discusión," Linea Militar, *El Diario*, January 6, 1988, p. 6. On the accusation against Guzmán of "Hoxhism," see, in the same document, p. 7.
5. Washington Irving, *The Life of Mahomet* (Leipzig: Bernh, Tauchnitz, 1850).
6. But he must have found a certain satisfaction in reading about the early tribulations com-

mon to prophets: "The greatest difficulty with which Mahomet had to confront at the outset of his prophetic career was the ridicule of his opponents. Those who had known him from his infancy—who had seen him a boy in the streets of Mecca and afterward occupied in all of the ordinary concerns of life, scoffed at his assumption of the apostolic character. . . . Some who had witnessed his fits of mental excitement and ecstasy considered him insane." Irving, *The Life of Mahomet*, pp. 57–58.

7. Ibid., p. 49.

8. During the 1960s and 1970s, the Shining Path's political enemies used the term "sacred family" to refer to those guerrilla leaders linked by diverse and, at times, complicated family ties.

9. José Carlos Mariátegui, letter to Samuel Glusberg, April 30, 1927. The letter is published in *Correspondencia de Mariátegui*, vol. 1, p. 273. The quotation is written precisely as it appears in the Shining Path document.

10. "Bases de Discusión," Linea Militar, *El Diario*, January 6, 1988, p. 6.

11. With minor modifications by the Shining Path, the quotation is taken from Mao Zedong's *On Prolonged Guerrilla War* (Peking: Ediciones en Lenguas Extranjeras, 1967), p. 263.

12. Ibid., p. 264.

13. On the possible influence of Jomini, a military theoretician, on the Maoist concept of "interior ideology" and "exterior ideology," see John Shy and Thomas W. Collier, "Revolutionary War," in *Makers of Modern Strategy*, ed. Peter Paret (Princeton, N.J.: Princeton University Press, 1986), pp. 843–44.

Chapter 4

1. Interview with Héctor López Martínez, May 6, 1987.

2. Both the "brigade" and "division" were relatively small departments within the National Police, each with a few dozen detectives. The use of military terminology simply reveals the compulsive desire among the police to imitate the military's tone, form, organization, and even operative structure. Often, this produced pathetic results.

3. For more on Zárate, see Chapter 17.

4. In 1978, the antidrug police under Ipinze's command arrested Rodríguez López's wife and a Colombian woman in a Lima cocaine laboratory. Rodríguez López was neither arrested nor mentioned in the police report and the two women were released without charge on the orders of a judge who later received free airline tickets from Rodríguez López. Ipinze as well as the police captain in charge of the case appeared in documents soon afterward as recipients of Rodríguez's favors. On the case known as "Villa Coca" (linked to Rodríguez's organization), see articles published in *Caretas*, particularly from July to August 1985 and June to December 1986. Specifically on the police, prosecutor, and judicial investigations into Ipinze, see the police report dated January 28, 1986, signed by Generals Alberto Suárez Caballero and Raúl Chávez Gonzales, particularly pp. 37–40. Also see the later opinions filed by special prosecutor Miguel Espinoza and investigative judge Hugo Príncipe Trujillo.

5. Aside from the accounts that appeared in the Peruvian press, this episode appears in James Mills, *The Underground Empire* (Garden City, N.Y.: Doubleday, 1986).

6. Rivera Llorente remains a fugitive to this day. For more detail on this escape and the investigation, see ibid.

7. This does not mean, however, that more "pragmatic" sectors within Popular Action,

more experienced in managing these issues, would have made a different choice. From the beginning, the majority within the Parliament, controlled by Alva Orlandini, blocked Luque's promotion and favored the careers of the Ipinze-Jorge group. Later, after they gained control over the Interior Ministry, corruption grew explosively, to the point where for all intents and purposes it dominated the ministry.

Chapter 5

1. The military government's preoccupation about "subversion" stemmed from its fear of an eventual explosion of an urban guerrilla war, in the style of organizations active in the continent's southern cone, and especially in light of its experience with Sutep, general strikes, and street clashes with rioting strikers. This worry was heightened by the memory of an urban riot that took place on February 5, 1975, the successful general strikes of July 19, 1977, and May 22, 1978, and Sutep's growing aggressiveness in spite of the dogged persecution of its leaders.
2. Interview with Héctor López Martínez, former interior vice-minister, July 20, 1987.
3. Ibid.
4. Report 008-GNC-77, March 16, 1977, Naval Intelligence Headquarters, Navy Ministry.
5. Ibid.
6. In terms of the quality, reliability, and importance of information, the highest classification is A/A/1.
7. SIN Report 1379, June 27, 1977.
8. Report 863 SIE, July 19, 1977.
9. SIN Report 3219, December 28, 1977.
10. Intelligence Report 17-DPE from Civil Guard Central Intelligence, December 6, 1978.
11. SIE Report 1343, April 30, 1979.
12. Intelligence Report 09 DPE, May 24, 1979.
13. *Caretas*, no. 566, August 20, 1979.
14. SIN Report 3076, September 6, 1979.
15. "Agent Report," October 1979.
16. Ibid.
17. Ibid.
18. Intelligence Report, Ayacucho, October 2, 1979.
19. Report: Operation "Morococha," Monterico, October 12, 1979.
20. Ibid.
21. Ibid.
22. Ibid.
23. SIN Report 4076, December 18, 1979.
24. SIN Report 149, January 17, 1980.
25. SIN Report 486, February 18, 1980.
26. DIGIS Report, February 21, 1980.
27. Ibid.
28. DINSE-FAP Report 339-FL, February 22, 1980.
29. Ibid.
30. SIN Report 922, April 4, 1980.
31. The emphasis is the author's. GRP/DINT Report 382, April 9, 1980.
32. However, it appears that there was a certain preoccupation among the middle ranks of the armed forces, which never jelled. Something of the debate filtered to the press, although—

perhaps because of the source of the information—it arrived distorted. On February 2, 1980, *Caretas* mentioned that "a sector of the armed forces is cooking up reports of ghost guerrillas, hoping to stir up the pot." It must be remembered that, in these months, there was an intense and reasonable fear that the electoral process would be sabotaged. This fear was used in order to deactivate the alarm that, apparently, some did try to raise.

Chapter 6

1. "The Hand of the M.O.T.C.," *Caretas*, no. 603, June 16, 1980. The Movement of Laborers, Workers, and Peasants is one of the primary "groups generated" (front groups) by the Shining Path.

2. The elevation of "Mao Tse-tung thought" to "Maoism," an academic decision that was undoubtedly audacious and had concrete political objectives, was not made until 1982. See Chapter 15.

3. On general policies and strategic policies, see Chapter 19.

4. MOTC, "La celebración del Primero de Mayo por el Proletariado Revolucionario," 1980, p. 2.

5. Ibid., p. 4. The emphasis appears in the original MOTC document.

6. Ibid., pp. 4–5. The uppercase emphasis is in the original document.

7. Ibid. The emphasis is mine.

8. On the basic concepts of war, see Chapter 19.

9. See Chapter 1.

10. MOTC, "La celebración," pp. 6–11.

11. Piedad Pareja Pflucker, *Terrorismo y sindicalismo en Ayacucho* (Lima, 1981), pp. 82–83.

12. "¡Desarrollemos la Creciente Protesta Popular!" September 1979, p. 15.

13. Pareja, *Terrorismo*, p. 91.

14. Ibid.

15. Intelligence Report 001, Civil Guard Intelligence Headquarters, February 13, 1981.

16. Interview with Germán Medina, July 30, 1987.

17. Interview with *Elba Carrasco*, Cangallo Agrarian League, 1986.

18. "Paladín," August 5, 1980. Taken from Pareja, *Terrorismo*, pp. 92–93.

19. Interview with Germán Medina, July 30, 1987.

20. Interview with *Elba Carrasco*, Cangallo Agrarian League, 1986.

21. The children of several members of the "sacred family" lived in neglect and abandonment in Ayacucho for much of the first eight years of the war, even though in several cases well-off relatives uninvolved in the insurrection lived nearby. This Dickensenian aspect to the fight was not easy to understand. And the disdainful comments made by Shining Path members about Andrés Vivanco Amorín, who dedicated his last and best years to protecting war orphans, must be understood in this context. It perhaps combines something of the traditional disinterest, rooted in the culture of the Hispanic conquerors, for casual or later children, with the symbolic gesture of sacrificing the family to an all-consuming cause.

22. Interview with Germán Medina, July 30, 1987.

23. Ibid.

24. *A World to Win*, June 1986, p. 71.

25. I have guided myself with the same typed version, based on captured documents, made by Ayacucho police headquarters in 1981 and mentioned in Chapter 3.

26. *A World to Win*, June 1986, p. 71 and typed version.

27. In light of the tremendous difference in the conditions surrounding the Albanian insurrection and that of the Shining Path, the accusation is off the mark even from an exclusively
military point of view. For a brief review of the insurgency in Albania, see Walter Lacqueur,
Guerrilla (Boston: Little, Brown, 1976), pp. 224–26.

28. See, for example, "Sendero y el Ejército Popular," part of the paper "Bases de Discusión," *El Diario*, January 6, 1988, p. 7; and *A World to Win*, July 1986, p. 71.

29. "Bases de Discusión," p. 7.

30. Ibid.

31. Robert Taber, *The War of the Flea* (London: Paladin, 1970).

32. Intelligence Report 001, Civil Guard Intelligence Headquarters, February 13, 1981.

33. Interview with Héctor López Martínez, May 6, 1987.

34. Ibid.

35. Ibid.

36. Pareja, *Terrorismo*, p. 48.

37. Interview with Héctor López Martínez, May 6, 1987.

38. Pareja, *Terrorismo*, pp. 52–63.

39. In statistical terms, there were 177 dynamite attacks in 1980, 76 with Molotov cocktails,
35 robberies of explosives, 3 robberies of weapons, 67 demonstrations and distributions of propaganda calling for "armed struggle," and 4 assaults on radio stations to transmit propaganda.

40. Pareja, *Terrorismo*, p. 94, and Intelligence Report 001, GC Intelligence, February 13,
1981. The Shining Path refers to the attack as "the first annihilation, this is to say an attack on
the living force of the enemy. For the first time, reactionary elements . . . were executed." *A
World to Win*, June 1986, p. 71.

Chapter 7

1. *Caretas*, no. 630, January 5, 1981.

2. Ibid.

3. Ibid.

4. Patricio Ricketts, "Zonas Liberadas," *Caretas*, January 26, 1981.

5. *Caretas*, no. 668, October 12, 1981.

6. Ibid.

7. *Caretas*, no. 631, January 12, 1981.

8. Information Report 228-DS-03.00, appendix 1, May 7, 1981.

9. Intelligence Report 001, DIRINGC, February 13, 1981.

10. On Willy Esquivel, see Chapter 20.

11. Intelligence Report 001, DIRINGC, February 13, 1981.

12. This was the third plenary session since the first conference in September 1979.

13. For a more detailed analysis on the Shining Path war classification criteria, see Chapter
19.

14. Except where noted, references to events, discussions, and agreements during the third
plenary come from a version typed in 1981 by the Ayacucho Police Headquarters—"¡Viva la
Lucha Armada!"—based on captured notebooks and notes.

15. See "Crack Secret Police Outfit to Combat the Shining Path's Offensive," *Andean Report*,
March 1987.

16. *A World to Win*, June 1986, p. 71.

17. Robert Taber, *The War of the Flea* (London: Paladin, 1970), p. x.

Chapter 8

1. JOOPP-ZE, "Apreciación de la situación en la Zona de Emergencia del Departamento de Ayacucho."

2. Decree Law 046, Article 1.

3. Ibid.

4. For example, this was the case of Segundo Centurión, a farmer and activist detained in the department of San Martín.

5. Decree Law 046, Article 7.

6. *Caretas*, no. 643.

7. Curiously, one demand was not only for the direct transmission of television programs from Lima, but also for the addition of a new television channel.

8. Interior Ministry, "Cronología de los hechos en Puno," April 20, 1981.

9. *Caretas*, no. 645, April 1981.

10. Ibid.

11. *Caretas*, no. 646, May 4, 1981.

12. Ibid.

13. However, until this moment, the Shining Path had dynamited seven electrical towers, few compared with the dozens that would be dynamited routinely in later years. Yet in terms of economic damages, the cost was already high.

14. *Caretas*, no. 656, July 13, 1981.

15. *El Comercio*, July 15, 1987.

16. For more on the attack, see JOOPP-ZE, "Apreciación de la situación en la zona de emergencia del departamento de Ayacucho"; and "Apreciación de Operaciones," November 1, 1981.

17. Ibid.

18. *Caretas*, no. 665, September 21, 1981.

19. JOOPP-ZE, "Apreciación de la situación en la zona de emergencia del departamento de Ayacucho"; and "Apreciación de Operaciones," November 1, 1981.

20. "Interview with Abimael Guzmán, 'President Gonzalo,'" *El Diario*, July 24, 1988, p. 20.

21. Karl Marx, *The French Civil War*, with an introduction by Friedrich Engels. These Soviet editions also contain additional commentary by Lenin.

22. John Shy and Thomas W. Collier, "Revolutionary War," in *Makers of Modern Strategy*, ed. Peter Paret (Princeton, N.J.: Princeton University Press, 1986), p. 826.

23. Marx, *The French Civil War*, p. 827.

24. Franz Borkenau, *European Communism* (New York: Harper Brothers, 1953).

25. John Armstrong, ed., *Soviet Partisans in World War II* (Madison: University of Wisconsin Press, 1964).

26. See the corresponding footnote in Chapter 3.

27. Mao Tse-tung, *On Protracted War*, p. 235.

28. In the excellent *Guerrilla* (New York: Harper and Row, 1963), Charles W. Thayer makes a fascinating comparison between the competing guerrilla insurrections of the Chetniks, led by Drakha Mikhailovich, and Tito's partisans. (Thayer served under Tito for a time as a liaison officer for the Allied command.) At the beginning of the war, Thayer noted, all available information suggested that Mikhailovich, a decorated military professional surrounded by a staff made up of top officers from the Yugoslavian army, had the advantage over Tito, a politician without conventional military experience and whose officers had more enthusiasm than professional knowledge. Yet four years later, the Chetniks were destroyed and the partisans were pursuing the Germans throughout Yugoslavia. What happened? As a general observation,

Thayer repeated what has been sustained by many of the best theoreticians and practitioners of guerrilla insurgency: military training tends to be an obstacle, not an advantage when put up against the extreme demands of flexibility, adaptability, and paradoxical actions that guerrilla warfare requires, especially in its initial phase.

But Thayer makes an additional observation that goes to the core of the theme discussed in this chapter. Faced with the savagely repressive and indiscriminate tactics employed by the Germans, Mikhailovich tacitly capitulated and virtually ceased operations. As Thayer points out, "The Germans knew that the Achilles heel of a guerrilla movement is not the elusive guerrilla in the forest, but the family and property he leaves behind." In contrast, Tito was not intimidated in the least by the effectiveness of the retaliation. As has been evident in other cases, the Communists were not at all interested in restoring the previous social order. Up to a point, the total destruction carried out by the Germans made their work easier. And as Thayer adds, "Of course, as repression increased, he could expect more recruits from those left without a roof or family." Tito's genius was to make the most of each increase in recruits or weaponry, but this all would have come to naught without his willingness to accept the abysmal sacrifices that war professionals refused to bear.

On this theme, see in particular Thayer's chapter titled "The Leadership."

29. It has to be added once again that the need for self-sacrifice was also understood by some non-Communist leaders. In his introduction to Thayer's book, Fitzroy MacLean, an outstanding British officer expert in guerrilla warfare during World War II, quotes T. E. Lawrence: "We knew that we had won over a province when we were able to teach the civilians to die for our idea of liberty."

30. From the fourth plenary forward, all Shining Path militants had to make the "promise," which might be better termed a vow. Although the language may vary, the meaning remains the same. "I commit myself to Comrade Gonzalo, leader of the Communist Party of Peru and the world revolution. I commit myself to the Central Committee of the Communist Party of Peru. I commit myself to Marxism-Leninism-Maoism, the Guiding Knowledge of Comrade Gonzalo, to accept my responsibility as a member of the Communist Party of Peru and never betray the party or the people. I commit myself with bravery, decision, and courage to fight against imperialism and feudalism until the liberation of the oppressed peoples of the world is achieved. I commit myself to struggle and offer my life to the world revolution."

31. Manuel Jesús Granados, "Ideology of the Communist Party of Peru–Shining Path," *Socialismo y Participación* (March 1987).

32. Shining Path manuscript. Written in Lurigancho in 1985.

33. Martin Van Creveld, *Command in War* (Cambridge, Mass.: Harvard University Press, 1985).

Chapter 9

1. See Chapter 19.

2. From this vantage point, it is difficult to resist pointing out that these other insurrections, led from the beginning by military professionals, experienced neither a faster growth nor greater success. In terms of military professionals who led insurrections, perhaps the most notable case was that of Giorgios Grivas, head of the Cypriot EOKA. Nevertheless, this insurrection was markedly smaller than the ones mentioned here.

3. *Caretas*, no. 663, September 8, 1981.

4. Using the Shining Path's translation, the "Three Rules" are:

- Obey orders during actions.
- Take not a single needle or length of thread from the masses.
- Turn over everything captured.

The "Eight Warnings" are:

- Speak courteously.
- Honorably pay for what is bought.
- Return everything borrowed.
- Pay for everything damaged.
- Do not hit or harm the people.
- Do not trample crops.
- Take no liberties with women.
- Do not mistreat prisoners.

5. *Caretas*, no. 665, September 21, 1981.
6. Interview with Héctor López Martínez, April 20, 1987.
7. Ibid.
8. In a veritable institutional resurrection, Luque returned from retirement years later, in 1987, as chief of the Interior Ministry's intelligence service. His performance was less than hoped for. It should come as no surprise, given that much of his reputation rested on antiterrorist operations carried out in the 1970s in collaboration with, for example, the Argentine services that arrested Montonero activists in Lima. However, his failure was not due to the dubious moral or legal dealings inherent in such actions, but because this experience acted as a prism that distorted his perception of the Shining Path insurrection.

Chapter 10

1. *Nueva Democracia* 1, no. 34 (July 1981).
2. In the Soviet Academy of Sciences' *Dictionary of Philosophy*, written under the supervision of Yudín and Rosenthal, of course during the most virulent years of Stalinism, the summary of Stalin's contributions to philosophy took up more space than the combined pages dedicated to Plato, Aristotle, Kant, and Hegel.
3. *Nueva Democracia* 1, no. 34 (July 1981), p. 2.
4. Ibid., p. 4.
5. *Perú Económico* 3, no. 6 (June 1980). Taken from *Nueva Democracia*.
6. *Nueva Democracia* 1, no. 34 (July 1981), p. 5.
7. Ibid., p. 6.
8. *Debate*, no. 5, August 1980. Taken from *Nueva Democracia*.
9. *Nueva Democracia* 1, no. 34 (July 1981), p. 13.
10. Ibid., p. 15.
11. Ibid., p. 16.
12. Ibid., pp. 17–18.
13. Ibid., p. 18.
14. Vladimir Lenin, *Proletarian Revolution and the Renegade Kautsky*, taken from *Nueva Democracia*, p. 20.
15. This is a not very subtle reference to Hugo Blanco, a Trotskyite parliamentarian.
16. *Nueva Democracia* 1, no. 34 (July 1981), pp. 20–21.

17. Ibid., p. 22.

18. Ibid., p. 23.

19. Throughout *New Democracy*, he is referred to as "Deng Hsiao-Peng" or the older form of "Teng Hsiao-ping."

20. The Trotskyites had experienced this state of affairs much earlier. Unlike orthodox Marxism, however, Trotskyism was an inheritance that had not developed under the full and prolonged use of power.

21. *Nueva Democracia* 1, no. 34 (July 1981), p. 25.

22. Ibid.

23. See Chapter 15.

24. *Nueva Democracia* 1, no. 34 (July 1981), p. 26. The emphasis is in the original.

25. Ibid., pp. 28–29.

26. Ibid., p. 29.

27. Ibid., p. 31.

28. Ibid., p. 34.

29. Ibid., p. 38.

Chapter 11

1. *Caretas*, no. 699, October 19, 1981.

2. Ibid.

3. Ibid.

4. Ibid.

5. Supreme Decree 026-81-IN, October 12, 1981.

6. This was based on Articles 2 and 23 of the 1979 Constitution.

7. His testimony was received with skepticism in Lima as well as Ayacucho. But in the end, this was the least of his problems. Villaverde, who had managed to escape the Shining Path cadre who wanted to kill him on October 11, was finally found and shot down by the Shining Path in Ayacucho several months later, a short distance from the Ninth Station.

8. Sonia Goldenberg, "Tambo, el Puesto Acribillado" (with photographs by Oscar Medrano), *Caretas*, October 19, 1981.

9. Nota de Información No. 01-EEI-"Vivanco" DIRINGC-EEI, November 9, 1981.

10. Ibid.

Chapter 12

1. Interview with General Carlos Barreto Bretoneche, August 1, 1987.

2. But it was the army that finally handed over about fifteen Thompson radios.

3. "If the action taken by the government aspires to be efficient . . . it is essential to establish an adequate administrative structure. The best plans, programs, and policies will be nothing more than good intentions unless the mechanism to implement them at the national level exists." Robert Thompson, *Defeating Communist Insurgency* (New York: Praeger, 1966), p. x.

4. On these "institutionalists," see Chapter 6.

5. Pliego de Instrucciones Operativas No. 01-GC-PP-GR, Estado Mayor de la II Región Guardia Civil, October 12, 1981.

6. JOOPP-ZE, "Apreciación de Situaciones de Operaciones," November 10, 1981.

7. This would prove to be a continuing problem over the following years. It should also be kept in mind that few available models were able to fly at altitudes above 13,200 feet, a common problem in Ayacucho. The model used by the air force was the Bell 212, which had a limited ability to haul large loads. Altitude made Soviet helicopters unusable.

8. Pliego de Instrucciones, p. 6.

9. JOOPP-ZE, "Apreciación de la Situación en la Zona de Emergencia del Departamento de Ayacucho," November 27, 1981.

10. Up-to-date or sophisticated weaponry is of secondary concern in a counterinsurgency war. However, the weapons used have to fit tactics and the kind of territory involved. Certain high-technology equipment, like night vision equipment and electronic sensors, could prove necessary in a war that involves mostly primitive or intermediate technology. But let it not be forgotten that the doctrine upon which both the police forces and the armed forces acted was based on their need to establish an overwhelming superiority of force over the guerrillas. Without it, troops trained on the basis of this assumption would necessarily feel hobbled.

11. Pliego de Instrucciones, October 12, 1981.

12. Ibid.

13. On "concrete pajamas and dynamite suppositories," see the interview done with De la Jara and published in *Caretas*, no. 663, September 8, 1981. In it, De la Jara (who, on the other hand, reveals himself to be badly informed about the dimension and plans of the Shining Path insurrection) underscores his conviction in democratic measures to confront states of exception, using words that have not lost their relevance. "But in applying maximum force . . . we have not given in to the temptation of using indiscriminate repression, nor have we abdicated our democratic credo. . . . democracy can be defended without recurring to measures that in the end may end in its ruin."

14. Orden de Operaciones Conjunto No. 2 "Vivanco," October 13, 1981.

15. The curfew was in effect from 10 P.M. to 5 A.M.

16. This included both rural and urban zones in Huamanga: Quinua, Tambillo, Acos Vinchos, Socos Vinchos, San Pedro de Cachi, and Chiara.

17. Orden de Operaciones Conjunto No. 2 "Vivanco."

18. Ibid.

19. On Alcántara, see Chapter 7.

20. JOOPP-ZE, "Apreciación de Situación de Operaciones," November 10, 1981.

21. John Ranelagh, *The Agency: The Rise and Decline of the CIA* (New York: Simon and Schuster, 1987), p. 424.

22. Victor Marchetti and John D. Marks, *The CIA and the Cult of Intelligence* (New York: Dell Publishing, 1980), p. 109.

23. Ibid.

24. Ibid., p. 110.

25. Ibid.

26. Ibid.

27. On this point, see also Salvatecci, Major (r) José Fernández, *Guerrillas y Contraguerrillas en el Perú*, self-published pamphlet, no date (approximately 1985), pp. 4–14.

28. Interview with José Gagliardi Schiaffino, former interior minister, July 1, 1987.

29. Interview with Héctor López Martínez, May 6, 1987.

30. *Caretas*, no. 670, October 26, 1981.

31. Ibid.

32. See Chapters 8 and 11.

33. The meeting had been held in a place called Piscotambo. According to police, it was there that a series of terrorist attacks had been planned, among them the looting of the "La Pequeñita" store.

34. Interview with Héctor López Martínez, April 20, 1987.

35. Ibid.

Chapter 13

1. Interview with José Gagliardi Schiaffino, July 1, 1987.
2. Ibid.
3. Ibid.
4. Interview with Héctor López Martínez, April 20, 1987.
5. Interview with José Gagliardi Schiaffino.
6. Ibid.
7. Ibid.
8. The first wanted list, dated October 13, had contained seventy names. Since it was issued, several had been captured and new names had been added.
9. JOOPP-ZE, "Apreciación de la Situación de Operaciones-EMC," November 1, 1981.
10. JOOPP-ZE, "Apreciación de la Situación en la Zona de Emergencia del Departamento de Ayacucho," November 27, 1981.
11. Interview with General Carlos Barreto, August 1, 1987.
12. JOOPP-ZE, "Orden de Operaciones Conjunto 'Rasuhuillca,'" December 7, 1981.
13. JOOPP-ZE, "Apreciación de la Situación en la Zona de Emergencia del Departamento de Ayacucho," November 27, 1981.
14. Interview with Héctor López Martínez, May 6, 1987.
15. DESCO, *Violencia Política en el Perú: 1980–1988* (Lima: DESCO, 1989).

Chapter 14

1. *Caretas*, no. 688, March 8, 1982.
2. Nelly Chávez was recaptured in Cajamarca at the end of August 1982. At the time of this arrest, she was living under the pseudonym of Sandra Mantilla. She was considered the Shining Path's political chief in Cajamarca and had managed to escape six previous arrests.
3. One of those killed, William Esquivel, had family ties to the Shining Path since its earliest days.
4. Interview with José Gagliardi Schiaffino, July 1, 1987.
5. Informe No. 01-9C-01-C, from GC general Walter Andrade, chief of police operations in the emergency zone, to the director in chief of the Civil Guard, "sobre acción subversiva en la ciudad de Ayacucho, la noche del 02 al 03 de marzo de 1982."
6. Ibid.
7. Ibid.
8. Interview with Héctor López Martínez, May 6, 1987.
9. Report of General Andrade.
10. *Caretas*, no. 689, March 15, 1982.
11. Ibid.
12. Interview with Héctor López Martínez, May 6, 1987.

13. Among these was the Star machine gun that Mata carried, seized in an attack on the Totos police station on December 31, 1981; a .38 revolver, taken after an attack in Tambo on October 11, 1981; and an M-1 carbine, captured in the assault on the Quinua station on August 15, 1981.

14. Interview with José Gagliardi Schiaffino, July 1, 1987.

15. Interview with Héctor López Martínez, May 6, 1987.

16. Report of General Andrade.

17. Meanwhile, Huamanga had been declared in a state of emergency with Supreme Decree 04-82-IN on March 3.

18. OCOMIN, Communique 002, March 6, 1982.

19. *Caretas*, no. 689, March 15, 1982.

20. *Puka Llacta*, no. 30, April 1982.

21. Ibid.

22. *Desarrollemos la Guerra de Guerrillas* (1982), p. 5.

23. Ibid., pp. 5–6.

24. *A World to Win*, June 1986, pp. 70–71.

Chapter 15

1. This same officer formed part of the Shining Path contingent that attempted to invade Sacsamarca in May 1983.

2. According to diverse Shining Path documents, seven guerrilla zones and eight operation zones were established during this period.

3. Along with the following quotations, this one is taken from manuscripts of notes taken during the meetings and copied for later transmission to the grass roots. The notes were both a schematic diagram of what was said and a record of what occurred. The close similarity of manuscripts drafted in many different places indicates that the final drafts had been submitted to Guzmán for approval before being copied and distributed to the organization's bases.

4. The word refers to the Maoist party known as Red Homeland.

5. In Cerro de Pasco, the escape attempt occurred long afterward but was successful. On June 30, a contingent of twenty-five to forty attackers seized the Cerro de Pasco jail, killing two Republican Guards and managing to free ten Shining Path members and three regular prisoners.

6. *El Pensamiento Militar del Partido*, December 1982, p. 19.

7. For example, see *Nueva Democracia*, July 1981.

8. The issue of the *Revolutionary Worker* published on October 21, 1983, the mouthpiece of the Maoist Revolutionary Communist Party in the United States, mentions the Shining Path's "insistence" on using "Maoism" in place of "Mao thought." Although it recognized that Mao represented a "qualitative advance," the *Revolutionary Worker* respectfully disagrees with their Peruvian comrades, maintaining that the Leninism era continues.

9. According to Shining Path documents that became available later, Conference II officially declared that "Maoism" was a new stage. Nevertheless, as has been noted, Guzmán had used the category previously. On this point, and on this early relationship with the American Revolutionary Communist Party, see "Bases de Discusión," Linea Internacional, *El Diario*, January 3, 1988, p. viii.

10. January 1981, in the "Cuarta Sesión Plenaria," upon beginning the "Cuarto Hito."

11. *El Pensamiento Militar del Partido*, December 1982, p. 13.

Chapter 16

1. Interview with Héctor López Martínez, May 25, 1987.
2. *Caretas*, no. 705, August 12, 1982.
3. Interview with Héctor López Martínez, May 25, 1987.
4. Ibid.
5. Ibid.
6. Memorandum from Abimael Guzmán to the university president, September 25, 1974.
7. The dispute, about sharing teaching duties and control of the Huamán Poma de Ayala high school—which was part of San Cristóbal de Huamanga National University—was one of the central battles in the fight between the Shining Path and opposition groups for control of the university and grass-roots groups in Ayacucho.
8. Request from A. Guzmán to the president of San Cristóbal de Huamanga National University, July 11, 1975.
9. Ibid., July 15, 1975.
10. Ibid., August 15, 1975.
11. Ibid.
12. See Chapter 18.
13. Literally, the "house of the Inca" in Quechua. Haya de la Torre used the word to stand for the changing, secret place where the head of a clandestine party lived.

Chapter 17

1. The "advisory committee to the interior minister" was installed on November 6, 1981. Initially, it included the SIN chief, Ludwig Essenwanger; the chiefs of the military intelligence services, Rear Admiral Ortecho, Major General Marchesi, and Colonel Portilla; the PIP intelligence chief, General Teófilo Aliaga; and GC colonel (later general) Juan Zárate.
2. Interview with José Gagliardi Schiaffino, July 1, 1987.
3. Interview with *Rogelio Ramírez*.
4. Interview with *Sergio Escalante*, April 15, 1987.
5. Interview with *Salvador Otárola*.
6. Ibid. Cooperation between Latin American intelligence and security services was especially intense and widespread in the 1970s. The standardized methodology of the "dirty war" produced kidnappings and murders throughout the world. Uruguayan parliamentarians like Zelmar Michelini and Héctor Gutiérrez were killed in Buenos Aires, as was former Bolivian president Juan José Torres. Dozens of Chilean refugees were murdered, among them General Prats. It is worth noting that, despite the border tension between Chile and Argentina that would push them to the brink of war within a few years, some dozens of Chilean police agents were based in Buenos Aires and cooperated closely with their Argentine colleagues.
7. The first documented kidnapping in Lima was that of Carlos Maguid in 1977. Along with Molfino, María Inés Raverta and Julio César Ramírez were also kidnapped. On this and earlier points, see Richard Gillespie, *Soldiers of Peron: Argentina's Montoneros* (Oxford: Clarendon Press, 1982), p. 257.
8. Interview with *Sergio Escalante*, April 15, 1987.
9. Interview with *Rogelio Ramírez*.
10. Ibid.
11. Ibid.

12. Ibid.

13. Interview with Héctor López Martínez, May 25, 1987.

14. Of course, Jorge ordered the basic information on Rodríguez López that existed in the intelligence service files destroyed.

15. When Ipinze took control of the PIP on August 4, 1980, one of his first official acts was to name Agurto head of his office of personal advisers.

16. Interview with Héctor López Martínez, May 25, 1987.

17. Since April 1982, there had been important arrests. Among them were young people who were nevertheless veteran Shining Path militants, like the Tullich Morales brothers (for the attacks on the Energy, Education, and Labor Ministries and Fiat-Peru). Most of those who had carried out attacks on the "Arenales Mall," the "Crillón" Convention Center, Hindú-hogar, Scala Gigante, and the Continental and Credit Banks were also arrested.

Chapter 18

1. Luján González had been accused by police of having participated in the attack on the Quinua police station.

2. Faced with the possibility of escapes from other prisons, the government decided to re-open hurriedly the island prison of "El Frontón," the prison where several previous generations of political prisoners had been housed, and transfer there all of the Shining Path prisoners currently in custody. Between the end of April and mid-May, the transfer was completed.

3. Piedad Pareja Pflucker, *Terrorismo y sindicalismo en Ayacucho* (Lima, 1981), p. 119. Beginning in July 1980, the number of policemen sent to the Canarias mine fluctuated markedly. In August 1980, there were only two policemen for several days. Later, the number gradually increased to thirty by September 2, then fell again to ten by September 11. This was approximately the number attacked in March 1982.

4. Technically, this was the second attack on the Canarias mine. On January 12, 1981, guerrillas had attacked with dynamite.

5. *Caretas*, no. 690, March 22, 1982.

6. At the time, a mine employee calculated that the systematic theft of dynamite since 1980 had reached 22,000 sticks per year at Canarias alone. *Caretas*, no. 690, March 22, 1982.

7. Supreme Decree, Interior sector, March 26, 1982. The same decree extended the state of emergency to the province of Angaraes, Huancavelica.

8. *Caretas*, no. 693, April 12, 1982.

9. Ibid.

10. Interview with Héctor López Martínez, May 25, 1987.

11. José De la Riva Agüero, *Paisajes Peruanos* (Lima, 1955).

12. Aurelio Miró Quesada, *Costa, Sierra y Montaña* (Lima, 1940).

13. Riva Agüero, *Paisajes Peruanos*, p. 70.

14. Ibid., pp. 71–72.

15. Ibid., pp. 72–73.

16. Ibid., p. 74.

17. Fernando Belaunde, *La Conquista del Perú por los Peruanos* (Lima, 1959), p. 23.

18. *Caretas*, no. 692, April 5, 1982.

19. François Borricaud, *Poder y Sociedad en el Perú Contemporáneo* (Editorial Sur, 1967), pp. 258–59.

20. According to statistics compiled by Civil Guard intelligence, at the beginning of April,

more attacks occurred in Lima than in Ayacucho: 650 compared to 397. However, the difference is misleading. The Lima number is inflated by 212 anonymous telephone threats as opposed to 11 in Ayacucho. But there had been 194 dynamite attacks in Ayacucho as opposed to 160 in Lima. And attacks on police stations, individuals, and other targets totaled 72 in Ayacucho while in Lima, attacks that were generally less serious totaled 24. The number of more serious attacks had also risen in other parts of the country. Along Peru's northern coast, the total was 109. In the northern Andes and central Peru (from Cajamarca to Junín), there had been 316. In the south, the totals were lower, and the least affected departments were those in the jungle.

21. Report from the *Caretas* correspondent in Ayacucho.

22. *Expreso*, August 15, 1982.

23. *Caretas*, no. 711, August 23, 1982.

24. Ibid.

25. *Caretas*, no. 712, August 31, 1982.

26. Interview with José Gagliardi Schiaffino, July 1, 1987.

27. Ibid., and *Caretas*, August 30, 1982.

28. Interview with *Juan Carlos Arenas*, May 22, 1987.

29. Ibid.

30. *A World to Win*, April 1985, pp. 16–19.

31. Interview with Héctor López Martínez, May 25, 1987.

32. *Caretas*, August 30, 1982.

Chapter 19

1. The document that was most frequently distributed was handwritten. For this analysis, I have used a typewritten version. The page numbers correspond to the typewritten version.

2. *El Pensamiento Militar del Partido*, December 1982, pp. 4–5.

3. Ibid., p. 11.

4. Ibid., p. 5.

5. Ibid., p. 2.

6. Ibid., p. 8.

7. Ibid., pp. 11–12.

8. Ibid., p. 12.

9. Ibid., p. 13.

10. Ibid., p. 25.

11. Ibid., p. 19.

12. Ibid., p. 17.

13. Ibid., p. 33.

14. Ibid., p. 35.

15. Ibid., p. 34.

16. "Sobre la guerra: Proverbios y citas," *Ediciones Voz Popular*, December 1981, p. 19.

17. Ibid., p. 13.

Chapter 20

1. Interview with José Gagliardi Schiaffino, July 1, 1987.

2. Ibid.

3. Nicholas Shakespeare, "In Pursuit of Guzmán," *Granta*, 1988, p. 181.

4. Ibid., p. 183.

5. In November 1976.

6. Oficio No. 61-82-MP-FSD from the Ayacucho Fiscalía Superior, October 4, 1982.

7. Interview with José Gagliardi Schiaffino, July 1, 1987.

8. Interview with *Alvaro Ramírez*, May 22, 1987.

9. Oficio No. 190-82-MP-Fiscalía Superior Departmental, November 19, 1982.

10. To add yet another twist to the complex political and family affiliations in Ayacucho, it is worth mentioning that a brother of Adriana's was arrested in 1981 as a suspected Shining Path leader. He was later freed. But at the same time, Adriana was Augusta la Torre's aunt and the niece of the former prime minister under the military government, Pedro Richter Prada. As they say in Peru, small town, big hell.

11. "The condemned of 'El Carmen,'" *Caretas*, no. 726, December 6, 1982.

12. Interview with Germán Medina, July 30, 1987.

13. Interview with Héctor López Martínez, May 25, 1987.

14. This included the provinces of Cangallo, Huanta, La Mar, Víctor Fajardo, and Huamanga in Ayacucho and the province of Andahuaylas in Apurímac.

Index

Path opposition to, 29–32, 66–67; legal defense of, 4–5; on legal Left, 122–27; medical history of, 190, 192–97; offer of asylum to, 189–92; on origins of conspiracy theories, 27; on Peruvian democracy, 126–27; on political theory made into practice, 23–24; on power, 98, 177, 186–87; and proclamation resulting from Central Committee third plenary session, 88; as professor, 193; on quota, 98, 104; on self-criticism of Huamanga prison attack commanders, 179–80; on two-line struggle, 25; use of literature in training of Shining Path cadres by, 25–28; use of Mariátegui writings by, 32, 123, 232; use of term "Maoism" by, 275 (n. 9); and Velasco Alvarado, 121; at Vilcashuamán, 197, 229–30; on war, 233–34; "We are the Initiators" speech of, 34–35. See also titles of specific Shining Path publications

Haya de la Torre, Víctor Raúl, 9
Herrera, Roberto, 224
Herrera Polo, Octavio, 258
Higa, Miguel, 81
Ho Chi Minh, 108
Hoxha, Enver, 67, 108, 120, 128, 130–31
Hoxhism, 66–67
Hoyos Rubio, Rafael, 15, 116, 199
Huamán, Juan, 260
Huamanga prison attack, 165–68; Central Committee analysis of, 177–78; government officials on, 170–71; Guzmán on, 179–80; López Martínez on, 166, 171, 204; and Republican Guard, 167, 169–70
Huamanga province, 60, 135, 141, 273 (n. 16), 275 (n. 17), 279 (n. 14)
Huamanguilla, 260
Huamaní García, Marcelino, 136
Huancapi, 60, 62–63, 64, 70
Huancaraylla, 250
Huancasancos, 70
Huancavelica, 48, 54, 70–71, 85
Huancayo, 109
Huanta, 60, 70, 135, 141, 279 (n. 14)
Huarochirí, 71, 109
Huarsaya, Zenobio, 226
Huasasquiche, Jesús, 169
Huayhualla, Julia, 170
Human rights, violations of. See Torture

Ideology: in orthodox Marxism, 120; of Shining Path, 122, 123, 186–87, 231–37; in training of Shining Path cadres, 29

Iglesias, César, 44
Institutionalists, 72–73, 140
Insurrections: Asian model of, 27, 68–69, 82–83, 108; Cuban model of, 95, 145–46; Shining Path's comparative analysis of, 27, 34, 270 (n. 2)
Intelligence gathering: by CIA, 146, 211–12; by Civil Guard, 47–50, 203–5, 277–78 (n. 20); Latin American cooperation in, 276 (n. 6, chap. 17); on Marxist activity in Ayacucho, 47, 48, 54; by PIP, 205–11; about Shining Path, 45–52, 54; by Shining Path, 84. See also Interior Ministry Intelligence Center; National Intelligence Service
Interior Ministry, 38–39, 43–44, 157–58, 159, 251–52
Interior Ministry Intelligence Center (Dimin): lost intelligence files of, 44–45, 54
International Communist Movement, 127–31
International Revolutionary Movement, 229
Ipinze, Eduard: background of, 40; Gagliardi Schiaffino requests resignation of, 159; and Luque Freyre, 45; named as head of PIP, 39; relationship with De la Jara, 113; and Rodríguez López, 111, 265 (n. 4); on Shining Path as drug-trafficking problem, 111–12; on Shining Path as foreign conspiracy, 110
Isbell, Billie Jean, 19–20, 264 (n. 6, chap. 2)

Jaén, 178
Jäger, Luis, 224, 226
Jáuregui Mejía, Jorge, 76, 139
Jáuregui Mejía, Victor, 259–60
Joint Operative Command of the Emergency Zone (JOOPP-ZE), 142
JOOPP-ZE. See Joint Operative Command of the Emergency Zone
Jorge Zárate, José, 40, 205, 277 (n. 14, chap. 17)
Junín, 71

Kajatt, Leoncio, 223
Kawata Makabe, Luis, 46, 248
Kim Il Sung, 120

La Convención, 46
Lagos, Edith, 80, 164, 239–42
La Mar province, 135, 141, 279 (n. 14)
Lambayeque, 71
Langberg, Carlos: in Apra, 9, 55; drug trafficking by, 9–10, 14, 210
La Oroya mining center, 71
La Pequeñita store, 144, 274 (n. 33)
Lara, Edilberto, 194